1x 9'
6/98

The Day the
Music Died

A Winter Dance Party tour poster

The Day the Music Died:

The Last Tour of Buddy Holly, the Big Bopper, and Ritchie Valens

LARRY LEHMER

Schirmer Books
An Imprint of Simon & Schuster Macmillan
New York

Prentice Hall International
London Mexico City New Delhi Singapore Sydney Toronto

Schirmer Books
An Imprint of Simon & Schuster Macmillan
1633 Broadway
New York, NY 10019

Printed in the United States of America

Printing Number

10 9 8 7 6 5 4 3 2 1

Library of Congress Cataloging-in-Publication Data

Lehmer, Larry.
    The day the music died : the last tour of Buddy Holly, the Big Bopper, and Ritchie Valens / Larry Lehmer.
        p.   cm.
    Includes bibliographical references (p.) and index.
    ISBN 0-02-864741-6
    1. Holly, Buddy, 1936–1959. 2. Richardson, J. P., 1932?–1959. 3. Valens, Ritchie, 1941–1959. 4. Rock musicians—United States—Biography. I. Title.
    ML420.H595L44   1997
    782.42166'092'273—dc21   97-19892
    [B]   LEH   CIP
                                                                                              MN

To the family and friends of Roger Peterson,
the often-forgotten victim of February 3, 1959

Contents

Preface and Acknowledgments ....*ix*

1 The Crash *1*

COMING TOGETHER

2 Big Beat from Texas *5*

3 The Big Bopper *26*

4 Getting Ready *37*

5 La Bamba *48*

THE WINTER DANCE PARTY

6 The Tour Begins *61*

7 The Tour Goes Bad *75*

8 The Tour from Hell *88*

9 The Flight *99*

AFTERMATH

10 A Star Is Born *115*

11 New Directions *128*

12 The CAB Report *135*

13 The Controversy *142*

14 Legacies *155*

15 Family Affairs *178*

16 The Fans *189*

17 Where Are They Now? *199*

18 The Last Tour *224*

Appendix A: The Plane *233*

Appendix B: Roger Peterson's Flying Career *239*

Notes and References *245*

Bibliography *251*

Index *257*

Preface and Acknowledgments

Buddy Holly. Ritchie Valens. The Big Bopper. Gone.

It was almost too much for my friend Harold Webster and me to comprehend as we trudged through the west end of Council Bluffs, Iowa, the afternoon of February 3, 1959, to pick up the bundle of Omaha *World-Herald* newspapers Harold was expected to deliver. A bitter north wind was at our backs as we approached the dropoff point, alternately offering our personal visions of a shared disbelief in what we had heard about the crash on the radio. How could this happen? What were these singers doing in Iowa and why wasn't everybody killed? Just where is Clear Lake anyway?

At thirteen, I was a year older than Harold. When we weren't in school or saddled with family obligations, we were probably together. Like most of our friends, we shared a passion for baseball, baseball cards, and rock 'n' roll music. Harold was a better baseball player than me, but I held my own in music. I was one of the first in the neighborhood to own a transistor radio and a record player. We subsidized our hobbies by helping friends on their paper routes or picking up litter at local drive-ins. We would scour the parking lot of a local drugstore, seeking receipts that, when the accumulation reached a certain dollar figure, were redeemable for merchandise. Our skimpy earnings went toward buying the latest *Hit Parader*, *Dig*, or one of the other teen magazines, which except for radio and *American Bandstand* were our only credible sources of information about rock 'n' roll.

To us, the only exposure our music seemed to get in the mainstream media in those days focused on riots, stabbings, shootings, or arrests at rock concerts, which seemed to be banned in as many places as they were held. Still, Harold and I were hoping to learn more from the *World-Herald* about the Iowa plane crash that had taken three of our favorite singers. We tore open the bundle, quickly found the news article, and started absorbing the meager details of the accident. Bad weather . . . small plane . . . four killed . . . tour goes on . . . investigation planned. We would have to wait for more information.

But outside of what we were fed by the teen press, there was precious little information on the accident forthcoming through the mass media. It was a minor irritation to adolescents like us. There was too much going on in our lives at that time to dwell on the past. Plus, we still had the music. In fact, with new material on Buddy Holly popping up with some regularity on the radio in the first few years after his death, you almost wondered if he were really gone.

But as time went on and as rock 'n' roll lost more stars under tragic circumstances—Eddie Cochran, Johnny Burnette, Sam Cooke, Bobby Fuller, Otis Redding, Frankie Lymon, Brian Jones, King Curtis, Duane Allman, Janis Joplin, Jim Morrison, Jimi Hendrix, Elvis Presley, John Lennon, Marvin Gaye—the early loss of three of rock's biggest stars in an Iowa farmfield started to take on mythic proportions. With each successive tragedy and the inevitable evocation of the Clear Lake crash, I was drawn back to my original questions. By 1974, my interest in the plane crash was at its peak.

In February of that year, *Crawdaddy* magazine featured a story by Tom Miller. The cover of the magazine carried the headline WHO KILLED BUDDY HOLLY? The story alluded to an investigation of the accident undertaken by members of Watergate Senate Committee counsel Sam Dash's staff, as a diversion from the tedious task of perusing government documents for hours on end. I was fascinated by Miller's work, which was rich in details previously unknown to me. There were names of bus drivers, ticket-takers, and nurses who had contact with the singers in their final hours and details of the accident itself. Superimposed on an illustration accompanying the article was part of the first page of the Civil Aeronautics Board's aircraft accident report from September 15, 1959. It was an impressive investigative work, I thought, and answered many of the questions I had as a young teenager fifteen years earlier. I was satisfied, for a while.

Two years later, I learned that a movie about Holly's life was in the works and that the movie was based on a book written by John Goldrosen. I bought a copy of the book and quickly turned to the section about Holly's last tour. Goldrosen's research, combined with Miller's earlier *Crawdaddy* story, painted a bleak picture of the Winter Dance Party tour. Besides the tragedy of the plane crash, the tour seemed doomed from the start. It seemed an odd proposition to me, in any case, that singers of this magnitude would subject themselves to such treatment. I was determined to learn more about the tour and the accident. I placed an ad in the Mason City *Globe-Gazette* in early 1976, seeking information from people who may have been at the Winter Dance Party concert at the Surf Ballroom in nearby Clear Lake on February 2, 1959, or who knew something about the crash. The ad drew just a few responses, but they started me down the path that ultimately resulted in this book.

The first person to respond was Elsie Juhl, on whose rented farm the plane had crashed. In a series of letters, she further piqued my interest by refuting many of the details of the Miller article. On my first visit to the area, Sharon O'Neill of Mason City told me about all the buzz around town about foul play.

I wrote to the CAB and got my own copy of the accident report before returning to the Mason City–Clear Lake area again. I visited the Surf for the first time, and maintenance man Leland Hammond let me in through a back door, giving me a guided tour through the dark and empty ballroom. I was given instructions on how to locate the Juhl farmhouse north of town. I stood there for the longest time, imagining the final moments of the plane's fatal descent. It was a chilly spring day with the stubble field behind the farmhouse looking much as it must have looked before Jerry Dwyer's Beechcraft Bonanza disintegrated in the Juhls' back yard.

In Clear Lake, I found Carroll Anderson, who was the manager of the Surf Ballroom in 1959. Anderson took time out from a busy lunch hour at the downtown Clear Lake cafe he was managing to grant me an interview at a front table. In Mason City, Cerro Gordo County Sheriff Jerry Allen invited me into his office, where he pulled out his file on the crash and started feeding me the details of his department's role in the investigation. He photocopied coroners' reports for me and answered all of my questions.

I soon realized that Miller's *Crawdaddy* story wasn't the result of an investigation after all but, rather, was a clever blend of fact and fiction. To me, the facts were more interesting than the fiction and I was determined to gather as many of them as I could. I started tracking down people and planned a vacation trip that would include stops in Beaumont, Texas, and Nashville, Tennessee.

In Beaumont, I was cordially welcomed in the house of J. P. Richardson's brother, Cecil, where we spent a balmy summer evening drinking Lone Star beer and discussing his late brother. Cecil, now deceased, was writing his own country songs at the time; he played for me a demo of a song he was preparing to ship to Nashville. He also put me in touch with J. P.'s manager, Bill Hall, who was working in Nashville at the time. While in Nashville, I also had two interesting interviews with Tommy Allsup, who had played lead guitar behind Buddy Holly on the Winter Dance Party.

Later that summer I tracked down Bobby Vee in Los Angeles and seemed to be making real progress toward the book I had hoped to write. But by late summer of 1976, my leads were drying up and my family was growing. With a wife and young son and another child on the way, I focused on my family life and building on my career as a sports editor at the *Council Bluffs Daily Nonpareil*. The book project was put on hold.

Over the next twelve years, there was an explosion of new information on Buddy Holly. The movie *The Buddy Holly Story* came out in 1978 and a group of ardent Holly fans had formed the enormously successful Buddy Holly Memorial Society. John Goldrosen updated his book with the help of John Beecher, who for years ran the Buddy Holly Appreciation Society in England. The Surf Ballroom started an annual series of tribute dances in 1979. In 1987, a movie came out on Ritchie Valens's life.

By this time, I had moved on to the *Des Moines Register,* the paper of record for the state of Iowa. Therefore, it was only appropriate that the *Register* acknowledge each February the tribute dances at the Surf, which drew fans from around the world. Finding new ways to handle an old story is a common newspaper problem. It was this problem that gave my book project new life.

In 1988, a colleague and good friend, Jim Pollock, was assigned the task of covering the tribute. In the course of his coverage, Jim visited the Surf and interviewed several members of Ritchie Valens's family, who were making their first visit to Iowa. Since Jim was vaguely aware of my earlier reporting efforts, he suggested that perhaps I would be interested in taking over the "tribute beat" through the next year leading up to the thirtieth anniversary of the crash. *Register* features editor Pat Denato approved a package of stories, including one on pilot Roger Peterson, the only Iowan killed in the crash.

As I started looking for new information, I met George Horton of Vining, Iowa, who has been searching Iowa for information about Buddy Holly for years. George, who has had a lock on the Iowa B HOLLY personalized license plate for many years, was responsible for discovering many of the photos of Holly's appearances in Iowa in 1958 and 1959. I first met George at a flea market in Marshalltown, Iowa. We spent nearly two hours talking about everything from George's then-current passion for the annual hobo convention at Britt, Iowa, to his past passions, which included an exhaustive study of native Iowa soils. But nothing compared to George's passion for Buddy Holly. After our conversation, he led me to his car in the muddy, gravel parking lot where he opened the trunk, revealing several boxes of what appeared to be magazines, papers, and smaller boxes.

"Take what you want," he said.

Over the next two weeks, I learned more about Buddy Holly and the Winter Dance Party than I had learned in the previous twelve years. Among George's collection were names of dozens of potential sources and even some original 4x5 photographic negatives taken by insurance adjusters and freelance photographers at the crash site that cold and dark morning of February 3, 1959. Fortunately for me, many others were as generous to me as George as I went through the fact-gathering process.

Roger Peterson's parents, Art and Pearl, shared the better part of an afternoon at the rural Alta, Iowa, farmhouse in which they raised their family decades earlier. They shared with me many of their most intimate thoughts of their son and their private collection of mementos, which they allowed me to take into nearby Storm Lake to photocopy at a stationery store. Peterson's widow, DeAnn, sat with me at the kitchen table of her Minnesota home, tearfully recounting Roger's courtship, their eventual marriage, and the joy of moving into their first home together, a cottage near the north shore of Clear Lake. She, too, shared generously, allowing me to take a wedding photo to use in the newspaper article and book.

In June 1988, the *Register* published its first in-depth story on Roger Peterson as part of a series of stories I wrote at the time of the dedication of a monument to the singers and pilot at the Surf. In the process, I learned of some long-lost crash photos and finally met members of the families of all three singers.

Jay Perry Richardson, the son of the Big Bopper, was presented with a watch owned by his father that had been discovered after the snow melted at the crash site. Maria Elena Holly, Buddy's widow, was present as the street running east of the Surf was renamed Buddy Holly Place. Connie Alvarez and Irma Norton, sisters of Ritchie Valens, returned to Clear Lake and quickly befriended Art and Pearl Peterson at the first gathering that included survivors of all four people aboard the Beechcraft Bonanza nearly thirty years earlier.

That fall, I visited Texas and New Mexico to learn more about Holly and Richardson. On the way, I visited Kevin Terry in Oklahoma. Kevin, a lifelong Buddy Holly fan, shared my interest in the accident and had spent many hours and thousands of dollars in long-distance phone bills in tracking down as many people associated with the crash as he could find. I have found Kevin's work to be thorough and accurate as we have shared information over the years. Kevin's early investigative work proved invaluable to my own project.

I spent several days in the Lubbock, Texas–Clovis, New Mexico, area, where I was struck by the similarities to my home state of Iowa. Lubbock is roughly the same size as Des Moines, and the area's topography is similar. The cottonfields around Lubbock are not unlike the corn and soybean fields that surround Des Moines. The people are similar, too: direct, plain-talking, and generally open and friendly.

In Clovis, I spent a full day with Vi Petty, the widow of Norman Petty, who produced most of the early hits of Buddy Holly and the Crickets at his tiny studio some one hundred miles and one time zone west of Lubbock. Vi and Billy Stull, who was chief engineer of the Petty studios at the time, ushered me around town, showing me the various Petty properties.

At the fabled studios on West Seventh Street where most of the early Holly material was recorded, Vi insisted that I sit at Norman's master console in the control room so she could take my picture while playing an old Holly master tape. In the studio itself, she played the familiar celeste accompaniment to the master of "Everyday." On our stop at the Mesa Theater studio, I was treated to an impromptu mini-concert in the empty theater. While Stull controlled the sound and lighting, Vi sang several songs, including a mutual favorite, "True Love Ways," to her appreciative audience of one. As her voice filled the theater with its shimmering strands of fine chain flanking the stage, it was a fitting tribute to her husband's acoustical genius.

Vi introduced me to Robert Linville, one of the Roses, a group that sang background on several Holly songs and toured with him and the Crickets in the fall of 1958. At the end of a busy day, Vi sat down with me in her home, a converted church called the Citadel, and spent two more hours answering my questions. Sadly, Vi died in March 1992.

Bill Griggs was no less gracious a host as I spent several days in Lubbock. Griggs is something of a night owl and frequently stays up into the wee hours taking telephone calls or working on some of the many projects he's associated with. As one of the cofounders of the Buddy Holly Memorial Society and its driving force for many years, Griggs is acknowledged as *the* expert on matters relating to Buddy Holly and the Crickets. As publisher of *Rockin' 50s* magazine, Griggs has shown his expertise is not limited to the boys from Lubbock.

While in Lubbock, I spent my days doing research at the Lubbock County Courthouse, tracking down sources or visiting the historical sites as provided by Griggs on a map of the city he distributes to interested parties. At night, he and I would share information and I would pore through his files for pertinent information. It was during one of these late-night sessions that we managed to pinpoint the exact location where the Winter Dance Party bus broke down in northern Wisconsin in the early morning hours of Feb. 1, 1959. We would later team up to locate Frankie Sardo, a member of the Winter Dance Party entourage who seemed to disappear from view shortly after the tour ended.

I also made stops in Dallas, Houston, and Beaumont during that Texas swing. In Dallas I made one of my many attempts to get an interview with Maria Elena Holly, Buddy's widow. Although Maria Elena declined my repeated requests, I spent several hours at the home of Ronnie Smith's sister in the Dallas area. Smith was the young singer from Odessa who was summoned to Des Moines to join the Crickets three days after the fatal plane crash. Smith was popular with the remaining members of the Winter Dance Party and appeared to be on the verge of stardom before substance abuse took over his life. In 1962, Smith died under tragic circumstances, and I was interested in his story. Smith's sister, Sherry, shared her memories with me in an emotional afternoon interview at her home and over lunch at Dallas's Hard Rock Cafe.

In Houston, Jay Perry Richardson opened his home to me to talk about his father, J. P. Although Jay wasn't born until a couple months after his father's death, he had spent the previous six months working with a Hollywood writer on a movie script and was overflowing with information. He was also working with Port Arthur writer Tim Knight on a book, which was later published by the Port Arthur Historical Society.

John Pickering, a lifelong acquaintance of Norman Petty and one-third of the vocal group the Picks, who backed up the Crickets on their first Brunswick album, was also gracious in opening his home to me. He and his wife, Vicky, prepared a buffet of Southwestern snacks for me to consume during our several-hours-long interview session in John's working den.

In the Beaumont area, I spent a pleasant evening with Tim Knight, who proved to be nearly as knowledgeable about the Big Bopper as Griggs was about Buddy Holly.

After returning from Texas, it was evident I was going to find enough material for my book. Before writing, however, I wanted to visit all of the towns of the Winter Dance Party. By the fall of 1989 I had completed my travels. During my last swing through Minnesota and Wisconsin, I was surprised to learn that many of the facilities that hosted the Winter Dance Party in 1959 were still standing. In fact, portions of the short wrought-iron railing that ringed the stage at the Kato Ballroom in Mankato in 1959 were piled behind the ballroom thirty years later.

By the time I started writing, I had visited every city in which the Winter Dance Party had played prior to the crash and had interviewed people who had witnessed each performance. I had found many people who were either at the crash site that day or had key roles in the subsequent investigation. I had visited with members of the families of Buddy Holly, J. P. Richardson, Ritchie Valens, and Roger Peterson, and had met many fans.

ACKNOWLEDGMENTS

Counting the twelve years my project was on hold, it took me more than sixteen years to complete my first draft of this manuscript. It took another three years of revision and refinement before it was ready to be published. Along the way, of course, I had lots of help.

First and foremost are the nearly four hundred people who shared their remembrances with me. Although many are mentioned in the notes at the back of this book, a few have made extraordinary contributions as I pieced together this project.

Much of what I have written about the Winter Dance Party tour has come from these people who were intimately associated with it, either as performers or in supporting roles: Tommy Allsup, Allen Bloom, Carl Bunch, Debbie Stevens (Dean), Dion DiMucci, Sam Geller, Waylon Jennings, Fred Milano, Frankie Sardo, and Bobby Vee.

I learned a great deal about the last show at the Surf Ballroom, the accident itself, and its investigation from Jerry Allen, Carroll Anderson, Eugene Anderson, Bob Booe, Jim Collison, Bob Hale, Elsie Juhl, Charles Mc-Glothlen, Elwin Musser, A. J. Prokop, Leo Sander, and Kevin Terry.

My knowledge of Buddy Holly and his West Texas–Clovis connection is more complete, thanks to Jerry (J. I.) Allison, George Atwood, Sonny Curtis, John Goldrosen, Bill Griggs, Ben Hall, Larry Holley, Buddy Knox, Robert Linville, Joe B. Mauldin, Echo McGuire Griffith, the late Vi Petty, John Pickering, Peggy Sue Allison Rackham, and Niki Sullivan.

Thanks, too, to the many friends, relatives, and associates of Ritchie Valens who shared their thoughts with me: Connie Alvarez, Donna Ludwig Fox, Bob Keane, Rosie Morales, Irma Norton, Earl Palmer, Steve Propes, Ted Quillin, Ernestine Reyes, Gil Rocha, Chan Romero, and Stan Ross.

These people helped me learn a great deal more about J. P. Richardson, the Big Bopper: Gordon Baxter, Jerry Boynton, Bud Daily, the late Bill Hall, Tim Knight, the late J. D. Miller, John Neil, the late Cecil Richardson, Jay Perry Richardson, Gordon Ritter, Ken Ritter, John Romere, Roy Dixon Shotts, and Adrianne Wenner.

The best source of information for Roger Peterson proved to be his family: his parents, Art and Pearl, his widow, DeAnn, his sister, Janet Dilley, and his brother, Ron.

Thanks, too, to those who offered their photographs as part of this project: Dr. Kenneth Broad, Bill Griggs, George Horton, Don Larson, Steven Lassiter, Larry Matti, Bob Modersohn of the *Des Moines Register,* Elwin Musser of the Mason City *Globe-Gazette,* Judy Peery, DeAnn Peterson, John Pickering, Jay Perry Richardson, Dick Strand, Tony Szikil, and Kevin Terry.

I would like to thank Jim Pollock for providing the spark that brought this project back to life and Sandra Choron, Jeanne Hanson, and Ed Knappman for their thoughtful advice in helping to shape and trim my manuscript. I also want to thank Richard Carlin and Debi Elfenbein, my editors at Schirmer Books, and Richard's assistant, Alicia Williamson, for clearing the path toward publication.

A special thanks to my wife, Linda, whose patience was tested on countless occasions as I interrupted family "vacations" to do interviews or visit newspaper libraries, and to my children—Aaron, Meghan, and Bret—who now may understand why they couldn't use the phone so many evenings while Dad was cooped up in his basement office.

The Crash

February 3, 1959, 12:50 AM

Roger Peterson was having second thoughts.

Gusty winds rattled the small Beechcraft Bonanza aircraft as pilot Peterson sat, cradling the steering yoke while waiting to take off from a remote northern Iowa airstrip. Snowflakes ricocheted off the windshield, accenting the deteriorating weather conditions that had developed over the previous few hours.

Peterson's friends and family had cautioned him against flying, but his impatient passengers were encouraging him to get into the air. In the back seat, singers Ritchie Valens and J. P. Richardson—known professionally as the Big Bopper, huddled in the cramped quarters trying to ward off the 18-degree temperature. For Richardson, who was battling a severe cold with a homebrew concoction of whiskey and mouthwash, it was all he could do to squeeze his 210 pounds into the small seat. Valens, who also was struggling with a bad cold, pulled up the collar of the winter coat he had received a day earlier and tried to catch up on some sleep.

In the front passenger seat, Buddy Holly was trying to persuade Peterson to get the plane into the air. But Peterson, an Iowa native, was well aware of how quickly weather conditions can change in the upper Midwest. Already the skies around Mason City, Iowa, were filled with snow flurries and the winds promised to make for a turbulent flight. Plus, Peterson knew his training did not include proficiency in instrument flying. But, the musicians pointed out, their tour bus had already left town for the next stop. Peterson represented their only hope to reach Moorhead, Minnesota, for their show the next night.

Reluctantly Peterson switched on the plane's landing lights and turned the Bonanza into the wind. As he applied the throttle, the six-cylinder Continental engine responded with a powerful surge and the plane's propeller bit into the frigid north Iowa air. The plane quickly gained speed as it rumbled down the runway, breaking ground little more than a third of the way down. As the Bonanza left the cold concrete behind, Peterson switched off the plane's lights and turned toward the lights of Mason City to the east. Continuing his turn, Peterson soon found himself pointed toward Fargo. With the lights of Mason City now behind him, Peterson had his hands full as he tried to steer the Bonanza through the snow and wind.

The winds made for a choppy ride. The overcast sky shrouded the stars and the landscape below was dark and barren. Peterson again switched on his landing lights and turned to his altitude gyro for assistance as he tried to boost the Bonanza to a safe cruising altitude. But a bright light from a farmstead soon exploded directly in front of the plane. As Peterson pulled back on the steering yoke, the Bonanza strained upward, narrowly missing a two-story farmhouse that lay directly in its path. A few seconds later, another light burst from another house. Peterson again pulled the Bonanza out of trouble.

Then another light appeared. This time, Peterson turned the Bonanza into a sharp right-hand turn. But the tip of the right wing caught the ground, carving a half-foot-deep furrow into the frozen stubble field. The wing started to splinter and was torn from the fuselage. The cabin of the Bonanza crashed into the turf as the wing gave way. All three singers were ripped from their seats, their restraining belts snapping under the force of the impact. The propeller blades snapped from the engine hub and the right-side cabin door popped from its frame as the plane started to skid.

The plane's momentum took it briefly to the air once more before it again collided with the frozen earth, this time on its nose. The cabin shattered on impact, scattering its famous occupants on ground where months earlier a bountiful crop had risen from the fertile Iowa soil.

Inside the wreckage lay Peterson, his body tangled in the plane's control cables. The boot on his right foot rose from the remnants of the disintegrated cockpit, pointing skyward.

As the crumpled cabin of the plane swayed gently against a barbed-wire fence while settling into its final resting place, the Bonanza gave up its final sounds—the hissing of ruptured hoses and gurgling of escaping mechanical fluids. Then it was quiet.

A dusting of snow fell sporadically throughout the night, brushing across the stilled bodies while pieces of the plane's cabin insulation fluttered in the persistent winds of a bitter Iowa winter.

Coming Together

Big Beat from Texas

Hit records. That's what brought Buddy Holly, J. P. Richardson, and Ritchie Valens together and deposited them in the upper Midwest in the middle of one of the deadliest winters of the last half century, touring two-lane blacktops in the dead of night aboard drafty converted schoolbuses. Although rock newcomers Valens and Richardson saw the tour as a great opportunity to realize their dreams, it was the last place Holly wanted to be. But he had little choice: He needed the money.

Although Holly and his band, the Crickets, enjoyed incredible musical success in the year that followed the 1957 release of their first hit, "That'll Be the Day," Holly's career was undergoing serious changes by late 1958. He had married that summer and moved from his native Texas to New York City. That led to a bitter break from his former manager, Norman Petty, and the eventual breakup of Buddy Holly and the Crickets. In New York, Holly continued to write and record songs in his Greenwich Village apartment. He had blueprints prepared for a studio to be built in his hometown of Lubbock, Texas, and had produced a record for an unknown singer named Lou Giordano.

But Holly was getting restless. He hadn't performed in two months and he couldn't get back to Lubbock to build his studio because of a financial dispute with Petty. He turned to an old friend, promoter Irvin Feld, who suggested he put together a tour for Holly. The tour was to mark a rebirth of his new career as a rock star. Holly, only twenty-two at the time, was all too familiar with the fickleness of the popular music business.

Although "That'll Be the Day" is regarded as a rock 'n' roll classic today, Holly had to record the song twice with different record companies before it made the charts.

Despite the rocky start, the success of "That'll Be the Day," and of Holly, was inevitable according to those who knew him. Music was popular in the Lubbock household of Buddy's parents, L. O. and Ella Holley (Buddy dropped the "e" from the family name at the beginning of his recording career). Holly, born September 7, 1936, the youngest of four children, learned to play the piano and violin as a youngster. Holly's first-grade teacher noted on his report card that "Buddy bothers his neighbors in school." He was active in scouting, soap-box racing, and enjoyed playing baseball. He went barefoot in the summer, rabbit hunting in the fall, and liked to read when forced inside, especially comic books, adventure stories, or science fiction.

Holly was elected king of the sixth grade at Roosevelt School. He started playing country music on guitar in seventh grade and tried his hand at playing the mandolin and banjo. Neighbor Wayne Maines helped expand Holly's guitar repertoire and soon Holly was entertaining classmates on the school bus by playing Hank Williams tunes, yodeling his way through "Lovesick Blues."

Holly and good friend Jack Neal appeared on a local television talent show as "Buddy and Jack" in 1952. Neal soon left the duo and was replaced by another Holly friend, Bob Montgomery. "Buddy and Bob" became regular performers on *The Sunday Party* program on radio station KDAV in 1953. In the years that followed, Holly played with many area musicians, from veteran country performers to other teenagers with a preference for more contemporary music. Buddy and Bob added bass guitarist Larry Welborn to their group in their latter high school years.

At this time, Holly appeared onstage in hand-crafted leather riding chaps, with his initials on one leg and the initials of his girlfriend, Echo McGuire, on the other. In many ways, Holly was a typical teenager. He preferred riding motorcycles and hunting and fishing to attending school. With Echo he was likely to attend a sporting event, go horseback riding or roller-skating, or grab a Hidey burger at the Hi-D-Ho drive-in. He was meticulous in his appearance, wearing wire-rimmed glasses, close-cropped hair, starched shirts, and pressed blue jeans. He spent many hours doing leatherwork, including hand-tooling a leather case for his guitar, and was an editor on the school paper. He joined his school's Vocational Industrial Club, and was released early from school each day so he could work a part-time job at a Lubbock print shop.

"He wasn't the most outstanding student I ever had," says Waymon Mulkey, Holly's vocational instructor. "He was highly interested in playing the guitar and the music business and not really interested in learning the vocation I was teaching."

Holly's late-night musical gigs often led to late-morning sleep-ins and class-cutting, which led to at least one brief suspension from school. Some of Holly's classmates say high school was a difficult experience for him.

"Lubbock, Texas, in 1954 and 1955 was very, very provincial," says Harold Womack, who was one year behind Holly at Lubbock High School.

"Buddy ran closer to the edge than I did." Another classmate, James Pritchard, says: "[Buddy] was pretty much of a loner, too. It was pretty hard on him around here for a while. A lot of people would laugh at some of the stuff he'd do."

Although country music was the general preference in the high plains country of West Texas, Holly and his young friends preferred other types of music. He and good friend Sonny Curtis used to spend late nights in Holly's car, listening to distant radio stations.

"They played blues and you couldn't hear blues back in those days, or black music," Curtis recalls. "It wasn't available [in Lubbock]."

By the time Holly became the first person in his family to graduate from high school in 1955, he was seriously considering pursuing a music career, thanks in large part to Elvis Presley. By mid-1955, Presley had already made several appearances in Lubbock. KDAV general manager "Pappy" Dave Stone and disc jockey Ben Hall had brought Presley to town in January and February as part of country shows at the local Fair Park Coliseum. Buddy and Bob were the opening act for the February 13 show.

Billed as the "Hillbilly Cat," Presley was an onstage spectacle never before seen in Texas. He dazzled them in Kilgore with his red pants, green coat, and pink shirt and socks, but fans in tiny De Leon shredded his pink shirt. In Amarillo, a female fan suffered a nasty gash on her leg at a Presley performance.

The shift in Holly's musical repertoire from country to rock 'n' roll was accelerated after meeting Presley. "He just blew Buddy's mind," Sonny Curtis says.

At the Cotton Club on April 29, 1955, Holly sat with Echo McGuire behind the stacks of cotton bales that separated Presley from his eager young fans, but Buddy and Bob were again the opening act on June 3 when Presley returned to Fair Park Coliseum. This time, however, Elvis brought along a drummer, D. J. Fontana. Soon Holly's group had a drummer, too: Jerry Allison. The group unleashed its new, harder rock sound at store openings, automobile dealerships, and roller rinks.

"We'd play at the opening of a pack of cigarettes," Allison says.

Holly even tried to look like his idol. "Buddy used to take burnt wooden matches, spit on them and paint his sideburns long," Holly friend Roy Rucker says.

Those were carefree days in Lubbock as Holly and his friends cruised down College Avenue, circling through the parking lot of the Hi-D-Ho where Holly once set up his equipment on the roof to perform.

"Buddy was electric," friend and fellow bandmate Niki Sullivan says. "In the middle of playing a guitar riff, he could drop down to the floor, his legs bent beneath him leaning back without his back touching the floor. He could move himself up and down, still playing the guitar, come out of that and start moving around."

Despite his local popularity, Holly's music hadn't become a full-time vocation. He spent much of his time in the months following his graduation from high school helping older brother Larry dig out a storm cellar for his new home or laying tile. Longtime girlfriend Echo McGuire was preparing to leave for Abilene Christian College, some one-hundred-and-fifty miles away.

In mid-October, Holly's group played with Bill Haley and His Comets and Elvis Presley on successive nights in Lubbock. Two weeks later, they performed with Marty Robbins. Holly caught the attention of Eddie Crandall, Robbins's manager and a Nashville talent scout. Crandall persuaded Jim Denny, former Grand Ole Opry manager and owner of Cedarwood Music Publishing, to sign Holly to a songwriters' contract and help schedule a January 1956 Nashville recording session for Holly with well-known producer Owen Bradley, who was helping Decca Records find a rockabilly singer to compete with Presley.

Seeking to make a good impression on Bradley, Holly borrowed $1,000 from his brother Larry and spent half of it on a new Fender Stratocaster guitar and the rest on clothes. "He bought green, pink, and red sports jackets and some red shoes and suede shoes," Larry Holley remembers. Holly also signed to spend two weeks on tour with country singing legend Hank Thompson. Holly recruited Curtis on guitar and Guess on bass for his touring band; drummer Allison was still in high school. "We were just Elvis clones," Curtis says. "We sounded just like Elvis."

At the conclusion of the tour, the trio strapped Guess's bass to the top of Holly's black-and-white 1955 Oldsmobile and headed to Bradley's quonset hut studio in Nashville. They made a brief stop in Memphis where Holly hoped to meet with Presley.

"Buddy made this wallet," Sonny Curtis remembers. "It had black flowers and in the middle, it had Elvis written in pink. Pink and black were big in those days. We stopped off at Sun Records. It was about four o'clock in the afternoon and there weren't [m]any people there, I think there was a girl there, and we had to go on to Nashville. Buddy said 'I sure would appreciate it if you'd give this wallet to Elvis.' So he just left it."

At Bradley's, two session musicians joined Holly, Guess, and Curtis in recording four songs, including two that would be their first Decca release: "Blue Days, Black Nights" and "Love Me." Curtis played lead guitar while Holly, following Bradley's instructions, just sang.

"We were nice boys from Texas and we were trying to put our best manners forward," Curtis says. "We were on our toes and it was 'Yes sir, Mr. Bradley' and 'Whatever you say, Mr. Bradley.'"

As Holly's group was returning to Lubbock, the nation's airwaves were filled with Presley's first release for RCA, "Heartbreak Hotel." Although the popular music charts were still dominated by Dean Martin, Tennessee Ernie Ford, Kay Starr, Les Baxter, and Nelson Riddle, rockers like Elvis, Bill Haley, and a group of young New Yorkers called the Teen-Agers were making their way into the Top 10.

Anxious to hear his own record on the radio, Holly wrote to Eddie Crandall in Nashville, who responded: "I can't say anything good at the present time. . . . Don't get discouraged. I know it's tough, but the break will come sometime. You have a fine little group." Finally, on April 16, Holly's first record was released. Holly's group soon went out on another tour through the Southeast, this time with Faron Young, Sonny James, Wanda Jackson, and Tommy Collins.

As Holly patiently waited for "Blue Days, Black Nights"/"Love Me" to climb the charts, his idol, Elvis Presley, was very hot indeed. Elvis seemed to be everywhere under new manager Colonel Tom Parker, a former carnival hustler who once developed an act of dancing chickens. Presley's onstage antics were the talk of the nation, thanks in great part to his exposure on the Dorsey brothers' television show. His leering, lopsided grin and grinding hips were a hit with teenage girls. Rumors proliferated that Presley stuffed anything from empty toilet paper rolls to lead pipe down his pants before appearing onstage. An estimated 25 percent of all Americans tuned in to watch Presley's appearance from the flight deck of the aircraft carrier *U.S.S. Hancock* on the *Milton Berle Show* on April 3, 1956.

Parker had negotiated a three-picture deal with movie producer Hal Wallis on behalf of his young star, who was accounting for half of RCA Victor's record sales at the time, about $75,000 worth each day.

It appeared, however, that Presley's appeal didn't extend to adults. In late April 1956, his scheduled two-week engagement at the Frontier Hotel in Las Vegas was cut to just one week because of a lack of interest by the older generation. It would prove to be a minor setback for Elvis and had no impact whatsoever on the teenagers of America, who were lapping up the new music, much of it from Elvis's hometown of Memphis. Although Carl Perkins was unable to make any appearances for two months because of an auto accident, he was doing solid business for Sun Records, with his hot-selling "Blue Suede Shoes."

Billboard took note of the Memphis rockers when reviewing Holly's first single: "If the public will take more than one Presley or Perkins, as it well may, Holly stands a strong chance." But the record wasn't a hit. Sonny Curtis thinks at least part of the reason is the Presley connection. "My feeling is that it just wasn't time and we sounded too much like Elvis," Curtis says.

"Also, I will say that Decca wasn't into promoting them real well. They probably sent 25 to San Francisco and called it a release. I don't know."

Decca estimated that the record sold just 18,000 copies. Although Holly's record failed to make the charts, another West Texan's did. Sam Phillips had another smash on his Sun label with "Ooby Dooby," a nonsensical rocker by Roy Orbison, who hailed from the tiny flatlands town of Wink, Texas.

Adding to Holly's frustration was the high-stakes race by the major labels to match Presley's phenomenal appeal with teenagers. No label wanted to be left behind. Gene Vincent, an ex-sailor from Virginia whose onstage antics were thwarted by a crippled leg, won a Presley sing-alike contest for Capitol Records and struck gold for the label with *Be-Bop-a-Lula,* recorded at Bradley's studio in Nashville. Decca's subsidiary, Coral, put its backing behind the hard-rocking Rock 'n' Roll Trio, which featured Johnny Burnette and guitar virtuoso Paul Burlison, former coworkers of Presley at Memphis's Crown Electric Co. Decca itself was getting into the act, recording rockabilly tunes by established country star Webb Pierce.

All across America, talent scouts were picking teens off street corners and shuffling them into studios. The message was clear: Rock music, especially music by young people for young people, was a big money-maker. Companies that could afford it turned their young singers over to image makers, who did their best to mold the performers into polite publicity machines. Besides teaching them manners, the publicists taught them to deal with the press. One of the most commonly asked questions of the era was "What will you do when rock 'n' roll dies?" The question Buddy Holly had foremost in his mind in mid-1956, however, was "When will my rock 'n' roll career begin?"

Holly returned to Nashville in July 1956. This time Holly brought old friend Allison, who had just graduated from high school, to play drums. One of the songs recorded was "That'll Be the Day," a song Holly and Allison wrote a few weeks earlier after watching the John Wayne movie *The Searchers,* in which Wayne frequently uses the song's title phrase. Sonny Curtis played rhythm guitar behind Holly's lead on "That'll Be the Day," but wasn't satisfied with the way his part of the three-hour session went.

"We just didn't get the right feel," Curtis says. "I don't think that song really needed a rhythm guitar."

Another song from the session, "I'm Changing All Those Changes," in which Curtis played lead, went much better. "We were so excited with it, saying 'Boy that sounds great,'" Curtis says. "When we left the studio, we were really flying." But none of the songs recorded that July in Nashville would be released in 1956.

Despite Holly's deepening frustration of a stalled career, rock music was cutting deeper into the fabric of American culture in late summer 1956.

Within weeks after Elvis started production of his first feature film, *Love Me Tender,* several rock stars gathered in Hollywood to make musical cameos in a Jayne Mansfield rock 'n' roll movie, *The Girl Can't Help It.* Even Elvis managed to break new ground on September 9 when he made his first appearance on *The Ed Sullivan Show,* just weeks after Sullivan vowed he would never allow Presley's antics on his stage. Television rating services estimated that 54 million viewers, 82.6 percent of the audience, watched the Sullivan show that night.

RCA released eight Presley singles in September 1956 alone. One of those releases, "Love Me Tender," from his movie of the same name, sold more than 850,000 copies before its release and would begin a five-week run at the top of the *Billboard* charts in early November.

All pumped up with nowhere to go, Holly made another tour supporting Hank Thompson in September and October with Curtis, Guess, and Allison.

———— • ————

September 19, 1956

Whatever we may think of rock 'n' roll, even if we dismiss it as merely teenage music, there is no getting permanently out of earshot. It catches up with you sooner or later on television or radio, in a restaurant, in the five and ten cent store, or from the mouths of babes.

If with regret, we've got no choice but to admit rock 'n' roll is part of our national culture, for the present, anyway. . . . Musical considerations aside, most of us could live happier without that nerve-jangling piano, that neurotic sax, and those jack-hammer rhythms. Rock 'n' roll has got to go. . . .

Rock 'n' roll may belong to the teenager, but the earache is ours. As the man says: Never send to ask for whom the record plays. It plays for you.

—*Downbeat*

Holly and his band continued to build a solid reputation around Lubbock. As their popularity grew, the *Lubbock Avalanche* ran a photo of Holly and his bandmates performing at the Cotton Club. Teenage dancers in the photo had their eyes covered with black bars, to protect their identities. The *Lubbock Evening Journal* sent a reporter to the local youth center to interview Holly for an October 23 story comparing him to Presley.

Decca summoned Holly to Nashville for one more shot at recording a marketable song. But Sonny Curtis was no longer part of the group.

"It wasn't going anywhere," Curtis says of his recording career with Holly. "Buddy and I sort of had a misunderstanding anyway. Buddy was wanting more and more to play lead and I didn't really envision myself as a rhythm player. It didn't seem like a very glamorous role to me." Instead, Curtis signed up as a guitarist for Slim Whitman, a star on the *Louisiana Hayride* radio show out of Shreveport.

En route to Nashville, Holly and Don Guess drove several hundred miles out of their way to visit Holly's longtime, but now occasional, girl-friend, Echo McGuire, who had transferred to a church college in distant York, Nebraska, from Abilene Christian that fall.

Holly's Nashville session ultimately resulted in another Decca record—"Modern Don Juan" backed with "You Are My One Desire"—which was released in late December, but Holly knew his days with Decca were numbered.

After returning to Lubbock, he sought a new career path. Curtis thinks that was a brilliant decision.

"He and Jerry Allison got a gig in Lubbock at the skating rink," Curtis says. "They had Friday and Saturday night be-bop deals for teens. . . . Man, they got so tight playing together, just drums and guitar, it just had a terrific feel."

Holly and Allison recorded a dozen songs in a small Lubbock studio in late 1956 as they worked on perfecting their sound.

As expected, sales were sluggish on Holly's second Decca release, and by early 1957, the label dropped him. Even though he was without a record-ing contract, Holly hadn't given up his dream of being a rock 'n' roll star. It was hard for the Lubbock teenager to sit still with all that was happen-ing around him.

The music industry was in the midst of a tremendous boom, thanks to teens, who were buying roughly two-thirds of all records sold in the Unit-ed States. Record sales in 1956 totaled more than $300 million, up from $219 million three years earlier. In 1956, RCA-Victor sold more than 13.5 million Elvis Presley singles and 3.75 million Presley albums. Presley was named businessman of the year by *The American Weekly* after earning more than $1 million in 1956. That was ten times what baseball's highest-paid player, Ted Williams, would earn in 1957.

Holly and Allison started a new group, adding guitarist Niki Sullivan, a hotshot young golfer who had visions of competing on the professional tour, and bass guitarist Larry Welborn. Holly's next move became apparent on February 13, 1957, when two new entries popped onto *Billboard*'s Hot 100: "Party Doll" by Buddy Knox and "I'm Stickin' with You" by Jimmy

Bowen. Knox and Bowen were fellow West Texans whose records had been recorded at the same tiny studio just one hundred miles northwest of Lubbock, in Clovis, New Mexico, where Holly had recorded some demos a year earlier. Impressed with the sound of Knox and Bowen's hits, Holly scheduled a recording session for February 24, 1957, at Norman Petty's studio in Clovis.

Petty was gaining a reputation for making rock 'n' roll hits with what was called the Tex-Mex sound, a blend of Texas swing, honky tonk, and boogie woogie. In 1955, Petty had recorded Roy Orbison's first record, *Ooby Dooby* (later re-recorded for Sun).

Recording at Petty's was much different than working at other studios. All recordings at Petty's had to be done at night. Train tracks ran within blocks of the studio and the main east-west highway running through Clovis passed within feet of the front door. Instead of scheduling a set number of hours for a session, Petty offered unlimited studio time to make a record. For $75, an artist could spend as much time as necessary to record two songs. Petty's wife, Vi, offered snacks and sodas from a well-stocked kitchen at the rear of the studio. Next to the kitchen was a sitting room, which offered an area to recuperate from the lengthy recording sessions. Vi Petty also served up polite conversation, often reassuring nervous young artists.

"It was sort of like sitting in your living room," Buddy Knox says.

Norman Petty had come a long way from the day in 1940 when the thirteen-year-old set up a recording studio in his parents' living room with a disc cutter he bought from Sears, Roebuck and Co., on the installment plan. Petty was always fascinated by music. As a third grader, he was the leader of the LaCasita School rhythm band. He learned to play the piano by ear and in junior high formed his own musical group, the Torchy Swingsters. Petty was also fascinated by electronics. His parents were dismayed when a young Norman took apart the family radio, but were relieved when he was able to put it back together in perfect working order.

As a teenager, Norman had his own program on Clovis radio station KICA, playing the organ. Through high school he dated Violet Ann Brady. After his graduation in 1945, Petty was drafted into the Air Force, while Brady attended the University of Oklahoma to study classical music. They wed on June 20, 1948, and lived briefly in Dallas where Norman was a part-time engineer at a country-music recording studio. They also formed the Norman Petty Trio, comprised of Petty, Vi on keyboards, and guitarist Jack Vaughn. The trio was a successful pop group in the late 1940s and early 1950s, playing lounges and Air Force bases around the country.

In 1952, Petty recorded "Mood Indigo" by the trio, but was unable to find a record label to take a chance on his group. Frustrated, Petty borrowed money to press the record himself, which he then released on his own label,

Nor-Va-Jak ("Nor" from Norman, "Va" from Violet Ann, and "Jak" from Jack Vaughn). In 1954 the record was released nationally on RCA's "X" label and sold almost a half-million copies, prompting *Cash Box* magazine to name the trio most-promising new small instrumental group in the nation.

As royalties for "Mood Indigo" rolled in, Petty started building his life-long dream: a state-of-the-art recording studio. In 1955, Petty started remodeling an old Clovis grocery store at 1313 West Seventh Street. The next building west was a garage operated by Petty's parents; an apartment at the rear of the garage would be Norman and Vi's home. Working with experts and engineers, Petty spent an estimated $100,000 on his project, stocking the studio with the best equipment available, including tape equipment which allowed him to refine the relatively new technique of multitracking.

Jimmie Self, a local country singer and longtime friend, was one of the first to record in the new studio. Then came Orbison, Knox, and a steady succession of young West Texas rock 'n' rollers, including Holly.

"You produced a hit for one Buddy [Buddy Knox]," Holly told Petty. "You can do it for me."

Holly's group arrived in Clovis early in the evening of February 24 but didn't begin to record until around 11 PM, Niki Sullivan recalls.

"Norman was having a hard time getting us all set up," Sullivan says, pointing out that truck traffic was particularly noisy, too. "Norman was a real stickler," bass player Larry Welborn says. "He wanted everything to be just right."

The session for "That'll Be the Day," a song recorded the year before in Nashville, ran into the early morning hours. "We cut and cut and cut and then they went back and took one of the first cuts we had done," Welborn says.

Finally the musicians headed back to Lubbock with their records. "We bought five acetates at three dollars apiece," Jerry Allison says.

Petty soon started to shop the record around, using the connections he had developed with his trio. He started with an old friend, Mitch Miller, at Columbia Records in New York. Miller had made a brief foray into rock in 1955, when Columbia signed a pair of teenagers from Oklahoma, rockabilly singers Lorrie and Larry Collins. The Collins duo never managed a break-out hit, although it was right on target for the teenage audience with such songs as "Beetle Bug Bop," "The Rockaway Bop," "I'm into My Teens," and "Rock and Roll Polka." Their clean-cut appeal earned them plenty of TV exposure and lots of touring dates, but none of their songs ever charted. It was a rare miss for Miller's label. In 1955, when given the opportunity to sign Elvis Presley to Columbia, Miller passed. But Miller, who had channeled so much of his energy into producing popular hits in the early 1950s, was waiting for the rock 'n' roll fad to pass, choosing to focus instead on the softer pop ballads of song stylist Johnny Mathis. So, it was not much of a surprise when Miller passed on the Crickets, too.

After being rejected by Miller, "That'll Be the Day" eventually landed in the hands of Bob Thiele of Coral Records, a subsidiary of Decca that had dropped Holly just months before. By mid-March, Thiele had persuaded Decca to release "That'll Be the Day" on another subsidiary, Brunswick. Because of Holly's Nashville recording of the same song on Decca the previous year, it was decided to attribute "That'll Be the Day" to the Crickets, with no mention of Holly. Indeed, the contract with Brunswick was signed by only three Crickets: Niki Sullivan, Jerry Allison, and Joe B. Mauldin, who had replaced Larry Welborn on bass the week after the record was cut.

Meanwhile, Petty started two months of negotiations, which eventually led to a solo deal for Holly on Coral. The agreement with Coral included Holly's forfeiture of royalties from his earlier Nashville recordings.

With Holly's recording career apparently on track again, Petty advised him to get a manager if he hoped for a real career. Holly agreed.

"I want you," he told Petty.

Within days after recording "That'll Be the Day," Welborn left Holly's group. Joe B. Mauldin replaced Welborn on bass in time for the Crickets' first public appearance at the Elks Club in Carlsbad, New Mexico, on March 2, 1957.

While waiting for the release of "That'll Be the Day," the Crickets kept busy: Sullivan drove a flower truck, Mauldin shined shoes, Allison worked at a grocery store, and Holly helped lay tile with his father and brothers. Holly also helped Petty build an echo chamber for his studio, in the attic above Petty's father's service station next door.

Petty had long been fascinated by the richness that a controlled echo can add to a sound. He had tried the technique in mid-1956 when Sonny West arrived to record "Rockola Ruby" and "Sweet Rockin' Baby." But, since Petty had no way of generating a satisfactory echo in his small studio at the time, he rented the Lyceum Theater in downtown Clovis for a one-shot recording session. Now, with some tile experts available and his father's space available, he saw an opportunity to realize another dream.

L. O., Larry, and Travis Holley did the job in one night, crawling about with flashlights as Buddy handed up tiles. "It didn't look like it would work to me," a skeptical Larry Holley says. "It was all slanted, with triangles and stuff. . . . It didn't have to be pretty. We didn't even have to grout it." Petty's echo chamber had a speaker at one end, some sewer pipes in the middle, and a microphone at the other end. Petty sent the sound from the studio via cable to the speaker. The microphone would pick up the sound and send it back to the control room where, when it was mixed with the pickup from the studio, it would create an echo effect.

On May 11 the Crickets were invited to the studios of Amarillo television station KFDA to audition for a spot on the Arthur Godfrey *Talent Scouts* network television show. Although Niki Sullivan didn't go to the audition, he doesn't think things went well. "I don't think Buddy's heart was in it," Sullivan says. The Crickets never appeared on the show.

Brunswick finally released "That'll Be the Day" on May 27, but the song didn't make the rock 'n' roll charts until August. "It seemed like it took forever," Jerry Allison said.

Meanwhile, Norman Petty took advantage of the opportunity to further his own career as a recording artist. Although Mitch Miller had passed on the Crickets a few months earlier, the artists and repertoire (A&R) chief at Columbia Records signed the Norman Petty Trio to a recording contract. The Trio's middle-of-the-road pop music was more suited to Miller's tastes. However, their first Columbia single, *The First Kiss,* barely dented the charts during its five-week run in the late summer 1957. It would be the last song by the trio to have any national success.

By early July, *That'll Be the Day* had become a breakout hit in Buffalo, New York, and Philadelphia, with national sales of about 50,000. Very pleased Decca officials offered to fly the musicians to New York later that month for a promotional visit. Meanwhile, Petty had booked the Crickets for their first tour with Irvin Feld, a pioneer rock promoter. The eleven-week tour was to start right after Labor Day. Feld, who noticed *That'll Be the Day* had made the rhythm and blues charts earlier in the summer, also booked the band into theaters in Washington, Baltimore, and New York for the first three weeks in August, before his national tour began in New York. Petty also arranged for the Crickets to perform on Alan Freed's week of concerts in New York around Labor Day.

Before shipping them out of Texas on July 28, Petty left nothing to chance for his young musicians. He bought them clothes in downtown Lubbock and opened a checking account for them at the Clovis National Bank. Before they boarded their flight to New York in Amarillo, Petty gave each of the singers a complete set of instructions of how to take care of business while on the road, including reading their bibles and sending their money back to Clovis for safekeeping.

Decca executives put the Crickets up in New York's Edison Hotel and showed off their new stars at a string of cocktail parties and receptions with music business associates. The Crickets then moved on to make their first appearance at the Howard Theater in Washington, D.C., on August 2, with the Cadillacs, Clyde McPhatter, and Lee Andrews and the Hearts, all black performers. Unbeknownst to the Crickets, Norman Petty, and the promoters, the white group had been booked onto the rhythm and blues circuit.

"[We thought] they were black," Feld aide Allen Bloom says. "They sounded like a black act. We had only heard the record. . . . When these white kids jumped on stage, there was a big hush in the audience . . . but everything went fine."

Two or three days into their stint at the Howard, the Crickets were faced with their first crisis: Holly lost his voice. "Buddy was sick," Sullivan says, adding that fear may have been a factor, too. "It was our first week of being in the spotlight. One day you're a tile-setter and the next day you're in front of a black audience doing the one thing you've wanted to do all your life. All of a sudden you're here and it's all on your shoulders."

Norman Petty, who was attending a Columbia Records convention in the Washington, D.C., area and promoting his Trio's own record, was summoned. Petty suggested that Sullivan take over the lead singing chores. "I filled in for two days and [then] Buddy was back at it," Sullivan says.

The crisis afforded Petty his first chance to see Holly on stage. He was stunned after seeing Holly in his bright red jacket with white pants and red shoes. "After I saw that I decided [the loud clothes] would have to go," Petty later said.

Sullivan's guitar was stolen in that first week, but Holly and the Crickets had few other problems in Washington. However, performing at Harlem's Apollo Theater two weeks later proved to be unnerving for the Texans. "We were told before we got there that if you can play the Apollo, you can play anywhere in the world," Sullivan says. "You've got to prove yourself to the audiences there. They've seen it all."

Holly and the Crickets were a disaster. "We got maybe a polite hand-clap for two or three seconds, but that was it," Sullivan remembers.

Midway through their week at the Apollo, Holly suggested the band perform "Bo Diddley."

"The place went wild," Sullivan says. "That saved our butts. We passed the Apollo. We cut up, we danced, we did everything. . . . We acted like complete rubber-legged idiots and they liked it. That's what they wanted to see."

By the end of the week at the Apollo, "That'll Be the Day" had sold a half-million copies. With the song racing up the charts, Petty was busy back in Clovis putting together two albums: a solo release for Holly on Coral and a Crickets' LP for Brunswick.

A session was scheduled with a New York photographer for promotion photos and a shot for the Crickets' album cover. The group went shopping.

"Finding four suits of the same kind was even tough in New York back then," Sullivan says. "We found four alike, but there was not enough time to do enough critical tailoring . . . the shoulders drooped a little, the sleeves were big and the pant legs looked like barrels." Allison remembers that the gray suits cost about $75 apiece and "there was enough room for another family to move in." The cover shot for the *Chirping Crickets* album was taken that weekend on the roof of the Brooklyn Paramount Theater, using the natural blue sky as a backdrop.

The Crickets' whirlwind introduction to the world of popular music continued that weekend as they made their first television appearances, on Alan Freed's New York City program and on Dick Clark's *American Bandstand.* On August 30, the Crickets began a seven-day stint on Freed's third anniversary Labor Day concerts at the Brooklyn Paramount theater featuring many of the top acts of the day. Freed's concerts were all-day affairs, with performers doing two or three songs several times throughout the day. Between the live music acts, the motion picture *Gunshot Ridge* was shown.

The Crickets were in illustrious company on Feld's "Biggest Show of Stars," which opened in Pittsburgh, Pennsylvania, on September 6. Included were Fats Domino, Clyde McPhatter, LaVern Baker, Paul Anka, the Everly Brothers, Chuck Berry, Eddie Cochran, and Buddy Knox. "LaVern Baker used to call it 'Can You Top This?'" Feld aide Bloom says. "It was an incredible show."

Just before leaving New York, Holly and the Crickets became good friends with the Everly Brothers, a pair of youngsters from Kentucky who had cracked the Top 10 that summer with "Bye Bye Love." "The Everlys looked at us as farm boys," Sullivan says, referring to the Crickets' casual dress, which usually consisted of blue jeans and T-shirts. At the Everlys' suggestion, the Crickets upgraded their wardrobes with Ivy league clothes. By the time the eighty-day tour would end in Richmond, Virginia, on November 24, the Crickets traveled some 19,000 miles and perform in twenty-four states and five Canadian provinces.

While the Crickets enjoyed their onstage performances, touring soon proved to be a drag. "There was a lot of boredom," Sullivan says. "Backstage there was nothing to do but wait."

The entourage traveled in two buses, where performers frequently slept as they traveled through the night. "Trying to sleep was impossible," Sullivan says. "There was always somebody who'd take their damn instrument or horn along and tune it." Says Buddy Knox: "You were confined either to a hotel room, a stage, or a bus twenty-four hours a day. There was no outside activity at all. There were more crap games going. I saw Fats Domino drop something like fifteen thousand dollars in a crap game between shows. We'd never seen anything like that before. It was like Alice stepping through the looking glass."

"That'll Be the Day" replaced Paul Anka's "Diana" at the top of *Billboard*'s popular music chart on September 23. About a week later, the song became a million-seller, as the tour crossed the Mason-Dixon line into the segregationist South. Even though Holly and the Crickets had been raised in the South and attended racially segregated schools in Lubbock, they weren't prepared for the treatment they received on that tour. "That was the worst of the times we had," Sullivan says. "The black [performers] could not stay in the white hotels and the whites were not really all that welcome in the black hotels." Allison calls the situation "ridiculous."

"We played some shows where there was actually a curtain down the middle of the audience," he says. "There'd be black on one side and white on the other. We couldn't believe it." The white performers of the Biggest Show of Stars were not allowed to perform on the same program with the black performers for several southern shows, even though "That'll Be the Day" was riding high on the rhythm and blues charts.

With a deadline approaching for the completion of the Crickets' album, Petty came up with a creative means to record the group, which was scheduled to rejoin the tour in Tulsa, Oklahoma, on September 28. Because the Norman Petty Trio was performing at the Officers' Club at Tinker Air Force Base in Oklahoma City that night and the Crickets were to perform at the Oklahoma City Municipal Auditorium on the next night, Petty took along some portable recording equipment and scheduled a late-night recording session at the club. Holly and the Crickets drove the 105 miles to Oklahoma City after their Tulsa show and, in the early hours of the morning of September 29, recorded four songs in a makeshift studio in a corner of the club: "Maybe Baby," "An Empty Cup," "Rock Me My Baby," and "You've Got Love."

Sellout crowds were common on the Biggest Show of Stars, which was three-fourths completed by November 2, when Holly's first single on Coral, "Peggy Sue," debuted on *Billboard*'s charts as the tour dipped into the Midwest on its way back to New York. When the musicians stopped in Omaha, Nebraska, on November 4, Holly tried to reach Echo McGuire at her college in York, some one-hundred-and-fifteen miles away. "He kept trying to call me, but I was in class and they wouldn't call me out of class," McGuire says. "He was hoping I could come to Omaha, it was like a two-hour drive. By the time they got hold of me, it was already too late to go over."

The grueling tour continued to work its way east, finally reaching Virginia and North Carolina in late November. "We were extremely tired," Niki Sullivan says. "We'd had little sleep. We worked hard, and long hours.

On one of the last nights on the bus, the Drifters sang "How Deep Is the Ocean." It was very quiet. They must have sung for twenty minutes. Man, I got tears, I think everybody got tears in their eyes. We were tired."

After appearing on *The Ed Sullivan Show* on December 1, the Crickets returned to Lubbock for a few weeks' rest before returning to New York to perform on Alan Freed's Christmas holiday shows. But the touring grind had taken its toll on Sullivan. "I'd had it," remembers Sullivan, who quit the group the day after returning to Lubbock. "When we got back home to Texas and I got some good food, I said there ain't no way I'm going to live like this."

But the other three Crickets were thoroughly enjoying the new lifestyle. "It was a change from not having enough money to buy gas for a car to being able to buy a new car with cash," Allison says. Indeed, Holly promptly purchased a new coral pink 1958 Chevrolet Impala coupe in Clovis. He also visited his dentist in Lubbock and had his front teeth capped.

Just before Christmas, Buddy had hoped to resume his relationship with Echo McGuire, who would be home for the holidays during her school break. But McGuire had a new boyfriend, fellow student Ron Griffith. The couple planned to marry in the spring. "I told [Buddy] what I had decided," Echo says. "From that point on, I put him aside."

———— •—• ————

December 21, 1957

Memphis, Tenn. — The career of rock 'n' roll singer Elvis Presley will be temporarily halted soon.

The 22-year-old singing sensation received his Army draft notice on Friday. As a result, his income will dip from some $50,000 a performance to $78 a month as a private. That amounts to at least a $500,000 loss to the U.S. government in taxes from Presley's projected income for 1958. Nevertheless, Presley, who is to be inducted on January 20, took it all in stride.

"I'm kinda proud of it," he told reporters. "It's a duty I've got to fill and I'm going to do it."

———— •—• ————

Presley's manager, Col. Tom Parker, soon asked the Memphis draft board to delay Presley's induction by a couple of months which would, in effect, cut the government's losses of Presley tax revenue. Of course, the $350,000 loss faced by Paramount Pictures if Elvis couldn't complete a scheduled motion picture may have been a factor, too. Elvis received a sixty-day deferment, prompting one member of the Memphis draft board to resign in disgust.

Record sales in the U.S. were estimated at $400 million in 1957 with Elvis-licensed products grossing an estimated $55 million.

Buddy Holly's "Peggy Sue" hit the one-million mark in sales the same day Freed's Christmas show debuted at the Paramount Theater near Times Square on December 27. Fans were enthusiastic, tearing at the clothes of anyone who ventured through the stage door, including stagehands. While in New York, Holly and the Crickets made their first television appearance as a three-piece band on the *Arthur Murray Show* on December 28, performing "Peggy Sue."

The Crickets caught their breath for three days after completing the Freed shows on January 5. They then did a seventeen-day tour of the northeast for Irvin Feld, made a second appearance on *The Ed Sullivan Show,* toured Australia for a week, recorded in New York and Clovis, and made another short tour through Florida.

But the Crickets' greatest conquest lay immediately ahead as they started a twenty-five-day swing through England on March 1. On the second day of the tour, the Crickets found themselves sharing a stage with American comedian Bob Hope on the *Sunday Night at the Palladium* television show. Besides being the group's first lengthy tour outside the United States, the British tour also was the first in which Holly and the Crickets were clearly the stars. All of the supporting acts were British, and none were rock 'n' rollers. Unlike American tours which played largely to teenagers, the British tour was more like a cabaret experience, with jugglers and mimes sharing the bill.

The Crickets were big in England even before their arrival. All three of their British releases—"That'll Be the Day," "Peggy Sue," and "Oh Boy!"— had cracked the Top 10. That was no small feat considering that the British Broadcasting Corporation had banned rock 'n' roll from the radio.

The British pop-music newspaper *Melody Maker* acknowledged Holly's visit, and that of Paul Anka, who was in the country at the same time: "Rock solid are the concert halls of Britain. Gyrating like rival sputniks round the provinces are these two rocking package shows headed by Paul Anka and Buddy Holly and the Crickets. The Beat, like it or not, is here."

English music critics were generally impressed by the Crickets, referring to the band's abnormally large sound for a trio and the engaging stage presence of Holly. Trying to summarize Holly's appeal, Keith Goodwin of the *New Musical Express* wrote:

Without doubt, the Crickets are the loudest, noisiest trio I've ever heard in my life.

But as far as the audience was concerned, everything was just fine. They loved the group's spirited lusty rock 'n' roll style and they went for Buddy's easy going natural stage personality in an equally big way.

The tall Texan cavorts around stage quite a bit, but his gyrations are not nearly as wild as the Elvis Presley type. Drummer Jerry Allison attacks his kit with murderous intent, but bassist Joe Mauldin remains relatively calm and looks rather miserable most of the time.

Before leaving England on March 25, the Crickets recorded "Maybe Baby" for the BBC's popular *Off the Record* television program.

Despite having toured for twenty-five straight days in England, Holly and the Crickets had just two days off before starting a forty-four-day tour in New York with Alan Freed. Dubbed "The Big Beat," it was a typical Freed attraction with fourteen acts, including Chuck Berry, Danny and the Juniors, the Diamonds, Jerry Lee Lewis, and Frankie Lymon. In some cities Freed booked as many as three shows in one day, similar to his New York City productions. The Big Beat was to rock through sixty-eight performances before wrapping up.

It was a riotous tour, with Jerry Lee Lewis and Chuck Berry carrying on a noisy feud after Freed declared that Berry would close the show instead of the flamboyant Lewis. Consequently, Lewis engaged in an unequaled display of one-upmanship, leaving a trail of shattered pianos in his wake. Primarily because of Lewis's escapades, The Big Beat was page-one news in many of the cities it played. NBC's *Today* program featured Jerry Lee on one of its early morning broadcasts as part of a series on the teenage phenomenon.

As the tour began its final week, the Big Beat landed in Boston for a Saturday night concert on May 3, 1958. For Freed, the Boston show offered an opportunity to make good in a city where he had had trouble in the past. Following riots at a Freed show in April 1957, Boston banned live rock 'n' roll shows. But Boston Mayor John B. Hynes relented in the weeks before the Big Beat was scheduled to arrive and the ban was lifted. Nevertheless, the Boston show was disastrous.

"[The fans] got to raising cain and throwing chairs when Larry Williams was on stage," Jerry Allison remembers. "Then they got to carrying on again when we were playing and they turned on the houselights. Alan Freed tried to get them to turn the house lights down and go on with the show." Police refused Freed's request, and Freed again took the mike and allegedly told the audience of six thousand: "I guess the police here in Boston don't want you kids to have a good time." As the angry fans streamed from the arena, incidents flared. *Variety* reported that "15 persons, including six women, were stabbed, slugged, beaten or robbed by berserk gangs of teenage boys and girls following the jam session. . . . A dozen police cars were rushed to the area as the teeners raged out of control."

In the wake of the riot, most of the remaining Big Beat shows were canceled and Boston Mayor Hynes again banned rock 'n' roll shows from his city.

With the end of the Big Beat tour, Holly, Mauldin, and Allison finally found themselves with some free time, their first real break in almost ten months. They tried very hard to catch up on some of the fun they had missed while on tour.

They flew into Dallas on their way home, bought motorcycles, and rode them the 320 miles to Lubbock. The Crickets spent much of the next two months together, taking life relatively easy. Norman Petty put them to work, too, in an extensive remodeling of his Clovis studio. The Crickets helped with landscaping, including building a fountain.

The Crickets also spent some time cruising the streets of their hometown, basking in the glow of rock 'n' roll stardom. Holly also proved to be generous with his church and family as he started to cash in on his success. He repaid Larry Holley the $1,000 he had borrowed before his first recording session in Nashville, and took a group of family members and friends on a fishing trip to northern New Mexico, near the small town of Chamas.

On June 19, shortly after "Rave On" broke onto the charts, Holly found himself in a New York recording studio without the Crickets. Holly and Petty were in New York attending to other business when Petty heard that the Crickets' label, Brunswick, had painted itself into a corner with Bobby Darin. Darin was a determined twenty-two-year-old pop singer who had tried to break into show business as a pianist and drummer, only to come up short each time. He and another aspiring young musician, Don Kirshner, recorded radio commercials to earn money to make demo recordings of their own compositions before Decca signed Darin to a one-year contract in March 1956.

When Darin's career went nowhere on Decca, he landed another one-year contract in 1957 with Atco, a subsidiary of Atlantic. Darin was a flop with Atco, too, and the label was expected to drop him. Brunswick was going to take a chance on the young singer, however, and had recorded Darin singing two of his own compositions—"Early in the Morning" and "Now We're One"—which were to be released under the group name of the Ding Dongs as soon as Atco dropped Darin.

But Darin's Atco release of "Splish Splash" was an unexpected hit and the label renewed Darin's contract at the last moment. With Brunswick unable to release the Ding Dong sides, Petty suggested that Holly record the songs using the same Darin arrangements.

Within forty-eight hours, Holly recorded both sides and the records were released simultaneously—Holly on Coral and Darin on Atco, under the

Rinky Dinks name—and each made the charts. It was the first Holly record without the Crickets backing him, but it wasn't the last. The Crickets would never record exclusively as a trio again.

By midsummer, Holly and the Crickets were ready to tour again, but no major package shows were available because a national recession began to have an impact on the rock music business. So Petty arranged with General Artists Corporation (GAC) in Chicago for an eleven-day tour through the upper Midwest with just two acts: the Crickets and a western swing band, comprised of local musicians and high school band teachers and headed by Tommy Allsup, a session guitarist Holly had used at Petty's studio. The bands traveled in two cars, Holly's new powder blue Lincoln and a DeSoto station wagon that pulled a trailer containing the bands' equipment. The tour opened in Angola, Indiana, on the Fourth of July.

Unlike the big package tours where the performers were paid by the organizers, this was the first Crickets tour where the band members were responsible for collecting their pay themselves. As they soon found out, some promoters were always ready to take advantage of young rock 'n' rollers. "I remember when somebody would try to dock us, Holly would jump right up and say 'Here's the contract and this is what you owe us. You pay us or else,'" Mauldin says.

The tour wound through Illinois, Iowa, Wisconsin, Michigan, Minnesota, and Wisconsin. Unlike previous tours, travel was relatively easy and the entourage even had time to relax between shows. Allison remembers the stop in Waterloo, Iowa, where they rented a boat and went waterskiing on the Cedar River. Mauldin recalls trying to walk across a row of logs in the river. "We tried to walk across those logs and they started turning and we fell into the river with our clothes on," Mauldin says.

Allsup recalls that there always seemed to be cash on hand on that tour. Whenever a band member needed cash, Allsup remembers, Holly would "just reach in the glove box, grab a handful of money and throw it in the back seat."

While the summer of 1958 had already seen major shifts in Holly's career—the compact summer tour and recording with musicians other than the Crickets—there were major personal changes as well.

Holly and Allison had discussed the possibility of a double wedding in late summer, Allison to longtime girlfriend Peggy Sue Gerron and Holly to Maria Elena Santiago, whom he had met in New York earlier that summer. They had hoped to finalize arrangements following their short summer tour. But Gerron, a "cradle Catholic," and Allison, a Baptist, faced opposition within their families over their plans to wed. Nevertheless, Allison and Gerron were wed within days of his return to Lubbock from the summer tour, eloping to Honey Grove, Texas, on July 22. "That kind of rearranged Buddy's plans," Peggy Sue says. The Allisons delayed their honeymoon until Holly was married to Santiago on August 15.

Holly had met Santiago just weeks earlier. Maria Elena, a native of Puerto Rico who lived with her aunt in New York, was a receptionist at Peer-Southern Music in New York, which handled Norman Petty's publishing business. Holly invited Maria Elena to dinner the day he met her and proposed to her on that first date. They were married at the home of Holly's parents in Lubbock. Right after the wedding, the Hollys left with the Allisons for a short honeymoon in Acapulco.

As Holly and Allison contemplated their futures as married men in the sweltering Mexican sun, another Texan also was gearing up for a major shift in his life. J. P. Richardson, a popular disc jockey from Beaumont, had finally hit the big time after several attempts as a country singer had fallen short. Richardson had found the right combination under the pseudonym of the Big Bopper. His recording of "Chantilly Lace" broke onto the charts the same day as Holly's "Early in the Morning," destined for a six-month run and a spot in the Top 10.

The Big Bopper

Hit records were probably the last thing Jiles Perry Richardson, Sr., saw in the future of his eldest son when J. P., Jr., was born on October 12, 1930, in Sabine Pass, Texas. An itinerant oil field worker, the senior Richardson towed the family home, a twenty-foot trailer, from rig to rig along the Texas Gulf Coast before moving to Beaumont in 1940 to work in the shipyards. In Multimax Village, a huge wood-frame government housing project, young J. P., Jr., learned to play the guitar. At the age of thirteen, he wrote his first song, about a naval captain meeting his son during World War II. "It was a real sad tear-jerker," recalled Cecil Richardson, J. P.'s younger brother.

At Beaumont High School, Richardson earned the good-natured nickname Killer, because of his prowess as a lineman for the school's Royal Purples football team. Despite his substantial size, Richardson was an easygoing sort, according to Cecil. "J. P. never had a fight in his life," Cecil Richardson said. "People would chew him out and tears would come to his eyes. By the time it was all over, he was their friend." Richardson won a high school choir contest for his rendition of "Old Man River," and showed his good humor at a school assembly when he brought the house down performing "The Old Maid Song," a song about a burglar who gets trapped in a house.

After Richardson graduated from high school at sixteen in 1947, he enrolled at Lamar College, first studying to be a detective and later a lawyer. At Lamar Richardson again found himself on a football field, playing the cymbals in the marching band. Richardson paid his way through school, working as an oil field roughneck until his knee gave out. After meeting one of the owners of local radio station KTRM, who was teaching a class at Lamar, Richardson was hired as a part-time radio announcer. One of Richardson's early assignments was doing sound effects during broadcasts of games of the local Texas League's Beaumont Explorers baseball team.

The shy Richardson was immediately popular with his coworkers. "You could embarrass him easily," says Bonnie Cornwell, KTRM continuity and traffic editor. "But he was outgoing and friendly."

Richardson quit college to become a full-time staffer at KTRM in 1949, hosting the Club 990 Show from 9 PM until midnight. As the smooth-talking head waiter of the mythical Club 990, Richardson was very popular among Beaumont's radio audience. Richardson's brother Cecil would sometimes do the sign-off, and then the brothers would file the records before taking off for an early morning tennis match.

KTRM soon featured Richardson on a second show, which he cohosted in the afternoon with his pet frog, Aloysious, a child's rubber squeeze toy. "The frog 'talked,'" says John Neil, a KTRM engineer and son of station owner Jack Neil. "You could almost understand what the frog said, but not quite, thank goodness." Richardson's sidekick was alleged to use language not allowed by the Federal Communications Commission.

By 1952, Richardson was the top-rated disc jockey in the Golden Triangle of Beaumont, Orange, and Port Arthur. Radio still ruled the airwaves in southeast Texas, where television had not yet gained a foothold. The nearest TV stations were in Galveston and Houston and reception was so poor that few residents had even bothered to buy receivers.

Around this time, Richardson met Adrianne "Teetsie" Fryou, the daughter of a Louisiana sugar-cane farmer, who had moved to Beaumont after graduating from high school in Montegut, Louisiana, to assist a sister as she gave birth. "It was love at first sight," she says. They were married on April 18, 1952.

In January 1953 Richardson was promoted to supervisor of announcers at KTRM. Those announcers included some of Beaumont's more colorful characters. One was Wortham "Slim" Watts, a tall, skinny singer who had his own band, the Hillbilly Allstars, and frequently sported a pair of pearl-handled revolvers at work. Watts once shot himself in the foot while practicing fast draw.

Another station personality was Gordon Baxter, who had jumped to KTRM from a station in neighboring Port Arthur. "Gordon never knew anything about music," KTRM announcer Jerry Boynton says. "Gordon was the world's best storyteller, though. His shows were virtually all talk, with him telling long stories and most of his stories were about his sponsors." Future country star George Jones also did a short stint at KTRM.

KTRM was a wacky place to work. Announcers would set alarm clocks to go off during each other's newscasts and turn cats and dogs loose in the studios. Richardson felt comfortable at KTRM from the beginning. During his off-air hours, he frequently just hung around the building or took a guitar into a production studio and sang to himself. "J. P. did a lot of taping, just experimental taping," says Bonnie Cornwell. "He would try to figure a new way of presenting a commercial or a new idea for programming or his songs."

Richardson also regularly did remotes from Jack's Tires, playing records and doing commercials from the showroom and mingling with the gathering crowd. "Business would go up whenever he broadcast from there," owner Jack Baxter says.

As rhythm 'n' blues music started becoming popular in Texas's bigger markets, KTRM owner Jack Neil decided to try a similar show on his station with Richardson as host. "Bopping was one of the terms [used in rhythm and blues music]," Cecil Richardson says. "J. P. was a big man. He needed a good colorful name for his radio show and so he just called himself the Big Bopper."

Says Gordon Baxter: "The Bopper was a distinct and separate personality from J. P. In person he was quiet, chunky, smiling, crew cut hair, the man on the staff everybody loved. He was shy, and a very straight arrow [who] never doped or drank."

The Big Bopper character, on the other hand, was a jive talker who played rhythm and blues records. "That was a pretty naughty kind of music for its day and J. P. wanted to be just on the edge of smutty with everything he did," Boynton says. "He believed there was great humor in touching on the very edge of smuttiness." Few listeners associated the Big Bopper with Richardson. "And that was the way he wanted it," good friend Boynton says.

In fact, Richardson was chagrined by KTRM's practice of opening the studio to the public on weekends, when people could come in and watch the announcers on the air. "He didn't care for that at all," Boynton says. "When he adopted the Big Bopper thing, he'd lock the doors and wouldn't permit anybody to come in and watch him."

Despite Richardson's reticence to be observed, the formula for his show was successful. The program's ratings soared. For its first three weeks, the Big Bopper Show ran for 30 minutes, three times a week. It was expanded to five times a week for one week before being allotted a full hour from Monday through Friday. Richardson also was becoming seriously interested in performing the type of music he was playing over the airwaves. "He did a lot of ad-libbing while the record was going on," reported J. D. Miller, a Crowley, Louisiana, record producer who knew Richardson from promotional trips to Beaumont.

Miller was one of the busier people in the Louisiana music business. After first producing records at Cosimo Matassa's studio in New Orleans in 1946, Miller opened his own studio in Crowley that fall. He specialized in recording regional artists such as Slim Harpo, Lightnin' Slim, Lonesome

Sundown, Lazy Lester, Doug and Rusty Kershaw, and Clifton Chenier, a Port Arthur native who took up playing the accordion while working in the oil fields near Lake Charles. Beaumont radio personality Clarence Garlow recorded for Miller's Features label in 1951.

On a 1954 trip to Crowley, Richardson visited Miller's studio just after a rhythm and blues session for local pianist Leon "Peaches" Stirling. Miller startled Richardson by suggesting he do a session himself.

"What do I do, Jay?" Richardson asked.

"You do exactly what you do on your show when you're playing a record," Miller said. "Just ad-lib anything that comes into your mind."

Miller let the tape roll as the musicians laid down a blues bass line and Richardson ad-libbed some lyrics. The result was a song later called "Boogie Woogie." Although the song would not be released until the 1970s, Miller was impressed with Richardson's early studio work.

"He was so good at ad-libbing," Miller said. "He may never do it twice the same way, but every time he did it was good." Miller hoped to work with Richardson again, with the intention of getting something on acetate.

"But he got his draft papers," Miller said.

Richardson was drafted into the army on March 16, 1955. After basic training in Fort Ord, California, he spent most of his mid-1950s army career at Fort Bliss in El Paso, Texas, where he was an instructor in the M-33 computerized radar system in the early days of the Nike missile program.

"It was tough," says Teetsie Richardson, who starched soldiers' uniforms for twenty-five cents each to supplement J. P.'s $82-a-month salary. The Richardsons became friends with another young couple from Beaumont, James Broussard and his wife, who lived down the street. They frequently got together with the Broussards to play cards, drink beer, and swap stories, until James Broussard was released from the army early to attend mortuary school in Houston.

After his discharge as a corporal on March 15, 1957, Richardson returned to KTRM. "He grew up a lot [in the service] and he became very serious," fellow announcer Roy Dixon Shotts says. "He really wanted to get on with things. He was ambitious." One of Richardson's goals was to begin in earnest the recording career that had almost started at J. D. Miller's studio before he joined the army. Prior to his discharge, Richardson contacted Miller about scheduling a session only to find that Miller was temporarily out of business while trying to move into a new studio.

With his recording plans put on hold, Richardson focused on returning to the top of the Beaumont radio scene. He approached his boss, Jack Neil, with a scheme to attempt to break the world's record for continuous broadcasting. An El Paso disc jockey had stayed on the air for 122 hours in

1956, claiming the record. "When J. P. came back from the service, he was broke," Jerry Boynton says. "The whole purpose of the Jape-a-thon was not for the fun of it, but to make money. He really needed it." Neil refused at first, but eventually realized the commercial potential of such an undertaking. Teetsie reluctantly agreed to the stunt. "I thought he was crazy, but I knew he had to make a comeback," she says.

A temporary studio was set up in the lobby of the Jefferson Theater in downtown Beaumont, where spectators could watch the event from the sidewalk through the wide glass windows. Richardson began broadcasting at noon on April 29, 1957, after undergoing a complete physical examination. He was to be checked by a physician twice a day and was placed on a high protein, sugar, and starch diet to keep his energy up. An accountant was on hand to certify the exact start and stop time of the event, which was expected to run six days.

To relieve the aches and pains of continual broadcasting, Richardson took cold showers ten times a day, during KTRM newscasts. The local YMCA contributed frequent massages, and a barber shaved Richardson daily while he was on the air. Chain-smoking L&M cigarettes and chain-guzzling Seaport coffee, the strain of the Jape-a-thon was almost too much for Richardson as it ground on. By the eighty-eighth hour, Teetsie Richardson was administering oxygen to her tiring husband.

"He did almost give it up one time," Cecil Richardson says. "He actually cried for his mother over the air."

Fellow disc jockey Gordon Baxter drove his MG onto the sidewalk in front of the theater every morning at 5 AM in an effort to give Richardson a chuckle and keep his spirits from flagging. A steady stream of radio personalities trickled into the Jefferson Theater lobby to offer encouragement to the glassy-eyed Richardson, while curious fans queued up outside. A chalkboard marked Richardson's progress, with hourly updates.

On the ninety-ninth hour, in the fifth day, Cousin Louie Buck stopped by with a case of Lone Star beer and Nehi Upper 10 soda, although Richardson was partial to ice-cream malts blended with a couple of raw eggs. At the one hundred and twenty-first hour, as Richardson approached the record, the crowd started to build outside the theater.

Gordon Baxter was with Richardson at the end, when the hallucinations came. "He called it going to the cinema," Baxter says. "He said he felt like he kept dying and coming back."

Finally, just after 2 PM on Saturday, May 4, Richardson set the record while "All Shook Up" by Elvis Presley went out over KTRM. "When he broke the record, he wasn't aware of it," Cecil Richardson says. Gordon Ritter remembers, "He was just like a walking corpse at the end. It was unbelievable." Teetsie Richardson says, "It was scary."

Richardson accepted congratulations from his fellow disc jockeys and played one more record, "Cattle Call" by Dinah Shore, before being loaded onto a stretcher by ambulance attendants and taken out of the theater to the cheers of a crowd estimated at two thousand. Richardson had stayed on the air for 122 hours 8 minutes, played 1,821 records, and earned $746.50 from KTRM for his overtime work.

Richardson was given oxygen as he was transported to Baptist Hospital in Beaumont. "When it was over, he slept for twelve hours, woke up and drank a quart of orange juice, then slept for another twelve hours," Cecil Richardson says. Although the Jape-a-thon earned $4,000 for Beaumont-area charities and Richardson lost thirty-five pounds from his 240-pound frame, he later told reporters he would never repeat the stunt.

However, Richardson built on his reputation with other stunts. He once rolled eggs down Pearl Street in downtown Beaumont at Easter. On another occasion he and Slim Watts raced from Beaumont to nearby Nederland while riding Yazoo lawn mowers. One of the more ambitious stunts was a race against Baxter from Beaumont to Lake Charles, Louisiana, Richardson driving a new Buick on U.S. Highway 90 and Baxter piloting a motorboat down the Neches River and across the intracoastal waterway.

Shortly after the start of the race, the cocky Baxter cut the cord to the boat's motor after starting it. When the motor died, Baxter was unable to restart it and he had to be rescued while Richardson cruised to victory. Richardson's reward was a ride down Pearl Street in a wheelbarrow pushed by Baxter. Richardson arrived for his wheelbarrow ride with a cushion and an umbrella. As the pair passed the local firehouse, firemen doused them with a fire hose.

Just a few months out of the service, Richardson had reclaimed his reputation as one of the Golden Triangle's premier radio personalities at a time when the national wildfire of rock 'n' roll was starting to consume the urban areas of Texas.

Houston record salesman Bud Daily, who also had an office in Dallas, kept Richardson current with the latest trends. Daily's father, H. W. "Pappy" Daily, was involved in virtually every aspect of the music business, from producing records to distributing them and owning the jukeboxes on which they played. "I'd go down and get a six-pack and take it to the control room and sit there and pull records out of my sample bag for him to play on the air," Bud Daily recalls.

Ironically, it was Richardson's preference for popular music that led to his attempt to be a country singing star in 1957. One day Richardson derisively told fellow disc jockey Slim Watts that "anybody can sing country music." Enlivened by the challenge, Richardson went to see longtime friend and country-music promoter Bill Hall, who was organizing concerts in Beaumont Auditorium. Hall, who had been the Richardson family paper boy when J. P. was growing up in Multimax Village, had already produced Beaumont musician George Jones and ran a small recording studio on Magnolia Street.

Before long, Hall submitted several songs J. P. had written to Glad Music, a Houston music publishing company owned by "Pappy" Daily. Almost immediately, Daily had Slim Watts in Houston's Gold Star studio cutting a pair of instrumentals Watts had cowritten with Richardson. Soon "Lonesome"/"Cotton Picker" on Daily's "D" label was getting local airplay.

Next, Daily had Richardson record two of his songs, "Crazy Blues" and "Beggar to a King," which were released by Mercury Records in late 1957. Although the recording sold fairly well for Richardson, "Beggar to a King" did even better for other artists who recorded it, including Benny Barnes on Daily's Starday label. Richardson returned to Houston in the spring of 1958 to record "Teenage Moon" and "The Monkey Song." Although Richardson's first record was pure country, he tried to branch out with his second recording to reach the fast-growing teenage market.

"Teenage Moon" was a countrified anthem obviously aimed at teens, but "The Monkey Song" was more of a rockabilly sound. The lyrics referred to an old high-school girlfriend who later married the manager of a jewelry store. Richardson's hiccupy chorus was closer in style to Buddy Holly than to George Jones. "It was too sweet, too gushy . . . it did not sell," Gordon Baxter says.

It became apparent to Richardson that his future wasn't in country music. "That bothered him some," Teetsie Richardson says. "But he was the type of guy that didn't let anything bother him too much."

Richardson started looking at rock 'n' roll, the music of choice for the country's young people and quickly becoming the choice of southeast Texans, too. "Then Jape settled down each night in the empty news booth and started writing the songs that made him immortal," Gordon Baxter says. "I was working in the control room just across the soundproof glass from him and all I could see of him in there in the dark was the glow on the end of his cigar and feel the steady rock beat . . . coming through the floor of that old wooden building. He put pile drivers into his music."

Rock 'n' roll was headed down a path Richardson found appealing in early 1958, with novelty tunes such as "Short Shorts," "Lollipop," and "Dinner with Drac" were making dramatic climbs up the charts. In April 1958, Ross Bagdasarian employed studio trickery to make recording history. Recording as "David Seville," Bagdasarian steamrolled his way to the top of the charts with "Witch Doctor," a nonsensical number that record-buyers found irresistible, largely due to the squeaky incantations of the title character. To achieve the Witch Doctor's distinctive high-pitched sound, Seville simply recorded his regular voice at half-speed and replayed it at normal speed.

Even as "Witch Doctor" began its inevitable slide, another novelty tune was rising to take its place. On June 9, country singer Sheb Wooley's "The Purple People Eater" assumed the No. 1 spot on the *Billboard* Hot 100, a position it would maintain for half the summer. As in Seville's tune, speed-ed-up voices were the keys to the tune's success. Among many other dee-jays, Richardson played the song on his radio show. "He always called it the 'Purple Peter Eater,'" John Neil says. "I told him, 'J. P. you're going to have to learn how to pronounce that.'"

Richardson proceeded to what he saw as the next logical step. With friend Gordon Ritter, he wrote a song called "The Purple People Eater Meets the Witch Doctor." In the mid-1950s, the Ritter brothers, Gordon and Ken, were television celebrities in Beaumont. Nephews of famed country singer Tex Ritter, they also were active in country music. Gordon Ritter headed a country band and was the star of a television show on Channel 6 (KFDM-TV) in Beaumont. Ken Ritter was the emcee of the show. After Richardson performed one of his country recordings on the show in 1958, he and Gordon Ritter retreated to the Pig Stand restaurant across the street.

Ritter suggested they combine the key elements of Seville's and Woo-ley's hits into one song, "Purple People Eater Meets the Witch Doctor." They stayed up all night working on the song. "The next morning we threw away everything we'd written and went to the radio station and worked on it again," Ritter says. Within days, the Ritter brothers joined Richardson to record the song at KTRM after the station's midnight sign-off. Ken Rit-ter and Bill Hall chipped in $25 apiece to hire some back-up musicians, and Gordon Ritter was tabbed to sing the tune.

Richardson was assigned the duty of taping the session because he was the only one who knew how to create the speeded-up voices. Demos were sent out and Gordon Ritter was signed by RCA records. Working with New York session musicians, Gordon Ritter re-recorded "Purple People Eater Meets the Witch Doctor" for RCA, to be released under his performing name of Rick Johnson.

But there was the legal problem of how to deal with David Seville and Sheb Wooley, whose songs provided the inspiration for the song. "RCA got a little nervous and indicated they probably wouldn't release the record," Gordon Ritter says. Gordon Ritter was still in New York working with RCA when Richardson made plans to cut "Purple People Eater Meets the Witch Doctor" himself, under his radio name of the Big Bopper.

Pappy Daily agreed to record the song in Houston, but insisted that Richardson come up with another tune for the flip side. "He hadn't really done a lot of preparation for this record," says Jerry Boynton, who drove

Richardson to the session. When he arrived at Richardson's home early Sunday morning, J. P. was sitting on his couch, playing with his guitar.

"It's about time for you to decide what in the hell you're going to put on the other side of this record," Boynton said. "What is it going to be?"

Richardson started improvising lyrics, blurting out something about "Chantilly lace and a pretty face."

"All right," said an enthusiastic Boynton as they headed for the car.

Says Cecil Richardson: "He started writing the song [on paper] in Liberty, Texas, and had it done by the time they arrived in Houston."

Pappy Daily had arranged for some of his top studio musicians to play on the session: Link Davis on saxophone, Buck Hinson on bass, Charles R. "Doc" Lewis on piano, Hal Harris on guitar, Bill Kimbrough on drums, and Sonny Burns on guitar. Bill Quinn was the engineer. Davis was well known for his own recording of "Big Mamou." Harris had played on several George Jones sessions, including his rockabilly tunes in 1955–56. Burns also had a lot of experience working with Jones, including cutting a couple of duets on Starday. Burns had also recorded his own rockabilly tune for Starday, "A Real Cool Cat."

After the session Daily played the song for the musicians, who all liked it but didn't care for the title "That's What I Like." After a short deliberation, the song was dubbed "Chantilly Lace."

Richardson was in high spirits after returning to Beaumont. "Man, I think I've got a hit on my hands," he told John Romere, his best friend since Lamar.

Ken Ritter thought it was a hit, too. "We were really amazed when we sent them to Art Talmadge [at Mercury Records] and he turned them down." Mercury had dropped Jape Richardson after his two country records fell short of expectations. Even changing his performing name to the Big Bopper failed to sway Talmadge. Ritter took the songs back to Daily, who released the record on his D label. "It became a hit the first day it came out on D," Bill Hall said. "Houston went wild over it."

"The record started out with the 'Purple People Eater' side getting the airplay and that's the side we started pushing," says Ken Ritter, who also placed the song with producer Bill Lowery of NRC Records; Joe South, then an eighteen-year-old from Atlanta, Georgia, covered it for NRC. South's version first charted in *Billboard* on July 19, 1958, reaching No. 47 before falling off after three weeks. By then, the Big Bopper's version had been picked up by Mercury, thanks to the strong sales on D. That move effectively killed the career of Gordon Ritter's recording alter-ego, "Rick Johnson."

Colorful Texas radio station owner Gordon McLendon also took a liking to the song. When he bought radio station WGRC in Louisville, Kentucky, he instructed his disc jockeys to play "The Purple People Eater Meets the Witch Doctor" continuously, up to twenty times per hour. McLendon's theory was that people would get so fed up with hearing the song that they would tune away for awhile, but come back later to see if the station was still playing it. The recognition for his station was worth the aggravation, McLendon reasoned.

However, Louisville police and the local telephone company disagreed. The police received several calls complaining that something had obviously gone terribly wrong at the station while the phone company complained that the calls to the station were jamming up their switchboard.

Fortunately for J. P. Richardson, many radio stations were discovering the flip side of his record. "It started switching over in places like New Orleans and Dallas and, when it turned over, it was a monster," says Ken Ritter.

John Neil remembers the first time he heard "Chantilly Lace" on one of KTRM's competing stations in Beaumont. "They introduced it as a new song by Fats Domino," Neil says. "They didn't want the competition to get [any credit] on the air at all."

The other stations eventually came around and soon all of America was listening to the song. Offers to lip-sync the song on television followed, but presented an unusual problem. "Chantilly Lace" was virtually ad-libbed in the studio, it was not in rhyme, or synchronized with the music. Richardson and Jerry Boynton worked hard in the KTRM studio to perfect the lip-synching technique. "It was a very difficult thing for him to learn to do right," Boynton explained. "He probably practiced more hours doing that than anything I ever saw him do."

On August 9, 1958, a national audience saw the zany antics of the Big Bopper for the first time on *The Dick Clark Saturday Night Beech-Nut Show* in New York while friends and family watched on television back in Beaumont. "The Bopper was something else," Gordon Baxter recalls. "A flamboyant personality in a long-coated Zoot suit with a dangling chain and a broad-brimmed hat and pegtop pants. He would come on and command a stage, steal the show. He was all over the place." Two days after the Clark appearance, "Chantilly Lace" broke onto *Billboard*'s Hot 100.

After returning to Beaumont, Richardson was a special dinner guest of Houston radio station KXYZ at the Houston Executive Club. He also made his first major public appearance in New Orleans at Pontchartrain Beach on August 21, performing on WTIX Fun Night with Gene Vincent and the Blue Caps, Don Gibson, Dale Hawkins, Sanford Clark, and other pop stars. Don Jacobs, a former reporter at the *Beaumont Enterprise*, was in New Orleans at the time for summer camp with his U.S. army reserve transportation battalion. With Bill and John Neil, he caught Richardson's performance that night.

"He started singing 'Chantilly Lace' and it didn't sound right to me," Jacobs says. After finishing the song, an obviously upset Richardson stormed down the back stairs of the stage. The Beaumont contingent of army reservists caught up with him.

"They can't play in my key," Richardson fumed.

"He was having to sing too high," Jacobs says. "He was pretty upset about that."

Shortly after that, Richardson made a promotional tour of the east coast. "I didn't like [his going on the road] at all," Teetsie Richardson says. "He didn't like it either. It took him away from us. He was very close to [daughter] Debbie." KTRM engineer J. C. Dorrell says: "['Chantilly Lace'] changed things drastically. He started his road shows in earnest at that time. Really, he didn't work [at KTRM] much after that. He was so in demand."

"Chantilly Lace" was a bona fide national hit in late 1958. At one point, *Billboard* called it the third most played record in the country. It was released in thirty-seven other countries, usually making the bestseller list in its first week of release. Furthermore, George Jones had his first Top 10 hit in three years with another Richardson tune, "Treasure of Love."

Richardson's manager, Bill Hall, booked him on a tour that would start in nearby Liberty, Texas, and take in much of the Southeast before working its way north. By the time Richardson arrived in New York to make a second appearance on *The Dick Clark Show* on November 22, his follow-up recording of "Big Bopper's Wedding" and "Little Red Riding Hood" were also getting good support nationally. The record was *Billboard*'s spotlight pick, and *Cash Box* made the record its "Disk of the Week," and it was a "Best Bet" in *Variety*.

Getting Ready

Late Summer 1958

Tim Gale of General Artists Corporation reports that his initial "Summer Dance Party" package grossed about $50,000 for its two-week stint just concluded.

On the windup date in North Dartmouth, Massachussetts, the package pulled better than 3,500 people.

"It's simply a new twist on the dance business," Gale says. "Except in this case you not only have a band for dancing but the accompanying acts are danceable, too."

Gale says it was quite possible that if the current success with the smaller package units continues, the practice might well be extended.

"The thing has been publicized by word of mouth from New England all the way through many areas of the Midwest with the result that we've had many inquiries about the next package to go out. Things look very good at this point," Gale added.

—*Cash Box*

In Clovis, New Mexico, Norman Petty was busy recording the steady stream of would-be rock stars who found their way to his studio in late summer 1958 following the success of the Crickets.

Holly, meanwhile, started making the adjustments to married life. After returning from their honeymoon, he and Maria went apartment shopping in Manhattan. They found a $1,000-a-month corner one-bedroom apartment on the fourth floor of the Brevoort building at Ninth Street and Fifth Avenue in Greenwich Village.

Holly soon returned to Lubbock, eager to try producing. Instead of producing his own band, however, Holly wanted to record Lubbock disc jockey Waylon Jennings. Jennings, a native of nearby Littlefield, had gained quite a reputation as a singer through his performances at remote broadcasts of his station, KLLL. The station's studios atop the Great Plains Life Building in downtown Lubbock were a gathering place for song pushers and local musicians, including Holly and the Crickets.

On September 10, Holly produced Jennings performing "Jole Blon" and "When Sin Stops Love Begins" at Petty's. Both songs featured Holly on guitar and King Curtis on saxophone. Holly had met Curtis, a twenty-four-year-old Fort Worth native, on an Alan Freed tour, and flew him from New York for the all-night Clovis session. Two songs by the Crickets—"Reminiscing" and "Come Back Baby"—were also recorded at these sessions. They would be the last songs Holly would record in Clovis.

Later in September, Holly and the Crickets went to New York to prepare for another Irvin Feld tour, the Biggest Show of Stars. Accompanying the Crickets were the backup singing group the Roses and Holly's wife, Maria Elena. While most of the performers traveled by bus, Holly and Maria Elena drove in his third new car of the past twelve months, a taupe Cadillac, while the Crickets and Roses traveled in his DeSoto station wagon. The Roses carried a mattress in the back of the station wagon so weary singers could catch up on much-needed sleep.

The Biggest Show of Stars wasn't as much fun for Holly and the Crickets as previous tours. With two of the band members now married and one of the wives with them, there were few opportunities for the hijinks that had helped overcome the boredom and sheer exhaustion of touring. Robert Linville, one of the Roses, noticed Holly's apparent preoccupation with business on the tour. "You knew he had something on his mind," he says.

Holly told Mauldin and Allison they should break from Petty and move to New York, where they would be closer to their record company, music publisher, and booking agents. They would also be free of Petty, whose management style Holly now found to be stifling. "Buddy was unhappy that Norman didn't believe in movie magazines or that kind of publicity," Allison says. Many of the Crickets' musician friends were appearing in the rock 'n' roll movies that were popular at the time, but Petty objected. "Norman said, 'No, that's not the right kind of thing for you all to be doing,'" Allison says. While Holly was not pleased with Petty's management, others blamed his marriage to Maria Elena for the eventual break from Petty.

Relations between Maria Elena and both Pettys were strained, at best. The Pettys knew her well before Holly, through their dealings with Peer-Southern Music. "She was so cute and I teased her, I guess, about her accent," Vi Petty said. "It was all in fun. It wasn't anything to put her down." Maria Elena believed, according to Holly biographer John Goldrosen, that Petty actively tried to dissuade Holly from marrying her: "Norman told Buddy that I was a cheap girl who tried to get picked up by practically every entertainer who walked in the office—that I'd run around with a lot of men." Goldrosen points out that Maria Elena's professional experience and family connections in the music business threatened to undermine Petty's control over Holly.

Waylon Jennings says that's exactly what happened. "The thing that broke up [Holly's relationship with Petty] was Maria Elena. She knew what Norman was doing. . . . He was getting the biggest end of the pie. . . . I think [Buddy and Maria] just said there's another way."

Petty did not accompany his musicians on the fall 1958 tour, but met them in New York following their last show in Richmond, Virginia, on October 19. After a short meeting between Petty and the Hollys, the rest of the entourage was abuzz with rumors of an impending breakup. "We just didn't believe it," Linville says.

Norman and Vi Petty and Peggy Sue Allison were in the control room at New York's Pythian Temple studio on October 21, 1958, when Holly recorded his famous string session with Coral producer Dick Jacobs. Holly recorded four songs that night, accompanied by a full complement of violins, violas, and cellos: "Raining in My Heart," "True Love Ways," "It Doesn't Matter Anymore," and "Moondreams." They were Holly's first recordings in stereo. Peggy Sue was struck by the strange combination of a young Texas rock 'n' roller being backed by an older, rather stuffy group of classical musicians from New York.

"That certainly wasn't their kind of music," she recalls. "It was sort of like everybody had their tongue in their cheek. I think they had quite an attitude. It was quite a stressful session because of it." The lush arrangements are considered to be among Holly's prettiest songs. In later years they served to fuel the controversy over what direction Holly was headed as a performer.

Holly and the Crickets remained in New York long enough to fulfill two television obligations for Dick Clark: one on the Saturday night show on October 25 and the second on the afternoon *American Bandstand* on Tuesday, October 28. The *Bandstand* appearance would mark the last time Buddy Holly would perform with his old friends from Lubbock, lip-synching to "It's So Easy."

Between the musical obligations, Jerry and Peggy Sue Allison looked at apartments with her former high school classmate Joe B. Mauldin. "We looked at apartments big enough to accommodate Jerry, myself, and Joe B. because he did not want to live alone in New York City," Peggy Sue recalls.

After the *Bandstand* performance, the Allisons and Mauldin flew back to Lubbock, while Buddy and Maria Elena drove back in their car and the Roses returned in the station wagon. Mauldin and Allison went to Clovis to wrap up their business dealings with Petty before their move to New York. But Petty persuaded the Crickets they'd be better off in Clovis. "We weren't that anxious to move to New York [anyway]," Allison remembers.

When Holly arrived in Clovis, Allison and Mauldin told him they wouldn't be moving to New York. When Holly found he couldn't persuade his friends to make the move, he told them to take the name of the Crickets while he pursued a solo career. "If it doesn't work out, we'll get back together," Holly told Allison, before returning to New York.

In Clovis, the Crickets planned their future without Holly. Earl Sinks of Amarillo replaced Holly on vocals and guitar and Sonny Curtis was added on guitar. The "new" Crickets longed to tour again, but met with resistance. "Norman just wanted Joe B. and me to hang around the studio and play sessions," Jerry Allison says.

In New York, Holly was trying to put together a new life without having to go on the road again. He managed to obtain a release from his writing contract with Petty, but was having a difficult time collecting his record royalties, which were paid directly to Petty and deposited into the Crickets' bank account in Clovis, an account only Petty had access to. Petty ignored Holly's frequent requests for payment, citing a vague ongoing accounting process that would eventually lead to a fair distribution of the band's accumulated wealth.

Frustrated, Holly turned to well-known New York entertainment attorney Harold Orenstein. As Orenstein began communications with Petty on Holly's behalf, Holly tried to concentrate on his music. Through his marriage to Maria Elena, he was cultivating an interest in Latin music. Through his association with session guitarist Tommy Allsup, he was becoming interested in jazz. Holly also kept busy writing songs, recording them in his apartment on a professional, portable Ampex tape recorder he had bought from Petty.

Holly socialized with other young performers who also spent much of their time in New York, such as the Everly Brothers, Buddy Knox, and Eddie Cochran. The young musicians gathered at one another's apartments or at small clubs to make music together. Holly stayed in close contact with his brother Larry Holley, frequently calling Lubbock late at night to seek personal advice. He tried to hire Larry as his manager at one point.

Holly had new publicity photos taken by fashion photographer Bruno and began wearing thicker, squarer-frame glasses. He took acting lessons at Lee Strasberg's Actors' Studio and started working out at a gym. "He was trying to develop his physique a little bit more," Larry says. "It was working. . . . He started putting on a little bit of muscle."

Holly was also looking well beyond his own performing days. He yearned to have his own studio in Lubbock and had already bought the land and had blueprints prepared for a combination house and studio, to be built by his father. Musicians would be able to live and record in the same building, an arrangement Holly found so appealing at Norman Petty's studio in Clovis. Indeed, under the original plan, Petty was to provide guidance to Holly in the proposed operation. Before moving to New York, Holly had formed his own record company (Prism Records) and publishing company (Taupe) in Clovis. Holly, Petty, and Ray Rush of the Roses singing group were to be co-directors of the new companies. Business cards for Prism list Petty's Clovis address as headquarters for the new company.

In New York, Holly produced a record by an unknown singer named Lou Giordano. Holly wrote the A side of the record, "Stay Close to Me," and teamed with Phil Everly to sing the falsetto background on the flip side, "Don't Cha Know," an Everly composition. But with Petty still in control of Holly's finances back in Clovis, he had little choice but to approach old friend Irvin Feld. He invited Feld to dinner and told Feld of his frustrations in dealing with Petty.

"You know, all my money is tied up," Holly explained.

"Why don't we put a tour together for you?" Feld suggested. "You can make some money, and save some money."

Since September, Feld had worked with General Artists Corporation (GAC) in a co-venture called GAC-Super Productions. The basic concept was to use disc jockeys in targeted cities to plug Feld's touring shows comprised mainly of young, up-and-coming talent. The shows were billed at bargain admission rates, usually under a dollar. Teens could also get discounts on records from participating local music shops. Feld saw this as a means of combating the growing popularity of disc jockeys' teen hops, which were siphoning off the big crowds that turned out just a year or so earlier for huge touring rock extravaganzas. For GAC, the arrangement offered a steady supply of potential clients.

Because Feld already had a major winter tour planned, he asked GAC to help put together a smaller tour for Holly. GAC suggested a dance party tour in the upper Midwest. Few tours ventured into this sparsely populated area although it was full of ballrooms and small dance halls. Promoters were pleading for such a package, and Feld aide Allen Bloom was tempted by the big-profit potential of sending a small group of musicians. An early itinerary prepared by GAC showed the proposed tour making stops in major cities such as Chicago, Milwaukee, St. Paul, Des Moines, and Louisville. But it also listed small towns such as Mankato and Montevideo, Minnesota; Fort Dodge, Iowa; Appleton, Wisconsin; and Spring Valley, Illinois. "We were not familiar with a lot of the cities they had booked," Bloom recalls. "Our expertise was in bigger shows and bigger cities. We didn't do dances."

In December 1958, Feld and Bloom started assembling talent for the GAC show. Besides Holly, they put together an impressive roster of performers for what promised to be a popular touring unit:

- Dion and the Belmonts: a group of New York teenagers who had a couple of minor hits in the previous six months, "I Wonder Why" and "No One Knows." A new release by the group, "Don't Pity Me," was getting good airplay when they were booked onto the tour. It would be the group's second tour of the Midwest in five months, having made a similar circuit in September.

- Ritchie Valens: A teenager from southern California, Valens's recording of "Come On Let's Go" was a national hit in the fall, but had especially strong sales in the Midwest. His follow-up, a ballad called "Donna," was working its way into the Top 20 late in the year. It would be Valens's first national tour.

- The Big Bopper: J. P. Richardson was busy recording follow-up singles and tunes for his first album, which Mercury planned to release in February 1959.

- Frankie Sardo: A little-known New York pop singer, the Italian-born Sardo entered show business as part of a comedy team after returning from service in the Korean war. Sardo released several records, but they didn't chart. Sardo hoped that a new recording, "Fake Out"/"Class Room," on a major label, ABC-Paramount, would give him his big break. "Fake Out" had broken out in the Midwest, leading to the invitation to join the Holly tour, which would be called the Winter Dance Party.

Feld hired Sam Geller of Baltimore, Maryland, to be the tour manager. Geller, a brother-in-law of the Clovers' manager, Lou Krefetz, had extensive experience working the R&B circuit and had been tour manager the previous September for a Midwest tour including Dion and the Belmonts.

Holly and Feld worked out an unusual financial arrangement for the tour. Holly was to receive a share of the profits and a salary, an arrangement Feld had found profitable on an earlier tour with Clyde McPhatter. Holly was paid around $3,000–$3,500 a week, which he shared with his band. Dion and the Belmonts received $1,000–$1,200 a week and Valens and the Big Bopper $700–$800. After the Winter Dance Party, Feld was to become Holly's manager. Holly needed the cash that the Winter Dance Party would provide before he headed to Europe for another tour Feld was planning. And he needed a band.

Holly made a brief visit to Lubbock to celebrate Christmas with his family and to put together a backup band for the Winter Dance Party. One of his first stops was at KLLL, where he visited with Waylon Jennings. He handed Jennings a bass and said, "You've got two weeks to learn to play this thing. . . . I want you to go to work for me." Holly also spent some time in a KLLL production studio with Jennings and station co-owner Slim Corbin, recording one of his new compositions, "You're the One."

Holly and old friend George Atwood got together for a cup of coffee at a Walgreen's drug store. There Holly showed Atwood the plans for his studio in Lubbock. Atwood was impressed with the grand structure. "He was going to have his own pressing plant there, he was going to have his own trucks deliver the stuff. He was going to do it from square one."

Just before New Year's, Buddy and Larry Holley took a long drive around Lubbock. Larry was perplexed by a barrage of questions from his younger brother. "I could never figure out what he was digging at," Larry says. "But I could see that he was disturbed about something. I know that Maria did get on his nerves pretty much because she had such different ways about her. . . . Those were very tense times for him. He was not a real calm person. He'd get uptight."

Buddy said, "I wonder why it is that when you get married your stomach starts just bothering the heck out of you?"

Larry said, "Well, you might have an ulcer, Buddy, ain't no telling."

On December 30, Holly drove to Odessa where he recruited old friend Tommy Allsup to play guitar and drummer Carl Bunch for his touring band. Allsup had met Bunch at Petty's studio when Bunch was recording with a popular Odessa band, Ronnie Smith and the Poor Boys. The next night, Larry Holley drove his brother and Maria Elena to the Lubbock airport where they caught a flight home to New York City.

Saturday, January 3, 1959

Dear Sirs,
    We are very interested in the Big Bopper's recordings. We have a fan club but we do not have enough pictures or details to have a good club. We look in Movie Life and TV Screen magazines every month but can not find any articles on him. We would like very much if you would send us some pictures of him. We think he is the greatest.
    Yours truly,

Fans from Johnson City, Tenn.

P.S. Make more records.

J. P. Richardson received lots of fan mail after the success of "Chantilly Lace." Unlike many recording stars, he tried to answer as many as he could himself. Despite the adulation of his fans and his love of writing and performing, Richardson was looking forward to the day when he could stop touring and settle down. He thought a lot of the young rock 'n' roll stars he had to deal with were obnoxious. They were good performers, but they were too cocky for Richardson's taste. Plus, the strain of performing continuously was tough on Richardson physically. "He would sing until he was hoarse," Cecil Richardson said. "He would cut lemons in half and eat them to hold his voice."

Richardson and Bill Hall formed Big Bopper Music to handle publishing of his newer songs and started to build a small studio in Beaumont's South Coast Insurance Building on Pearl Street. As the Richardsons and friends John and Dixie Romere covered the walls of the studio with egg cartons, they dubbed the place "the chicken coop." Although he tried not to perform any more than necessary, Richardson helped out brother-in-law Woodrow Due on more than one occasion; Due was in charge of the union at Gulf State Light and Power Co. and often asked him to handle master-of-ceremony duties at union social functions.

On one of his last trips to Beaumont, Richardson went drinking with his old friend John Romere. Sitting in a local bar, Richardson told Romere he wasn't going to stay in the business long, just the two or three years he would need to make enough money to buy a radio station and settle down. The staff members of KTRM had a going-away party for Richardson before he returned to a house he had rented in Montegut, Louisiana, for his pregnant wife and young daughter to stay in while he was on the road. As Woodrow Due said, Teetsie "was about ready to domino." Her mother would be right across the road in case of an unusually quick labor.

In Montegut, Richardson caught up on some fan correspondence and autographed one hundred photos to be used in a promotion by an Australian radio station for a tour that was to start right after the Winter Dance Party. The Australian tour would earn Richardson $1,750 a week, a good start on his dream of owning a radio station.

After Richardson's short stay in Montegut, Teetsie Richardson drove her husband to the New Orleans airport where he boarded a Chicago-bound plane toting a briefcase containing horn arrangements for "Chantilly Lace" and a pint of whiskey to help pass the boredom of long bus rides across the snow-swept upper Plains.

———•◦•———

January 1959

> Waylon Jennings, 21, of Littlefield, left for New York Monday [January 19] to become a member of "Buddy Holly and the Crickets" of "Peggy Sue" and "What'll [*sic*] Be the Day" fame.
>
> Jennings will have his own record on the market in two or three months. He will tour the midwestern states beginning January 23.
>
> Mrs. Jennings and their two children, Terry Vance and Julie Rae, will reside in Littlefield.
>
> —*Lamb County* (Texas) *Leader*

———•◦•———

A bitter winter wind swept across northwest Texas as Carl Bunch's mother drove her son and Tommy Allsup from Odessa to Lubbock, where they picked up Jennings on the way to the airport at Amarillo to catch a flight to New York City.

Jennings was stunned after arriving in New York. "Talk about a culture shock," Jennings says. "We went down the very next day after we got there and Buddy bought suits, blazers, ascots . . . and these gangster hats. We cocked them on the side of our heads. We were hot."

The band spent several days practicing before leaving for the start of the tour in Chicago. "We rented a rehearsal hall," Allsup says. "You'd have to carry stuff up three or four flights of stairs." Rehearsing was a full-time job for Bunch. When not practicing with the other musicians, he would play along with Holly's records, trying to duplicate Jerry Allison's licks. "It was hard work for me," Bunch recalls. "I was a perfectionist and I wanted to get it perfect and I couldn't. I was scared to death that I wouldn't be able to please Buddy."

At the same time, Allsup was teaching Jennings how to play the bass, which he had never played before. "I very quickly memorized everything Buddy did," Jennings says. "I didn't learn to play the bass, I memorized the notes."

Holly pushed hard to make the new group sound like the old Crickets. "When we left New York City, you could listen to us and we sounded like J. I., Joe B., and Niki Sullivan," Bunch says. "We were good."

On at least one occasion, Maria Elena tried to cook for the musicians. "She about killed us cookin'," Jennings says. "She tried to cook beans and burned them. Can you imagine burning beans? Buddy said, 'Don't say anything. Just eat them.'"

Food aside, spending all that time with the Hollys didn't set well with Bunch. "I felt ill at ease," Bunch says. "[Buddy and Maria] had some hard words before he left New York. . . . They were having some difficulties." Bunch indicates that Maria Holly precipitated most of the disputes by telling Holly how to handle his life and career now that he was in the big city. Holly resisted Maria's advice. "You don't tell Buddy what to do with his life or his music. He was real serious about the music."

Allsup didn't feel the same tension sensed by Bunch. "[Buddy and Maria] seemed to get along pretty good. She was pretty hot-tempered. I didn't see anything out of the ordinary."

As the time to leave approached, Holly started breaking in a new Gibson guitar by playing with Allsup. "We recorded six things the night before we left his apartment," Allsup recalls. "We just put them down so we wouldn't forget them."

One night, Holly played Jennings's record of "Jole Blon." "I remember Maria Elena in the kitchen, burning the beans, hollering 'Waylon, I likes that. It gives me goose bumples,'" Jennings recalls.

As the musicians ate breakfast in Holly's apartment the morning they were to leave for Chicago, Holly and his wife each told of dreams of airplanes they had the night before. "[Buddy] said something about a plane crashing," Allsup says. "I didn't even think about it for years. I don't know if it was a premonition or if he had a dream."

Bunch is more certain. "Buddy had a premonition about his death."

Bad weather blanketed the United States as Holly, Allsup, Jennings, and Bunch boarded a Chicago-bound train at Grand Central Station. Tornadoes were reported in the Southwest and heavy flooding was reported in Ohio and Pennsylvania. For the week, at least one-hundred-and-ten weather-related deaths were reported and some 25,000 people were estimated to have been left homeless. One of the hardest hit areas was the Midwest. Up to ten inches of snow was dumped in eastern Iowa and bitterly cold temperatures dominated the nation's midsection. Snow emergencies were declared in Wisconsin, where three-foot drifts were common.

The train ride from New York to Chicago was no joy ride. "It was the worst ride of my life," Carl Bunch says. "Just shaking back and forth all night long. When we got to Chicago, I stepped off that train with a tom-tom under each arm and the wind hit me and blew me down that ice right out in the middle of the street flat on my fanny. And all that slush and ice, I like to froze to death. It was terrible." Tour manager Sam Geller also was surprised by what he saw when he arrived in Chicago: Ritchie Valens had arrived from California wearing just a light jacket.

Howard Bedno of Chicago's All State Distributing Company ushered Valens to various radio stations in the Windy City to promote the tour, and Danny Driscoll of Mercury Records did the same for the Big Bopper. The musicians were in Chicago just long enough to meet each other and run through their material with Holly's band and some back-up horn players hired for the tour. Brief promo records were cut to be sent to radio stations in cities in which the Winter Dance Party would play.

Bob Ehlert of GAC's Chicago office had taken care of logistical arrangements for the tour, including hiring the back-up musicians and chartering a bus. Although the musicians may have been adequate, the bus, it turned out, was not. It more closely resembled a school bus than the plush touring buses Geller was accustomed to with tours originating in New York City.

In addition, Howard Bedno was concerned that the shy Valens may have been in the wrong business. Noting Valens's good manners and limited wardrobe, Bedno tried to discourage Valens from pursuing a musical career, especially the hard touring of rock 'n' roll. "What are you doing in this kind of business?" Bedno asked the California teenager. "Why don't you get out of it and try something else?"

5

La Bamba

It was an uncompromising world that greeted young Richard Steven Valenzuela upon his birth in Los Angeles General Hospital in the early morning hours of May 13, 1941. The second son born to Concepcion Valenzuela, young Ritchie joined his half-brother, Bob Morales, in a lifelong struggle to escape the indigent lifestyle suffered by his hard-working parents.

Ritchie's father, Joseph Steve Valenzuela, was born in nearby Long Beach in the 1890s and worked as a cowboy in California in the early 1900s. His work took him to the Pacoima area of the San Fernando Valley, where he settled. Valenzuela served in the U.S. Army in World War I, where he was hit by mustard gas while fighting in the trenches. For the rest of his life, Valenzuela was plagued by sneezing fits.

After marrying Concepcion Reyes, the couple moved to a crude shack near the railroad tracks that ran through the town of San Fernando. In the early 1940s, Steve and Connie Valenzuela worked at a munitions factory in nearby Saugus. Steve Valenzuela's sneezing fits took a toll over the years, causing chronic nose bleeds. Eventually, he turned to alcohol to numb the pain. After his parents separated when he was three, Ritchie lived with Steve in Pacoima in the San Fernando Valley. Although poor, Ritchie was exposed to music at an early age. His father plunked Latin tunes on his guitar while Ritchie tried to keep pace on a ukelele or toy guitar. He also learned to play the trumpet, harmonica, and drums as a youngster. Ritchie enjoyed horseback riding and sometimes accompanied his father to his work on ranches in the Piru valley.

After Steve Valenzuela died of complications from diabetes in 1951, Ritchie moved in with his mother, Connie, who had remarried, and younger half-sister, Connie Ramirez. While Connie's husband, Ramon Ramirez, eked out a living in the asparagus fields near Saugus, she moved her family into Steve Valenzuela's old house in Pacoima. At times, Connie and her sister,

Mary Murillo, would head north to Cupertino, where they picked plums in the orchards of cousin Pete Gonzalez.

As Ritchie grew into his teens, Connie found it difficult to control him. Ritchie had lived with several relatives as a youngster. As a result, Ritchie attended several elementary schools in Pacoima, Norwalk, and Santa Monica. "It wasn't that he was a bad kid," says his aunt, Ernestine Reyes. "It was just that Connie couldn't give him what he needed."

By January 1955, Ritchie was getting very serious about his guitar playing. He bought a second-hand Sears guitar that he refinished in wood-working class at Pacoima Junior High. Relatives taught Ritchie some Latin songs, and soon he was carrying his guitar to school, giving impromptu lunch-time concerts. When pressed into babysitting duty at home, Ritchie would work on his guitar playing by singing to his younger siblings.

By December 1956, Ramon Ramirez had left Connie. Pregnant with another child and unable to make payments on the family house on Fillmore Street, Connie moved her family to a run-down house on Gain Street. "It was a tiny, tiny house," remembers Rosie Morales, who lived in the basement of the one-bedroom house along with her husband, Bob, while Connie's family occupied the main floor. Connie supplemented her $140 monthly widow's pension by working as a housekeeper and waitress at Del & Johnny's in nearby Sylmar. Despite her efforts, the family was so poor it had to drink from empty jars because glasses were too expensive.

By the time Ritchie started his sophomore year at San Fernando High School, he was living with his aunt Ernestine and uncle Lelo Reyes at least part of the time, while Connie concentrated on keeping her family together. That fall, Ritchie's reputation as a guitarist led to a tryout with a local band, the Silhouettes.

Gil Rocha, who had majored in drama and music at Valley College, had formed the Silhouettes in an effort to jump start his acting career. "I'll start a band, I'll make a record and it'll be well-known, then I'll get into the movies," he reasoned. He decided to have his band play rhythm and blues since "that wasn't being played by the other bands around town." Rocha started looking for a sax player but, when his drummer suggested he check out the hot young guitarist from San Fernando, Rocha asked Ritchie to come over. "He came to the door carrying a little green guitar and a real tiny amplifier," recalled Rocha. "I said to myself 'What kind of musician is this?'"

The polite teenager plugged in his amp and started through an impressive repertoire of Little Richard, Fats Domino, and slow r&b tunes. "This kid really knocked my shoes off," Rocha says. After Ritchie told Rocha he was just sixteen, the band leader told the youngster, "You can stop calling me mister. I'm Gil and you're Ritchie and you're in." After just a few rehearsals, Rocha knew the key to future success for his band: "It was us getting used to playing backup for Ritchie," he said.

The Silhouettes played their first dance on October 19, 1957, for the Lost Angels car club at the Panorama City Union Hall. The six band members shared the $35 fee they collected for their performance. After playing two more car club dances in December, Ritchie was making quite a reputation for himself, despite a fairly tame stage presence. "He wasn't shy, he wasn't laid back," Rocha said. "Because of his extraordinary talent he was up front, but not a braggart. He enjoyed performing."

The Silhouettes were an ever-evolving band, with members coming and going on short notice. On the weekends when they didn't have a paying performance they would practice, often in the garage of sax player Bill Jones. It was not unusual for neighborhood teens to gather outside the garage for an impromptu dance. Because the group performed several Little Richard tunes, Ritchie soon earned the nickname "Little Richard of the Valley." He experimented with his guitar style, too, pulling on the strings to create a crying sound. A poster for a January 18, 1958, dance at the San Fernando American Legion Hall invited teens to come hear "The Fabulous Lil' Richi' and His Crying Guitar."

Into the first weeks of 1958, Ritchie played the piano and drums during rehearsals and wrote original material for the band. "He could whip out anything in a few seconds," Rocha said. "Then next rehearsal, he'd change it again. Not that he forgot. He just wanted to improve what he'd done."

The Silhouettes had a busy February, playing six dates, including a free concert at San Fernando High School to help raise money for a new scoreboard. Aunt Ernestine and Uncle Lelo frequently provided the transportation, in their brand-new 1957 brown-and-beige Chevrolet.

Despite his busy schedule with the Silhouettes, Ritchie also worked parties on his own, collecting up to $15 each appearance. At one of those parties, Ritchie met Donna Ludwig, a sophomore at San Fernando High School. "Donna was bitchin'," Rocha said. "She had big blue eyes, blonde hair. She was loud. You could talk to her about anything and she was always happy and funny." For the next few months "[Ritchie and I] were pretty tight," Ludwig acknowledges, despite her father's objection to their dating. "I was pretty good at sneaking out the window," she says.

As bookings for the Silhouettes slowed that spring, Rocha was ready to quit the group when Ritchie's mother stepped in. Connie Valenzuela opted to skip the $65 mortgage payment on her house in order to rent the Legion Hall in San Fernando for a dance on May 2, 1958. "She made some tamales, got some Cokes and sold some things in the kitchen to make a few extra bucks," Rocha says. Rosie Morales, Ritchie's sister-in-law, remembers the semiformal dance, where she sold sodas and $1.25 tickets and helped check coats. "The hall was small, but it was packed," Morales says.

Connie Valenzuela made about $130 from the dance, but stood to gain a lot more if Rocha's plan to land the band a recording contract worked. Rocha asked a former classmate to tape his final appearance with the Silhouettes. The friend then took the tape down the street from his print shop to a fellow named Bob Keene, who ran a recording studio.

"Keene called me and said he wanted to talk to Ritchie," Rocha recalls. "I asked if he liked the band and he said, 'Naw, but I like the kid singing.'"

Bob Keene was one of those West Coast entrepreneurs that sprung up like mushrooms in the early days of rock 'n' roll. A clarinet player by trade, Keene formed his own band as a teenager and was touted with some hyperbole as the "world's youngest bandleader" before his career was interrupted by service in World War II. After the war, Keene's band played the southern California circuit before he started fronting the Artie Shaw band in 1952. He recorded his first album in 1953.

Keene formed the Keen label with partner John Simus in early 1957 and soon struck it big with Sam Cooke, whose first release on Keen—"You Send Me"/"Summertime"—reached No. 1 on the charts and sold two and a half million copies. Meanwhile, Keene started the Del-Fi label in late 1957. After some success with his first Del-Fi artist, pianist Henri Rose, Keene sold Rose's contract to Warner Brothers and used the proceeds to buy out his partner.

Keene's next project was an innovative young rock guitarist, Dick Dale, whom he recorded in a small storage room in the basement of his home. Dale would create the surf sound that inspired so many instrumental groups of the early '60s. Problems with Dale's father led to a split, however, and Keene was looking for new talent when he heard about Ritchie.

Keene saw Ritchie perform in a Saturday morning talent contest at the Rennie Theater in San Fernando. "The way he communicated with the audience, that's what really impressed me," Keene remembered. "I thought that if we can find the right song for him and get that to come off on record, we would have a very good act." Keene invited Ritchie to his house for an audition. After hearing Ritchie perform a disjointed version of "Come On Let's Go," Keene scheduled a June session in the Gold Star Studio.

Since Gold Star Studio had opened in Hollywood in 1950, it had become "the demo capital of the world," according to co-owner/engineer Stan Ross. "It wasn't expensive and they could play around with ideas and sound," Ross explained. The cost of about $15 an hour "sometimes even included the tape," Ross says. Gold Star's relaxed atmosphere was perfect for young rock 'n' rollers. The Champs had already produced a No. 1 hit at Gold Star with "Tequila," for the independent Challenge label. The independents could take their demos one block down Vine Street to have their records pressed. A label-printing plant was next door.

To get Ritchie ready for the recording session, Keene first started working on his song, "Come On Let's Go," which came from a commonly used Valenzuela family expression. "All he had was 'Well, come on let's go, let's go' and then he'd ramble on and on and on," Keene says. "So we kind of made little arrangements out of those things, put a bridge to them and got the lyrics so they made a little sense."

Stan Ross was engineer for the session, which Keene presided over with a firm hand. "He was a very dominating type of personality," session drummer Earl Palmer says of Keene. "If you had a little bit of fear, he utilized it." Although long, the session went well. "[Ritchie] was kind of shy," session bass player Carol Kaye thought. "As soon as he started singing a little bit, you could tell that he had a lot of talent."

As long as the session was, Keene says he took nearly as long to edit the tape. Keene estimates he made forty-six edits before "Come On Let's Go" was ready to master. "We had a lot of trouble with Ritchie, because there were breaks in there and he couldn't feel the time," Keene says. "So we had to manufacture the time. We had to count down and keep clipping and put back in the editing to make it come out right." Ritchie later recorded "Framed" for the B-side.

Keene persuaded Richard Valenzuela to take Ritchie Valens as his recording name. "If you send something out by Valenzuela to a pop radio station, they'd throw it in the basket and wouldn't even listen to it," Keene says. That settled, Keene ordered five hundred copies of the record from Allied Records (a local manufacturer) and began promoting it. One of Keene's first stops was the weekly disc jockey meeting at radio station KFWB, which was No. 1 in Southern California. "We'd all listen to different records and vote on them," says Ted Quillin, one of KFWB's top-rated jocks at the time. "Sometimes they'd vote them on the playlist and other times they'd say, 'Naw, it's a dog.'"

Quillin met Keene and Valens in the hallway prior to the meeting. Quillin, who learned Spanish while working around El Paso, Texas, attempted some small talk. "I said, 'Hey, Ritchie' and I hit him with some slang thing in Spanish," Quillin recalls.

A slightly bewildered Valens paused for a second before replying. "I don't understand Spanish," he said. Despite the apparent language barrier, the KFWB jocks gave "Come On Let's Go" a thumbs up and it was soon on the station's playlist.

When the early pressings quickly sold out, Keene ordered Allied to crank up production. The record soon sold 225,000 copies, and Keene was busy ushering his new star from disc jockey to disc jockey and appearances at their record hops.

"Come On Let's Go" went into national distribution in late summer. Keene drove his wife, their young son, and Valens to San Francisco for a performance. As Valens sat in the back seat with Keene's son, he started playing a Mexican folk song. "That's where I heard 'La Bamba' for the first time," Keene recalls. "I told him, 'Let's do something with that.' He says, 'I can't do that.' He really believed Mexico was his home. He was very loyal to his Mexican heritage."

In early September, "Come On, Let's Go" was given a national boost when *Cash Box* named it "Sleeper of the Week" and *Billboard* made it its "Spotlight" tune. Valens no longer had time for school. Keene says quitting San Fernando High School probably saved Valens's life. "If he'd been there, he probably would have been killed," Keene says. "He came from a very rough town."

Keene started planning a national tour to give Valens greater exposure, but he wanted to give disc jockeys something more than "Come On Let's Go." He suggested that Valens record "La Bamba" as a follow-up, but Valens had other ideas. "He called me with the hook for 'Donna,'" Keene says. "'I've got a girl, Donna is her name' and then he would ramble on and on." Keene says he and his partner in Kemo Music Publishing Co., Herb Montei, took Valens's idea and finished the song. Keene then summoned session musicians to the basement of his home in Silver Lake to get the song on tape.

Later that day, Valens called Donna Ludwig from his aunt Ernestine's home. "She must have cried or something, because he said 'Oh, don't cry. Wait. Let me play you this song,'" Ernestine remembers. "So he started singing the song to her on the phone." Donna was surprised by Ritchie's song. "He had just mentioned casually, 'I think I'll write a song for you,'" she says. "It was never mentioned again. The next thing I know he called me on the phone and said 'I want to play this for you.' And he sang 'Donna.'"

Soon Keene booked studio time at Gold Star to add instrumentation to "Donna" and record a flip side. Keene again pressed Valens on "La Bamba," and he finally agreed.

Although Valens had first heard "La Bamba," a traditional Mexican wedding dance, at family gatherings as a child, he didn't know the words to the song. "We finally had to ask his aunt Ernestine for the lyrics," Keene says.

Before leaving on a ten-day trip to the East Coast, Keene left an acetate copy of "Donna" with the program director at KFWB. To his surprise, he heard the record on his car radio as he returned to his office.

Another person surprised to hear the song on the radio was Donna Ludwig. "A bunch of us were driving down the street in my car," Ludwig says. "I heard it and I said, 'Oh, my God' and we all started screaming, I started crying. We pulled over and listened to it."

Keene and Valens spent a couple of days in Chicago before proceeding to New York where Valens made his national television debut on Dick Clark's *American Bandstand* on Connie Valenzuela's birthday, October 6. Valens appeared on other television shows on this east coast swing: the Alan Freed show in New York, the Buddy Deane show in Baltimore, and the Milt Grant show in Washington, D.C. He also performed at several record hops, flying in a wide range of aircraft. "We landed in back of a factory on grass to pick up some people" at one point, Keene recalls, adding that Ritchie "sang in a log cabin with a bunch of kids around" at another stop. When Keene and Valens returned to California, there were more than 100,000 orders for "Donna" and "La Bamba."

Valens then began what would be a steady stream of local appearances at Pacific Ocean Park, Disneyland, and El Monte Legion Stadium, the pinnacle of success for a young Latino singer where the latest dance crazes were performed with great fervor. West Coast stars, such as the Penguins, the Coasters, and Bobby Day frequently played El Monte. Valens was sometimes backed up at the stadium by drummer Sander "Sandy" Nelson or future Beach Boy Bruce Johnston on keyboards.

Valens and his family remained close, despite his hectic schedule. "His mom worked hard," Gil Rocha says. "She had two jobs at times to keep her family clothed and fed. Ritchie stayed home and took care of the baby-sitting while Connie worked and he played that darn guitar to himself all the time." Valens also played children's songs like "The Paddiwack Song" to entertain his young sisters, Connie and Irma, and baby brother, Mario. "He was very helpful," Rosie Morales says. "He used to talk to [older half-brother] Bobby, give him some advice. It seemed like *he* was the older one. He would tell Bobby to 'quit drinking, to take care of Rosie and the kids. You're a married man, you have kids.'"

Despite his rising national popularity with the release of "Donna," Valens still occasionally performed for friends. On Halloween, Valens was preparing to go to a party at the house of a friend, Gail Smith, when he came to the rescue of his aunt Ernestine, who had forgotten to buy treats for some trick or treaters. While she dashed to the store, Valens kept the youngsters entertained by singing "The Paddiwack Song" for them.

Valens teamed with Ted Quillin at KFWB and a local pizza chain in a promotional contest that offered a top prize of a house party with Valens entertaining. Valens and Quillin became quite close, and Valens was a regular visitor to Quillin's North Hollywood home.

"After 'Come On Let's Go' came out, he forgot that he was shy," Donna Ludwig says. "He came to San Fernando High School and was guest star at an assembly. The people would not go back to class. Everybody was clapping and stomping up and down. They had to get Ritchie off the stage and they still couldn't get us out of the auditorium."

With "Donna" racking up impressive sales, Keene intensified his promotional efforts. Although Keene had lots of expertise in the studio and in working with disc jockeys to promote his artists, he had never been involved with handling an emerging national rock 'n' roll star. Keene engaged General Artists Corporation, which had an office in nearby Beverly Hills, to help Valens get the exposure he wanted. Keene also hired Muriel Moore, who worked down the street from the Del-Fi offices as Frankie Laine's secretary, to operate a fan club for Valens. Valens bought a fancy blue and black, rhinestone-studded stage outfit from Nudie's in North Hollywood.

"He was getting into a little bit more flash and that was never him," Donna Ludwig says. "He was always pretty straight. I saw him in a plaid jacket one time and I almost died laughing."

"Who put you in that?" Ludwig asked.

"Bob bought this for me," Valens replied. "How do you like it?"

"It's terrible," Ludwig said.

By mid-November, "Donna" hadn't quite made the charts, but it was getting good reviews in the trade press. In the November 15 issue of *Cash Box*: "Ritchie Valens . . . turns in a beautiful rock-a-ballad performance on 'Donna,' a lovely name tune. Sound and song are terrific. Watch this one closely. On the flip, 'La Bamba,' Ritchie belts out a thrilling cha cha number singing only in Spanish." Two days later, *Billboard* made the song "A Billboard Pick."

Valens was performing for GAC in Hawaii on November 24 when "Donna" appeared on the *Billboard* chart for the first time. Three days later, on Thanksgiving, the future success of "Donna" was threatened by a freak occurrence. "The record-pressing plant burned down," Keene says. Keene quickly shuffled the pressing operation to a Midwest plant. Soon, the song broke out as a No. 1 hit in Chicago.

Despite the success of "Donna," the relationship between Valens and Ludwig had cooled considerably by late 1958. "After he started making records, he was gone," Ludwig says. "He met other people and I did, too. [But] we never lost our affection."

Valens's popularity was snowballing in early December 1958 as he returned to Gold Star to record eight new songs for his first Del-Fi album. "Donna" was one of the most played songs in the country, and England's Tommy Steele covered "Come On Let's Go," a record that would eventually crack the British Top 10. Bob Keene released another Valens single that month, an instrumental called "Fast Freight." But, instead of releasing it under Valens's name, it carried the name of "Arvee Allens."

Valens continued to make local appearances, including an assembly at his old school, Pacoima Junior High. Although it was not known at the time, the school principal accidentally recorded the assembly on a transcribing machine, a taped record that would later be duplicated by Bob Keene as one side of a Valens album.

Valens was set for another trip to the East Coast to appear on Alan Freed's annual Christmas shows but, before he left, he had one piece of personal business to attend to. "He wanted to buy a house for his mom," aunt Ernestine Reyes says. "When he first started his career he said, 'Tia, if I make it big, we're not going to live here in Pacoima any more. We're moving to Beverly Hills.' He wanted a swimming pool." Valens settled for an 1,100 square foot, pink-stucco tract house with turquoise trim, in Pacoima. With Ernestine as cosigner, Valens took $1,000 Bob Keene had given him as an advance on royalties and made a down payment on the $13,500 house. "To him it was like a mansion," Donna Ludwig says. "He thought he'd died and gone to heaven."

Valens began his eleven-day run on Freed's Christmas Jubilee of Stars at Loew's State Theater on Times Square in Manhattan on Christmas Day. During his stay in New York, he renewed an acquaintance with Diane Olson, a girl he had met during his earlier trip to New York. Olson had been persuaded by a friend to attend the Alan Freed show that fall. After the show, the girls went backstage. "As soon as I walked into the crowded room, I could see only one person—Ritchie," Olson told Dee Spencer of *Movie Life*. "I fell in love with him that moment."

Trade publications were predicting big things for Valens when he returned to California in early January 1959. With "Donna" and "La Bamba" emerging as a double-sided hit, his records were expected to earn him at least $100,000 for the year. He had been booked, along with J. P. Richardson, for a major tour of Australia beginning in Sydney on February 22. After that, there was to be a March 7 appearance on the Perry Como show, and GAC had set up four weeks of theater engagements in Baltimore, Washington, Philadelphia, and New York.

His first album was scheduled to be released in mid-February, and Valens also filmed a brief appearance for an Alan Freed movie, *Go Johnny Go*. Valens also found time to appear at several local dances in January. But the hectic lifestyle was taking its toll. Bob Morales told Valens biographer Beverly Mendheim that Valens had told him, "It's happening too fast. It's too confusing."

The frantic pace of the previous few months had slimmed Valens down a bit. "But not that much," Ernestine Reyes says. "He was very, very stout and big-muscled, but he hadn't lost that much weight. He was still a big boy." Donna Ludwig teased him about it. "Don't lose too much weight, there won't be anything to hold onto," she said.

Valens tried to take a few days off before flying to Chicago and the Winter Dance Party, his first major tour. On Monday, January 19, Valens held a party at his mother's new home. "I was supposed to be his date, but my father wouldn't let me go," Donna Ludwig recalled. "That was the last time I talked to him. We talked [on the phone] for a real long time. His mother kept asking him to get off the phone, because she wanted to be with him. He said, 'My mother is so silly—she thinks I'm going to get hurt.' I even tried to sneak out that night, but got caught."

The next night, on the eve of his departure for the Winter Dance Party tour, Valens went to Guardian Angels Church with his mother, fan club president Gail Smith, and Smith's mother. "Ritchie and I knelt down and prayed for a safe trip," Gail Smith told Beverly Mendheim. "On the way home, while our mothers sat up front, we were sitting in the back seat talking about the upcoming tour . . . Ritchie said, 'When I get back, I'm gonna get my T-Bird.'"

Ernestine and Lelo Reyes drove Valens and Bob Morales to the airport the next day. Aware that Valens always was concerned about the welfare of his mother and that he had a fear of flying, Ernestine prodded Valens to buy insurance. "Every time we'd go [past the Hollywood-Burbank airport and their small planes], he used to say, 'I'll never get in one of those S.O.B.s,'" Ernestine Reyes says. "He didn't like [buying insurance] very well, but I'd say, 'You never know, God forbid.'" Valens would try to dissuade his aunt by joking: "If the plane crashes in the water, I'll use my guitar as a boat. If it lands in the snow, I'll use my guitar as a sled." Despite his objections, Ernestine says Ritchie bought the insurance.

Just before boarding the Chicago-bound plane, Valens walked up to his brother and put his arms around him. "I want you to take care of my mother," he said.

The Winter Dance Party

January 23
Million Dollar Ballroom
Milwaukee, Wis.

January 24
Eagles Ballroom
Kenosha, Wis.

January 25
Kato Ballroom
Mankato, Minn.

January 26
Fournier's Ballroom
Eau Claire, Wis.

January 27
Fiesta Ballroom
Montevideo, Minn.

January 28
Prom Ballroom
St. Paul, Minn.

January 29
Capitol Theater
Davenport, Ia.

January 30
Laramar Ballroom
Fort Dodge, Ia.

January 31
National Guard Armory
Duluth, Minn.

February 1
Cinderella Ballroom
Appleton, Wis. (cancelled)

February 1
Riverside Ballroom
Green Bay, Wis.

February 2
Surf Ballroom
Clear Lake, Ia.

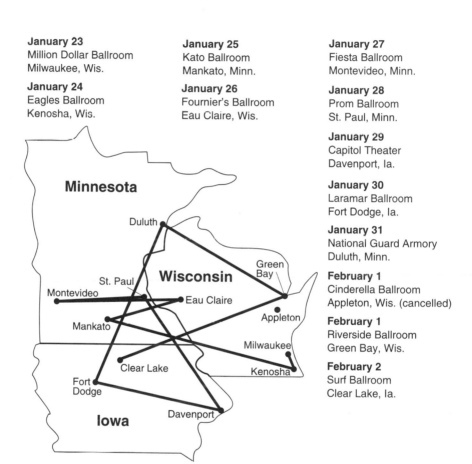

A map of the Winter Dance Party tour itinerary

The Tour Begins

Friday, January 23, 1959

> Milwaukee Braves pitcher Warren Spahn is voted the Wisconsin
> athlete of the year for the second time in three years.

Baseball was not the main subject of conversation as the Winter Dance Party bus skimmed along the western edge of Lake Michigan, bound for its opening performance in Milwaukee, Wisconsin, eighty-six miles north of Chicago. The temperature had dipped to 3 below zero in Chicago on Friday morning, prompting Ritchie Valens to call his mother in California to complain about the bitter cold. A concerned Connie Valenzuela told her son she'd mail him a topcoat. The weather was even worse in Milwaukee, which was buried under thirteen inches of snow a day earlier, the city's heaviest snowfall in twelve years. Four people had died from heart attacks while digging out in temperatures that reached as low as 17 below zero Friday morning.

With a population of just more than 500,000, Milwaukee was the biggest city in Wisconsin. An influx of German and Polish immigrants in its early days helped the city earn its blue-collar nickname, "America's Workshop." The city was best known for its many breweries, but its major league baseball team, the Braves, was a close second. The Braves, who won the 1957 World Series, repeated as National League champions in 1958, only to lose the series to the New York Yankees in seven games. Much of the winter sports talk in Milwaukee centered around the Braves' hopes for 1959. Would third baseman Eddie Mathews bounce back from a .250 season? Would pitcher Bob Buhl's sore arm heal? How much longer could thirty-eight-year-old starter Warren Spahn hang on?

Rock 'n' roll fans may have been questioning the future of their favorite music as well. Local pop-music station WISN incurred the wrath of its regular listeners in mid-1958 when it programmed five straight hours of rock music. Some six hundred protest calls later, the station returned to its regular programming. Furthermore, disc jockey Charlie Hanson burned some two hundred rock discs in the station's courtyard to emphasize its anti-rock commitment.

Despite the frigid weather, the singers were looking forward to getting their show on stage. After checking into a downtown hotel, they again boarded the bus for the trip to George Devine's Million Dollar Ballroom, a few miles west of downtown Milwaukee on Wisconsin Avenue. The ride took longer than expected. "We couldn't find the place," Carl Bunch recalls. "When we finally found it, Buddy asked, 'What time does this eight o'clock gig start?' It was like nine-fifteen then."

Because union rules required a local band appear at Devine's dances, Larry Ladd's Entertaining Band, which specialized in light pop tunes of the '40s, was booked to play on the same evening. The group drew a lukewarm response from the packed house as it filled in for the late-arriving rockers. It was obvious that swing music was not what Milwaukee teens wanted that night. The crowd was getting increasingly impatient as it waited for Frankie Sardo to take the stage to open the first show of the Winter Dance Party. "The people were ready to riot," Bunch says. The musicians were impatient, too. "Before we walked out [on stage], I was shaking like a leaf."

Waylon Jennings, Tommy Allsup, and Bunch spent most of the night backing up the other acts before Holly closed the program. Holly kicked off his initial performance of the Winter Dance Party with a surprise. Instead of opening with one of his more familiar hits, he sang "Gotta Travel On," a recent hit by Billy Grammer.

As Holly moved into more familiar songs, Bunch tensed up. "When [Buddy] started to play "Peggy Sue," I was about twice as fast as he normally played it and it was real hard for him to slow me down," Bunch says. "But before it was over, I finally got my sea legs under me and began to feel like I was part of the group."

———— ◆ ————

January 24, 1959

It was crazy, daddy—the goings-on Friday night at George Devine's Million Dollar Ballroom.

Nearly 6,000 young people turned out to hear such rock 'n' roll stars as Buddy Holly and the Crickets, Big Bopper, Dion and the Belmonts and Ritchie Valens. If you haven't heard them, you haven't lived, man.

The show was billed as a 'winter dance party,' but there was little room to dance once the show got underway. The youngsters jammed the front of the huge stage about 50 deep in a row and 20 to 25 rows deep. Others threatened to fall out of the crowded balconies.

It's obvious the Big Beat still has a hold on the kids and it takes steady nerves to withstand the sound. Electric guitars boomed through two loudspeakers with the force of two symphony orchestras in full sway, and the twitching rock 'n' rollers invoked screams that surely melted the snow on the roof of the ballroom.

Backed by the Crickets—two young guitarists and a drummer—Buddy Holly rocked his beanpole figure onstage, clutched his little guitar against his loud, red coat and jerked his way through Peggy Sue. His voice was scarcely audible over the raucous guitars, but he itchy-twitched in grand style, and that's what the kids wanted.

Dion and the Belmonts, three handsome lads who barely escaped the clutches of the girls reaching over the stage to grab their legs, offered their recording hit, "I Wonder Why," a big beat ballad.

The liveliest performance was Big Bopper, a chubby crewcut cat, who sported a leopard skin coat and white bucks. He stomped and shuffled his weight around with ease and—surprisingly enough—he had the voice to match his bulk. Everybody demanded and got his hit version of "Chantilly Lace."

A comparative newcomer was the 17-year-old, Spanish lad, Ritchie Valens. Only the squares don't know that Ritchie's hit "Donna" is now among the Top 10 tunes in the country. When he sang it here, his audience swayed back and forth as if hypnotized by the slow love song.

The crowd ranged from Great Lakes sailors and couples in their 20s down to sharp-as-a-tack and well-coiffured boys and girls looking scarcely more than 10 or 12 years old. All had one thing in common—they turned up their noses at a swing band which filled in the time prior to the rock 'n' roll acts.

George Devine beamed broadly, reporting it was his most successful rock 'n' roll show to date.

Yes, George. It was a fine blast!

—Joe Botsford, *The Milwaukee Sentinel*

A warming trend pushed the temperature in Milwaukee above zero during Friday night's show. With the temperature holding steady above zero after the show, some of the singers returned to their hotel; others explored downtown Milwaukee. The tour was off to a good start, despite the frigid weather.

Fortunately, Saturday promised to be an easy day. The Winter Dance Party would turn over the Million Dollar Ballroom stage to polka king Frankie Yankovic while it headed down the road a bit, some thirty-four miles south to Kenosha, Wisconsin.

The musicians arrived in Kenosha (pop. 54,368), an industrial center nestled along the shore of Lake Michigan, on Saturday morning. Jazz musician Lionel Hampton got his first musical instruction there at the Holy Rosary Academy. Eagles Ballroom, the site of Saturday night's dance, was located in the long lakefront area of the city. Separating the ballroom from the gray waters of Lake Michigan was Lake Front Park where Joe Louis trained in 1937 for his world heavyweight championship fight with Jim Braddock.

The weather was improving by the time the singers arrived in Kenosha, climbing to 24 degrees by noon. Saturday's moderating temperatures were good news for Jim Lounsbury, a Chicago television personality who had booked the Winter Dance Party into Kenosha. Lounsbury was the host of one of the earliest television dance programs to feature rock 'n' roll, *Bandstand Matinee* on WGN-TV in Chicago. Lounsbury started his show in June 1954, three full years before Dick Clark began *American Bandstand.* By the late 1950s, Lounsbury was hosting record hops in the Chicago area six nights a week, in addition to his Saturday afternoon TV show.

When Lounsbury learned that GAC was booking dates for the Winter Dance Party, he bought one, hoping to use his Chicago base. Unfortunately, GAC's Bob Ehlert had already sold a Chicago date for February 8 to the Aragon Ballroom. So, Lounsbury took his show some fifty miles north to Kenosha. He also took the opportunity to add one singer to the Kenosha program, his wife, aspiring rock 'n' roller Debbie Stevens. Stevens had recorded a couple of records in 1958, but hadn't cracked the big-time. At the Winter Dance Party she would perform her newest recording, "If You Can't Rock Me."

Lounsbury made several trips to Kenosha in the days preceding the show to promote it. He distributed posters and enlisted Ed Auxner, a young disc jockey at Kenosha radio station WLIP, to help handle master of ceremonies duties. Lounsbury's promotional efforts paid off. An article in the *Kenosha News* before the concert focused more on Lounsbury than the singers, carrying the headline: JIM LOUNSBURY TO BE IN TOWN. Lounsbury also arranged to have Valens and the Big Bopper appear on his 3:30 to 5 PM TV show that Saturday. After Valens lip-synched his way through "Donna" and the Bopper did the same with "Chantilly Lace," the singers returned to Kenosha with Stevens while Lounsbury wrapped up his television show and headed to a teen hop on the south side of Chicago.

Lounsbury had to cut short his duties at the hop in order to make it to Kenosha for the Winter Dance Party. He turned over the Chicago hop chores to a friend and headed toward Midway Airport where he had chartered a Beechcraft Bonanza to fly him to Kenosha.

As the area braced itself for another cold night, hundreds of Kenosha teens lined up for tickets before the doors of the Eagles Ballroom opened at 7:30 for the 8 PM dance. Hundreds more "scooped the loop," Kenosha's version of cruising. Although teen dances were common in Kenosha, usually held at the Union Ballroom or Polonia Hall, it was unusual to bring in a package as loaded with stars as the Winter Dance Party. Even the Eagles Ballroom was more accustomed to holding high school proms than rock 'n' roll shows. The oval ballroom featured a grand ceiling and indirect lighting. Fancy trimmed columns surrounded the dance floor and full-length mirrors around the dance floor made it appear even larger than it was.

One of those waiting to pay $1.50 to attend the Kenosha show that night was Tom Rotunda, a fourteen-year-old who played guitar in a group called the Rhythm Teens. "We stood in line and just froze to death," Rotunda recalls. "The line went from [the second-floor ballroom] all the way out the door and down the street." While Rotunda waited for the doors to open, the musicians were unloading their equipment from the bus and setting up inside. Frank Zabukovec was backstage, collecting dues of $1.30 from each musician for Kenosha Local No. 59 of the American Federation of Musicians. The auxiliary police were receiving last-minute instructions on what to look for as they patrolled the dance floor. Auxner mingled with the singers as he prepared to handle master of ceremony duties until Lounsbury arrived.

Fans pressed toward the stage, some jumping on it to sit just a few feet from the musicians. It was a well-dressed crowd, with several males wearing ties and sailors wearing white uniforms. Although a NO SMOKING IN BALLROOM sign was clearly visible near the stage, many fans chose to ignore it. "The place was just jam-packed, smoky," Rotunda says.

Eileen Doyle, a fifteen-year-old sophomore at St. Joseph High School, went to the concert hoping to get close to her idol, Ritchie Valens, as he performed her favorite song, "La Bamba." During the first part of the concert, Doyle stood with friends at the rear of the ballroom. But during an intermission, they pressed closer to the stage to catch Valens's act. "When people started to surge forward, we were pressed between the stage and the people. So when he [Valens] walked out and put his cigarette butt out, I was right there." Doyle retrieved the butt as a memento. Joe Santiloni thinks Valens was the biggest hit of the night. "The girls went absolutely nuts. You could hardly hear him," he says.

By the time Lounsbury arrived from Chicago, the show was half-completed. He chatted with the singers backstage between acts and took over as emcee.

Downstairs, Tony Szikil, a young photographer, was wrapping up work at a wedding reception. After work, he was to meet other photographers at the Eagles Club for some socializing. "When [the other photographers] joined me at ten thirty, I went upstairs to see what was happening [at the dance]," Szikil says. Szikil entered the ballroom and started shooting pictures as he approached the stage. Lounsbury saw Szikil and called him onstage, where he was introduced to the singers and stayed for the rest of the evening, shooting pictures from the wings.

As the concert wound down, some of the singers hung around the ballroom, talking to fans and signing autographs. Joan Mesner got a special treat from Dion: "He signed my arm. He dotted his 'i' with the mole on my arm." Shortly after Mesner collected her souvenir, she joined other Kenosha teens who were noisily scooping the loop. "Downtown Kenosha was almost like the Fourth of July," Joe Santiloni says. "Cars all over, beeping their horns."

Meanwhile, the singers piled aboard the bus for the 381-mile all-night trek to their next stop: Mankato, Minnesota.

<hr />

January 25, 1959

A horde of recording stars will invade the Prom [Ballroom] Wednesday night for a teen dance. In person will be Buddy Holly and the Crickets, Ritchie ("Donna") Valens, the Big Bopper, Dion and the Belmonts, and Frankie Sardo. Wow!

—Bill Diehl's "Look 'n' Listen" column for the *St. Paul Pioneer Press*

A cold front was pressing hard into the upper Midwest, dumping snow in northern Minnesota and sending temperatures plummeting once again as the bus headed west out of Kenosha.

The singers tried to catch some sleep as the bus bounced along the two-lane highways that straddled Wisconsin and Minnesota. Some stretched across the seats; others tried the luggage racks. None were comfortable. "Trying to sleep at night on that bus was ridiculous," Jennings recalls. Dion was incensed by the conditions. "It wasn't a bus. . . . It was a piece of shit," he remembers.

In the early morning darkness and increasingly heavy snow showers, the bus slipped through the narrow valleys of the rocky western Wisconsin hills, rising through close-walled coulees to a rounded plateau and dipping again into open country, surrounded by forests of evergreen and fertile farmlands. Snow was falling heavily when the bus arrived in downtown Mankato at midday. The singers checked into the Hotel Burton to relax before their performance at the Kato Ballroom that night.

Most of the singers relaxed in their rooms, but a few spent some time at Frederickson's Cafe, across the street. There Bunch met a young waitress named Cathy Chatleain. "We were quite infatuated with each other," Chatleain recalls. Chatleain invited Bunch to her home, where she introduced him to her family.

By evening, more than four inches of snow had accumulated on Mankato's streets, making travel impossible in some hilly parts of the city. After the bus inched slowly into the gravel parking lot behind the Kato, ballroom manager Jerry Martinka helped the musicians set up on the unusual crescent-shaped stage. The big stage easily accommodated the big bands that frequently played the Kato, and a horseshoe-shaped extension took smaller bands right onto the dance floor. A short wrought-iron railing ringed the stage to remind performers of the two-foot drop to the dance floor. A series of steps on either side were the only paths to a small dressing room behind the stage. To get to the dressing room, performers passed coatracks made of galvanized pipe and a series of benches, which were usually full of Kato patrons.

Owners Herb and Jerry Martinka kept things hopping at the Kato, especially on weekends. On the Friday and Saturday before the Winter Dance Party arrived, a pair of polka bands—Whoopee John and Clem Brau—drew large crowds, despite the weather. Teen dances also did well, despite often being held on school nights. Two off-duty Mankato police were always on hand, with firm instructions to enforce a no-drinking rule. Teen dances were always over by 11:30 PM and parents were admitted free. "We were in on the ground floor of rock and roll and used [disc jockey] Bill Diehl of WDGY [in Minneapolis]," Jerry Martinka says. "Bill used to come down and emcee hops."

Bill Diehl was a mighty busy fellow in 1959. First there were his duties as a disc jockey for top-rated WDGY in Minneapolis with his drive-time patter: "It's the Top 40 Show and I'm Bill Diehl, the Rajah of the Records, the Deacon of the Discs, the Premier of the Platters and the Wizard of the Wax, with all the musical facts. From four to seven we go from forty to one." Then there were Diehl's entertainment writing duties at the *St. Paul Pioneer Press* newspaper, which he had joined as a copy boy in 1943. Finally, there were the teen hops that were the inevitable windfall from successful rock 'n' roll radio programming in the 1950s.

"Many times I would emcee four dances in a night," Diehl says, noting that he would often spend just a few minutes at each one. "I'd give away some records, promote the next week's dance, pocket fifty bucks, and drive like hell to the next one.

"We could do no wrong. I would go out to appear in a town like St. James, Minnesota, and they'd meet you at the edge of town and give you a police escort into the armory. Towns fought to have you come."

Jerry Martinka didn't have to fight very hard to persuade Diehl to make the seventy-mile drive to Mankato to emcee the Winter Dance Party. Diehl had lunched with Holly a year earlier when Holly appeared in Minneapolis and was looking forward to meeting him again. "He was very scholarly," Diehl says. "I always called him the Glenn Miller of rock. . . . This was not the stereotypical rock and roll star. This was a fellow who made sense."

Diehl's on-air promotion of the Mankato and St. Paul shows undoubtedly had a lot to do with the estimated 1,500 teenagers who paid $1.50 each to crowd into the Kato for the show. "Everybody listened to WDGY," says Judy Peery, who attended the show with classmates from Good Council Academy.

Dianne Cory, a freshman at Mankato High School, collected Diehl's autograph that night as she roamed the ballroom in search of souvenirs. By the time the evening had ended, she had collected autographs of most of the performers, an autographed Frankie Sardo Fan Club membership card, and had snapped several photos of the singers with her Kodak Brownie camera.

As the show began, the kids pressed close to the Kato's stage to get a better look at the singers. Some found a seat at the front of the stage where a four-foot section of the wrought-iron fence was missing. The Kato was packed with girls in pedal pushers and crew-neck angora wool sweaters bedecked with "virgin pins." Some girls with "steadies" wore their boyfriend's class ring, tightly wrapped with matching angora yarn. Boys with Brylcreemed pompadours and confetti tweed sport coats skirted the crowd, some with dates, others nervously checking out the knots of girls congregating in front of the stage. Between sets, the singers posed for photos and signed autographs. Cory remembers them being in a joyful mood, especially Sardo and Valens. "They were cutting up and being silly," Cory says.

Judy Peery and her friends were celebrating Peery's recent eighteenth birthday. Among them was Kathy Chatleain, who looked forward to seeing her new friend, Carl Bunch, perform. Between sets, Chatleain and Bunch cozied up on one of the settees behind the stage while her friends snapped pictures. "We were backstage talking about how we were having a birthday party for Judy and we invited them over," Chatleain says.

When Holly began to sing, Curt Schueneman, a nineteen-year-old graduate of Mankato West High School, stood to one side of the stage. On the opposite side was Sue Vee, the girl he had broken up with just days earlier, with her date. "'That'll Be the Day' was our No. 1 song," Schueneman remembers. "I'd look at Holly and I'd look at her and the songs would come on and my throat would hurt. I used to sing 'That'll Be the Day' to her when we were holding hands, trying to imitate Buddy. I didn't do that well, but she liked it.

"I was watching her and her date through the whole show. It was terrible."

After the show, Judy Peery returned to the upstairs apartment she shared with her mother in North Mankato, unaware that her friends had invited the singers to her home. "I didn't know anything about it until this cab pulled up in front of the house and these guys got out," Peery says. Besides Bunch, Carlo Mastrangelo and Fred Milano of the Belmonts showed up for the surprise birthday party. "My mom just about had a fit," Peery says. "It was a real small apartment, but she loved it. She had a real good time." The singers serenaded Peery with "Happy Birthday" and posed for pictures.

After about an hour, Bunch and the Belmonts returned to their rooms at the Hotel Burton for a good night's rest before the Monday night show at Eau Claire, Wisconsin, some 167 miles to the east.

It was another bitterly cold morning as the singers filed out of the Burton and onto the bus for the five-hour drive back to Wisconsin. It was near zero as the bus lurched out of Mankato.

Instead of sleeping, as they did on the overnight ride from Kenosha to Mankato, most of the singers found other escapes from the tedium of a long bus ride. "It was joke-telling time," Frankie Sardo says. "We laughed a lot. We joked a lot. We teased a lot."

Carl Bunch says: "There was a lot of craziness on that bus. Absolute craziness. We played a game called skunk. The idea of skunk is to get somebody to repeat themselves or say something stupid. I got skunked over and over and over. I was just out to lunch.

"One day we stopped at a gas station to get something to snack on. Dion decided he was going to skunk the guys around the station. He stood outside in the cold, trying to open a bottle of Coca-Cola in the coin return. He stood there until a man finally came over there and took the Coke out of his hand and opened it in the opener. Everybody just broke up laughing."

Fred Milano prefered to play poker, but Bunch was not among the card players. "Buddy warned me once that they played a lot of cards on the bus," Bunch says. "He said, 'Son, you don't make enough money to play. You let the big boys play, and you watch.'" Dion says: "We didn't have videos, we didn't have tapes to listen to, we didn't have computer games, we didn't have TV. All we had was each other."

Eau Claire (pop. 36,000) was the largest metropolitan center in northern Wisconsin. Winter sports were very popular in the area, but Eau Claire also had a baseball team in the Class C Northern League, the Braves. Hank Aaron hit his first professional home run in Eau Claire as an eighteen-year-old shortstop in 1952, and Milwaukee native Bob Uecker started his pro career there in 1956, hitting .171 and making nine errors in forty-five games.

The Winter Dance Party bus pulled into the parking lot of the Hotel Eau Claire in mid-afternoon. After checking into the downtown hotel, the singers bused the half mile to Fournier's Ballroom to begin setting up their equipment. Temperatures rose into the teens as the musicians grabbed some hamburgers and French fries at the Crosstown Cafe before returning to their hotel rooms to rest up for that night's show.

The smarter kids in Eau Claire had bought their tickets for Monday night's dance ahead of time for $1 at Meyer Music on Barstow Street. Everybody else paid $1.25 for the program, which was sensibly scheduled from 7 to 10:30 PM on a school night. There was no break from the weather, though, with temperatures sliding into single digits by showtime.

The ballroom was deteriorating on the outside, with imitation brown brick tarpaper sagging over its aging wooden frame. The inside, with its knotty pine floor and walls, was only slightly better, but it didn't really matter to the teenagers who "cruised the gut" on Barstow Street and snacked at the Dog-N-Suds Drive In and Ptomaine Tommies. More than 1,000 teens crowded onto Fournier's lower-level dance floor where security man Clarence Jackson was more of a greeter than an enforcer. The dance floor was rumored to have springs under it to aid dancers, but there was little dancing that night as the singers offered their hits.

In the second-floor dressing room, Steve Meyer took a break from running Fournier's public address system by chatting with the singers. "I talked mostly to Ritchie Valens," Meyer says. "It was difficult to talk to Buddy

Holly. He just didn't want to talk and I didn't want to pry. A little bit sullen. That's the way he was even on stage. The Bopper was sick . . . something like a cold."

Frankie Sardo was first to come down from the dressing rooms, followed by Dion and the Belmonts, Valens, the Big Bopper, and Holly. Don Larson, a seventeen-year-old Holly fan, pressed closer to the stage as his idol took the stage. Larson had been waiting for the moment for ten months, ever since his parents had bought him the *Chirpin' Crickets* album for his seventeenth birthday. "I can remember standing at the bandstand, only two or three feet from Buddy and I looked up on stage and saw Waylon Jennings and Tommy Allsup and Carl Bunch. I told my friend, 'Those are not the Crickets up there.' . . . I just resigned myself to the fact that something must have happened to the rest of the Crickets, and Buddy just came by himself."

After the show, the singers loaded their equipment back onto the bus and returned to their hotel. From there, Holly, Richardson, and other tour members walked two blocks to Sammy's Pizza Palace where they tried several of its thirteen varieties of pizza, including some top-of-the-line $1.50 specialties. The singers unwound in booths at the rear of the restaurant, away from the horde of teens that regularly descended on Sammy's after a big event. Holly raised a few eyebrows among employees, however, when he paid the bill.

"He whipped out a roll of bills, gave her two twenties and said, 'Keep the change,'" employee Curt Tweith recalls. "That was really a big deal."

The singers returned to the hotel on a cold, windy night as the temperature again flirted with the zero mark. They rested before once again heading back to Minnesota, to the tiny town of Montevideo, some 240 miles of blacktop to the west.

The singers had the dubious distinction of waking in the coldest state in the nation on Tuesday morning, January 27. It was 26 below zero in Lone Rock, Wisconsin, although it only reached 2 below in Eau Claire as the singers embarked on another day of traveling through the frozen upper Midwest.

It wasn't long before the entourage fell into its routine of card-playing, story-telling, and cat-napping. Inevitably, the bus filled with music. "We had these acoustical guitars, so we spent a lot of time on the bus making music," Dion says. Says Carl Bunch: "One of the funniest things I ever heard was Dion trying to sing country music: 'I nearly died when I tought youse had left me.' With the Bronx accent and country lyrics, it was really funny."

Jennings recalled: "Dion was the biggest hillbilly on earth. He loved country music more than anybody I ever saw. He loved Hank Williams. . . . It was pretty boring [on the bus] a lot of the time, but we had a lot of fun when we were singing."

The bus passed lime-pit–filled hillsides, flat natural prairie, and the St. Croix River valley before cutting through the heart of the twin cities, first St. Paul then Minneapolis. The bus emerged from the metropolis past towns named Cosmos, Blomkest, Prinsburg, and Clara City before pulling into Montevideo. With a population of around 5,600, Montevideo was the smallest city the Winter Dance Party was scheduled to visit. The weather warmed into the mid-teens by late afternoon when the singers arrived at the Hotel Hunt in downtown Montevideo.

It wasn't long after the group's arrival that Bunch made a chilling discovery: He had lost his performing outfit. "He [Holly] got real angry with me," says Bunch, who apparently had left the uniform in the dressing room at Eau Claire. "Oh God, I don't know what happened," Bunch told Holly. "Somebody must have gotten on the bus and stolen them."

Holly replied: "I wouldn't dig that hole any deeper, son, you're going to have to crawl out of it." Fortunately, Bunch had other clothes that were similar to the stage outfits.

Tour manager Geller, meanwhile, inquired around town about bus repairs. The tour bus was running smoothly enough, but was having trouble keeping out the northern plains' frigid air. Lack of heat had become a constant annoyance. "The bus was third class," Geller says. "We had ample room, individual seats and all that, but I had never made a tour in the wintertime out west. I couldn't believe [how cold it got]."

Although relatively small, Montevideo was the biggest town for many miles around. "Lots of area teenagers would drive over to 'Monte' to drag the main, visit the bowling alley, the roller skating rink or the back alley of Main Street," says Ruth Benson Leppke, who was a junior at Montevideo Central High School in 1959.

Among the bigger attractions were the Tuesday night teen dances at the Fiesta Ballroom. The decor of the Fiesta reflected the tradition of Montevideo's sister city in Uruguay. Colorful sombreros, maracas, and other Latin musical instruments graced the ballroom's walls. Waitresses wore colorful printed skirts and peasant-style blouses. The ballroom's logo had a sombrero jauntily perched on the "F" and a scarf trailed behind the word. When ballroom owner Clarence Burns first started his teen dances, he required his young patrons to provide a parent's permission slip before entering. Once teens were admitted, they couldn't leave the building until the show was over.

Burns also didn't allow smoking in the Fiesta during teen dances. Assistant manager Glenn Gayken monitored the men's restroom and waitress Sandra Ryer checked the women's restroom to make sure the teens weren't smoking or drinking. If a youngster was believed to be drinking, he (or she) was detained in the office until a parent came.

"I remember we would make our [soda] pops look like a drink [by mixing Coke with Seven-Up]," says Jane Ellefson, who attended the Winter Dance Party. "Burns would look at our drinks and say, 'Well, which one of you girls got the Coke tonight?' It was just kind of a joke."

The Winter Dance Party was an extra-special event, the second big rock 'n' roll show to hit Montevideo in a week. It was just a week earlier that the Big Beats had rolled into town. "It [the ballroom] was really full," says Ellefson, who pressed toward the stage, a Brownie camera clutched tightly in her hand. "I learned from experience that you had to be close to get a decent picture."

Bob Bunn, a twenty-one-year-old guitar player with a local band, the Rockin' Rebels, was one of those at the foot of the stage, watching Holly's fingers as they danced across his Fender Stratocaster guitar. "Everybody just stood and watched him," Bunn says. "He played pretty much one song after another. He didn't talk too much, he just said, 'Thank you.'"

Dick Strand, a high school senior from Madison, Minnesota, also wedged near the stage to watch Holly. Wearing the horn-rimmed style of glasses associated with his idol, Strand finally got a good look at Holly. "I didn't know who he was until he sang 'Peggy Sue,'" Strand admits. "In those days there wasn't the TV coverage and all that stuff where you'd get so familiar with the looks of the people." Strand also was impressed by the Big Bopper. "He just shook the stage," Strand says. "He had a mouthful of chewing gum and was stomping on the stage."

After the show, Ellefson collected most of the singers' autographs on a sheet of yellow paper. Bunn hung around to talk to the singers, but was disappointed. "I tried to talk to [Holly] afterwards, but there were too many people. I tried to talk with Dion, but he was way above us. He was just like he was on cloud nine . . . he treated us like peons."

High school sophomore Diane Bagus, who was at the show with some girlfriends, was more successful attracting the stars' attention. "A bunch of us girls were giggling [as we talked to the singers]," she says. "I just said, 'If you guys want something to do afterwards, just come on over.'" Shortly after the dance broke up, several of the singers showed up at the Bagus house, about a mile from the Fiesta.

Larry Pray, a Montevideo teenager who once had a party at his house with Gene Vincent's band, says he wasn't at Bagus's party that night, but he has heard about it. "That was that real wild party," Pray says of what turned out to be one of the most talked-about social events of the southwestern Minnesota teen set that year.

Stories of the party probably exceeded the event itself. Bagus thinks Holly, Valens, the Big Bopper, and Dion were at her house. "They weren't rowdy or anything," Bagus says. "They were talking about touring. They were really tired and beat." Before the singers left, Bagus had them sign their names on her bedroom wall.

The singers then went to the Highway Cafe on Highway 212. There Wanda Quilitz of Madison, Minnesota, collected autographs from the singers on the inside of a popcorn box. Also stopping at the cafe was Bunn, who saw the singers' bus in the parking lot. "I had an old guitar in the back of my car and I was going to have them autograph it," Bunn says. "He [Holly] was in such a hurry, I just sat down and introduced myself and had just a few words with him."

Holly asked, "Is it always this damn cold in Minnesota?"

Bunn replied, "No, it gets a lot colder."

The singers slept in on Thursday morning.

Geller arranged to leave the bus with the balky heater in Montevideo for repairs and contracted with a local bus service to provide transportation to St. Paul, 155 miles east of Montevideo. GAC would then send another bus to St. Paul to take the singers to their Friday engagement in Davenport, Iowa.

While the singers slept, Simon Olson, the owner of the Montevideo charter bus company, prepared to drive the singers to St. Paul. Olson and one of his employees, Loran Kratz, took the 1958 Ford charter bus to the front of the Hunt Hotel, where they helped the singers load their equipment. While the singers' old bus was driven to a local garage, Olson pointed his blue-and-white vehicle toward the Twin Cities and drove off.

Photo of Buddy Holly sent out by General Artists
Corporation (GAC) to promote Winter Dance Party.
(Courtesy Larry Lehmer collection)

Photo of Big Bopper sent out by
GAC to promote Winter Dance Party.
(Courtesy Larry Lehmer collection)

Photo of Ritchie Valens sent out by GAC to
promote Winter Dance Party.
(Courtesy Larry Lehmer collection)

Norman Petty at the famous console where he produced some of Buddy Holly and the Crickets' greatest hits in his Clovis, New Mexico, studio.
(Kenneth Broad)

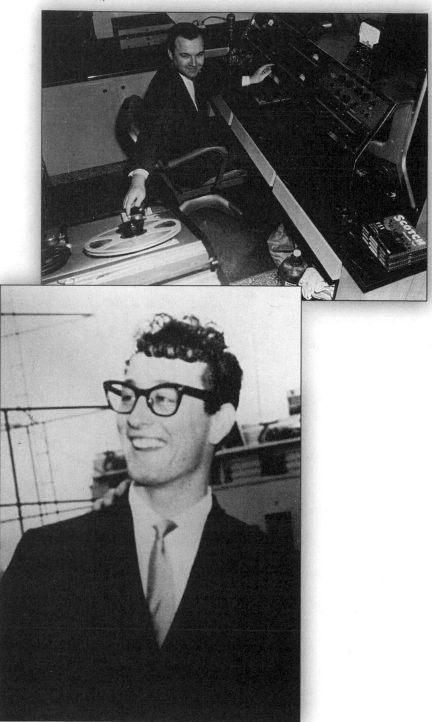

Buddy Holly outside Norman Petty's studio in Clovis, New Mexico
(Copyright © John Pickering)

The Picks—John Pickering, Bill Pickering, and Bob Lapham—did the vocal backing on several songs for Buddy Holly and the Crickets in 1957. *(Copyright John Pickering)*

J. P. Richardson and his bride, Teetsie, pose for pictures at the house of his brother-in-law in Beaumont, Texas, following their April 18, 1952, wedding. *(Jay Perry Richardson)*

J. P. Richardson selects a record at the beginning of the Disc-a-thon in the lobby of Beaumont's Jefferson Theater on April 29, 1957. *(Jay Perry Richardson)*

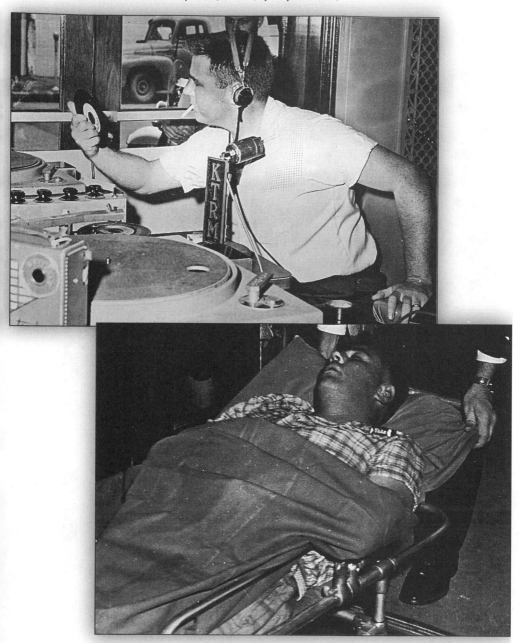

J. P. Richardson is wheeled to an ambulance to be taken to Baptist Hospital in Beaumont on May 4, 1957, after completing the 122-hour 8-minute Disc-a-thon. *(Jay Perry Richardson)*

J. P. takes on his Big Bopper personality in this Mercury Records publicity photo, which also appeared on the cover of his first Mercury album. *(Courtesy Larry Lehmer collection)*

Ritchie Valens shows off his flamboyant guitar style to an appreciative
audience at the Eagles Ballroom in Kenosha, Wisconsin, on January 24, 1959.
Emcee Jim Lounsbury and bass player Waylon Jennings *(right)* enjoy Valens's performance.
(Photo by Tony Szikil, Kenosha, WI)

The Big Bopper clowns around with the crowd at the Eagles Ballroom
in Kenosha, Wisconsin, on January 24, 1959. *(Photo by Tony Szikil, Kenosha, WI)*

Fans crowd the stage to collect autographs from Ritchie Valens, Dion DiMucci, the Big Bopper, Jim Lousbury, and Frankie Sardo *(bottom)* during the Winter Dance Party performance at the Eagles Ballroom in Kenosha, Wisconsin, on January 24, 1959. *(Photo by Tony Szikil, Kenosha, WI)*

The Big Bopper and Judy Peery backstage
at the Kato Ballroom in Mankato, Minnesota,
on January 25, 1959 *(Courtesy Judy Peery)*

Jim Lounsbury, the Big Bopper, Debbie Stevens,
Frankie Sardo, and Buddy Holly at the
Eagles Ballroom in Kenosha, Wisconsin,
on January 24, 1959 *(Photo by Tony Szikil, Kenosha, WI)*

Gathering around the birthday cake at Judy Peery's apartment following
the performance at the Kato Ballroom in Mankato, Minnesota, on January 25, 1959,
are Cathy Chatleain, drummer Carl Bunch, Fred Milano, and Carlo Mastrangelo
of the Belmonts, and Judy Peery. *(Courtesy Judy Peery)*

Kato Ballroom in Mankato, Minnesota
(Courtesy Larry Lehmer collection)

Call AM 9-6100 for Booth Reservatio

TUES., JAN. 27   "TEEN HOP
Coral   and ABC Paramount Artists

Buddy HOLLY & The Cricket
with such stars as

BIG BOPPER, Ritchie VALENS an
DION and The BELMONTS. Adde
Attraction Frankie SARDO!

Ticket stub from the January 27, 1959,
performance of the Winter Dance Party
at the Fiesta Ballroom in Montevideo,
Minnesota *(Courtesy Dick Strand)*

The Fiesta Ballroom in
Montevideo, Minnesota
*(Courtesy Larry Lehmer
collection)*

Tommy Allsup plays guitar behind Dion and the Belmonts at the Winter Dance Party show at the Fiesta Ballroom in Montevideo, Minnesota, on January 27, 1959. *(Courtesy Jane Ellefson)*

Waylon Jennings, Buddy Holly, and Tommy Allsup share a mike at the Fiesta Ballroom in Montevideo, Minnesota, on January 27, 1959. *(Courtesy Jane Ellefson)*

An intent Buddy Holly strums his famous Stratocaster at the Laramar Ballroom in Fort Dodge, Iowa, on January 30, 1959.
(Collection of the late Sharon Kay Lassiter)

A young Waylon Jennings at the Laramar Ballroom in Fort Dodge, Iowa, on January 30, 1959
(Collection of the late Sharon Kay Lassiter)

Buddy Holly clutches the shaving kit that contained
his pistol as he leaves the Laramar Ballroom in
Fort Dodge, Iowa, following the Winter Dance Party
performance on January 30, 1959.
(Courtesy Roger Kleve)

The Riverside Ballroom in Green Bay, Wisconsin *(Courtesy Larry L. Matti)*

Frankie Sardo eyes his Coca-Cola backstage at the Riverside Ballroom in Green Bay, Wisconsin, on February 1, 1959. *(Courtesy Larry L. Matti)*

With Carl Bunch in the hospital, Ritchie Valens takes a turn at the drums behind Tommy Allsup and Waylon Jennings during February 1, 1959, show of the Winter Dance Party at the Riverside Ballroom in Green Bay, Wisconsin. *(Courtesy Larry L. Matti)*

This close-up photo of Buddy Holly, taken backstage at the Riverside Ballroom in Green Bay, Wisconsin, following the February 1, 1959, stop of the Winter Dance Party is the last photo taken of the singer to be published. *(Courtesy Larry L. Matti)*

Surf Ballroom, Clear Lake, Iowa *(Courtesy Larry Lehmer collection)*

The stage at the Surf Ballroom in Clear Lake, Iowa, where Buddy Holly, Ritchie Valens, and the Big Bopper made their final appearances on February 2, 1959. (Bob Modersohn/The Des Moines Register)

Beechcraft Bonanza 35, a 1947 model similar to the one that carried Buddy Holly, Ritchie Valens, J. P. Richardson and Roger Peterson to their deaths north of Clear Lake, Iowa, on February 3, 1959. (Courtesy Beech Aircraft Corporation)

The Tour Goes Bad

The moderating temperatures continued Wednesday as the Winter Dance Party made an uneventful 155-mile jaunt to the Prom Ballroom in St. Paul, retracing part of the route it had taken the day before. Although skies were cloudy and a cold front sliced across the northern part of Minnesota, the temperature climbed into the upper 20s by Wednesday afternoon.

The new issue of *Variety* brightened the day for at least one Winter Dance Party member: Valens's "Donna" climbed one spot to No. 4 on the *Variety* charts, and the flip side, "La Bamba," was No. 17. On the bus, Valens and Bunch were forming a solid friendship. "[Ritchie] was more my age," Bunch explains. "We used to joke with him and tease him about not having a girlfriend. Waylon had to chase them away, I couldn't buy one, and [Ritchie] didn't have one. He was forever practicing and working, carrying his guitar with him."

Frankie Sardo, who was Valens's roommate on the overnight stops, says: "He was a sweet kid. To me, it was like having a kid brother. I loved this kid's guitar playing. He taught me a couple of guitar chords. And I loved the song "La Bamba." We all would stand in the wings when this kid was onstage. We would be singing offstage with him."

Dion, too, was impressed with Valens. "He was one of the greatest rhythm guitar players I ever heard, and he sang with a passion. Ritchie was very quiet and very lonesome. You were just drawn to him to make him kind of relax. He became like a younger brother to me, and Buddy became like an older brother."

The whole entourage was beginning to sound like family. "[Richardson] was like a father to me," Carl Bunch says. "Buddy had kind of turned me over to him to keep me out of trouble. He watched out for me and kept me from getting in too much trouble. But Dion and the Belmonts were pretty wild, and I wanted to run around with them and carry on."

The singers were in a good mood when Simon Olson dropped them off at a St. Paul motel before returning to Montevideo. St. Paul was one of the bigger cities that the Winter Dance Party would pass through. With a population of around 350,000 it was more than fifty times larger than Montevideo. The Twin Cities formed the eighth-largest metropolitan center in the United States with a population of 1.5 million, half of all the people who lived in Minnesota. The Winter Dance Party arrived with much less fanfare in St. Paul than it did in the smaller cities, although Minnesota governor Orville Freeman had proclaimed February as American Music Month in Minnesota. Disc jockey Bill Diehl was hoping teens would start celebrating a few days early at the Winter Dance Party he was set to host at the Prom Ballroom in St. Paul.

The Prom was one of the classier ballrooms in the entire Midwest. From its neat brick exterior and well-lit marquee to its rows of gleaming booths amid a checkered tile floor leading to its hardwood dance floor, the building was superior to most used by the Winter Dance Party. Harry Given, a former bandleader and piano player from St. Paul, and one of the hall's four co-owners in 1959, did much of the booking. Given preferred bands similar to his house band, the Jules Herman Orchestra.

"There were a lot of second thoughts about the early rock days about whether or not this is what we wanted to have in our building," Given says.

Following a mid-1956 showing of *Rock Around the Clock* in Minneapolis, a group of teenagers had snake-danced around town, breaking windows. The movie's run was immediately canceled. When Minneapolis radio station WSPT banned Elvis Presley records later that year, the station received several threatening phone calls. A rock was thrown through the station window with a note saying: "I am a teenager—you play Elvis Presley or else we tear up this town." However, things had settled a bit by the time of the Winter Dance Party.

In promoting the dance, Given worked closely with Diehl, whose late-afternoon program on 50,000-watt powerhouse rocker WDGY was the top-rated show in the Twin Cities. Diehl emceed many shows for Given, and had originally met Holly in Minneapolis on Alan Freed's 1958 Big Beat tour. Diehl was happy to see Holly again, nine months after they had shared lunch. "He remembered it all," Diehl says. "He remembered everything. That impressed me."

Holly introduced Diehl to the rest of the performers before the curtain went up on the 7:30 PM show. "I remember Ritchie Valens being very shy," Diehl says. "This was all kind of new to him. And I remember the Big Bopper with his jacket. I remember the crowd. We had over 2,000 people. It was over capacity, really. And orderly. No rioting or anything. It was fantastic."

Included in the huge crowd were Mike Ulahakis and his girlfriend, Pat Ek, of faraway Rhinelander, Wisconsin. They had seen Holly twice in Wisconsin in the summer of 1958. That winter Ulahakis was a college student in River Falls, Wisconsin, and Ek was attending college in Eau Claire. "We used to like to dance," explains Ulahakis. "We used to follow bands all the time." So Ek caught a bus to Hudson, Wisconsin, Ulahakis borrowed a friend's 1955 Mercury convertible, picked her up in Hudson, and drove on to St. Paul where he plunked down $2.50 for a pair of tickets to the show.

"The Big Bopper actually stood out more than Buddy Holly did, with the coat and the telephone ringing. That song was more popular than anything Buddy Holly had had in quite a while," Ulahakis remembers.

Diehl also was impressed with Richardson as they swapped backstage stories about their radio careers. "He was laughing and saying that if he could do it, anybody could do it," Diehl says.

Also backstage was twelve-year-old Timothy D. Kehr, a regular at Prom rock shows. He was not a fan of any of the singers and could not play a musical instrument. Kehr's interest was in the business of music. With the help of his father, a family friend of Harry Given, Kehr pursued his interest at the Prom. "The music was onstage, a lot of the other stuff was backstage, the comings and goings of what the music business was really like," Kehr explains. "There was some age difference between us, but I was fairly knowledgeable. So I could hold my own in a conversation."

Kehr knew most of the radio personalities in the area, and had met Dion and the Belmonts on a visit the previous fall. Kehr was also well known by the off-duty St. Paul policemen employed by Given for security. "So they just kind of left me alone," Kehr says. His access to the singers included the dressing room in the basement, where the members of the Winter Dance Party were playing cards. Kehr had brought a photograph of Holly with the original Crickets, hoping to get it autographed.

"Some of the other guys were making fun of the photograph," Kehr says. "He [Holly] had had his teeth capped [since the photo] . . . and everybody said it looked like Buddy had his whole face capped because it was such a drastic difference."

Backstage, Diehl recalls, the musicians were excited by the turnout.

I can still see Buddy Holly going over and talking to Ritchie Valens. I saw him patting him on the back and talking to him and they'd peek out and look at the crowd. I'm sure Buddy was telling him to just relax and don't be nervous. Buddy was kind of a parent figure.

[Holly was] this tall, slender fellow running around, making sure that everything was right. . . . He'd make sure that the lighting was right, that the band instruments were right and that all the speakers were working. He was a very, very thorough fellow.

Holly's attention to detail parallels that of one of his biggest fans that night, local musician Sherwin Linton. Linton, who had moved to the Twin Cities in 1958 to attend broadcasting school, caught Holly and the Crickets at their Big Beat show. Linton had been so impressed that, when he had a publicity photo shot of his own band, he duplicated a well-known pose of Holly's group snapping their bowties.

Even though Linton was busy making plans for his wedding, he took time to catch the Winter Dance Party show. He arrived just in time to catch Holly's set but was disappointed. "I wasn't able to get anywhere near the stage area," Linton says. "It was difficult to hear the performance well. What I could hear sounded good, but I couldn't hear it well. The screaming of the girls was tremendous. Whenever he'd start to sing anything, it was nothing but screams.

"I was disappointed that Jerry Allison and Joe Mauldin weren't there. I was aware of that right away. . . . It was Buddy Holly and he had a good band, but it wasn't quite the same."

By the time the Winter Dance Party wound up its show around 10:30 PM, the temperature had risen into the mid-30s, well above the predicted high of mid-20s. The unexpected moderation also forced weather forecasters to alter their prediction of a below-zero low Wednesday night.

With a new bus lined up for the rest of the trip and the promise of better weather, the singers spent a restful night in the Twin Cities before heading south, toward Davenport, Iowa, three hundred and twenty miles away.

—◆·◆—

Thursday, January 29, 1959

New York — Peter Tripp, 34-year-old disc jockey at New York's WMGM, was recovering Thursday from a 200-hour sleepless broadcasting marathon.

Tripp slept for nearly 14 hours following completion of his 8½-day stunt in Times Square.

Another well-known disc jockey, Dave Hunter in Jacksonville, Florida, was continuing his marathon, which started at the same time as Tripp's.

Radio-marathon veteran J. P. Richardson could identify with Tripp's ordeal. But the Winter Dance Party was having troubles of its own Thursday morning. Although the temperature was holding steady around 30 degrees, the new bus creaked along the Mississippi River basin in drizzly weather, barely staying ahead of a cold front that was cascading over the plains from Canada. Like its predecessor, the bus was having trouble keeping out the cold.

When it reached Davenport, Iowa's third largest city with a population of 60,000, the Winter Dance Party took on a new identity, if just for one night. Fred Epstein, owner of Davenport radio station KSTT, booked the Winter Dance Party into the Capitol Theater, offering Davenport its first sit-down rock concert. Epstein also offered two shows, at 7 and 9 PM. By clearing the house between shows, Epstein was able to recoup some of the high cost of the Winter Dance Party. Because there was no room for dancing in the theater, Epstein changed the name of the show to the "KSTT Concert of Stars."

Epstein's station was locked in a ratings war with WOC. Both stations catered to teens, playing rock 'n' roll and holding frequent teen hops. WOC touted its "Good Music Survey" and had the "Morning Mayor of the Quint Cities" in deejay Ed Zack, but Epstein claims his station was number one, largely on the strength of his top-rated, drive-time jock Mark Stevens. Epstein tapped Stevens as master of ceremonies and heavily promoted the concert on his station and in the local newspapers. Certificates for a fifty-cent discount from the $1.50 admission were distributed widely, at the Capitol and its sister theaters, the Fort and Rocket, in nearby Rock Island, Illinois.

For Stevens, the Winter Dance Party offered a rare opportunity to work with some of the bigger names of rock 'n' roll. Most of Stevens's previous off-air work had consisted of spinning records at teen hops, not surprising considering that he was just fifteen years old. "I was just a snotty-nosed kid," says Stevens, who dashed from his classes at Davenport West High School to make it to the station in time for his 3 PM program. "I was the most popular guy in school, besides the football team."

Stevens was setting up tape equipment at the Capitol when the Winter Dance Party bus arrived, parking in the alley behind the theater. The singers were not happy. "They had a bus with no heater," Stevens says. "They were all bitching about it when they got off the bus."

While the musicians prepared for the first show, the Capitol filled, mostly with teens, although a handful of parents also dropped by. Stevens recorded interviews with the singers backstage and chatted with them between acts. "The madman was the Big Bopper, who was a jock and I kind of looked up to because he was a big-time operator," Stevens says. "I was pretty well impressed. He was a nut, backstage and on stage." As the evening progressed, Valens became very ill with flu-like symptoms, Stevens says.

While the musicians performed, the temperature dropped from the mid-30s and the drizzle turned to sleet, glazing Davenport's streets and area highways and causing several accidents. Flights in and out of the Quad-City airport were canceled, and the sleet was expected to turn to snow during the night with accumulations of three inches in Davenport. Up to four inches was expected in northwest Iowa, where the Winter Dance Party was to perform in Fort Dodge the next night.

After the Capitol performance, the musicians dashed around the corner to spend the night at the Hotel Davenport. Richardson, who was developing a cold, called home from his hotel room, and Jennings slipped across the river to visit some Illinois night spots with some fans. After returning to the hotel, Holly visited Jennings in his room. "He woke me up," Jennings recalls.

"How would you like to go to England?" Holly asked.

"Good," Jennings replied.

"Well, don't say anything to Tommy or Goose [Bunch], because I'm not going to take them," Holly said. "I'm going to get back with J. I. and Joe B."

If Holly was getting back together with his old bandmates, Jennings asked, what did he need him for?

"I want you to open the show," Holly replied.

———— • ————

Friday, January 30, 1959

Jacksonville, Fla. — After 9 days, 9 hours, 9 minutes and 9 seconds, WZRO disc jockey Dave Hunter ended a 225-hour broadcasting marathon from the showroom of a local auto dealer. After Hunter was driven home in an ambulance, he ate dinner and settled into a 17-hour nap.

———— • ————

Hunter was still sleeping when J. P. Richardson and the rest of the Winter Dance Party checked out of the Hotel Davenport Friday morning on a blustery winter day. Davenport had been one of the state's warmer spots overnight with the temperature holding in the teens. In the northern part of the state, however, temperatures stalled just above the zero mark, and bitterly cold conditions Friday night were expected to drop temperatures well below zero throughout the state.

About thirty miles west of Davenport, with the temperature still in the teens and an inch of newly fallen snow on the ground, the Winter Dance Party bus stopped providing heat altogether. The bus was driven slowly into Mac's Shell Station in Tipton, Iowa, where station owners Bob and Betty McGregor referred the troupe to Gaul Motor Co. next door. Betty McGregor then phoned the Tipton newspaper, *The Conservative,* to tell the editors about the stars in town. "But they thought I was kidding, so they wouldn't come down," McGregor says.

At Gaul, the bus trouble was easily diagnosed: All nine heaters on the converted school bus had frozen. It would take several hours for them to thaw and be cleaned out. As mechanic Martin Young began defrosting the heaters, the singers scattered throughout the eastern Iowa town of about 2,100.

"I remember everybody getting real irritable about the cold," Bunch says. "It was like 'What's going to happen next to stop us from being able to do this [tour]?'"

Holly and several others remained in the showroom, many sitting on a bench near some new 1959 Edsels. Holly pulled a bucket-type tractor seat from a display and plopped down on it. "I'm a reindeer salesman," he quipped to the amusement of his friends.

Ritchie Valens led another group across the alley to the tiny Meet and Eat Cafe, where Esther Wenck and Betty Murray were serving up hamburgers and hot beef sandwiches to a packed lunchtime crowd. Even though the cafe had just a handful of tables and a few seats at the counter, a jukebox was squeezed in against one wall.

Valens stood at the jukebox and asked waitress Wenck: "Would you like to hear the song I made famous?"

Says Wenck: "I thought he was kidding. I said yes."

Several Tipton residents then were treated to an impromptu performance as Valens sang along to "Donna."

"I still thought he was goofin'," Wenck notes. "I still didn't think it was him."

Several of the singers swarmed into the T & M Clothing Store, where they contributed profusely to the local economy. "They all had lightweight clothes on," co-owner George Tevis remembers. "They were cold and they were buying everything in the store. Pants, jackets, everything."

Although Betty McGregor wasn't able to persuade editors of *The Conservative* to interview the singers, the paper later acknowledged the unscheduled Winter Dance Party stop: "The group caused a great deal of interest because of their popularity among teen-agers and because their conversations were conducted in a language intelligible to musicians but mystifying to nearly everyone else."

It took Young four hours to thaw the heaters, and the Winter Dance Party didn't leave Tipton until after 3 PM, less than five hours before a scheduled appearance at the Laramar Ballroom in Fort Dodge, about two hundred miles away.

The rest of the trip to Fort Dodge was slow, but uneventful. Fort Dodge (pop. 28,000) had come under the intense scrutiny of health officials after a mysterious virus spread rapidly through the city in November. As many as two thousand Fort Dodge residents had been stricken with the virus, which caused nausea, vomiting, and diarrhea. A team of federal health officials descended on the city in January in an all-out effort to determine the source of the virus. When it was discovered that the pet dog in many families was stricken with similar symptoms, the Iowa state veterinarian was dispatched to the city to take case histories of the sick dogs.

The Winter Dance Party bus with its balky heater slipped through the winter darkness in temperatures in the low teens and with two inches of freshly fallen snow on the ground, en route to a concert in a city full of sick people and dogs.

The bus was late arriving in Fort Dodge. "We were worried," says Dick Derrig, an assistant manager at the Laramar Ballroom.

Bob Geer, fifteen-year-old son of Laramar owner Larry Geer, remembers the group's arrival. "They had a bus that smelled bad. I'm sure it was no fun traveling on."

Bill McCollough, a local disc jockey at KWMT who was to emcee the show, agrees. "It was an old ratty-looking bus," McCollough says. "It was pretty tacky."

The venerable Laramar probably looked good to the singers as they unloaded their equipment from the parking lot behind the ballroom. The building was constructed in 1903 as the Fort Dodge Armory and Auditorium. By the time Larry Geer bought it in 1952, the ballroom had featured virtually all the famous dance bands since the mid-1920s.

Geer immediately started to cultivate the teen crowds. When rock 'n' roll struck in the mid-1950s, Geer instituted regular Friday night dances for youngsters. Although his teen dances were very popular, he faced stiff competition the night the Winter Dance Party arrived in town. The state tournament–bound Fort Dodge High School basketball team drew almost two thousand fans who watched them lose 65–62 to Waterloo West that January 30, and St. Edmond drew another thousand for its 51–49 loss to

Pocahontas Catholic. The city's three movie theaters also drew good crowds, but Fort Dodge's true rockers queued up outside the Laramar.

Girls in poodle skirts, saddle shoes, and car coats stood in line, teasing their pageboy fluffs while their boyfriends annoyed them with sick jokes ("Mommy, Mommy! Come quickly and bring the marshmallows, Daddy's on fire.") Across the street, the singers checked into $3-a-night rooms at the Hotel Cornbelt. The Big Bopper slipped away to Tom's Lunch, two doors down from the Laramar. There he ate a hamburger and chatted with Bob Geer.

"I don't think he really liked going on one-nighters around the Midwest at that time of the year," Geer says. "He was talking about his family back home in Texas."

An estimated one thousand people filed into the Laramar, each pausing to have a hand stamped by ticket-taker Katie Cain. One of those was Jerry Estes, a sixteen-year-old from Storm Lake, Iowa, who braved the blustery weather conditions to drive the sixty miles to Fort Dodge without his parents' permission. "We kind of all just decided we were going to go," Estes says. "We were pretty sure what our parents would say, so we decided to just take our punishment later. . . . We had a lot of trouble driving over. The wind was whipping across the road."

It was worth the trouble, Estes says. "It was just packed in there. You could hear very well and occasionally you could actually get to see them. It was standing room only."

During the show, Bob Geer observed the singers backstage. "Dion was definitely enjoying the 'teen idol' image and sweeping the gals off their feet. I have a feeling that he spent a little time in the bus with some of the gals."

McCollough, a twenty-two-year-old who had a Top 40 show on KWMT each afternoon, also remembers Dion and the Belmonts. "Dion was totally standoffish. Absolutely aloof," he recalls. "The Belmonts wore pants that were right off the hanger. You could still see the creases in them."

During the show, kids sneaked downstairs to smoke. Derrig and a handful of other local men helped Larry Geer patrol the ballroom, keeping things orderly.

Eddie Simpson, a freshman at nearby Callendar High School, found brief refuge from the crowd on the ballroom floor by fleeing to the Laramar's balcony, an area usually reserved for the parents who were admitted free to the teen dances. "We were looking right down on the stage," Simpson says. "We sat there and watched the whole thing. I can remember when they announced Buddy Holly and he stepped out on the stage. He had been standing back in the backdrop and everybody went nuts when he started singing."

Jerry Estes agrees that Holly was a fitting climax to the show. "He really brought down the house."

After the show, the singers loaded their equipment on the bus and congregated in the basement of the Laramar. Simpson and two friends, Gary Onnen and Phil Swanson, stopped to use the basement restroom when they spotted the singers sitting in a booth. "They were just getting ready to go," Onnen says. "The dance had been over for quite awhile. . . . They were stars, but they were as common as could be. They just sat and talked to us." After visiting for a few minutes, the three fans left, Simpson stopping just long enough to pilfer an 8x10 glossy photograph of Ritchie Valens from a lobby display.

Meanwhile, emcee McCollough made his way down the stairs where he started a conversation with Holly. "He was complaining about the bus," McCollough says. "How it was drafty and everything and he was going to catch his death of cold, he thought. I had been taking some flying lessons and was just about to the point of soloing. So, I opened my big mouth and said, 'Well, why don't you let me fly you?'"

"That's really a great idea," Holly answered.

Surprised by Holly's reply, McCollough started back-pedaling. "I can't really," he said.

"Could you call somebody and get us a plane?" Holly asked.

"Yeah, I can do that," McCollough said.

Bunch recalls the conversation. "Buddy was flying crazy," he says. "Buddy believed you could land a small airplane on a housetop if you had to. He really liked to fly. He had been bugging us for days."

Allsup agrees that Holly was anxious to get things moving. "We'd talked about it [flying] several times. Buddy liked to fly. He thought there was no way a small plane would crash. He was used to flying out there in West Texas where you could land in a field."

McCollough called his flight instructor, who declined the offer to fly the singers the three-hundred-and-sixty miles north to Duluth. Ballroom owner Larry Geer, a pilot with twenty-two years' experience, also warned the singers that to fly into the upper Midwest darkness in sub-zero temperatures and uncertain weather would be risky at best. After considering the matter for awhile, the singers decided to retire to their rooms in the Corn Belt and take their chances with the bus on Saturday.

Holly called his pregnant wife in New York. "Buddy would call from the tour and say how unhappy he was," Maria Elena later told the *Chicago Tribune.* "'Buddy,' I'd say, 'Why don't you come home?' He'd say, 'Maria, you know me. I have to finish.' Besides, we needed the money."

Saturday, January 31, 1959

The forecast was not good when the singers awoke in 1 below zero weather in Fort Dodge on Saturday morning. Cold as that was, the morning low in Duluth, Minnesota, was 24 below. The singers expected to be in Duluth by late afternoon when, they hoped, it would be substantially warmer.

By the time the bus reached Minneapolis and St. Paul at midday, it was still well below zero. Although the bus heating system was unable to provide enough warmth for the singers, temperatures were rising inside the bus. "Tempers got a little short at times," Allsup recalls. "Mainly because guys were feeling bad, not getting any rest. I don't think anybody was actually mad at anybody."

Says Bunch: "It had gotten really tedious trying to live on that bus. There was no place to lay down and it was always cold. Real bad. It got to where we were joking with each other and we were calling [Dion and the Belmonts] Moron and the Bellhops, and they were calling us Bloody Holly and the Rickets."

As if the weather and bus problems weren't enough, one of the singers introduced another threat to the tour. "One of the Belmonts had a pistol," Allsup says. "We'd be going down the road and he'd point it down the aisle at the bus driver. He'd click it and go 'Bang—the bus driver's dead,' and Holly said, 'Man, don't do that. You act like you've never seen a gun before.'"

At one point, Jennings recalls, the bus driver took control of the situation. "Freddie [Milano] was waving that gun around and clicking it," Jennings says. "The bus driver stopped the bus."

Frankie Sardo says: "Freddie would play Billy the Kid."

Milano's Luger earlier had created quite a stir during one of the overnight stops on the tour. Tommy Allsup and Waylon Jennings were in adjoining rooms, connected by a shared bathroom. Milano was visiting Allsup and Jennings in one of the rooms. "A guy was raising hell with us for making noise," Allsup recalls. "He finally started banging on our door. He was banging on one door and Fred went down to the other door and just cracked it. He pointed his gun at that guy and clicked the hammer. That guy ran over to his room. You could hear him piling furniture against his door."

Milano insists that it was simply a case of self-defense. "He pulled a knife on us," Milano says. "He came to the door with a knife. When somebody pulls a knife, you've got to be prepared for that. I wouldn't just go pulling guns on anyone."

Despite the increased tension among the weary performers, the bus pushed on to Duluth.

It's doubtful that any of the members of the Winter Dance Party would quarrel with Duluth's claim to being "America's Coolest Summer City." The temperature was still well below zero when the singers checked into the Hotel Duluth for a short rest before their show at the National Guard Armory. Had the weather been more hospitable, the singers may have better enjoyed their visit to Minnesota's third-biggest city (pop. 105,000). A common complaint of Duluthians was that the city has "nine months of winter and three months of poor sledding." Indeed, the breaking up of the ice on Lake Superior each spring was a major event.

The winds were howling off the frozen waters of Lake Superior, one block east of the armory, when the singers arrived to set up for the 8 PM show. "The smell of that diesel [from the bus] coming off that ice would just literally stone you," Bunch says.

The weather was becoming a deadly serious matter for the Winter Dance Party. Temperatures approaching 35 below zero were predicted for Duluth that night, and the tour was booked for a 1:30 PM show Sunday in Appleton, Wisconsin, some three hundred and twenty miles away. With the Duluth show to run until midnight, tour manager Sam Geller had no choice but to have his entourage travel through the night while the singers tried to sleep.

Given the bus problems, Geller made arrangements to keep the vehicle in the basement of the armory, away from the frigid temperatures outside. Hopefully, he'd deliver a warm bus at the end of the show to help the singers rest for Sunday's doubleheader at Appleton and Green Bay.

Meanwhile, fans crammed into the massive armory. Ron Sapik and a group of buddies, all of whom who were joining the army within days, took a case of beer and a quart of peppermint schnapps to the show as they celebrated their last few days of freedom. Sapik was surprised to find that Ritchie Valens stole the show from Holly.

"When he sang "La Bamba," he got down on his knees and he leaned all the way back with his head almost touching the floor and he was looking up in the air. He had his guitar strapped across his chest. He put on a good performance."

After the show, Sapik remembers: "It was so cold out, we just ran for our cars."

The warmed bus was brought from the basement to the stage area, where it was loaded before the singers climbed aboard for one of the longest night rides of the tour.

The Tour from Hell

The bus left the Lake Superior basin, piercing the winter darkness through densely wooded forests of poplar and birch. Near the town of Hurley, the bus turned south on U.S. Highway 51. Screened by ragged trees and brush—the marks of forest fires that had gutted the area over the years—the road ran through a barren, rocky land with few farms and little cultivation.

It was here that the bus died, wheezing to a stop up a slight incline, some ten miles south of Hurley. The singers soon found that this was no place to be stranded. Nothing on the bus was working and snow was waist-deep alongside the desolate highway. Geller decided to keep the singers in the bus and wait for help.

"I didn't know where the hell I was. Everything froze," Geller recalls. "I'm looking for traffic. Nothing. I'm worried about it. The kids in back were freezing."

The singers burned newspapers in the aisle of the bus to keep warm, opening windows on one side of the vehicle to let the smoke escape. In the pitch-black darkness outside, the sound of the howling wind and snapping tree limbs reminded them of their desolation.

Carl Bunch broke out a couple of bottles of whiskey he had bought in New York City and shared them with his fellow musicians, who huddled under blankets, trying to keep warm. "It was pitiful," Bunch says.

For Frankie Sardo, the bitter cold brought back unpleasant memories of his duty in the U.S. Army during the Korean War. "I thought Korea was the last time I was going to be cold," Sardo told Dion. "I can't believe this. I didn't think I'd ever have to experience this again."

Dion told stories about life in New York; Holly shared tales from the Plains of West Texas. "We were like kids," Dion says.

The wait was longer than the singers expected. Soon, some of the chilled entourage started to question the wisdom of waiting.

The trumpet player from the band said, "We can't stay on this bus, man. They'll read about us in the paper tomorrow."

Headlights in the distance spurred Geller into action. He jumped from the bus and waved down the car, which turned out to be driven by a county sheriff. The sheriff drove Geller to Hurley, where he found an old crankhandled telephone and woke the operator. After hearing of his group's predicament, she said, "Oh my God, you'll freeze to death." The sheriff called for help from Hurley and nearby Ironwood, Michigan, to rescue the singers.

But back at the bus, the singers weren't waiting. "We were flagging down cars," Dion says. Every car they stopped took a few singers into town. Soon, only Dion, Valens, Sardo, and Bunch were left on the bus, drinking up what was left of Bunch's New York whiskey. Eventually they, too, were rescued.

In its first half century, Hurley, Wisconsin, gained a reputation as one of the rowdiest towns in the world. Indeed, lumbermen of the nineteenth century used to boast that "the four toughest places in the world were Cumberland, Hayward, Hurley, and Hell, and that the first three were tougher than the last." Hurley's lusty reputation lured novelist Edna Ferber to town. She spent several days at the grand Burton House hotel, gathering details for her novel, *Come and Get It*.

Tucked among pine trees several miles south of town was a resort called Little Bohemia where John Dillinger and his mob hid in 1934. When government agents surrounded the place, the mobsters escaped amid a hail of bullets. For several years after the incident, Dillinger's father operated a small roadside stand at the site, where for twenty-five cents tourists could check out the bullet holes and some of Dillinger's personal possessions that were left behind in his hasty escape. But, by the 1950s, the vice was mostly gone.

Hurley was quiet as the singers arrived. The 24-below-zero temperature doubtless had something to with it. "We went into Hurley knowing it was wilder than hell," Jennings says. "We thought, 'Oh, this will be fun.' . . . But they had cleaned it up. . . . We stayed in the other town."

Jennings was one of the lucky ones. Richardson, Holly, and Jennings managed to get rooms at the St. James Hotel in Ironwood, just a few blocks to the east. The rest of the musicians ended up at Hurley's Club Carnival on Silver Street, a notorious place in its heyday, but an all-night cafe when the Winter Dance Party arrived.

Ritchie Valens called his manager, Bob Keene, in California where it was still late evening. He managed to connect with Keene at a restaurant in Santa Monica. Valens complained that his toes were freezing. Keene told him to get on an airplane and come home the next day.

Although most of the musicians settled in for a long night at Club Carnival, Bunch was not among them. Bunch had put several layers of socks on his feet and stuffed them back inside his boots when the bus broke down. Soon his feet started to sweat and the sweat froze around his feet. By the time he was rescued, Bunch was in such pain they drove him directly to Grand View Hospital near Ironwood. There they cut the boots and socks from his swollen and disfigured feet.

After checking Bunch into the hospital, Geller was driven back to the Iron County Garage in Hurley, where a wrecker was dispatched to the crippled bus. The bus was towed back to the garage where it was discovered that a piston had gone through the engine block. The mechanics could not repair the damaged engine, and Geller needed to get the Winter Dance Party to Appleton, some two hundred miles away, in time for the 1:30 PM dance. When it became obvious that the singers could not make it to Appleton in time, Geller called the owner of the Cinderella Ballroom and canceled the show, the first time in his road experience that he had to cancel. He then made arrangements to get his show to Green Bay. Some of the singers went by Greyhound bus; others went by train.

It was a tired, somber group of musicians that reassembled in a downtown Green Bay hotel late Sunday afternoon. There was some good news for Valens, however. The winter coat his mother had promised to send had arrived.

J. P. Richardson settled in the warmth of his hotel room to call his wife in Montegut, Louisiana. He complained about a head cold, and told his wife how much he was looking forward to returning home and getting a good night's sleep. Despite his illness, Richardson made light of the difficulties he had endured on the Winter Dance Party. "He laughed about it," Teetsie says.

Meanwhile, Geller made arrangements for a new bus to arrive from Chicago the next morning.

The temperature had risen above zero and was around the day's high of 5 degrees when the singers gathered Sunday afternoon. The frigid temperatures, combined with recent snows, left many of the city's streets hard packed and slippery. Green Bay police responded to thirty-two traffic accidents that weekend, but the lousy driving conditions didn't keep teens away from the Riverside Ballroom. They were lined up for three blocks as the singers arrived in taxi cabs.

The crowd looked just as big from inside the cavernous ballroom, where ticket-takers attempted to control the flow of kids trying to buy tickets before 8 PM, when the price would rise from ninety cents to $1.25. But the crush of youngsters proved too much. The door to the ballroom gave way to the weight of the mob.

The Riverside had been Green Bay's premier ballroom since it was constructed in 1929 by Joseph Blecher. That first year, the ballroom was given over to the Green Bay Packers for a scrimmage when it was too cold to practice outdoors. Blecher claimed that bandleader Lawrence Welk and his Hotsy Totsy Boys became the Champagne Music Makers during a radio broadcast from the Riverside, at the urging of sponsor Miller High Life, "the champagne of bottled beer." Before Red Nichols's band appeared at the Riverside, Blecher had his wife, Marie, and two daughters paint nickels with red nail polish to be given as change that night.

The Blechers retired in 1945, yielding to a series of managers over the next few years before Lloyd and Phyllis Aude took over. The Audes were the first to feature rock 'n' roll acts at the hall. Lloyd Aude teamed with a local disc jockey, Bill Walters of WDUZ, who emceed most of his teen dances, including the Winter Dance Party, and interviewed performers for later broadcast.

Walters took over a small room to the side of the stage and set up a tape recorder for interviews while the singers were setting up their own equipment. While the singers set up, Walters spotted an old friend, Bob Ehlert of GAC, who had come from Chicago to provide encouragement to Geller and the musicians.

There was another reunion of sorts that night, between Holly and a group of teenagers from Wausau, Wisconsin—brothers Terry and Bob Oestreich, twin sisters Judy and Joan Bender, and Larry Matti—whom Holly had met on tour the previous summer. The youngsters had planned to catch the Winter Dance Party in Appleton, but when the show was canceled, they came to Green Bay instead. During the show, the Wausau teens stayed in the offstage interview room with Walters, where they talked with the singers about the weather and continuing bus problems.

Larry Matti, who spent much of that evening taking photos of the singers, recalls: "I think they were kind of beat." Despite their lack of sleep and continuing travel problems, the singers never let their despair show on stage.

At least two thousand people jammed the Riverside that night. The hardwood dance floor, which was almost as long as a football field, allowed room for dancing near the back, but most fans pressed toward the stage.

With Bunch still in the hospital, the show was without a drummer. Fortunately, Carlo Mastrangelo of the Belmonts had some drumming experience. He handled drum chores for all the groups that night, except his own. When Dion and the Belmonts sang, Valens sat in on the drums.

Holly was impressed with Mastrangelo's drum work. "He was going to take him away from me," Dion recalls. "He offered him twice as much money as I was paying him."

Backstage, Richardson and Frankie Sardo were cutups, posing for photos for Matti. Matti's camera also caught a somber Ritchie Valens, who looked much older than seventeen.

By the end of the show, Bill Walters had his interviews, Judy Bender had autographs of most of the singers, and Larry Matti had his photos.

Everybody packed up and went home. But, for the singers, there was an early-morning wakeup call for the three-hundred-and-forty-mile trip to Clear Lake, Iowa, the next day, a journey that was expected to begin in temperatures near 20 degrees below zero.

———————◆———————

Monday, February 2, 1959

> Punxsutawney, Penn. — Bad news. There will be six more weeks of winter.
>
> That's according to the groundhog at Gobbler's Knob on the edge of Punxsutawney, who saw his shadow when he briefly emerged from his home this morning.
>
> He quickly ducked back inside, no doubt due to the 10-below-zero temperature.

———————◆———————

It was another bitterly cold morning when the musicians woke in Green Bay. The temperature had bottomed out at 19 below zero, but that was downright balmy compared to where they were headed that morning. Their route would take them within a few miles of Lone Rock, Wisconsin, the coldest place in the United States with a minus-36 reading. But two factors were in the singers' favor: They had a new bus and the weather was expected to moderate again. The high pressure center that had kept the upper Midwest in the deep freeze for several days was moving east. Temperatures in the mid-20s were forecast for the Clear Lake–Mason City, Iowa, area where the Winter Dance Party was to play on Monday night.

But as the bus swooped toward the Mississippi River bluffs near Prairie du Chien, it started to act up. Even though temperatures had risen into the teens, the bus was unable to keep the entertainers warm. The driver pulled into a service station for assistance. While mechanics worked to repair the faulty heaters, the entourage took advantage of the break to take care of some personal business.

At Richardson's request, Geller went in search of a bottle of whiskey, which the singer could mix with mouthwash in an attempt to battle the cold that had been nagging him for days. Richardson went to a nearby store where he hoped to find a sleeping bag to make traveling more tolerable. The tour was to head north again after Monday night's show, four hundred and forty miles to Moorhead, Minnesota, with two shows scheduled for Tuesday night.

Holly phoned his lawyer in New York but did not like what he heard. He told bandmates that even the threat of legal action against Norman Petty had not freed up the royalties he thought he was owed. Holly was cursing about it when he got back on the bus. Jennings recalls, "He came back on the bus and he was mad. I mean he was bad mad, the maddest I ever saw him."

Holly's mood was in stark contrast to a happy Richardson, who returned to the bus toting a sleeping bag. "Man, I'm gonna be warm tonight," he said.

After leaving Prairie du Chien, the singers again crossed the Mississippi River into Iowa. The singers wound their way through hilly northeastern Iowa before arriving in Clear Lake around 6 PM, just two hours before the Winter Dance Party's show at the Surf Ballroom, but too late for a scheduled 4:30 PM personal appearance at the Record Salon in nearby Mason City. The singers split up to catch a quick dinner, some going to Witke's Cafe across the street from the ballroom and others going to Peterson's Cafe nearby.

As the singers ate, teens from all around north central Iowa began to arrive at the ballroom in Clear Lake, a town of about six thousand known as "Iowa's Fun Capital." The Surf Ballroom had played an important role in the social life of Clear Lake residents since 1933, when Carl Fox tempted fate by having it built on the lake. Two earlier Clear Lake ballrooms had been destroyed: The White Pier Ballroom on the lake's east shore was blown away by a tornado in 1931, and the Tom-Tom Ballroom was destroyed by fire just a few months after its summer opening in 1932. The Surf officially opened for business on April 17, 1934, with a $1 dance on its 90-by-120-foot hardwood floor. Fox sold his ballroom to a Chicago firm, and it, too, was consumed by fire, following an explosion in the early morning hours of April 20, 1947. The new owners had the ballroom rebuilt across the street, where it opened on July 1, 1948.

Known as the Surf of the Four Seasons, the arched ceiling of the ballroom was painted blue where projections of stars and clouds created the illusion of an open sky. With palm trees stationed around the ballroom floor and the swirling clouds overhead, the sensation was so realistic it is said that male patrons who had a bit too much to drink could be seen relieving themselves under the trees.

The Surf was one of the first ballrooms in the state to feature rock 'n' roll, under manager Carroll Anderson, who took over in 1950. Anderson had booked the Winter Dance Party into the Surf after his friend Bob Ehlert of GAC told him of an open date. Anderson priced his tickets at $1.25 for the weeknight show and advertised his standing policy of allowing parents in free—to prove to the parents he was running a fine, wholesome activity. Anderson got Bob Hale from local radio station KRIB to emcee on Monday, February 2. The twenty-five-year-old Hale, who was in his first job at a radio station, was eager to work with major recording stars.

In a strange turn of events for the Winter Dance Party, the temperature was still rising as teens lined up for Monday night's show at the Surf. The rising temperature was a good sign for an area that had had twelve days of sub-zero temperatures in January. Plus, while most of the rest of the state was receiving measurable snow Monday evening, northern Iowa was expected to get just a trace.

Inside the ballroom, senior floorwalker Harvey Luth helped the singers set up equipment and do sound checks. In the parking lot behind the stage, Geller attended to some last-minute details with the bus. He told the driver to keep the bus running to keep it warmed up while the singers were performing.

Inside, Bob Hale sat at a table in the Surf lounge, sipping hot drinks with J. P. Richardson and Buddy Holly and discussing their three pregnant wives. They also talked about the stench of bus travel. After each evening's performance, the singers would shed their sweaty clothes and toss them in the back of the bus. The odor from the ripening clothes sometimes forced the singers to open the bus windows, despite the numbing cold. Holly was disappointed to learn that Clear Lake didn't have a place where he could get his laundry done that night.

Holly also complained about the way things were going with his business dealings back home. "I've got to do something to get this stuff straightened out," he told Hale. "One problem with being on the road, you don't know what's going on back there.'"

As the kids spilled into the Surf, filling every available booth and table, Luth and his team of floorwalkers strolled among them, looking for potential trouble. Luth presented an imposing figure, with a husky body spread over his six-foot frame. An operator of a lakeside resort by day, Luth donned a tuxedo for his nighttime duties at the Surf.

During the evening, most of the singers made their way through the crowd to manager Carroll Anderson's office, which was just off the lobby. Holly and Anderson talked as if they had known each other for years. "We talked about hunting squirrels," Anderson says. Holly also mentioned the troubles with the bus, and asked Anderson if there was any way he and his band could catch a flight to their next show in Moorhead, Minnesota.

"They wanted to get ahead so they could get their laundry done and get a few things out of the way and get a good six or eight hours of sleep, which they said they dearly needed," Anderson says.

Anderson tried to reach Jerry Dwyer, who ran a charter service at the Mason City airport, but Dwyer was attending a meeting of the Mason City Junior Chamber of Commerce. Anderson then located a young pilot who lived just a few blocks from the ballroom, Roger Peterson. Peterson agreed to fly the singers. "That was the only time I saw Buddy that he was adamant," Frankie Sardo says. "Nobody was going to talk him into getting back on that bus. Nobody."

Sardo once again opened the show and the Big Bopper followed as the crowd pressed toward the stage. Clear Lake police chief Nels Larsen moved vigilantly through the crowd as the singers performed their songs. Teenage girls in angora wool sweaters with rabbit fur collars and flat ballerina shoes swayed to the beat while chomping Teaberry gum. By the time Ritchie Valens went through his set, no one in the crowd of more than 1,200 was dancing. The show was a hit.

The singers were in high spirits backstage, where Richardson and Valens were observed Indian wrestling between acts. Emcee Hale remembers Richardson kept things loose backstage by telling jokes. Onstage, Richardson was still battling a fever. Midway through his frantic performance he was forced to change out of his sweat-soaked jacket.

Carroll Anderson says the crowd was responsive and respectful. Even Dion, a veteran of many similar shows, says the Clear Lake performance was exciting.

During a short intermission, before the closing sets by Dion and the Belmonts and Holly and the Crickets, fans lined up for autographs. John Hurd, a sophomore at Mason City High School, had Holly autograph a promotional copy of "It Doesn't Matter Anymore," which he had received as one of the first teens through the door earlier in the evening.

During the break, several singers left the autograph table near the stage to make phone calls from the ballroom's lobby. Valens called his home in

Pacoima and talked to his half-brother Bob. The brothers talked about getting together after the Winter Dance Party in New York, where Valens was to be presented a gold record for "Donna."

Holly phoned his wife in New York. He complained about the conditions of the tour and said that morale was low among the singers. He told her that he was going ahead of the others to make arrangements for the next night's show. "He didn't tell me he was going to fly," she told Holly biographer John Goldrosen.

Holly wasn't the only one to call Maria Elena that night. Jerry Allison and Joe B. Mauldin were hoping to get in touch with Holly from Texas to try to patch things up. They, too, were getting ready to sever their relationship with Petty, and hoped to rejoin Holly. Although the Lubbock Crickets were unable to reach Holly in Clear Lake, they left a message in Moorhead, asking him to call them when he arrived there the next day.

Meanwhile, word of the planned flight filtered out to the rest of the entourage. Richardson, whose cold didn't seem to be getting any better, wanted to be included. He approached Jennings and asked, "If it's all right with Buddy, would it be all right with you if I took your place?"

Jennings, feeling sorry for the flu-stricken Richardson said, "If it's all right with Buddy, it's okay with me."

Ritchie Valens also approached Allsup about taking his seat on the flight, but Allsup refused.

Between acts, Hale and some stagehands did some minor rearranging on stage before Dion and the Belmonts took the spotlight. Holly would be playing drums for the Belmonts. To keep the fans from noticing Holly behind the drum kit, Hale placed the cymbals right in front of his face. After Dion's performance, Hale had Dion introduce all the band members, except the drummer.

Then Hale pointed toward the drums and said to Dion, "We didn't get this guy's name. What's his name, Dion?"

Dion replied, "'Oh, that's our new drummer, umm, Buddy Holly, Buddy Holly."

After the crowd roared its approval, Holly did "Gotta Travel On." Then Jennings joined Holly for a spirited version of "Salty Dog Rag" before the rest of the band joined them on stage. Holly's last number, "Brown-Eyed Handsome Man," was a rousing jam with the entire entourage. Last to join the musicians onstage were Richardson, carrying his trademark telephone, and Hale, doing his best to stay with the rhythm on a tambourine.

"That was kind of a jam, a farewell," Hale says. "It was a big joke."

As the fans filed from the Surf, Holly and his band relaxed in a dressing room next to the stage before catching a ride to the Mason City airport. After sending Jennings to the ballroom's snack bar for hot dogs, Holly learned that Jennings had given up his seat on the plane to Richardson. When Jennings returned, Holly teased his bass player.

Leaning against the wall in a chair as he ate a hot dog, Holly said, "Well, you're not going on that plane with me tonight, huh?"

When Jennings said, "No," Holly replied, "Well, I hope your old bus freezes up again."

Jennings snapped back, "Well, hell, I hope your old plane crashes."

Carroll Anderson, who was to drive Holly, Allsup, and Richardson to the airport, was helping load the singers' baggage in the back of his station wagon when Holly sent Allsup back into the ballroom to make sure they had gotten everything.

In the ballroom, Valens was signing a few last-minute autographs when he spotted Allsup. Once again he pleaded to take Allsup's seat on the plane. When Allsup again declined, Valens persisted, suggesting they settle the matter by a coin flip. Reluctantly, Allsup flipped half a dollar and Valens said, "Heads I go, tails you go." It came up heads.

Valens joined Holly and Richardson in Anderson's station wagon, with Anderson's wife and son. Allsup then asked Holly to pick up a letter his mother had sent to the Moorhead post office, giving Holly his wallet for identification.

As Anderson drove from the Surf, Geller was looking for the three stars who failed to show up for the warmed-up bus. When he was told that the singers had left for the airport, Geller was upset about their planned flight to Fargo. "I would have put my foot down on that," he later recalled.

Bob Hale and his wife, Kathy, were among the last people to leave the Surf as they headed to their nearby cottage. On their way home they noticed that a weather front had passed through the area during the concert. Light snow was blowing across the road in front of the headlights of Hale's car. His thoughts turned to the singers as he told his wife, "This is no night to be flying."

In Lubbock, Larry Holley was listening to the radio before turning in for the evening. He heard them play some of Buddy's songs and mention the bad weather in the upper Midwest. Realizing that Buddy was touring in that area, Holley said a little prayer for his youngest brother. "If I knew he was flying, I'd have said a long prayer," Larry Holley later recalled.

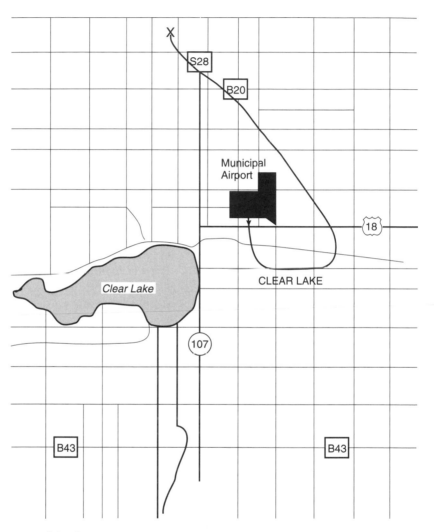

Map of the flight path

The Flight

Few pilots would be enthused at the prospect of a midnight flight in a single-engine plane from a dimly lit Iowa airstrip on a blustery winter night. But it was business as usual for Roger Peterson. Peterson, a life-long Iowan, was all too familiar with the state's unpredictable weather. His job as a pilot for the Dwyer Flying Service in Mason City sometimes required him to work unusual hours. Despite the apparent drawbacks, it was perfect work for the twenty-one-year-old who had ambitions of becoming a commercial pilot.

Peterson was raised in a converted one-room schoolhouse on the family farm near Alta, Iowa, a community of about 1,200 about one hundred and ten miles southwest of Clear Lake. There were two girls and five boys in Peterson's graduating class at Fairview Consolidated School in 1954. Peterson's parents, Art and Pearl, had attended the same school.

An average student, Peterson was "one of the most likeable kids in the class," according to Thomas Cameron, a grade-school friend. "He was always a happy kid," Roger's sister, Janet, says. "As I remember him, he was always smiling." DeAnn Lenz, who had transferred from Sibley to Fairview when in fifth grade, noticed Roger immediately. "He had automatic rosy cheeks and he had beautiful eyes," she recalls. "*Very* beautiful eyes."

Peterson played on Fairview's baseball and basketball teams, the only sports offered by the small school. The playing floor was so close to the walls, the only place for spectators was on the small stage at one end of the gym. Peterson's high, arching set shot was known to frequently ricochet off the low ceiling. One year, when Fairview had just eight baseball players, Roger's sister, Janet, played so the team wouldn't have to forfeit its games.

By the time they were juniors in high school, Roger and DeAnn were steadies. By the time they were seniors, Roger was class vice-president and joke editor for the Fairview school annual, *The Fairview Hi-Lites*. After graduation, DeAnn went to business school at Mankato, Minnesota, while Peterson worked as a construction worker and truck driver and joined the National Guard.

He also became interested in flying. Several of his neighbors bought planes while still students at Fairview. "I wasn't old enough to drive a car, but I could fly," says neighbor Bruce Anderson, who flew two and a half miles to high school as a fourteen year old. Jim Frederickson, a teacher and coach at Fairview, remembers the young Alta fliers: "When school was out, they'd run for their planes and they'd buzz the school buses. The superintendent would have a fit.".

Roger Peterson started flying lessons in the fall of 1954 and, soon after that, his father bought a Piper J-3 Cub and cleared a spot on the family farm for the two-seater aircraft. Peterson was issued a private pilot's license on October 16, 1955. He flew whenever possible, building up his flying hours. Sometimes he took along his younger brother Ron, to act as observer as he worked on his instrument rating, placing orange plexiglass on the inside of the cockpit windows and wearing blue goggles to make it appear black.

In the fall of 1957, Peterson enrolled at Ross Aviation School in Tulsa, Oklahoma. "It was a complete package deal," Ron Peterson recalls. "You pay so much and you get so many licenses for it." But Peterson wasn't in Tulsa long enough to pick up any ratings. His father, Art Peterson, came down with a rheumatic heart condition that winter and Roger returned home.

As Art Peterson recovered, Roger took over most of the farm chores. In February 1958, he enrolled in the Graham Flying School in Sioux City. For two months, Peterson shuttled between Alta and Sioux City. He was issued a temporary commercial pilot license on April 2, 1958.

A few weeks later, Art Peterson heard that Jerry Dwyer in Mason City was looking for a pilot. "[Roger] went over and applied, but Dwyer told him to go on home and keep on working on his ratings," Art Peterson says. "[Dwyer] called the next morning and wanted Roger to go to work."

DeAnn remembers the day well: "He was pretty excited about it. His one dream was always to be an airline pilot. We felt this would probably be a stepping stone."

Dwyer's Flying Service had grown to become one of the most successful in Iowa, since Hubert J. "Jerry" Dwyer began operations at the Mason City airport in May 1957 after operating a similar flying service at Charles City, Iowa.

Peterson moved to Clear Lake while DeAnn continued to work in Storm Lake and planned their marriage. They were married on September 14, 1958, in the St. Paul Lutheran Church at Alta, the first wedding in their new church. After a brief honeymoon in Colorado, the Petersons settled into one half of a small cottage on North Shore Drive in Clear Lake. Within a few weeks, DeAnn landed a job in the accounting department at KGLO-TV in Mason City.

From the start, Roger was busy. He was the only full-time pilot working for Dwyer in 1958. Because he was still working on his instrument and instructor ratings in late 1958, Peterson did mostly charter work. That work took Peterson to the East Coast and throughout the upper Midwest, but was sporadic. "You just never knew when a job was going to come up," DeAnn explains. "He liked it."

Peterson often discussed his career goals with his good friend Charles McGlothlen, a mechanic at Dwyer's. "He wanted to fly executive airplanes," McGlothlen recalls. "He didn't want to fly those puddle-jumpers."

At the time of the Winter Dance Party flight, Peterson had an application for a job on file with Northwest Airlines in Minneapolis, according to Art Peterson.

Roger Peterson finally was awarded a temporary certificate as a limited flight instructor on January 27, 1959, after a test flight with Dwyer in a Cessna 172 two days earlier. Although most of Peterson's flight tests were taken in Cessna aircraft, most of his charter work was done in a Beechcraft Bonanza that Dwyer had purchased in June 1958. The 1947 vintage aircraft had been through nine owners before Dwyer bought it.

"It was in pretty tough shape," McGlothlen notes. "I went clear through that son-of-a-gun. Overhauled the engine, rebuilt the landing gear. I had everything re-upholstered. I had everything stripped out of that thing."

On Sunday, February 1, Peterson flew the Bonanza to Des Moines in the afternoon and to Minneapolis that evening. DeAnn went along on the evening trip and the couple met with Roger's sister, who worked for Northwest Airlines in Minneapolis. "It was a beautiful night to fly," DeAnn recalls. "He said, 'Do you want to fly a little bit?' At that time I was afraid if I leaned one way, the plane would go, too, but I took the wheel. I was really a little afraid. But it was such a gorgeous night."

With no flights scheduled on Monday, February 2, Peterson went to the airport around 8 AM, and spent most of the day riveting a Cessna 120 with McGlothlen. He went home around 5:15 and had dinner with DeAnn. McGlothlen drove Peterson to a meeting of the Clear Lake Junior Chamber of Commerce later that evening while McGlothlen's wife, Judye, stayed with DeAnn at the cottage.

A short time later, Carroll Anderson tracked down Peterson at the Jaycee meeting and asked if he could fly some people to Fargo. Peterson agreed and the flight was tentatively scheduled for 12:30 AM, just thirty minutes after the scheduled end of the Winter Dance Party performance at the Surf Ballroom.

While Buddy Holly, J. P. Richardson, and Ritchie Valens had them rocking at the Surf Ballroom a few blocks away, Peterson left the Jaycee meeting to start preparations for the flight to Fargo. Borrowing McGlothlen's car, Peterson drove to the Mason City airport where he checked the weather conditions. Then, Peterson picked up McGlothlen at the Jaycee meeting and returned to the Petersons' cottage where DeAnn and Judye were waiting for them. They were more concerned about the weather conditions than about who would be Peterson's passengers.

"I can't even remember him saying who [the passengers] were," DeAnn says. "I don't think either one of us had heard of Buddy Holly." The conversation focused on the weather. Light snow was falling and the temperature was in the teens. "We kept asking him if he really thought he ought to take the flight," Charles McGlothlen says. "I told him not to go that night. His wife told him not to go and Judye told him not to go. [The weather] looked too awfully bad."

The McGlothlens left the Peterson cottage around 10 PM. Charles McGlothlen later told CAB investigators that Peterson "seemed to be in a very good mood all the time." After the McGlothlens left, Peterson called the airport for a weather update and napped until around 11 PM. At 11:20, Peterson again called the airport. Visibilities were at least ten miles at the reporting stations, and all had ceilings of at least 4,200 feet. Light snow was falling at Minneapolis and a cold front was expected to pass through Fargo at 2 AM.

Peterson then called Jerry Dwyer to ask for help preparing the plane for the trip, and left for the airport.

"Normally when he walked out I would have gone back to bed, but I can remember looking out the front window when he went to the car . . . and I watched him," DeAnn says. "I had a funny feeling and I didn't know what it was. [It was] like something was going to happen."

Dwyer and Peterson arrived at the airport at the same time. Dwyer followed Peterson into the drive. "The first thing we did was go to the Tower to check the weather conditions," Dwyer later told CAB investigators. "Roger told me that he had checked several times earlier. . . . As far as weather for the whole trip was concerned, we both agreed that he might have to stay overnight at Fargo, North Dakota, due to the fact that they predicted a front to move in to Fargo at approximately 3 AM. We then went over to Dwyer Flying Service, turned on the lights in the hangar and began an inspection of the aircraft. . . . We then both checked the airplane over completely and then rolled the plane outside. . . .

"Roger got in and started the airplane to warm it up and I would say he ran it approximately eight or ten minutes. I was in our office at this time.

When he shut it off, I went out and personally filled both tanks with 80 Oct[ane] gas. Then Roger put chocks under both main wheels and then got back in and started the airplane again. . . . About 12:20 AM he ran the airplane a few minutes more and then shut it off around 12:30. We went in the office and wrote a ticket for the trip. Roger then told me that the passengers were supposed to be there at about 12:30. It was approximately 12:40 when [Surf Ballroom manager] Carroll Anderson drove in."

Dwyer told CAB investigators, "Mr. Anderson introduced them [the singers] to Roger. He did not introduce them to me, but I heard the introductions and this was the first time I realized who our passengers were to be. We all went back into the office and they paid individually [$36 apiece] for the trip. We talked for about four or five minutes, basically about where the boys were from and one thing I specifically remember is that Buddy Holley mentioned that he had been taking flying lessons and that he had hoped one of these days to buy a Cessna and fly these trips himself when he was fully capable."

Anderson recalls those few moments in Dwyer's office. "We were [measuring on a map] how far it was to Fargo and how much farther it was to Lubbock, Texas, and how much farther it was to California where Valens lived."

Dwyer told the CAB: "We then went outside and the fellows got in the airplane. I don't recall how they sat in the back seat, but I do remember that Mr. Holley sat in the right front seat. I remember specifically because Buddy Holley got in the plane before Roger and then had to get out to let Roger in first." Carroll Anderson agrees with the seating arrangement. "Holly was the last one in," Anderson remembers. "He got in and pulled the door shut. He sat in the front seat opposite the pilot."

Dwyer told CAB investigators: "They started the airplane and then taxied North out of our taxi strip and then turned West and taxied up to our terminal building. I got in my car and drove over to the terminal building and then I went upstairs into the tower. Mr. Bryan was on duty and I asked him if Roger had filed a flight plan yet[,] as one of my requirements of charter flying is that the pilot should always file a flight plan. Mr. Bryan said he [Peterson] had not filed a flight plan as yet, but had contacted him [Bryan] by radio and said that he would file a flight plan as soon as he got into the air. He sat on the North end of the North-South runway and sat there for several minutes. I would say that at this time it was approximately 12:50 or 12:55 AM on the morning of February 3.

"[Peterson] turned on both landing lights and I stepped outside the tower onto the platform and watched them take off. I would say it was a very normal take off. He broke ground about one-third the way down the runway and turned his landing lights off at approximately 150 feet of altitude.

I would say the climb out was quite normal and he leveled off South of the field at approximately 800 feet. This is higher than usual for a daytime pattern, but quite normal for night time flying. He made a 180-degree turn to the left and took up about a straight North heading."

Carroll Anderson says, "We saw them off. It was spitting a little snow, it was February weather. It was cold but it was clear above. You could see real good. There were gusty winds but they got off in good shape and they took right off into the horizon."

Dwyer continued the story for the CAB investigators. "I stepped back inside the tower and asked if Roger had filed a flight plan yet. [Bryan] told me that [Peterson] had not. So I asked Mr. Bryan to give him a call on the radio and tell him that I wanted him to file a flight plan both ways. There was no answer. He tried another time or two and once more[,] throwing the master switch so that all the transmitters would be transmitting as he thought Roger might have changed frequencies. I again stepped outside of the tower and could still see the white tail light of the airplane northeast of the field.

"The airplane still appeared to be approximately at the same altitude. The airplane took up what appeared like a North West heading and I could still see the white tail light. When the airplane was directly North of the field, I noticed by watching the white tail light in reference to the red lights on the two towers on the North edge of the field the airplane appeared to be going down at a very slow rate of descent as it went farther away from us. I would guess that it was approximately four miles north of us. I thought at the time that probably it was an optical illusion."

Ruth Pickering was dog-tired.

After spending the better part of a dark and blustery, dead-of-winter day painting the kitchen and scrubbing the windows of her farmhouse northeast of Clear Lake, it was time to complete her solitary project.

It was 1 AM as she coaxed her weary arms upward one last time, hoisting freshly washed curtains to the window of her kitchen. She was startled by the dancing light of a small airplane, piercing the snow squall that was peppering the polished glass. Quickly realizing the airplane was headed directly for her house, Pickering dashed toward the door, pausing just long enough to flick on her yard light.

As the light flooded the farmstead, Pickering was relieved to see the plane rise quickly, narrowly missing the house and a barn as it strained to clear a grove of trees comprising a windbreak just north of the farm.

But a few hundred yards away, Pickering's neighbor was awakened by the sound of the airplane as it approached his house. Farmer Reeve Eldridge heard the familiar sound of an accelerating engine as the plane flew directly over his house. "That was the last I heard of it," Eldridge says. "By the time I got up and looked out the windows, he was on the west side of the house."

Down the road from the Eldridge farm, Elsie Juhl was having a tough time sleeping. The gusty winds of the cold, snowy night rattled her two-story frame farmhouse. As her husband, Albert, slept on, Elsie heard "the worst motor noise I've ever heard.

"I knew it was a plane. It was so low, I thought it was going to hit our house."

Another Juhl, Elsie's son, Delbert, lived next door in a small one-story house with his wife and two small daughters. They, too, heard the plane pass almost directly overhead. "The wife was up with one of the girls, and she said the plane blew snow on our windows," Delbert Juhl says.

As the Juhls returned to sleep, Jerry Dwyer was trying to make radio contact with Peterson. When his attempts proved futile, he contacted airports on Peterson's likely route to Fargo in an attempt to locate the Bonanza.

After returning to his Clear Lake home, Dwyer called the Fargo airport around 3:30 AM and was told they had not heard from Peterson. Finally, Dwyer asked authorities in Minneapolis to issue an alert. The alert notice was sent to all stations at 5:16 AM CST. At 6:41, the 10th Air Force Search and Rescue Coordination Center was alerted.

DeAnn Peterson was expecting her husband home by 6:30 so she could drive the couple's car to work. "When I woke up and he wasn't there, I had a feeling he *wasn't* going to be there," she says. She got a ride to work with a friend.

"We went past the flying service and I looked for Roger's car," DeAnn says. The green Ford Fairlane was there. "I *knew* it was going to be there. It wasn't any surprise. We got to work and I had that feeling. I was just waiting for something."

Before returning to the airport, Dwyer called an old friend, Bob Booe. Booe, who was with Dwyer at the Jaycees meeting when Carroll Anderson first tried to line up the flight the night before, was a pilot and also one of Roger Peterson's friends. Dwyer told Booe about Peterson's disappearance and asked if he could help while Dwyer conducted an air search. Booe, who had recently left his job with a Mason City radio station and was packing for a move to Cedar Rapids, agreed to help. Dwyer returned to the airport, which was shrouded in fog, around 8 AM, just moments before Booe arrived.

"The first place I went was up to the tower and they still had no news whatsoever," Dwyer told CAB investigators. "I didn't know what to do, so I stayed around the terminal building approximately until 9:15. I decided I just couldn't sit there and decided I would go fly and try to follow the same course that I thought Roger would have taken. I was only approximately eight miles northwest of the field when I spotted the wreckage. I believe the time was approximately 9:35 AM. I called the tower by radio and told them I had found the wreckage and told them to send the police and two ambulances immediately. I kept circling over the field until they got there, so as to help guide them in."

At the Cerro Gordo County sheriff's office in Mason City, Chief Deputy Duane Mayfield—who was temporarily in charge of the office, because Sheriff Jerry Allen was in St. Louis on county business—took the call from the airport. Mayfield dispatched the rest of the sheriff's staff, deputies Bill McGill and Lowell Sanquist, to the site.

Meanwhile, beneath Dwyer's circling plan, Delbert Juhl had joined his parents in their farmhouse. Talk centered on the previous night's storm and the early morning noise. Elsie Juhl looked out her window toward the farms of neighbors Gus Punke and Oscar Moffett, but saw nothing unusual. Looking up, she saw the plane circling the area. "That had never happened before," she notes.

Ruth Pickering noticed unusually heavy traffic speeding up the road that ran past her home. "I couldn't imagine what in the world happened," she says. "I thought about that airplane."

McGill and Sanquist soon arrived at the Juhl farm, although no wreckage was visible from the gravel road. Delbert Juhl opened the gate for McGill, who turned into the Juhl driveway and headed west, past the small house. That's when he saw the wreckage, about one-half mile west of the Juhl farmbuildings. McGill drove around 570 feet of skidmarks to reach the Bonanza, a balled mass of steel resting against a barbed wire fence separating the Juhl farm from those of Punke and Moffett.

The plane had first touched the ground with its right wing, which had ripped from the fuselage and disintegrated as the rest of the plane slid across the field to the northwest. The only large component still attached to the plane was the left wing. Trapped inside the twisted cockpit was pilot Peterson, his body entwined in cables and wrapped around the plane's instrument panel. All that was visible was one of his boots, pointing skyward. Seventeen feet to the south was the body of Valens, clothed in a black wool overcoat and a black wool suit, with the left leg of the suit split to the hip, his head pointing south. A few feet away lay Holly, the seams of his full-length yellow leather-like jacket split in the back from the force of the impact, his head pointing southwest. Thrown about forty feet across the fence into a picked cornfield on the Moffett farm was Richardson, lying partly on his right side with his head pointing south. Fine snow that fell after the crash had drifted slightly about the bodies and the wreckage.

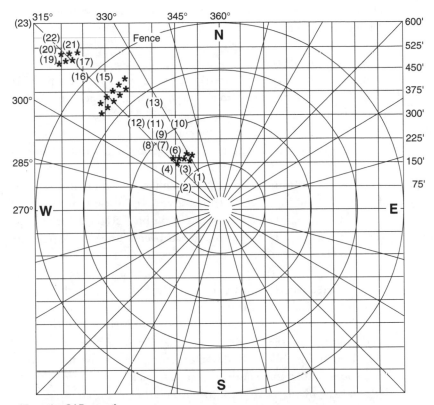

[From the CAB report]

*First contact :: Earth gouged out approximately 6 inches deep for 57 feet, no parts.
(1) Small piece of center section. (2) Nose wheel fairing. (3) Right ailerons. (4) Part right wing.
(5) (*) Other parts of right wing. (6) Right wing leading edges. (7) Cabin visor. (8) More of right
wing. (9) Bottom engine cowl. (10) More of right wing with fuel filler cap. (11) More of right wing.
(12) Part of cabin door frame. (13) Exhaust stack and piece of engine case. (14)*Small pieces
of debris. (15) Cab door. (16) Tail cone. (17) Coat. (18) *Small pieces of debris. (19) Nose
gear. (20) Right gear. (21) Heading indicator (found caged). (22) Major portion of wreckage
with left wing, engine, left gear in wing, and tail section up against a fence. (23) Radio beyond
fence. RE: Beechcraft "35", N–3794N
5NNW Mason City, Iowa, 2/3/59, 0100C

Distribution of the wreckage

The deputies soon were joined by three Iowa Highway Patrol officers who helped secure the scene, and ambulances were called to the site. Jerry Dwyer returned to the airport. "The minute I looked at [Dwyer's] face, I knew something was wrong," recalls Booe, who had been gassing planes and running the flying service in Dwyer's absence. "He got out of the airplane and said, 'They're out here. I think they're all dead.'" Dwyer took off for the scene by car.

"I'm sitting there all the time like a lump on a log and I realize, holy cripes, I'm in the midst of a story," says Booe. He called radio station KCRG in Cedar Rapids with the first bulletin that some prominent people may have been killed in an aircraft accident near Clear Lake. KCRG then alerted the American Broadcasting Company and the wire services.

Booe made a brief visit to the crash site before he started telling the world about the crash. "I started feeding phone reports out of there," Booe explains. "These are prominent guys. You don't sit on their names while they notify their next of kin because this is a very significant story."

Bob Hale was doing the news that morning on KRIB. "I picked up a bulletin that the wreckage of a light plane had been found on the outskirts of Mason City," Hale says. "I read that and let it go. I didn't even think about it. I wasn't even sixty seconds into the next tune when the phone rang. It was Carroll Anderson on the private line. . . . He said, 'Bob, Ritchie Valens, the Big Bopper, and Buddy Holly are dead.' I just about threw up.

"I opened the mike and I knocked the record right off the turntable . . . and I put this on the air, repeating what Carroll Anderson had said. I just reached over and grabbed a Buddy Holly tune. So we just started playing all day. I had to have a guy come in, I was just sick to my stomach. Then I called UPI and the phone started ringing from all over the country."

In Beaumont, Texas, first word of the crash came out on one of KTRM's competing stations. "Someone who was listening then called us," explains John Neil, the engineer at KTRM that morning.

Says Gordon Baxter: "Jack Neil picked up the phone. . . . Jack listened a while, turned white as a sheet, said 'Oh, shit' in a very small voice and hung up the phone. He turned to us and said, 'J. P. is dead.'"

John Neil says the staff reacted in disbelief. "He was supposed to be on that damn bus, so we just didn't pay any attention to the phone call. Then a few minutes later, it came across our wire."

Says Roy Dixon Shotts, who also was in the KTRM studio that morning: "Several of us were talking about what we should do. Of course all of J. P.'s family lived around there and we weren't about to go half-cocked on a story like that, yet we knew other people were doing it. . . . I took the bulletin in to Robert Hooker, who was on the air at the time, and I handed it to him. Robert just went into shock and absolutely refused to put it on the air. He just wouldn't read it. Someone else read the bulletin on the air. It was traumatic."

Teetsie Richardson heard the news in Montegut, Louisiana, from her older brother, who had heard it on a New Orleans radio station. Accompanied by a doctor, Teetsie's brother told her of the crash, and they began packing for a return to Beaumont.

In Lubbock, Sky Corbin was sitting in for Waylon Jennings at KLLL. His brother, Slim, and Hi-Pockets Duncan were working a remote when he saw the bulletin of the crash. He tore the news from the teletype and caught his breath before returning to the control room. He interrupted the remote to read the bulletin.

"Boys, I'm sorry to interrupt, but I'm afraid I have some very bad news," Corbin said, before telling Lubbock that Holly and his band had been killed. "The phone started ringing off the wall," Corbin says. "All day long people asked me questions. Waylon's folks called from Littlefield. I put this on the air assuming the relatives had been notified."

In nearby Littlefield, KVOW also carried the news that Buddy Holly and the Crickets were dead. Tommy Jennings, Waylon's brother, heard the news at his repair shop and ran home to comfort his stunned family. "It was terrible," says Jennings's mother, Lorene Gilbert. "We didn't know who was on the plane." It was several hours before Waylon called to say he was all right.

Niki Sullivan was awakened from a sound sleep by a telephone call from a friend who had heard news of the crash on the radio. Sullivan called his mother and asked her to call Holly's parents. After Sullivan's mother determined that Ella Holley hadn't heard of the crash, she asked her not to listen to the radio until she arrived. Ella Holley soon received more curious phone calls from friends. She tuned in KLLL on her radio.

By the time Mrs. Sullivan arrived, Ella and L. O. Holley had heard the news. The Holley house soon filled with relatives and friends. The Corbin brothers had just arrived when Ella Holley approached them.

"Sky, you know how we heard about Buddy?" she asked.

"I assume your pastor told you," Corbin replied.

"No, we heard you read it on the radio."

"Oh, my God, I'm sorry," the stunned Corbin replied. "It never entered my mind that you wouldn't have been notified before they put that out on the news."

"Don't worry about it," Ella Holley said. "That's all right. We'd just as soon have heard it from you as anybody else."

Buddy's brother Larry had been checking on some of his tile jobs in Lubbock when he took a lunch break in Pansy's Cafe around noon and heard the news from a waitress. "So I got on the phone there at the cafe and couldn't get nobody," Larry Holley says. "Every phone of everybody I knew was busy so I knew something was bad."

Bob Keene was driving to work on Sunset Boulevard when he heard news of the crash on his car radio. "I heard 'and now the late, great Ritchie Valens,'" Keene says. "It was just like somebody hit me in the stomach with a ball bat."

Valens's mother, Connie Valenzuela, was washing clothes in a second-hand machine on the back porch of her home in Pacoima when she heard news of the crash on the radio. As she sat in her living room in stunned disbelief, friends and relatives started arriving.

Young Connie Ramirez was walking home from school when some other kids told her that her brother Ritchie was dead. "I yelled and screamed that they were alive," she recalls. "As I got close to our house, I stopped and looked around. There were all these cars and people. When I opened the door, Mama was sitting in a chair and looked up. By the look on her face, I knew it was true. I screamed, 'Mama!' and I screamed, 'Ritchie, no!' I just ran to her and buried my face in her lap."

While local authorities secured the crash site for Civil Aeronautics Board investigators, Chief Deputy Mayfield was busy at the sheriff's office, much of his work created by Booe's dispatches from the airport.

"The publicity hounds were after me," he said. "I had to make recordings until almost midnight that night—Canada, Hawaii—radio stations and papers from almost all over the world."

Mayfield also notified A. J. Prokop, supervising inspector of the Federal Aviation Agency at Des Moines, Iowa. Around 10:45 AM, Prokop called the CAB's Bureau of Safety in Kansas City, Missouri, to report the accident, the first in Iowa in 1959. Meanwhile, Carroll Anderson was summoned to the crash site to provide the first tentative identification.

It was a confusing scene at first. Anderson was able to identify the bodies, but five billfolds were found. The fifth belonged to Thomas Douglas Allsup of Bellflower, California. It was hours before it was discovered that Allsup had given his billfold to Holly.

Back at the airport, an anxious Charles McGlothlen worried about his friend Roger Peterson, whose body was still trapped in the wreckage.

> Lord, it was terrible. I wanted to go out to the wreck, but [Deputy] Lowell Sanquist wouldn't let me go and he says, "You don't want to see it." I was sitting there, stewing and fretting. I had just rebuilt the airplane and I thought, "My Lord, what could I have done wrong?"

Nobody was really sure what was going on. There were telephone calls from all different places and people and news people. It was really a zoo.

Dwyer was in and out and calling people because most of the calls were to him. And a lot of it was news media trying to find out what was going on because of the popular group that got killed. Nobody cared about Roger.

DeAnn Peterson was working in the accounting department at KGLO-TV in Mason City when word of the crash danced across the newsroom's teletype. At about the same time, Judye McGlothlen and Barb Dwyer arrived at the station and waited in the lobby while a receptionist led DeAnn to her visitors.

"I went down the stairs and I knew, I just knew," DeAnn recalls. "They took me to a doctor's office and they gave me a sedative. I remember in the doctor's office I said, 'We've got to call down home.'"

Art Peterson remembers: "We didn't know about it until eleven o'clock that morning. It came out on the radio earlier in the morning, but we didn't hear it."

That afternoon, Art Peterson headed to Clear Lake to see what he could do for his son.

Jim Collison was at his desk at the Mason City *Globe-Gazette* newspaper when the call came that a plane had crashed about fifteen miles away, near Clear Lake. Collison, who had been on his $90-a-week job as courthouse reporter for less than a year, never got to the courthouse that day. He and photographer Elwin Musser were sent to the crash site.

"The city editor was insistent that we get in there and get the facts, get the story, get it back, and make a scoop," Collison recalls.

Collison and Musser drove to Clear Lake in separate cars, Musser alone and Collison with editor W. Earl Hall and city editor Thor Jensen. By the time they got there, the area was sealed. They waited about a half mile from the crash site.

"All I knew when I left the *Globe-Gazette* was that there was a plane down," Musser says. "I got out there and then I had to wait. I sat in my car part of the time, listening to the radio. I heard them say the Buddy Holly group was in that plane. . . . That was the first I knew what it was."

After acting coroner Ralph Smiley arrived around 11:15 and conducted his preliminary examination, the media finally were allowed to view the wreckage. Also surveying the scene was Glenn Buchanan, office manager of the W. L. Patton Insurance Agency, which held a liability policy for the city of Mason City. "They still hadn't touched anything," Musser notes. "They were just moving around observing. We were in a deadline and I had to leave."

Collison and Musser dashed back to the *Globe-Gazette* together to work on that afternoon's paper. "I was riding back to get my pictures developed because the AP was hollering for them," Musser says. "Collison didn't think it was going to be that big a deal. And I told him, 'Hey man, this is big.'"

Ed Christensen, superintendent of the identification bureau of the Mason City Police Department, was summoned to the scene along with Officer Dick McKinney to take fingerprints from the bodies for positive identification. Christensen's job was made all the more difficult by the ten hours' exposure to bitter temperatures, which froze parts of each victim's body. The fingerprinting was put off until the bodies thawed.

Smiley did a brief examination of each singer's body before sending them to local funeral homes. After permission was granted by Civil Aeronautics Board officials, the deputies used metal-cutting tools to remove Peterson's body from the plane. The task took two hours.

Smiley examined the bodies further at the funeral homes and arranged for an autopsy of Peterson's body with Dr. George T. Joyce, a Mason City pathologist. As employees of the funeral homes sorted through the personal belongings of the victims, Smiley was doing the same, gathering information on each as he filled out the certificates of death as required by the Iowa State Department of Health. He also collected $11.65 in cash from each of the victims for coroner's fees.

Aftermath

A Star Is Born

Tuesday, February 3, 1959

Rod Lucier's morning cup of coffee proved to be a real eye-opener. He was sitting in a Moorhead, Minnesota, restaurant when a friend came in and said, "Rod, did you hear about the plane crash?"

"What plane crash?"

"The rock 'n' roll stars that were on the show tonight, their plane crashed."

Lucier, a disc jockey at radio station KVOX in Moorhead, had a lot at stake if the news were true. Besides being the emcee of Tuesday night's scheduled seven-thirty and nine-thirty Winter Dance Party shows at the Moorhead National Guard Armory, Lucier was the sponsor of the show.

When promoter T. B. Skarning of Minneapolis had first contacted Lucier about booking the show, it seemed like a good buy. Because there were a few open dates in the tour that General Artists Corporation was anxious to fill, Skarning offered the entertainment to Lucier for $750, about half the original cost. After renting the armory, publicizing the show, and selling several hundred advance tickets, Lucier found himself with a concert missing its three biggest attractions.

GAC's Bob Ehlert called Lucier from Chicago and told him the shows were canceled. Lucier spread word through Fargo and Moorhead radio stations and the Fargo *Forum* newspaper. But callers to the radio stations were insistent that the show go on as a tribute to the dead singers. Given the community's response and his personal financial stake, Lucier headed to the Comstock Hotel to talk with the surviving entertainers of the Winter Dance Party.

Ironically, the overnight bus ride from Clear Lake to Moorhead was one of the smoothest legs of the entire Winter Dance Party tour. There were no problems as the bus cruised through the remote upper Plains. Tommy Allsup got his best night's sleep of the tour, curled up in J. P. Richardson's sleeping bag in a rear seat that ran the width of the bus. "I stayed pretty warm," Allsup recalls.

The singers arrived at the Comstock around noon, unaware of the accident. When they pulled up to the hotel, Geller assumed Holly, Valens, and Richardson would be there waiting for them. As most of the singers slept on the bus, Geller and Allsup entered the hotel and asked the desk clerk, "Has Buddy Holly checked in here? The Big Bopper? Ritchie Valens?"

The bewildered clerk didn't answer, but pointed at Richardson's picture on the television in the lobby.

"I thought it was an advertisement for the concert at first," Allsup says. He and Geller stood in shocked silence as they watched a news report of the crash. Geller returned to the bus and broke the news to the rest of the troupe.

"We sat on the bus for I don't know how long, just crying," says Frankie Sardo. "All of us were in a state of shock."

The entourage checked into the hotel, where Geller planned to have the singers spend the night before heading back to Iowa and a Wednesday night performance in Sioux City. But when he called Irvin Feld in Washington, D.C., Feld said not to cancel any shows. Feld was already working to line up replacements for the dead singers.

"They told me the old showbiz crap, 'You've got to go on,'" Geller says. "What the hell could I do?"

The singers knew what to do.

"The first thing we all did, we ran to the phones and called our folks or whoever we had at home and said we're here, we're safe," remembers Fred Milano.

Waylon Jennings was one of the last to call his family back in Littlefield. He was surprised to learn that the local radio station was reporting that Holly's band had been killed, too, leading his relatives to think he was dead.

After calling his relatives, Allsup says the reality of the situation started to sink in at midafternoon when he received a phone call from Feld.

"Well, you know you've got to go ahead and do that show tonight," Feld said. "If you and Waylon leave, the show is going to break up. Remember the old adage, 'The show must go on.' You're all professionals. We'll take care of you when you get back up here. We'll give you the balance of what we were paying Buddy."

A phone call to Holly's parents in Lubbock convinced Allsup that a show that night would be a fitting tribute. The Belmonts also decided they should continue after receiving supportive telegrams from friends.

"Here we are in Moorhead, it was lonely," Dion recalls. "We were baffled. Devastated, actually. To get some telegrams and just feel like you're part of something was a big help."

As lonely as Dion and the Belmonts felt in Moorhead, they were not as isolated as Carl Bunch, who had spent most of the previous three days in Grand View Hospital near Ironwood, Michigan, recovering from frostbitten feet. "They just looked at me," Bunch says of his hospital stay.

Midafternoon Tuesday, Bunch was rolled down a hall of the hospital in a wheelchair to take a call from his mother.

"What are you gonna do?" she asked.

"When my feet thaw out I've gotta get back out on the road," Bunch replied. "I've got a job here."

"No, what are you gonna do *now*?" she asked, more insistently.

"Well, it's gonna take another day or so and the doctor says I'll be able to walk and everything will be OK and I'm gonna go back on the road."

Bunch's mother sighed before responding. "You don't know they were killed, do you?"

Bunch was shocked. "I didn't know what to do," he remembers.

Meanwhile, from his office in Washington, Feld coordinated replacement talent with aide Allen Bloom, who was in Charlotte, North Carolina. Bloom had another, much larger show on the road at the time, so he suggested taking some acts from the bigger show to replace Holly, Valens, and Richardson. The other show had opened in Columbus, Ohio, on January 23, the same day the Winter Dance Party started, and was in the last week of its seventeen-day run.

Feld agreed with Bloom's suggestion and sent Jimmy Clanton and Frankie Avalon to the next Winter Dance Party stop in Sioux City from Chicago, where the bigger GAC show was playing. Feld also hired Debbie Stevens, who had performed at the Winter Dance Party show in Kenosha.

When Lucier met with the Winter Dance Party singers at the hotel, he learned of the change in plans for Tuesday night's show. With the Fargo *Forum* already on the streets with news of the cancellation, Lucier again contacted all the radio stations with news of the rescheduled show while making a plea for local talent to fill the bill. Lucier began a hectic afternoon of trying to piece together a 9 PM show while being bombarded by the media, and the call for talent went out.

Charlie Boone of KFGO agreed to replace Lucier as emcee and broadcast the plea for musicians on his station. "The listener response was overwhelming," Boone recalls.

One of those respondents was a fifteen-year-old sophomore from Central High in Fargo, named Robert Velline. Within a year, he would be better known as Bobby Vee.

Robert Velline sat in silence as he listened to news of the crash on the radio while eating lunch in his Fargo home. Holly was his favorite singer. At the time, Velline and his brother, Bill, were forming a band with Jim

Stillman and Bob Korum, although the group had not yet performed in public.

"We were kind of looking for someone to guide us and get us started," says Bill Velline, a nineteen-year-old who worked in a dental lab by day and played lead guitar in rehearsals at night. After school, the group heard about the search for bands. They called the radio station to try to get on the show and were told to show up early. They could be the opening act.

With the reality of their debut sinking in, the band members swung into action. Within three hours they had bought matching outfits from J. C. Penney and sweaters from a local thrift shop. After assembling their stage outfits, the singers returned to their homes for dinner with one final assignment: to think of possible names for the band before its debut.

Rod Lucier's concerns about his $750 investment in the Winter Dance Party proved to be unfounded Tuesday night, because more than two thousand people jammed into the 1,700-seat Moorhead Armory. "As it turned out, people were lined up outside because of all the national publicity," Lucier says. "It was the biggest show I ever had."

Two fans who made it inside before the fire department closed the doors at 8 PM, one hour before the show began, were Pat Berg and her date, Bruce Nokleby, students at Concordia College in Moorhead. Berg remembers "a certain sadness" at the start of the concert.

Emcee Boone says: "I don't know if people came to the armory expecting to see coffins laid out in front, but there was a curiosity factor because of the publicity given the tragedy." According to Boone's manager, Burnell Bengtsson, "It turned out to be like a big wake."

While Bobby Velline and his band set up onstage, Frankie Sardo opened the show in a somber fashion. "[Sardo] went out and did a whole maudlin tribute to the three of them," Bobby recalls. Sardo's rendition of "Donna" and Valens's other numbers failed to inspire the audience. "It was hard for him and it was hard for the audience, too," says Nokleby.

After Sardo departed the stage, Velline was still trying to pull things together for his band, which was next. Bill Velline had forgotten his guitar strap and none of the other band members had bothered to come up with a name. So when Boone was ready to introduce the band, he turned to Bobby, who blurted out the first name that popped into his head, the Shadows.

The Velline brothers copied the tight harmonies of the Everly Brothers on "Bye Bye Love" and ran through a few other numbers by Ronnie Hawkins, Jerry Lee Lewis, and Little Richard. Berg and Nokleby say the Shadows rescued the night.

"I think Bobby Vee was so good that, after a while, the music sort of took over and everybody sort of just fell in with the music," Berg recalls. Nokleby agrees: "It started to shake after that."

Bengtsson says Bobby Velline's performance was haunting. "When he sang, he sounded like Buddy Holly. Everybody gasped. It was really a strange feeling."

At least one other local group performed that night, Terry Lee and the Poor Boys.

Later, a three-man band of Allsup, Jennings, and Carlo Mastrangelo made what would be their only appearance as "Buddy Holly's Crickets" before an appreciative audience of clapping, screaming teens.

In Mason City, Tuesday afternoon's edition of the *Globe-Gazette* was a hot seller. A banner headline topped Jim Collison's non-bylined story on the crash: FOUR KILLED IN CLEAR LAKE PLANE CRASH. Two page-one photos of the crash site as well as smaller head shots of Holly and Valens ran on the front page. Inside were shorter stories on the singers and the pilot.

Collison's main story, as printed in the *Globe-Gazette* and distributed nationally by the Associated Press, read:

> Four persons, three identified as nationally famous rock 'n' roll singers, died early Tuesday in a plane crash five miles north of Clear Lake.
>
> The three singers were Buddy Holly, 22, Texas, Ritchie Valens, 21, Los Angeles, and J. P. Richardson, 24, of Louisiana, known professionally as the "Big Bopper."
>
> Also killed was the pilot of the plane, Roger Peterson, 21, Clear Lake.
>
> The entertainers had appeared at the Surf Ballroom Monday night and were to appear at Fargo, N.D., Tuesday night.
>
> Other members of the troupe which appeared at Clear Lake left after the show by chartered bus for Fargo. They are Dion and the Belmonts, Frankie Sardo and the Crickets, of which Holly was the singing star.
>
> Apparently Holly, Valens and Richardson decided to fly in order to arrive ahead of the troupe and make advance preparations. The single-engine, four-place Beechcraft Bonanza left the Mason City Municipal Airport shortly after 1 AM. It crashed about seven miles northwest of the airport. The plane was owned by the Dwyer Flying Service, Mason City.
>
> The trip to Fargo was expected to take about 3½ hours. When

no word of the plane's arrival was heard, Jerry Dwyer, owner of the flying service, went out to look for the party. He was delayed several hours because of early morning fog.

Dwyer discovered the wreckage on the Albert Juhl farm at about 9:30 AM.

It was obvious that the pilot had been flying on a straight northwest line and was at a very low angle to the ground when he hit. The field slopes slightly toward the northwest.

The left wing of the plane seemingly struck the ground and plowed a furrow for about a dozen feet before it crumpled and the body of the plane hit. It dug a shallow depression in the stubble field and the wing fell off as the rest of the plane bounced. It struck the ground again about 50 feet farther northwest and then skidded on the ground about two city blocks until it piled up against a fence.

The wreckage was a jumbled mass which would not have been recognized as a plane. Along the skid path small bits of the plane and its contents were strewn. There was a man's shoe, a traveling bag and small pieces of plane, including parts of the instrument panel. The bag was the largest piece except for the wing, the jumble against the fence and three bodies.

One body was broken and entangled in the wreckage. Two bodies were lying about 12 feet south and southwest of the plane. Another body was lying about 40 feet northwest of the plane. No bodies were positively identified at the scene.

Newsmen and others were barred from the scene until 11:30 AM after Dr. Ralph E. Smiley, acting coroner, arrived.

Authorities do not yet know the cause of the accident. Some believe, however, that ice may have formed on the wings or windshield, making a forced landing necessary.

Dwyer said he didn't have the "faintest idea" why the plane crashed. He said the craft was in good condition. He said Peterson was a competent pilot and weather conditions were favorable for flying.

He estimated that the plane crashed only "a couple of minutes" after taking off.

Dwyer said that Peterson did not file a flight plan. Dwyer became worried when Peterson failed to report back from Fargo and checked other airports in Iowa, Minnesota and the Dakota area.

The bodies were taken to funeral homes in Clear Lake.

Two investigators from the Civil Aeronautics Administration were sent from Des Moines to investigate the cause of the accident.

Peterson was married less than a year ago. His wife is employed in the accounting department of KGLO-TV. They were living in the Armsbury Cottages on North Shore Drive in Clear Lake.

Peterson came to Clear Lake from Storm Lake. He taught flying for the Dwyer Flying Service.

The troupe, on its fourth national tour, was booked by General Artists, Chicago. The booking firm said when other artists heard of the deaths, they volunteered to keep the tour going. These included Bill Haley and his Comets, Bill Parsons and Frankie Avalon—all rock 'n' roll favorites.

C. E. Stillwagon, an air safety investigator for the Civil Aeronautics Board (CAB), flew from Kansas City to Des Moines, where he met Tuesday afternoon with A. J. Prokop, supervising inspector of the district office of the Federal Aviation Administration (FAA), and two other FAA inspectors, Fred Becchetti and Eugene Anderson. The CAB was responsible for investigating all fatal accidents, with help from the FAA. The probable cause and actual findings were in the hands of Stillwagon, who would author the final report.

With Prokop at the controls of a rented Beechcraft Bonanza, the quartet proceeded to Mason City. The party arrived at the crash scene around 5 PM and began its investigation.

Prokop remembers his first impressions. "It was out in a dreary, open, no-trees, no-nothin' field," he recalls. "Just one fence line across the field. . . . It looked like the wreckage had gone in at a pretty good speed. . . . It didn't hit flat. It couldn't have, the way she was torn up. It looked like it was maybe a wing down."

A light snow was falling in Clear Lake Tuesday night where what remained of the plane was left on the Albert Juhl farm. A steady stream of cars inched along the gravel roads bordering the crash site, their occupants craning their necks to get a glimpse of the wreckage of rock 'n' roll's first great tragedy. Guards turned away those bold enough to try to enter the adjacent farm fields.

After darkness, when the guards took some time off for dinner, Albert and Elsie Juhl drove out to the wreckage for the first time, with their son Delbert. There they saw several young people scouring the crash site. Elsie Juhl noticed some of them leaving with clothing belonging to the victims. Having seen the wreckage firsthand, the Juhls returned to their farmhouse, longing for a return to the quiet life they had enjoyed before Roger Peterson flew Jerry Dwyer's Beechcraft Bonanza through a good twenty rods of rich Iowa topsoil.

A light snow that fell overnight in Clear Lake hampered FAA officials who returned to the crash scene Wednesday morning to begin their investigation in earnest. Prokop began checking the records to find out whether Peterson had filed a flight plan, where he was going, what the weather was like when he took off, and what his flying qualifications were.

Anderson and Becchetti spent part of Wednesday combing the site for scraps of wreckage and examining the balled-up aircraft. They programmed the plane's path on the ground after the initial contact, and drew diagrams of where the various parts of the disintegrating plane and passengers' bodies came to rest in the two-block long crash area. The investigators also took several photos, and a winch and flatbed trailer were brought in to remove the mangled wreckage. Dwyer's mechanic, Charles McGlothlen, was there when the plane was lifted onto the trailer.

"They hooked a winch on a boom truck on the main spar and started to pick it up," McGlothlen recalls. "It just unrolled." The flatbed then carried the plane to a secured hangar at the east end of the Mason City airport, where it was dismantled, piece by piece.

The CAB also took over one of airport manager Dick Mettler's offices in the basement of the airport's administration building to use as headquarters for their investigation.

Meanwhile, the Ward and Wilcox funeral homes were busy making arrangements with the families of the victims of the accident.

Buddy Holly's brother and brother-in-law, Larry Holley and J. E. Weir, arrived in Mason City Wednesday morning. "I was almost in a daze from the trauma," Larry says. "There was snow all over the ground and we saw the crashed plane. Of course the bodies had been taken in, but everything else was laying about like it was. Somebody had stacked some nice jackets and some of them I had bought Buddy were in the bunch. . . . They asked me if I wanted those and I said, 'I don't believe I do.'"

As he left the crash site, Holley reclaimed his brother's shaving kit from the frozen earth. Because the devastated Holley was not up to the task of identifying his brother's body, the job fell to Weir.

Holly's body was loaded aboard a chartered plane and left the Mason City airport only to be grounded for the night in Des Moines because of bad weather. Another private plane was dispatched to pick up Richardson's body from the Ward Funeral Home Wednesday afternoon. Valens's body was loaded aboard a train, headed for his hometown of Pacoima. Roger Peterson's body was prepared for burial at Wilcox Funeral Home before being turned over to Dr. George T. Joyce for an autopsy.

A Wednesday afternoon story written by Dave Dale in the Mason City *Globe-Gazette* said records by the singers were in extra-heavy demand.

In Bakersfield, California, an eighteen-year-old disc jockey at radio station KFXM was preparing to record a song he had written as a tribute to the dead singers. Tommy Dee had been in his first week on the job when he got word of the crash Tuesday morning. On his way home that evening, Dee wrote his song, "The Three Stars," in about twenty minutes. Dee recorded his song with a group known as Carol Kay and the Teen-Aires.

Meanwhile, Maria Elena Holly flew to Lubbock from New York with her aunt.

Before the singers left Fargo Wednesday morning, Tommy Allsup and Waylon Jennings were trying to decide what to do with the Crickets. What had started as a makeshift band had turned into a tight rock 'n' roll unit before Bunch wound up in the hospital and Holly was killed. Stranded some 1,300 miles from home, less than twelve hours from their next performance and with twelve days left to go on the tour, things didn't look good.

After running through their limited options, Allsup and Jennings decided to check on Bunch to see if they could regain their drummer and if he could call on one of his old bandmates in the Poor Boys, singer and guitarist Ronnie Smith. Although Smith's rockabilly style was more reminiscent of Elvis Presley than Buddy Holly, he was well known in West Texas as a talented performer.

When Allsup phoned Bunch in Ironwood he was pleasantly surprised to find that Bunch was ready to leave the hospital. Bunch also arranged for Smith to join the Crickets Thursday, at the Val Air Ballroom in Des Moines.

Bunch caught a flight to Sioux City, where he was joined Wednesday afternoon by new tour members Jimmy Clanton, Frankie Avalon, and Debbie Stevens. Shortly after their arrival in Sioux City, the replacements were interviewed by local radio and television reporters.

Clanton told them how he had started his career while in high school in his hometown of Baton Rouge. His first hit, "Just a Dream," had vaulted into the Top 10 in late summer 1958, just before his eighteenth birthday.

Avalon was an eighteen-year-old Philadelphia native who had shot to stardom a year earlier with "De De Dinah." Avalon's "I'll Wait for You" was sliding off the charts and his latest song, "Venus," had just been released when he got the call to head to Sioux City.

Ironically, Clanton and Avalon had toured with Holly in the fall of 1958 on the Biggest Show of Stars tour and had appeared with Richardson on Ted Steele's 1958 Thanksgiving concerts at the New York Paramount. Clanton had also appeared in Iowa in September 1958 with Dion and the Belmonts as part of a teen-dance package featuring Bobby Darin and Jo Ann Campbell. Clanton was also featured with Valens in the motion picture *Go Johnny Go,* scheduled for an April release.

The Sioux City show proved to be difficult for the singers. The audience was very somber and responded with just polite applause.

"It was horrible," Carl Bunch says. "We couldn't get through the music. We'd break down crying. The audience would stand there like [they were at] a freak show."

Besides the emotional loss of his leader and friend, Bunch was also in pain because of his frostbitten feet. He could play no more than five minutes at a time before yielding to Carlo Mastrangelo.

After the show, Jimmy Clanton received a shock as he boarded the bus. "All [the dead singers'] clothes and guitars were there as if they had simply taken a few days off," Clanton later told Bill Griggs of the Buddy Holly Memorial Society. "It was an eerie feeling."

Thursday, February 5, 1959

Things were starting to return to normal in the Clear Lake–Mason City area, just two days after the crash. The investigation had shifted from the Juhl farm to the hangar at the Mason City airport where Jerry Dwyer's already demolished Beechcraft Bonanza was being further dismantled. Ben Neiderhauser of Waterloo, Iowa, was one of the experts checking over the wreckage while Charles McGlothlen nervously looked on. McGlothlen was so depressed over the death of his good friend Peterson, just months after he had rebuilt the Bonanza, that a doctor had placed him on tranquilizers.

Thursday afternoon's Mason City *Globe-Gazette* carried no articles about the accident, its investigation, or the singers. Reporter Jim Collison felt the story had run its course. "Buddy Holly never meant anything to me. . . . I wasn't a follower of that type of music. Obviously, I cared that somebody got killed in a crash, but no more than if it had been a John Doe. After you report the crash, there's not too much more you can do because the guy isn't from here. He has no connection with the community other than he crashed here."

The bus containing the new lineup of the Winter Dance Party made its way from Sioux City to Des Moines on Thursday, a distance of 193 miles, where Ronnie Smith joined Buddy Holly's Crickets. With Smith's arrival, the Crickets were again a complete band. Plus, Smith was a charismatic presence onstage. "Ronnie Smith and the Poor Boys were bigger than Roy Orbison and the Teen Kings in West Texas," Bunch says. "That's because of Ronnie."

Smith's arrival was a shot in the arm for a shattered band. Dion remembers Smith's debut performance at the Val Air Ballroom in West Des Moines. "He did this Presley imitation. He was such a good-looking kid. He was terrific."

Friday, February 6, 1959

Friday was a day for laying to rest two of the victims of the plane crash.

Roger Peterson was buried in the Buena Vista Memorial Cemetery near his hometown of Alta, and the Big Bopper was buried in Beaumont, Texas. Private Elvis Presley and his manager, Colonel Tom Parker, sent yellow roses arranged in the shape of a guitar to Richardson's funeral.

Richardson's friend Gordon Baxter paid him tribute over the air on KTRM as his body was carried from Broussard Mortuary to Forest Lawn Memorial Park. "I had stayed up all night with his coffin, but I couldn't go," Baxter recalls. "I played all of Jape's favorite records. . . . Jape loved Dixieland jazz. . . . Jape said if he ever went, he wanted to go New Orleans jazz musician–style. He did. I gave him that."

As the funeral procession wound through Beaumont, with thousands of fans lining the route, every radio in the funeral party was turned to KTRM, listening to Baxter.

"People stood out in the yards and heard him go by," Baxter says. "In the control room I swear to this day he was with me. Standing there cool and gentle, hand on my shoulder, saying, 'Bax, you got to make a happy sound.'"

The plane's manufacturer, Beech, sent chief investigator Otwell Aycock and technical representative Leo Sander from its Wichita headquarters in a company-owned Bonanza Friday to do their own investigation of the accident. Also on hand was Marvin A. "Ike" Iverson, an attorney from Des Moines. Iverson had been retained by J. P. Richardson's family to investigate the possibility of tort claims against the airport, aircraft manufacturer, aircraft owner, or pilot.

The Winter Dance Party stopped in Cedar Rapids Friday night, while a wake for Ritchie Valens was being held at the Noble Chapel Funeral Home in San Fernando, California. The previous four days had been trying for the Valens family as friends and relatives crowded into the tract house Valens had bought for his mother. Teenagers shuffled through the stucco house, offering condolences. Several went on to local churches where they prayed and lit candles. On Friday night, a rosary was said.

Bob Keene brought copies of Valens's unreleased album and presented them to Concepcion Valenzuela. "I originally wasn't going to play the album because it was too painful," she told the *Los Angeles Times* in 1987. "But

I finally put on a brave front and said to myself, 'I'm going to play them before I bury him,' and I did."

———◆———

Saturday, February 7, 1959

C. E. Stillwagon, Eugene Anderson, Fred Becchetti, and A. J. Prokop wrapped up their investigation on Saturday. Although a public hearing would be held later, their examination of the airplane and crash site was complete. Beech investigator Aycock also was completing his work in the area Saturday, interviewing farmers living near the crash site and examining the wreckage.

Although Aycock wrote the Beech report, his colleague Sander worked alongside him throughout the investigation. "To the best of my recollection it was considered by us a weather-related accident," says Sander.

Two more singers were buried Saturday.

Ritchie Valens was laid to rest in San Fernando, California, making the journey to San Fernando Mission Cemetery in a copper-colored hearse.

"It was probably the saddest day of my life," says Donna Ludwig Fox, Ritchie's former girlfriend. "I had nightmares for days. The night of the funeral I had a dream that Ritchie was sitting at the foot of my bed telling me he was all right."

More than one thousand people attended the services, including several policemen who were guarding against possible demonstrations by the many young fans who attended. The police proved unnecessary on the rainy, overcast day. While most of the attendees headed for the comfort of their cars, members of the Drifters car club gathered around Valens's grave, wearing the club uniform of jeans and black leather jackets. One of the members quietly read a poem he had written to Valens.

In Lubbock, Buddy Holly was buried following afternoon services by Rev. Ben Johnson at the Tabernacle Baptist Church. Although an estimated one thousand people attended Holly's funeral, his widow, Maria Elena, was not among them.

Peggy Sue Allison noticed Maria Elena's absence and feared there had been some sort of transportation miscommunication. She left the church and drove to the home of Holly's parents, where Maria Elena and her aunt were staying. Allison soon realized there had been no mix-up.

Maria Elena was packing her suitcase to return to New York.

The Winter Dance Party continued to grind its way through the upper Midwest, including a stop at the Aragon Ballroom in Chicago where Mercury Records officials had planned to present Richardson with his gold record for

"Chantilly Lace." As the singers headed back to Iowa for a Monday night concert at the Hippodrome in Waterloo, a young English singer named Cliff Richard was conducting a recording session before several hundred screaming fans in London, England. At the session, Richard and his band, the Shadows, recorded Valens's "Donna" and Holly's "That'll Be the Day," which would be released on his debut album later that spring.

An article in the February 9, 1959, *Billboard* called J. P. Richardson "a cleffer of some distinction," and GAC spokesman Tim Gale says of the fatal flight: "We always fought against the idea of them chartering their own planes. It's a terrible thing."

With three days remaining on the tour, Avalon left and was replaced by another young rock star from Philadelphia—Fabian.

While the tour was headed to Peoria, Illinois, for its next-to-last performances on February 14, Jerry Dwyer, who owned the Beechcraft Bonanza that had carried Buddy Holly, Ritchie Valens, J. P. Richardson, and Roger Peterson to their deaths, was meeting with a lawyer.

Dwyer and his wife, Barbara Jean, completed paperwork to incorporate their business, appointing themselves as directors of the corporation. One provision of the incorporation documents, article eight, exempted the private property of the stockholders from corporate liability.

That Saturday was also the day Valens's first album was to be released. Bob Keene had planned to call the album *Valens-Time Day* to coincide with its release on Valentine's Day. Keene put the release date on hold immediately following the accident.

The next day, Bill Parsons, whose recording of "The All-American Boy" was high on the charts, joined the entourage for the final Winter Dance Party shows at the Illinois State Armory in Springfield.

After the final show, the singers spent the night in Springfield before boarding the bus for one last ride together, to Chicago.

On Monday, Coral Records announced it would soon release an LP, *The Buddy Holly Story,* and Frankie Avalon's "Venus" made its debut on the *Billboard* charts. Meanwhile, the members of the Winter Dance Party exchanged autographs and photos of one another and said their final good-byes.

New Directions

> Rock 'n' roll is a disease that shall pass away as quickly as it was
> created. It is a sad thing for your country. It is nothing, nothing.
>
> —Cellist Pablo Casals, 81, *Time*

It was with great apprehension that Waylon Jennings, Tommy Allsup, Carl
Bunch, and Ronnie Smith boarded a New York–bound train in Chicago.
With Holly gone, their musical futures were far from clear. Allsup feared a
planned European tour was off. "It was set," Allsup says. "We were going
to be off two weeks, then go to Europe for four weeks. That was already in
the works with Irvin Feld."

Allsup and his bandmates were to meet with Feld in New York. "We
came up [to New York] to settle up with GAC. They were going to keep
booking us as the Crickets, but when we got back up there, [Norman] Petty was there with the other Crickets: Jerry Allison, Joe B. Mauldin, Sonny
Curtis, and Earl Sinks.

"GAC reimbursed me for the train tickets, but that's all they gave us.
They said, 'Well, we had to give Buddy a bunch of money before the tour
started, and when he got killed Maria Elena came over and got some money.'"

According to Feld aide Allen Bloom, "We did arrange to get quite a
bit of money to [Holly's] widow. We declared Buddy an employee so that
she could get an insurance check."

Then, there was the matter of all those "Crickets." Jerry Allison claimed rights to the name, although Holly had continued to call his sidemen the Crickets on the Winter Dance Party.

"Me and Jerry and Joe B. and Earl stayed up there in New York," Allsup recalls. "Ronnie Smith, Sonny Curtis, Waylon, and Carl went back to Texas."

The trip to Europe was, indeed, canceled.

While the FAA held a public hearing on the accident on February 18 at the Mason City airport, Feld and Allen Bloom pondered the future of the New York Crickets. One thing was certain: There would be no more dance parties.

"The show really didn't do that much business," Bloom says. "In fact, it was a financial failure. We lost money."

Record companies owning masters by Holly, Valens, and Richardson wasted no time capitalizing on public demand. Just seventeen days after the plane crash, Coral released a four-song EP, "The Buddy Holly Story." A month later, Coral released a complete LP by the same name. The LP reached the U.S. charts in May, where it remained for 181 weeks over the next five years.

Sales of Holly's single "It Doesn't Matter Anymore" took off after his death, beginning a fourteen-week run on the *Billboard* charts on March 1, 1959. It was Holly's second million seller, peaking at No. 13. When it slipped off the charts after May 31, it marked the last time a Holly single would be in the Top 100 in the United States. Overseas, however, Holly was much bigger. "It Doesn't Matter Anymore" reached No. 1 in England and Australia, where his records appeared on the charts throughout much of the 1960s.

Due to the strong sales of Holly's recordings immediately after his death, Coral searched for other Holly material. It obtained the tapes Holly had made in his New York apartment just prior to his departure for the Winter Dance Party and turned them over to New York producer Jack Hanson. Hanson overdubbed studio musicians and added vocal backing by the Ray Charles Singers to six songs. In July 1959, Coral released two of them on a single: "Peggy Sue Got Married" and "Crying, Waiting, Hoping." Neither song charted in the United States.

While Holly left behind a sizable catalog of recorded material, there was much less available from Valens and Richardson, who were both scheduled to start a tour of Australia on February 22. At the time of his death, Richardson was also scheduled to be on *The Ed Sullivan Show*.

Del-Fi released Valens's first album, *Ritchie Valens,* on March 9. Two of Valens's singles—"That's My Little Suzie" and "Little Girl"—were good sellers on the West Coast, but neither climbed into the national Top 50.

Bob Keene claims disc jockeys were reluctant to play records by artists who weren't around to promote the product.

"They've got to have personal appearances," Keene says. "Once you're dead, you're dead. . . . They dropped him like a hot rock."

Keene says he never saw any of the money Valens received for his work on the Winter Dance Party. "I should have sued them. It was their goof. A seventeen-year-old kid out there freezing his toes off. Allowing him to get on an airplane. They were definitely at fault."

Although Valens never saw his gold record for "Donna," Keene presented it to his mother at a dance at the San Fernando American Legion Hall in May 1959, the same month Keene announced plans to establish a memorial fund with profits from Valens's records. At that time Keene estimated record sales of more than 400,000 singles and 100,000 albums since Valens's death. Keene says he still got fifty letters a week from Valens's fans and that the number of Valens fan clubs had grown from thirty to fifty. Del-Fi was to release a Limited Valens Memorial Series of records, featuring four-color sleeves and gold labels. The first release was "Little Girl"/"We Belong Together" on May 30, Memorial Day.

Valens fan club secretary Muriel Moore remained on Keene's payroll for years after Valens's death. Club president Gail Smith says she got up to one hundred letters a week for several years after Valens's death.

Mercury Records bought a full-page ad in *Billboard* to eulogize the Big Bopper, and issued a press release announcing its record release plans for his remaining recordings. The release also said the label would double the artist royalty on all of the Big Bopper's recordings, with the proceeds going to his wife and children.

The Bopper's *Chantilly Lace* LP had been released just before the accident and a single was pulled from the album in mid-February: "Someone Watching Over You"/"Walking through My Dreams." Another single was released in April 1959—"It's the Truth Ruth"/"That's What I'm Talking About"—but neither of the posthumous singles made the charts.

Richardson's old friend at KTRM, Gordon Baxter, also wrote one of several tribute songs to the dead singers, "Gold Records in the Snow." The song was recorded by Benny Barnes and released on Pappy Daily's D label. Two former Beaumont-area residents had major national hits with Richardson songs within a year after his death: George Jones with "White Lightning" and Johnny Preston with "Running Bear."

Meanwhile, Waylon Jennings had returned to KLLL in Lubbock, where he resumed his career as a disc jockey. His recording of "Jole Blon" was released in March 1959 by Brunswick, around the same time the company released Lou Giordano's "Stay Close to Me," a song written by Holly. However, the sales of 45 rpm singles fell off 32 percent in the first seven months of 1959 compared to the same period a year earlier; Jennings's first release was not a success.

———•———

Saturday, March 14, 1959

> "There'll be an investigation into the financial accounts of one of the rock 'n' roll stars who died in that recent plane crash in Iowa. His heirs thought he had about $100,000 in the bank, but can only find $35,000. The discrepancy came to light when creditors pressed for payments of bills he owed."
>
> —Syndicated columnist Dorothy Killgallen

———•———

None of the singers killed in Clear Lake had wills at the time of their deaths. Their legal heirs were never in dispute. Because Holly and Richardson were married, their wives inherited the bulk of their estates; because Ritchie Valens was a minor, his mother inherited his estate. Because Holly was a resident of New York at the time of his death, part of his estate went to his parents. However, because they were all professional performers, recording artists, and songwriters, the actual "content" of their estates has been debated over the years, sometimes with great rancor. This was especially true for Holly, whose songwriting royalties continued to be paid directly to Norman Petty until 1976 when Paul McCartney bought the Holly catalog.

Relatives of all three deceased singers took their battles over royalties and publishing rights into the courts as they fought to sort through the complicated bureaucracy of the music business. Interestingly enough, there was little legal action over the fatal plane crash itself.

On June 26, 1959, the Valens estate filed a $1.5 million lawsuit in Cerro Gordo County District Court against Jerry Dwyer. The lawsuit was said to be the largest ever filed in the county at the time and alleged negligence for allowing the plane to take off. The suit claimed "it was a very stormy and snowy evening" the night of the crash.

Shortly after the lawsuit was filed, "our lawyer told us that if we ever wanted to take a vacation, we'd better take it now," Barb Dwyer recalls. "He said 'you might not be able to afford it later.'" Barb and Jerry Dwyer left their three young sons with relatives. "We were going to be gone two weeks, but we stayed three. We didn't know what we were going to come home to."

The lawsuit was settled out of court and was dismissed with prejudice on September 11, 1959, just days before the CAB report was completed. Each of the estates also received an insurance settlement of between $25,000 and $50,000.

In the spring of 1959, the Albert Juhl family planted hay in the field where the Bonanza crashed. "We had to go out and pick up quite a little debris where it slid so it wouldn't get in the mower," Delbert Juhl recalls. The Juhls tossed the parts of the plane into a tub.

"It took a lot of cleaning up after it thawed," Elsie Juhl says. "My husband and son found parts of the bodies [and] many personal belongings which we turned over to the sheriff's office. . . . We picked up bushel after bushel of parts of the plane. All summer, people would stop from all over, wanting to know where the plane crashed, and they were very happy to take a piece for a souvenir."

On April 7, 1959, the Juhls turned over several items to the sheriff's department, including glasses, dice, watches, and cigarette lighters. One of the watches was a white gold Omega with 44 diamonds around the perimeter. A local jeweler cleaned the watch, which he estimated to be worth $5,000 at the time, and found it to be in perfect running order. It was returned to Maria Elena Holly on May 9, 1959.

Even without Buddy Holly, Norman Petty kept busy in Clovis in 1959. At the conclusion of the Winter Dance Party, Holly had planned to produce a recording session for Lubbock piano player Don Webb. Instead, Webb journeyed to Clovis where he cut four sides for Petty.

By April, the Fireballs, an instrumental band that Petty was grooming for success, returned to Clovis to record. A contract with Top Rank records followed, and the Fireballs were serving as Petty's studio musicians by the end of the year. While the Fireballs toured the Midwest on a series of one-nighters in the summer of 1959, Petty upgraded his studio with stereo equipment.

Ronnie Smith, who had returned to Odessa with Carl Bunch and formed a new band called the Jitters, also recorded at Petty's shortly after returning from the Winter Dance Party. A marathon session led to *Lookie Lookie Lookie* and *A Tiny Kiss,* which were released on a Brunswick single on June 27, 1959.

"That was the longest recording session we, as a vocal group, ever had," says Robert Linville of the Roses, who sang backup on the Smith tunes. "Ronnie couldn't remember what to do on some of the songs."

The session for *Lookie Lookie Lookie* ran from 3 PM on a Saturday until 7 AM the next morning. "That's the only time I ever saw Norman Petty really irritated," Linville says. "After about eight hours, our voices totally gave out. He made us stop. We went into the back room to the kitchen. Just like kids, he poured three big old tablespoons of honey down our throats and gave us hot tea. He told us to sip on that for one hour and do not speak. And it worked. It cleared our vocal cords." For their efforts, the Roses were paid $42.50.

Tommy Allsup remained with the New York Crickets for a time after the Winter Dance Party. "We stayed up there about six weeks and did a bunch of TV shows around New York and Washington, Baltimore," Allsup says. "GAC couldn't get any bookings then because without Buddy Holly there wasn't any Crickets, so I said: 'Man, I'm going back to Texas.'"

Although he was afraid to fly after the accident, Allsup caught a flight back to Odessa. He did some session work at Petty's in mid-1959, including some with Bob Montgomery, who was learning the recording business from Petty.

The Texas Crickets—Earl Sinks, Joe B. Mauldin, Jerry Allison, and Sonny Curtis—never again recorded at Norman Petty's. Sessions in Los Angeles and New York in May 1959 resulted in eight songs, but no hits.

Except for the record-buying public and faithful fans, few people gave Buddy Holly, Ritchie Valens, or J. P. Richardson much thought once the shock of their tragic deaths subsided. With the possible exception of their hometown press, the mainstream media virtually ignored the trio until the movie *The Buddy Holly Story* was released nearly twenty years after their deaths.

Although Norman Petty skillfully released fresh Holly material for years after the crash, Holly's popularity in the United States fell far short of his fame in England. Across the Atlantic, a vibrant teen press kept Holly's image alive, influencing a whole wave of British youngsters, including Paul McCartney, John Lennon, and Mick Jagger.

Holly's former bandmates—Jerry Allison, Joe B. Mauldin, and Sonny Curtis—provided the instrumental backing for the Everly Brothers' Top 5 hit "'Til I Kissed You" in the fall of 1959, at about the same time as the Civil Aeronautics Board issued its long-awaited report on the accident.

The CAB Report

Here is the Civil Aeronautics Board (CAB) Aircraft Accident Report synopsis, which was adopted September 15, 1959, and released on September 23, 1959.

A Beech Bonanza, N3794N, crashed at night approximately 5 miles northwest of the Mason City Municipal Airport, Mason City, Iowa, at approximately 0100, February 3, 1959. The pilot and three passengers were killed and the aircraft was demolished. The aircraft was observed to take off toward the south in a normal manner, turn and climb to an estimated altitude of 800 feet, and then head in a northwesterly direction. When approximately 5 miles had been traversed, the tail light of the aircraft was seen to descend gradually until it disappeared from sight. Following this, many unsuccessful attempts were made to contact the aircraft by radio. The wreckage was found in a field later that morning.

This accident, like so many before it, was caused by the pilot's decision to undertake a flight in which the likelihood of encountering instrument conditions existed, in the mistaken belief that he could cope with en route instrument weather conditions, without having the necessary familiarization with the instruments in the aircraft and without being properly certificated to fly solely by instruments.

INVESTIGATION

Charles Hardin, J. P. Richardson, and Richard Valenzuela were members of a group of entertainers appearing in Clear Lake, Iowa, the night of February 2, 1959. The following night they were to appear in Moorhead, Minnesota. Because of bus trouble, which had plagued the group, these three decided to go to Moorhead ahead of the others. Accordingly, arrangements were made through Roger Peterson of the Dwyer Flying Service, Inc., located on the Mason City Airport, to charter an aircraft to fly to Fargo, North Dakota, the nearest airport to Moorhead.

At approximately 1730 (all times herein are central standard and based on the 24-hour clock), Pilot Peterson went to the Air Traffic Communications Station (ATCS), which was located in a tower on top of the Administration Building, to obtain the necessary weather information pertinent to the flight. This included the current weather at Mason City, Iowa; Minneapolis, Redwood Falls, and Alexandria, Minnesota; and the terminal forecast for Fargo, North Dakota. He was advised by the communicator that all these stations were reporting ceilings of 5,000 feet or better and visibilities of 10 miles or above; also, that the Fargo terminal forecast indicated the possibility of light snow showers after 0200 and a cold frontal passage about 0400. The communicator told Peterson that a later terminal forecast would be available at 2300. At 2200 and again at 2320 Pilot Peterson called ATCS concerning the weather. At the latter time he was advised that the stations en route were reporting ceilings of 4200 feet or better with visibilities still 10 miles or greater. Light snow was reported at Minneapolis. The cold front previously reported by the communicator as forecast to pass Fargo at 0400 was now reported to pass there at 0200. The Mason City weather was reported to the pilot as: ceiling measured 6,000 feet overcast; visibility 15 miles plus; temperature 15 degrees; dewpoint 8 degrees; wind south 25 to 32 knots; altimeter setting 29.96 inches.

At 2355, Peterson, accompanied by Hubert Dwyer, a certificated commercial pilot, the local fixed-base operator at the Mason City Airport, and owner of Bonanza N3794N (the aircraft used on the flight), again went to ATCS for the latest weather information. The local weather had changed somewhat in that the ceiling had lowered to 5,000 feet, light snow was falling, and the altimeter setting was now 29.90 inches.

The passengers arrived at the airport about 0040 and after their baggage had been properly stowed on board, the pilot and passengers boarded the aircraft. Pilot Peterson told Mr. Dwyer that he would file his flight plan by radio when airborne. While the aircraft was being taxied to the end of runway 17, Peterson called ATCS and asked for the latest local and en route weather. This was given him as not having changed materially en route; however, the local weather was now reported as: precipitation ceiling 3,000 feet, sky obscured; visibility 6 miles; light snow, wind south 20 knots, gusts to 30 knots; altimeter setting 29.85 inches.

A normal takeoff was made at 0055 and the aircraft was observed to make a left 180-degree turn and climb to approximately 800 feet and then, after passing the airport to the east, to head in a northwesterly direction. Through most of the flight the tail light of the aircraft was plainly visible to Mr. Dwyer, who was watching from a platform outside the tower. When about five miles from the airport, Dwyer saw the tail light of the aircraft gradually descend until out of sight. When Peterson did not report his flight plan by radio soon after takeoff, the communicator, at Mr. Dwyer's request, repeatedly tried to reach him but was unable to do so. The time was approximately 0100.

After an extensive air search, the wreckage of N3794N was sighted in an open farm field at approximately 0935 that morning. All occupants were dead and the aircraft was demolished. The field in which the aircraft was found was level and covered with about four inches of snow.

The accident occurred in a sparsely inhabited area and there were no witnesses. Examination of the wreckage indicated that the first impact with the ground was made by the right wing tip when the aircraft was in a steep right bank and in a nose-low attitude. It was further determined that the aircraft was traveling at high speed on a heading of 315 degrees. Parts were scattered over a distance of 540 feet, at the end of which the main wreckage was found lying against a barbed wire fence. The three passengers were thrown clear of the wreckage, the pilot was found in the cockpit. The two front seat safety belts and the middle ones of the rear seat were torn free from their attach points. The two rear outside belt ends remained attached to their respective fittings; the buckle of one was broken. None of the webbing was broken and no belts were about the occupants. Although the aircraft was badly damaged, certain important facts were determined. There was no fire. All components were accounted for at the wreckage site. There was no evidence of inflight structural failure or failure of the controls. The landing gear was retracted at the time of impact. The damaged engine was dismantled and examined; there was no evidence of engine malfunctioning or failure in flight. Both blades of the propeller were broken at the hub, giving evidence that the engine was producing power when ground impact occurred. The hub pitch-change mechanism indicated that the blade pitch was in the cruise range.

Despite the damage to the cockpit the following readings were obtained:

Magneto switches were both in the "off" position.

Battery and generator switches were in the "on" position.

The tachometer rpm needle was stuck at 2200.

Fuel pressure, oil temperature, and pressure gauges were stuck in the normal or green range.

The attitude gyro indicator was stuck in a manner indicative of a 90-degree right bank and nose-down attitude.

The rate of climb indicator was stuck at 3,000 feet per minute descent.

The airspeed indicator needle was stuck between 165-170 mph. The directional gyro was caged.

The omni selector was positioned at 114.9, the frequency of the Mason City omni range.

The course selector indicated a 360-degree course.

The transmitter was tuned to 122.1, the frequency for Mason City.

The Lear autopilot was not operable.

THE AIRCRAFT

The aircraft, a Beech Bonanza, model 35, S/N-1019, identification N3794N, was manufactured October 17, 1947. It was powered by a Continental model E185-8 engine which had a total of 40 hours since major overhaul. The aircraft was purchased by the Dwyer Flying Service, July 1, 1958, and, according to records and the testimony of the licensed mechanic employed by Dwyer, had been properly maintained since its acquisition. N3794N was equipped with high and low frequency radio transmitters and receivers, a Narco omnigator, Lear autopilot (only recently installed and not operable), all the necessary engine and navigational instruments, and a full panel of instruments used for instrument flying including a Sperry F3 Attitude Gyro.

PILOT

Roger Arthur Peterson, 21 years old, was regularly employed by the Dwyer Flying Service as a commercial pilot and flight instructor, and had been with them about one year. He had been flying since October of 1954, and had accumulated 711 flying hours, of which 128 were in Bonanza aircraft. Almost all of the Bonanza time was acquired during charter flights. He had approximately 52 hours of dual instrument training and had passed his instrument written examination. He failed an instrument flight check on March 21, 1958, nine months prior to the accident. His last CAA second-class physical examination was taken March 29, 1958. A hearing deficiency of his right ear was found and because of this he was given a flight test. A waiver noting this hearing deficiency was issued November 29, 1958. According to his associates he was a young married man who built his life around flying. When his instrument training was taken, several aircraft were used and these were all equipped with the conventional type artificial horizon and none with the Sperry Attitude Gyro such as was installed in Bonanza N3794N. These two instruments differ greatly in their pictorial display.

The conventional artificial horizon provides a direct reading indication of the bank and pitch attitude of the aircraft which is accurately indicated by a miniature aircraft pictorially displayed against a horizon bar and as if observed from the rear. The Sperry F3 gyro also provides a direct reading indication of the bank and pitch attitude of the aircraft, but its pictorial presentation is achieved by using a stabilized sphere whose free-floating movements behind a miniature aircraft presents pitch information with a sensing exactly opposite from that depicted by the conventional artificial horizon.

THE WEATHER

The surface weather chart for 0000 on February 3, 1959, showed a cold front extending from the northwestern corner of Minnesota through central Nebraska with a secondary cold front through North Dakota. Widespread snow shower activity was indicated in advance of these fronts. Temperatures along the airway route from Mason City to Fargo were below freezing at all levels with an inversion between 3,000 and 4,000 feet and abundant moisture present at all levels through 12,000 feet. The temperature and moisture content was such that moderate to heavy icing and precipitation existed in the clouds along the route. Winds aloft along the route at altitudes below 10,000 feet were reported to be 30 to 50 knots from a southwesterly direction, with the strongest winds indicated to be closest to the cold front.

A flash advisory issued by the U.S. Weather Bureau at Minneapolis at 2335 on February 2 contained the following information: "Flash Advisory No. 5. A band of snow about 100 miles wide at 2335 from extreme northwestern Minnesota, northern North Dakota through Bismarck and south-southwestward through Black Hills of South Dakota with visibility generally below 2 miles in snow. This area or band moving southeastward about 25 knots. Cold front at 2335 from vicinity Winnipeg through Minot, Williston, moving southeastward 25 to 30 knots with surface winds following front north-northwest 25 gusts 45. Valid until 0335." Another advisory issued by the U.S. Weather Bureau at Kansas City, Missouri, at 0015 on February 3 was: "Flash Advisory No. 1. Over eastern half Kansas ceilings are locally below one thousand feet, visibilities locally 2 miles or less in freezing drizzle, light snow and fog. Moderate to locally heavy icing areas of freezing drizzle and locally moderate icing in clouds below 10,000 feet over eastern portion Nebraska, Kansas, northwest Missouri, and most of Iowa. Valid until 0515." Neither communicator could recall having drawn these flash advisories to the attention of Pilot Peterson. Mr. Dwyer said that when he accompanied Pilot Peterson to ATCS, no information was given them indicating instrument flying weather would be encountered along the route.

ANALYSIS

There is no evidence to indicate that very important flash advisories regarding adverse weather conditions were drawn to the attention of the pilot. On the contrary there is evidence that the weather briefing consisted solely of the reading of current weather at en route terminals and terminal forecasts for the destination. Failure of the communicators to draw these advisories to the attention of the pilot and to emphasize their importance could readily lead the pilot to underestimate the severity of the weather situation.

It must be pointed out that the communicators' responsibility with respect to furnishing weather information to pilots is to give them all the available information to interpret this data if requested, but not to advise in any manner. Also, the pilot and the operator in this case had a definite responsibility to request and obtain all of the available information and to interpret it correctly.

Mr. Dwyer said that he had confidence in Pilot Peterson and relied entirely on his operational judgment with respect to the planning and conduct of the flight.

At Mason City, at the time of takeoff, the barometer was falling, the ceiling and visibility were lowering, light snow had begun to fall, and the surface winds and winds aloft were so high one could reasonably have expected to encounter adverse weather during the estimated two-hour flight.

It was already snowing at Minneapolis, and the general forecast for the area along the intended route indicated deteriorating weather conditions. Considering all of these facts and the fact that the company was certificated to fly in accordance with visual flight rules only, both day and night, together with the pilot's unproven ability to fly by instrument, the decision to go seems most imprudent.

It is believed that shortly after takeoff Pilot Peterson entered an area of complete darkness and one in which there was no definite horizon; that the snow conditions and the lack of horizon required him to rely solely on flight instruments for aircraft attitude and orientation.

The high gusty winds and the attendant turbulence which existed this night would have caused the rate of climb indicator and the turn and bank indicator to fluctuate to such an extent that an interpretation of these instruments as far as attitude control is concerned would have been difficult to a pilot as inexperienced as Mr. Peterson. The airspeed and altimeter alone would not have provided him with sufficient reference to maintain control of the pitch attitude. With his limited experience the pilot would tend to rely on the attitude gyro which is relatively stable under these conditions.

Service experience with the use of the attitude gyro has clearly indicated confusion among pilots during the transition period or when alternating between conventional and attitude gyros. Since Peterson had received his instrument training in aircraft equipped with the conventional type artificial horizon, and since this instrument and the attitude gyro are opposite in their pictorial display of the pitch attitude, it is probable that the reverse sensing would at times produce reverse control action. This is especially true of instrument flight conditions requiring a high degree of concentration or requiring multiple function, as would be the case when flying instrument conditions in turbulence without a copilot. The directional gyro was found caged and it is possible that it was never used during the short flight. However, this evidence is not conclusive. If the directional gyro were caged throughout the flight this could only have added to the pilot's confusion.

CONCLUSION

At night, with an overcast sky, snow falling, no definite horizon, and a proposed flight over a sparsely settled area with an absence of ground lights, a requirement for control of the aircraft solely by reference to flight instruments can be predicted with virtual certainty.

The Board concludes that Pilot Peterson, when a short distance from the airport, was confronted with this situation. Because of fluctuation of the rate instruments caused by gusty winds he would have been forced to concentrate and rely greatly on the attitude gyro, an instrument with which he was not completely familiar. The pitch display of this instrument is the reverse of the instrument he was accustomed to; therefore, he could have become confused and thought he was making a climbing turn when in reality he was making a descending turn. The fact that the aircraft struck the ground in a steep turn but with the nose lowered only slightly, indicates that some control was being effected at the time. The weather briefing supplied to the pilot was seriously inadequate in that it failed to mention adverse flying conditions which should have been highlighted.

PROBABLE CAUSE

The Board determines that the probable cause of this accident was the pilot's unwise decision to embark on a flight which would necessitate flying solely on instruments when he was not properly certificated or qualified to do so. Contributing factors were serious deficiencies in the weather briefing, and the pilot's unfamiliarity with the instrument which determines the attitude of the aircraft.

By the Civil Aeronautics Board:
/s/ JAMES R. DURFEE
/s/ CHAN GURNEY
/s/ HARMAR D. DENNY
/s/ G. JOSEPH MINETTI
/s/ LOUIS J. HECTOR

The Controversy

The CAB report did little to stop conjecture as to what had caused the crash. Few newspapers found the CAB report newsworthy, and those that did buried the item deep within their news columns. Even the teen press, which had kept the singers' memories alive for a few months following the accident, no longer had time for Buddy Holly, the Big Bopper, or Ritchie Valens.

Therefore, most impressions of the crash and its cause were formed by media reports in the days immediately following the accident, and by the rumors that arose in the subsequent months. Decades after the crash, mistakes that originated in early 1959 are still passed off as fact in newspaper and magazine articles and reference books. For example, one book places the crash in the foothills of the North Dakotan mountains during a blizzard. Another book said the very-much-alive Johnny Preston was one of the crash victims—and that the crash occurred in Ames, Iowa.

Nearly every story on the accident carried by wire services in the United States in the three days following the accident contained errors. Many mistakes were minor. For instance, J. P. Richardson's age was given as anywhere from twenty-four to twenty-eight (correct). One story gave Valens's age as twenty-one and another said Peterson was "about" twenty-five. Several stories erroneously stated that Richardson and Holly were single, a detail likely perpetuated by public relations people who thought knowledge of a singer's marriage would cost him many of his teenage female fans. Misspellings were common: Beechcraft was spelled "Beachcraft," Sam Geller became "Sam Geeler," Ritchie Valens was "Richie," and Frankie Sardo was "Franky."

GAC was guilty of mistakes, too. In posters and prepared newspaper ads for the Winter Dance Party, Sardo's recording of "Fake Out" was referred to as "Take Out." Newspaper ads had particular trouble with Dion and the Belmonts, referring to Dion as "Don" or "Diana."

A more serious error appearing in many newspapers on February 3 was that the plane had been consumed by fire and all four bodies badly burned. Almost all stories referred to weather conditions at the time of the crash, strongly suggesting that weather was the culprit.

For most fans, these were the final words on the accident. It's no wonder so many people have thought bad weather killed the singers. Those who knew the pilot may agree. Although the CAB report officially cited Peterson as the cause of the accident, most of those who knew him don't believe it. "[Airplane owner Jerry Dwyer] was real unhappy when he found out that they were saying it was Roger's fault," says Barb Dwyer, Jerry's wife. "Of course, nine times out of ten in an aircraft accident, it's pilot error."

Leonard Ross, one of Peterson's flight instructors in Sioux City, recalls: "I was flying that night. . . . There were snow showers in that area, but it wasn't that bad. Roger was a competent pilot and a good pilot. I could never understand what happened. I know Roger couldn't have gotten into any problem by flying on instruments. There's no way. There was no problem with Roger."

Bruce Anderson, one of Peterson's flying buddies from Alta, also doesn't believe his old friend was to blame for the accident. "I can't believe a little bad weather got him in trouble. We can't understand up here what went wrong because Roger was a better pilot than that.

"Everybody in this area thinks it was foul play of some kind. We think that those guys were high on something and [saying] go, go, go."

"Foul play" is a phrase you hear a lot around Clear Lake and Mason City when people discuss the crash, primarily because of the discovery of Holly's pistol at the crash site two months after the accident. The Clear Lake *Mirror-Reporter* reported the discovery April 9. The article noted that Albert Juhl had found a small six-shot German-made revolver with four unfired cartridges in the cylinder. The other two cylinders were empty. Juhl "fired all four bullets into the air," the story said, and "all discharged perfectly."

The article further stated that CAB authorities had been notified. Chief investigator C. E. Stillwagon reportedly said, "These investigations are never closed and this board will proceed at once on any evidence that has a bearing on the accident."

Discovery of the pistol fueled new rumors about the cause of the crash. For Roger Peterson's supporters, the gun offered a plausible explanation: Somebody shot Peterson or, at least, threatened him, diverting his full attention from flying the plane.

The rumor flames burned even hotter when an article appeared in the Mason City *Globe-Gazette* on April 10, 1959, under the headline PISTOL IN PLANE WRECK NOT FIRED. The article reported: "The pistol found in the wreckage of the light plane which crashed north of Clear Lake February 3 was not fired. . . . Authorities said Friday they were certain the pistol had not been fired. It contained four cartridges. The other two chambers in the six-chamber pistol were empty.

"A check of the coroner's official reports Friday showed that the pilot and passengers died from wounds received in the plane wreck."

Nearly forty years later, it's impossible to know if the Juhls actually fired the gun after picking it up from the field. In an interview on April 12, 1976, Delbert Juhl said: "I'm pretty sure we fired it." In March 1976, Cerro Gordo County Sheriff Jerry Allen confirmed that at least one shot had been fired. In a 1979 interview with Bill Griggs of the Buddy Holly Memorial Society, Allen again said one shot had been fired, by Albert Juhl.

But in an article in the February 1, 1989, *Globe-Gazette,* Delbert Juhl denies that he or his father fired the pistol: "I was with my father the day he found the gun and we gave that to [Deputy] Lowell Sandquist [*sic*]," said Delbert Juhl. "He [Albert Juhl] did not fire that gun." The conflicting stories have done nothing to lay to rest the "foul play" rumors surrounding the crash.

Dwyer's old mechanic, Charles McGlothlen, says he was unaware that a gun had ever been found, but recalls that FAA investigators had considered the possibility of a gun early in their work at the Mason City airport. "The thing that was throwing them was that they found an empty casing of a shell in the aircraft."

FAA investigators Eugene Anderson and A. J. Prokop disagree. "I don't believe it [a bullet casing] was ever uncovered in our particular investigation," Anderson says. Prokop also denies that a shell casing was found. "We sure didn't find one," he says. Furthermore, says Prokop, chief investigator Stillwagon "never mentioned [a gun] to me, either."

It was three months after the gun was found before Buddy Holly was identified as the owner. It was turned over to Holly's father in October 1959. Tommy Allsup had given Holly the pistol in 1958.

"I think I had it before we left on that [summer 1958] tour," Allsup says. "It was a little old .22-like target pistol. . . . [Buddy] had had some bad experiences riding those buses with some of those black acts when they were on that dance party tour the year before. . . . We were collecting money every night and he was just carrying it in his car. He wasn't sending it back to Petty like Petty wanted him to and he didn't want anybody robbing him."

According to Holly's former bandmates, it was common for Texans to carry guns, even in the 1950s. "It's fun to have a gun," Jerry Allison says. "Joe B. [Mauldin] and I both had a gun." Carl Bunch agrees: "Everybody in West Texas has got guns. And if you're carrying the kind of money Buddy was carrying, you've got to have some kind of protection."

Although stories have surfaced over the years that Holly used the gun to deal with unscrupulous promoters, Jerry Allison has no such recollections. However, Holly did use his gun on at least one occasion on his Midwestern tour in the summer of 1958, according to Allison.

"Somebody pulled up, a bunch of local hoodlums or thugs . . . and blocked the driveway [to where we were playing]. Buddy got that gun out . . . the car was like twenty feet away . . . and he pointed it right in the guy's face and said, 'Just sit there . . . one . . . two' and the guy moved."

Bunch doesn't recall Holly producing his pistol at all during the Winter Dance Party. "Buddy didn't go around flashing a gun. Buddy was cool."

It is difficult to prove that Holly's gun was anywhere but in its usual place in his leather shaving kit at the time of the crash. The kit was found about eight feet from his body in the snow. The false bottom, where Holly carried his pistol, was ripped out. It is doubtful that anyone on board the plane used Holly's gun to shoot Roger Peterson.

The best evidence is the autopsy of Peterson's body by Dr. George T. Joyce conducted on February 4, one day after the crash. Joyce's four-page autopsy report shows no evidence of bullet wounds to Peterson's body. Joyce, who was a thirty-nine-year-old pathologist with twelve years of private practice experience when he did the autopsy, did not know about the rumors that a gun may have been involved in the crash until he was asked in 1992 to review his autopsy report. After reviewing the report, Joyce was asked if any of the injuries to Peterson's body could have been caused by a gunshot. He answered: "No. There wasn't a thing."

There is also the question of motive: Why would anyone want to kill Peterson, or anyone else on the plane, especially while airborne? If it was a case of one of the singers wanting to commit suicide, it is doubtful they would follow such an unlikely scenario, taking others with them in the process.

Another persistent, and more plausible, theory blames the crash on some sort of disturbance on the plane which diverted Peterson's attention. Although Jerry Dwyer consistently turns down requests for interviews about the crash, he has discussed his theories informally with acquaintances.

"Jerry's got the conspiracy theory going," says Bob Hale, the emcee of the Winter Dance Party show at the Surf who has made several subsequent trips to Clear Lake and has become a friend of Dwyer's. "He still believes that there was a fight on the plane for whatever the reason. He says there's more to this, these guys weren't getting along."

But Hale, who spent several hours with them just before their deaths, doesn't believe the fight theory. "These were good friends. These guys were back-slapping buddies. There wasn't a bit of tension, jealousy, or bitchiness about any of these guys."

Drugs frequently are cited as the cause of any disturbance. The subject was brought up within hours of discovery of the wreckage, in a phone call to Hale from Bill Bennett of Minneapolis radio station WDGY. "Bill wanted to ask me about drugs," Hale says. "He was the only one. . . . I said these guys didn't even have a beer. . . . There wasn't an inkling of booze or drugs. . . . I was with them from the moment they got off the bus to the moment they got in the car [to the airport]. There was no booze or alcohol, nothing of that." Hale thinks Bennett was asking this question to "clear the air before the speculation started."

The drug rumor may have been fueled by a curious discovery made by those at the crash site the morning of February 3. "The field out there was strewn with candy bars," Charles McGlothlen says. "According to Lowell [Sanquist] and some of the other people out there, when a person needs a fix, candy is the only thing that will tide them over."

Mahlon A. "Curly" Hintzman, the mayor of Clear Lake at the time, was at the crash site twice on February 3 where he picked up bits and pieces of the plane. He estimated that two or three cartons of candy bars were scattered along the plane's path from where it first touched down to the fence.

Bob Booe isn't surprised at the rumors of drug use. "Even back then, marijuana was very common among entertainers," recalls Booe, who occasionally booked shows at the Surf Ballroom. However, those who were on the tour claim there was little, if any, drug use on the Winter Dance Party tour before the accident. Jerry Allison says there was no drug trouble on any of his earlier tours with Holly, either. "People drank, but it wasn't a problem. We never saw drugs at all."

After the accident, several tour members acknowledge that Ronnie Smith brought amphetamines from Mexico when he joined the band in Des Moines. "There were pills," Debbie Stevens says. "I remember the pills, because [Ronnie Smith] asked me if I wanted some."

Carl Bunch, Smith's lifelong friend, says: "Ronnie had some serious problems. He didn't share those problems with me. I knew that he used pills every now and then, but I didn't see him using the stuff. I kept trying my best to keep him away from the use of drugs because I didn't think we needed them. I thought they were hurting him."

Waylon Jennings also tried to persuade Smith to give up the pills, warning him that drugs could be fatal. Nevertheless, one of Smith's little white pills was ground up and dropped into a bottle of beer Jennings was drinking. "I just drank that one beer and I was up for two days," Jennings says. "I rode all the way from Chicago to New York on that damn train, awake. When I got to New York, I laid down and the bed started shaking."

But tour manager Geller says he was unaware of any drug use on tour before the accident, even by Dion, who later wrote in his autobiography that he drank alcohol by the time he was twelve, smoked marijuana when he was thirteen, and was using heroin at fourteen. Despite these claims, Dion says that he wasn't much of a drug user in 1959. "Not so much on that tour. . . . At the time I really wasn't that bad. Maybe I used some pills and did some drinking, but I wasn't really into anything. The Belmonts drank more than me, I didn't even like liquor."

Fred Milano, one of the Belmonts, says: "We weren't into drugs. . . . We would know if somebody was on drugs . . . drugs were in existence in New York, on the road there was no such thing."

There is no evidence that any of the people on the plane were drug users. Roger Peterson rarely touched alcohol, and drug use was virtually unheard of among the people he associated with. "In all the years I went with him, I probably was with him only once or twice when he drank," says his widow, DeAnn. "That was just a couple of special occasions . . . it was just something we never did."

Even though there was an autopsy on Peterson's body, there was no blood analysis, because the body had been arterially embalmed prior to the autopsy. "That was a mistake we probably made," says Dr. Joyce. "We were a little trapped [because of the embalming]. We couldn't really do a decent toxicological exam."

Holly, too, rarely drank, because of an ulcer, and was not known as a drug user. Neither were Valens or Richardson, although Richardson had been given Seconal, atropine, and regular doses of the pain killer Demerol in 1956 while in a U.S. Army hospital recovering from two hemorrhoid surgeries. Demerol is a brandname for meperidine hydrochloride, an addictive synthetic narcotic. Friends of Richardson say he was not dependent on any drug after leaving the service in 1957, and his 122-hour stint during the Jape-a-thon in full public view supports that position.

Ritchie Valens wasn't known as much of a drinker, although one of his former bandmates, Fred Aguilera, acknowledged that the Silhouettes sometimes had parties where alcohol was available: "Sometimes they would give us a drink or two or a little bit of wine or something and we'd all get nice and cheery." Another Valens friend, Louis "Skip" Raring, described a party where he and some friends once started smoking marijuana around Ritchie: "This *really* bothered him . . . I never heard from him again."

Nevertheless, some critics of the CAB report claim it was the quest for drugs that caused the crash, not Roger Peterson's inability to fly the plane. Proponents of the drug theory accurately point out that drugs would be difficult to obtain in most of the cities the Winter Dance Party passed through.

"You're not going to find [drugs] out there [in the Midwest] unless you've got some real tough connections," Carl Bunch says.

The most common drug-quest scenario has someone on board the plane trying to persuade Peterson to alter his route to include a stop in Minneapolis or St. Paul, a metropolitan area where, presumably, drugs were more readily available than in the Fargo-Moorhead area. But the flight path of the Bonanza was exactly as Jerry Dwyer and Roger Peterson had planned. When the plane went down it was on a direct heading to Fargo, some 35 degrees west of the Twin Cities.

The drug rumors eventually filtered back to FAA investigator Anderson. "I had heard rumors about [drugs] being found at the scene after the snow had melted," Anderson recalls. "Whether it was related or not, I don't remember, but I had heard of some packets of other material somewhere in the neighborhood of that scene. . . . It never came to light during our investigation."

Indeed, the CAB report never mentioned anything about the gun or a possible distraction in the cockpit. Apparently, C. E. Stillwagon, who authored the report, gave neither any credence. But investigator Anderson never fully agreed with the CAB findings. "I certainly do feel there was some interference inside the airplane . . . that restricted Mr. Peterson from doing what he was supposed to do."

Anderson thinks the investigation might have been handled differently had the investigators known that one of the passengers carried a gun. "You could do most anything with one of those stuck in your back," he says.

There is also the question of weight and balance in the plane. Those at the scene have placed Ritchie Valens and J. P. Richardson in the back seat, with Holly and Peterson in front. But a weight and balance report provided to CAB investigator Stillwagon by Jerry Dwyer clearly puts Richardson in the right front seat. In those weight and balance calculations, pilot Peterson's weight is given as 165 pounds, with the heaviest passenger, at 190 pounds, in the front passenger seat. The passengers in the rear seat weighed 145 pounds (Holly) and 165 pounds (Valens), according to Dwyer's figures.

Accurate weight and balance information is important in ensuring that a plane is safe to fly. The accuracy of the weight and balance information used for Roger Peterson's flight is questionable. The two primary considerations are the total weight of occupants, cargo and fuel, and the proper loading of the aircraft. According to Jerry Dwyer's weight and balance report, the Bonanza was carrying 961 pounds, some thirty-one pounds below the maximum "useful load" as determined by Beech engineers. But J. P. Richardson's actual weight was considerably more than the 190 pounds listed in the report.

When Richardson entered the army in 1954, he weighed 212 pounds. When he was discharged in 1957, he weighed 210 and was termed "overweight" by Army doctors. At the conclusion of the Jape-a-thon in May 1957, *The Vidorian* newspaper of Vidor, Texas, reported that Richardson's weight had dropped from 240 to 205 pounds during the five-day ordeal. It is likely that he weighed at least 210 at the time of the fatal flight.

Also not taken into account on the report were the heavy winter coats worn by Holly and Valens, or the carry-on luggage in the passenger compartment. The report estimated that a total of 43 pounds of baggage was on board, all loaded in the rear of the plane. The total cargo was very likely much closer to the maximum allowable limit and may have exceeded it, making the airplane more difficult to fly. The way the cargo was loaded also likely contributed to handling difficulties.

For the plane to respond properly to flight controls, it must be loaded so its center of gravity is within allowable limits. If the center of gravity (c.g.) is outside the prescribed limits, the plane's stability is affected and control forces can become erratic. For the Bonanza, the center of gravity needed to be located between 82.4 and 84.8 inches from the nose of the plane.

The weight and balance report signed by Jerry Dwyer, with Buddy Holly and J. P. Richardson in the wrong seats, listed a c.g. of 83.09 inches, well within the limits. However, because of an apparent mathematical error, the actual c.g. (even before correcting for the seating error) should have been 83.91. By simply putting Buddy Holly and J. P. Richardson in their proper seats, the c.g. moves to 84.47, much closer to the aft limit of 84.8. By calculating with a weight of 210 pounds for Richardson, the c.g. is at 84.72. Toss in a couple of coats and small baggage and the c.g. is beyond the allowable limits. For a plane such as the Bonanza, which is known for its sensitive handling qualities, this can create serious handling problems for a pilot.

According to the editors of *The Aviation Consumer Used Aircraft Guide*, a Bonanza with too much of its load at the rear experiences "decreased pitch stability and lightened stick forces. Considering the Bonanza's already light pitch control forces and its tendency to build up speed quickly, an out of c.g. Bonanza can really take a pilot by surprise."

Despite the weight and balance discrepancies, it is certain Holly was in the front passenger seat at takeoff. Holly loved to fly and had hopes of becoming a pilot himself. Indeed, just three months earlier, on November 5, Holly had taken a thirty-minute flying lesson with his brother Larry in a Cessna 175 at the airport in Lubbock. It was not unusual for him to take a front seat, where he could observe the pilot.

People who knew Holly say his eagerness to fly may have been a critical factor in the moments just before the accident. In testimony to CAB investigators, Dwyer told how Peterson taxied to "the North end of the North-South runway and sat there for several minutes." But why would Peterson sit for several minutes in the bitter north Iowa cold when he was cleared for takeoff on a night when there was no other traffic at the airport? "No reason unless he was checking all his instruments and adjusting them, but that wouldn't take very long," Charles McGlothlen says. "I don't know. Strange things happened all through that thing."

Outside of a brief communication to the tower that he would file his flight plan after becoming airborne, Peterson was not heard from again. Barb Dwyer says Peterson had been previously reprimanded for not filing a flight plan.

Some have suggested that someone other than Peterson tried to take control of the plane during the brief wait at the end of the runway. "There was speculation that they actually tried to take over the airplane and go to Minneapolis before they went on," McGlothlen remembers. "But that was speculation. Nothing ever got proved."

Another possibility is that Peterson was having second thoughts about proceeding and may have tried to call the flight off. Barb says Jerry Dwyer's pilots were given instructions not to take off if they had any reservations about doing so. "I wouldn't be surprised if [Holly] didn't insist on that guy taking off that night if there was any question or doubt," Tommy Allsup says. "[Buddy'd] probably say, 'Well, let's go. We can make it. You don't have anything to worry about.'"

Jennings is convinced that Holly could have coaxed Peterson into the air, even if against Peterson's better judgment. "We flew around West Texas several places—Odessa, Clovis—in those little planes," Jennings says. "The minute the plane got off the ground, Buddy'd start saying, 'Let me take the controls.' . . . He was really into that. I have often wondered if he talked that kid into it. . . . I'll bet you ten to one he did. If Buddy asked a kid that young, what would [the kid] do?"

Others have suggested that Holly may have been at the controls at some point in the brief flight. With its "throwover wheel," the Bonanza could be flown from either of the front seats.

However, it's unlikely anyone other than Roger Peterson was at the controls of the Bonanza as it bore down on Albert Juhl's farm. Peterson was the only one trapped in the wreckage and his body bore puncture wounds in the chest, likely from the control column. Plus, his right thumb was partially amputated in the crash, likely from his death grip on the steering yoke at the time of impact.

Dr. Joyce says it is reasonable to assume that Peterson was flying the plane, saying that the chest injuries were "consistent with that type of accident" and that the thumb amputation probably occurred at impact.

Even though Peterson may not have been shot while guiding the Bonanza on its short, fateful flight, there remains the possibility of distraction, intentional or inadvertent. But outside the flight's dramatic conclusion, it appeared to be very ordinary to those on the ground. Observers called it a normal takeoff, a normal roll toward the northwest, and a steady, if not level, flight toward its destination. Roger Peterson did not use his radio to indicate anything was wrong.

As Charles McGlothlen says, flying out of the Mason City airport at night can be an unnerving experience, even in good weather. "The most-used runway is the one that takes off over Mason City [to the east]. And all those bright lights and everything. He was going northwest and you turn in any north or westerly direction from there and it's black. Even in clear weather, and he had a snowstorm going on. I've flown up there a lot at night and it's really kind of eerie."

Bob Booe agrees: "I think pilot error was made and I think Roger in his transition [had] no reference on the horizon when he turned away from Mason City and was taking up his course northwest . . . there were no reference points on the horizon. I think he may have been in conversation, misread an instrument and flew the airplane into the ground. It was just a terrible accident."

As the CAB report correctly pointed out, Roger Peterson was not qualified to fly on instruments, although he had taken some fifty-one hours of instrument training. Peterson was enrolled in the Instrument Course at Graham Flying Service during February and March of 1958, where he received his first radio training. "When he began his training he seemed to be slightly overconfident of his own ability," instructor Charles Meyer told CAB investigators. "We gave him his instrument training in a Piper Tri-Pacer. He handled the airplane well on instruments, but when things would go badly with a flying lesson he would become disoriented in his radio procedure."

Peterson also took eight hours of instrument dual flight instruction from Lambert Fechter of Hartley, Iowa, in early 1958.

"Mr. Peterson was below average at the end of this time in that he had tendencies up into the sixth hour of developing severe vertigo, and allowing the aircraft to go into diving spirals to the right," Fechter told CAB investigators. But according to Charles Meyer, "We gave him forty-two hours of training while he was [at Graham] and during that time we did not notice that there was any tendency to fall off to the right in his flying."

On March 21, 1958, Peterson took an instrument rating flight test given by Mel Wood at Sioux Falls, South Dakota. The plane used was a Piper

PA-22, and Peterson used a vision restrictor, "a hood deal that you've got to raise your head way up to see outside," according to Peterson's flight instructor, Leonard Ross. Peterson failed the test. Deficiencies cited by Wood after the test were:

> Applicant had difficulty copying and interpreting ATC Clearances. Failed to orientate himself and comply with Air Traffic Control instructions given by Sioux Falls Approach Control.
>
> Failure to properly tune and use his omni radio, became confused and was unable to establish on course.
>
> Failed to establish holding procedures and identify station passage.
>
> Lost control of the aircraft, on two occasions, while reading approach charts and descended below his assigned altitude in a spiral attitude. At this point the flight test was discontinued, and no approach procedure, missed approach procedure or emergency procedure was accomplished.
>
> This applicant was very susceptible to distractions and became upset and confused during phase III of the flight test.

Ross, who also gave Jerry Dwyer his multi-instrument rating, was in the back seat when Peterson failed his instrument flight check. "I remember him doing only one thing wrong," he says. "I remember him being disoriented as far as tracking outbound from the VOR. He didn't know exactly where he was."

Normally, Ross says, a student would take a few more hours of training and take the test again. Peterson never again took the test. "The instrument rating is very, very important. You [commercial pilots] have to have that."

Peterson's radio problems may have been at least partially attributed to some hearing difficulties. A "loss of hearing in lower ranges" was detected in his left ear in an October 19, 1956, physical and a "hearing deficiency" was noted in his right ear during a March 29, 1958, physical. Peterson was granted a medical waiver in November 1958 after he passed a flight test in Des Moines, Iowa, with A. J. Prokop. Whatever Peterson's hearing problems were, they were unknown to his wife and parents, although Pearl Peterson says Roger may have had his hearing damaged by a childhood bout with scarlet fever.

From the date he failed the instrument flight test to the time of his death, Roger Peterson accumulated about 440 hours of flying time, but only eight of those hours were on instruments. The biggest chunk of the instrument hours was compiled on January 6, 1959, when Peterson took 3 hours 15 minutes of instrument instruction from Lawrence A. DenHartog of Eagle Grove at Mason City in DenHartog's Tri-Pacer.

"After takeoff, I had the colored goggles in my lap, and shortly thereafter, Mr. Peterson reached over and put them on," DenHartog told CAB investigators. "He had trouble orientating himself and flying the aircraft for at least 15 minutes after putting on the goggles. I would say that he had a false courage or was a little over-confident. . . .

The first thing I was going to have him do was some holdings. However, after taking off, I felt it was necessary to practice considerable straight and level flying for some time before practicing turns and holdings. Then after the 3:15 hours of instruction, given by me, I think Mr. Peterson was disappointed in himself and may have thought I was a little rough as a flight instructor on instruments.

On the afternoon, previous to the aircraft accident, I called Mr. Peterson at the Dwyer Flying Service, Mason City, Iowa, on the telephone and he told me that he had been busy getting his flight instructor rating but planned to take additional instrument instruction from me the next week.

At the time of his death, Peterson had around forty hours of solo night-flying experience, none of it on instruments. After takeoff, Peterson found himself deprived of the normal cues used to determine balance. The overcast sky hid the stars from view. He was flying over a remote section of rural farmland, with few lights visible on the ground. There were snow showers, further obscuring the view outside the window. Compounded by the thrust of the engine driving the Beechcraft forward at 170 miles per hour and the substantial winds, it is not hard to imagine Peterson becoming confused about the attitude of his aircraft. A more seasoned pilot likely would have relied on his instruments to show him what he could not sense. No one will ever know if Peterson relied on his instruments or not.

The CAB report suggests that Peterson may have relied on the attitude gyro and, because of his limited previous training, misread it. The CAB report discusses that the attitude gyro Peterson had used previously read in exactly the opposite manner to the Sperry model installed on the plane. If Peterson was relying on the Sperry attitude gyro, he probably thought he was climbing when, in fact, he was descending. The rate of climb indicator on the Bonanza was stuck at 3,000 feet per minute descent.

There is some evidence that Peterson may have realized he was in trouble in the final seconds of the flight. "I'm the last one that ever saw that plane," says Ruth Pickering, who spotted the landing lights of the Bonanza heading right for her kitchen as she hung curtains that night. "I knew it was going to hit the house, so I quick turned on the yard light and ran out-doors because I didn't want to burn up. . . . If I wouldn't have turned the yard light on, he'd have hit my house. He pulled up and missed the house, the barn, and the grove. I seen him go over the barn."

Pickering never understood why Roger Peterson didn't just keep on climbing after she warned him. "[The accident] really shouldn't have happened. I really gave him a warning when I turned that yard light on. He must have been confused."

Peterson apparently was still close to the ground as he approached the Reeve Eldridge farm a few seconds after averting disaster at the Pickering homestead. There he received another warning, Eldridge thinks. "We left the light on in the hallway for the children upstairs," Eldridge says, pointing out that there was a window near the light. "Apparently he was flying low and the light shone out that east window." Eldridge claims he could "definitely" detect a change in the sound of the Bonanza's engine as it passed over his house. "Apparently he saw the light and pulled her up. That's my guess."

A few seconds later, the plane crashed.

The attitude gyro recovered from the demolished Bonanza indicates that Peterson was in a sharp 90-degree right turn when the plane first touched the ground. Dwyer observed the plane heading to the northwest; and the plane's path along the ground also was to the northwest; it follows then that the turn must have been started very close to the impact point.

Perhaps Peterson was steering away from another light on the ground.

Perhaps someone persuaded Peterson to head to Minneapolis after all, and thinking he was climbing, he made a sharp turn toward the Twin Cities.

Perhaps Peterson could tell that conditions exceeded his skills and he decided to turn back toward the airport to wait until daylight.

Perhaps there was a disturbance in the cockpit, resulting in someone pulling the steering yoke too far to the right, driving the right wing into Albert Juhl's stubble field.

Perhaps.

"I just think that accident happened too soon, so quickly after takeoff," says Peterson's widow, DeAnn. "It's something that I just can't ever under-stand."

Ron Peterson, Roger's younger brother, who frequently helped with in-strument training on the Alta farm, comments: "In my mind, it's still not clear what took place and it will always be that way."

Pearl Peterson doesn't know what caused the accident either, but she's certain her son wasn't to blame. "When they can't find anything else, they blame it on pilot error," she says. "Who knows what happened? God only knows what happened."

Legacies

It has been decades since the voices of Buddy Holly, Ritchie Valens, and J. P. Richardson were permanently etched in the collective psyche of rock music fans. Rock contemporaries who also met untimely deaths at an early age—such as Johnny Ace, Frankie Lymon, Johnny Burnette, King Curtis, Clyde McPhatter, and Chuck Willis—generally are not as widely revered despite comparable contributions to the art form. But for Holly, Richardson, and Valens, the legacy continues to grow stronger. Their music is heard regularly emanating from classic-rock radio stations, compact disc players, automobile cassette decks, and scratchy 45s. Other artists still record their songs, creating a blue-chip market for their heirs and music publishers. Books have been written about all three, movies have been produced about the life stories of Buddy Holly and Ritchie Valens, and two scripts have been written for Big Bopper films.

Amazingly, there is still unreleased Buddy Holly material, which was recorded at Norman Petty's tiny Clovis studio more than thirty-five years ago. Eager fans wait patiently as Petty's estate and Holly's heirs negotiate for the release of the songs, promotional jingles, alternate takes, and studio chatter that will provide additional insight into the early days of rock 'n' roll.

Squabbles and disputes have become increasingly common in recent years as those closest to the singers try to protect their images while maintaining control of what made those images possible, their music. One of the bigger controversies centers on Norman Petty's business dealings with Holly. Most of Holly's family and closest friends say Holly wouldn't have had to tour with the Winter Dance Party if Petty had treated him fairly when managing his affairs.

"Buddy was broke [at the time of the Winter Dance Party]," Tommy Allsup says. "He needed the money. Only Norman had the power of attorney to write checks [on their bank account]." Petty did wield an extraordinary amount of control over Holly and the Crickets early in their career. Although Petty created a relaxed, carefree, and creative atmosphere in his recording studio, there was more to the man than someone whose sole interest was in perfecting his craft.

"Around the studio, he was amiable and smiling and he got the most out of you artistically," said lifelong acquaintance John Pickering, who sang backup for Holly as one of the Picks. "I don't guess Norman ever did a reckless unthought thing in his life. He would take chances, but they were calculated risks. I don't mean that he was afraid, he just had more sense. He was a very intelligent person."

Petty was smart enough to latch tightly onto Holly and the Crickets after getting them their first record deals. He handled their music publishing, shared songwriting credits, and signed on as their manager. He also had all their income deposited into a checking account, an account that only he had access to.

Rockabilly singer Buddy Knox, who had recorded at Petty's studio before Holly came on the scene, has a theory on why Petty had such a tenacious hold on Holly and the Crickets. "Norm made a mistake with us, he let us slip through his fingers. And he let Roy Orbison slip through his fingers. When Buddy Holly came along, he said 'Huh unnh, no way this boy's going to get away.'"

John Pickering gives Petty credit for launching Holly into the big time. "Buddy would never have been a national star if that studio had not been in Clovis, New Mexico," Pickering said. "He'd had his shot. Nashville had some great producers and he had one of the greatest. Anybody will tell you, Owen Bradley knows his business. All it proves is that Buddy had to do it his way or he couldn't do it as well.

"Buddy evolved. You can listen to his records and you hear him evolving. There was a big change from fifty-six to fifty-seven. Now what was the change? It was Norman Petty."

One of Petty's changes was in the songwriting credits for "That'll Be the Day." When Holly recorded the song in Nashville, Decca gave songwriting credits to Holly and Allison; the Brunswick version added Petty's name to the credit.

"Buddy and I had written it long before we went over to Clovis," Jerry Allison says. "When we got through recording it and [Petty got the record] deal, he said, 'Boys, I'm going to put my name on there. Since my name is familiar in the industry, it'll get more play.' I said, 'Well, I don't care if it gets more play or not. I don't want anybody else's name on it.' I wasn't even thinking about the money. I just wanted my mom and dad to see me and [Buddy's names] on it." Petty continued to cut himself in on songwriting credits throughout his association with the Crickets.

Niki Sullivan, who was with the Crickets on their first recording session at Petty's, agrees that Petty frequently contributed to the recording of songs in the studio. "Norman did help certain arranging through his demands of what he needed in the sound," Sullivan says. "[But] there were songs, for instance "That'll Be the Day" and "Peggy Sue," he had absolutely nothing to do with. . . . Norman didn't write that kind of music. If he did, he didn't need us."

Larry Holley says: "Buddy was generous with his songs to a point of being ridiculous. . . . He figured he could write a song a night. What the heck, he's rich in songs."

Sonny West, writer of "Oh Boy" and "Rave On," says his professional relationship with Petty was as strained as Holly's. After writing "Rave On," West almost reached a deal with Chester Oliver, the Texan who had released Roy Orbison's first recording of "Ooby Dooby." But when that deal fell through, West ended up at Petty's. Petty placed West's recording of "Rave On" with Atlantic Records and took over West's management. As with Holly and the Crickets, West's royalties were to be paid directly to Petty. Petty also added his name to the songwriting credits for both of West's best-known songs.

"I was young and they said that's the way things were done," West says.

Indeed, the practice of "cutting in" on songwriting credits was widespread in those days. Charlie Phillips, a young songwriter and aspiring singer from nearby Farwell, Texas, had recorded his own composition, "Sugartime," at Petty's in 1957, a session on which Buddy Holly played guitar. Although the song later became a hit for the McGuire Sisters, Phillips's version was less successful.

In Phillips's case, he shared songwriting royalties not with producer Petty, but with his manager, Otis "Pop" Echols. "I didn't mind him getting his cut because he trained me in the radio business," Phillips says. "He gave me a chance. I was a kid off the farm and I wanted to get off the farm.

"Those are the things that happen when you're a greenhorn behind the ears. You don't know the business."

In his lifetime (he died in 1984), Petty rarely defended himself publicly over the issue of "cutting in." "Norman just didn't like to talk about it," his widow, Vi Petty, said in a 1988 interview. "It just wasn't worth it to him, really." Vi also pointed out that it was her husband who sorted out the tangled contract mess Holly had created through his earlier attempts at rock stardom in Nashville; Petty eventually brokered the deals that freed Holly from his contracts with Cedarwood Publishing Company and Decca.

"Norman didn't know the full details on the whole thing at the time [the singers recorded "That'll Be the Day"]," Vi Petty said. "They had not told Norman that they had recorded it [for Decca in Nashville]. . . . Norman still had to work something out with the publishing people."

Vi Petty said her husband got more satisfaction out of creating music and recording it. Petty's technical expertise allowed him to set down his musical creations on tape from which Vi would later transcribe the melodies and chords onto lead sheets. Working with young rock 'n' rollers was frustrating for Petty, whose roots were deep in keyboard-based popular music. John Pickering says Petty hated rock 'n' roll, but stayed with it because of its income-generating potential.

"Norman had a deal with Columbia to record talent," Pickering says. "They wanted to get in on the West Texas talent situation because by that time Roy Orbison, Buddy, and others were doing well."

But Columbia's head A&R man, Mitch Miller, didn't like the new music any better than Petty did. Still, Petty continued to record just about anyone who found their way to Clovis. "I know what he was going through," Vi Petty said. "It was sad for him. He was just disappointed that the more he did for people, the less they appreciated him.

"Norman did all those sessions. He didn't charge any session fees. . . . I remember Norman doing so many songs for so many people and changing their words or melodies and never even putting his name on the song."

Whatever Petty's contributions were to the songwriting side of Buddy Holly, there is no question that his innovative recording techniques were major factors in the Crickets' "sound."

It was Petty who had Jerry Allison slap out the rhythm for "Everyday" on his knees. Petty also had Allison shun his drum kit on "Well . . . All Right," opting instead for a single cymbal. On "Not Fade Away," Petty had Allison pound out the beat on a cardboard box, the same technique that had worked so well on Buddy Knox's "Party Doll."

While Joe B. Mauldin was learning to play the bass in his early days with the Crickets, Petty recorded Mauldin separately from the rest of the band. Later, George Atwood would don a set of headphones in the studio and add the bass track to what Holly, Allison, and Sullivan had recorded earlier.

Larry Holley says Buddy was unhappy with some of Petty's innovations, such as adding background vocals. "Buddy didn't care for the Roses or the Picks much, either one. That was Norman's idea. Buddy would say, 'Who are we going to have, the Noses or the Picks?' He didn't like Vi's piano playing, either. She just pounds the thing, but with Norman there, he'd slip stuff on after they'd cut the session."

John Pickering agrees that Petty's musical talents did not include vocals. "Norman was not a singer," Pickering said. "He didn't think vocals. He couldn't tell you how to sing and never did."

Nevertheless, Petty took advantage of Holly's natural hiccuping-like song stylings, even though Holly objected at first. That style translated into big bucks as the Lubbock musicians broke into the major leagues in 1957. As their manager, Petty insisted that the singers send home most of their earnings when on tour.

Allison and Mauldin acknowledge that the Crickets sometimes held back the money they were supposed to send Petty, to buy anything from clothes to motorcycles. Tommy Allsup says that on the summer tour in 1958, "we were collecting money every night and [Buddy] was just carrying it in his car. He wasn't sending it back to Petty like Petty wanted him to."

Vi Petty said: "I remember so many times Norman saying, 'The boys have not sent any money. I guess I'm going to have to pay [their bills].' So they evidently thought they sent more money or they spent more money than they thought. The money was not there."

But Larry Holley insists that his brother didn't get the money due him from Petty. "Norman kept Buddy broke. Norman got all the money and then just passed out a little bit to the boys. He had control of the bank account. He even took their money and tithed to his church. That was making Buddy awful mad.

"He told Mother that he hated Norman with a passion there at the last. It was to the point that somebody could have got killed pretty easy. Norman said he'd starve Buddy to death, he'd just show him."

Although there's no way of accurately determining what each of those associated with "That'll Be the Day" made from the million-seller, it is possible to make an approximation.

Petty acknowledged that artist's royalties for the record were 5 percent for each single. Applying the royalty against the industry standard of 90 percent of the retail cost, that comes to 4 cents per record sold (5 percent χ 90 percent χ 89 cents). Mechanical rights would amount to 2 cents per song: 1 cent for the publisher and 1 cent for the songwriter.

Assuming sales of 1 million singles and a 10 percent management share of artist's royalties by Norman Petty, here is how the royalties would look for "That'll Be the Day":

Artist royalties: $40,000 ($4,000 for manager Petty; $9,000 for each of the Crickets: Buddy Holly, Joe B. Mauldin, Niki Sullivan, and Jerry Allison).

Mechanical (copyright) royalties for "That'll Be the Day": $20,000 ($10,000 for publisher Petty; $3,333 each for songwriters Petty, Holly, and Allison).

Mechanical royalties for flip side ("Looking for Someone to Love"): $20,000 ($10,000 for publisher Petty; $5,000 each for songwriters Petty and Holly).

Total payment of $80,000:

Norman Petty	$32,333
Buddy Holly	$17,333
Jerry Allison	$12,333
Niki Sullivan	$ 9,000
Joe B. Mauldin	$ 9,000

From this example, it is clear Petty would pull in 40 percent of the royalties, and almost twice as much money as Holly's $17,333. Furthermore, for every dollar collected in sheet music sales or broadcast fees for "That'll Be the Day," Norman Petty would collect 66 ⅔ cents (50 cents as publisher and 16 ⅔ cents as cowriter, along with Allison and Holly).

Vi Petty never thought her husband got enough credit for his role in the success of Buddy Holly and the Crickets. "I feel Norman was knocked out of a lot of what he should have gotten," she said. "He had the confidence in Buddy Holly and the Crickets. He never charged any sessions, everything he did was on his own. . . . All he had in mind was the good for everybody, not just for himself."

However, other musicians disagree. Says Niki Sullivan, "Buddy didn't get near what he had coming to him. A lot of people who worked with Norman or knew Norman, trusted him totally. . . . After all, he sat at his desk in a suit with a tie on and a Bible on the right upper corner of his desk. My father told me long before then . . . don't trust a man in business who has a Bible on his desk. Jesus, was he right."

Sonny West, whose recording of "Rave On" was released in January 1958, three months before Holly's version, never received any royalties for his record. West says: "The only statement I ever got from Atlantic, the statement they sent to Norman, said that it was still in the red because they hadn't sold enough to pay back their initial investment in it."

Royalties aside, West says that Norman Petty really didn't offer a lot of help to him and his band. "I think he was quite busy with the Crickets. He probably just couldn't spread himself that thin."

Pickering agrees that Petty had a difficult time hanging on to talent. "You can go talk with most anybody who ever recorded there and for some reason they don't ever go back," Pickering says. "They don't like it. And it all stems back to money.

"[Norman is] not ever going to be revered for his handling of money or his management of performers. I'm sure that if you talked to him he could have told you many good reasons for it, but the fact remains that I don't know of anybody that I've talked to or heard from who felt good about him after they were there."

It was money that eventually split Petty and Pickering. After relocating to Corpus Christi, Pickering says he drove to Clovis on three straight weekends to record at Petty's and received a total of $35 for his efforts. That was the last work he did for Petty.

The tile job the Holley family did for Petty in 1957 was the last work they ever did for Petty, too. Larry Holley says they were never paid for their efforts. "I don't remember Norman paying much of anything to anybody," Holley says. "He was a skinflint."

Buddy Knox lost some royalty money from his association with Petty, but doesn't blame Petty. Knox published some songs through Petty under the pen name of Jack Dixon. "I can't prove I was Jack Dixon," Knox says. "I've seen no royalties."

Sonny Curtis, whose personal association with Petty was minimal, says he benefited from that association. "When the Crickets left him, he was no longer interested in me," Curtis said. "He hassled me a little bit, but he was quite willing to let me go. I had to sit still for a couple of lectures about how I was never going to make it, that I'd wind up with a goose egg and that kind of stuff.

"I will give Norman credit for one thing. He was a sharp businessman and he got me with BMI [Broadcast Music, Inc.]. I thought BMI was a club of some sort. . . . All of a sudden BMI started sending me checks and I thought, 'Boy, what a great club.'"

Jerry Allison still feels taken advantage of, forty years after first meeting Norman Petty. "We were more interested in getting out and playing music and touring and having fun than we were the money and we assumed that everybody would be fair, especially Norman . . . but it wasn't that way."

Despite his disagreements with Petty, Allison says the Crickets were luckier than many of the groups they worked with in the 1950s. "Mostly, [Petty] took care of business real good," Allison said. "There were lots of acts back then that didn't get any of their songwriting royalties or anything."

Buddy Knox says the early days of rock 'n' roll were full of unscrupulous adults who took advantage of wide-eyed youngsters. "It's an unfair thing in our business because the records are still selling," Knox says. "They're still leasing the stuff out and there's still millions of dollars passing back and forth. We didn't know nothing. They said, 'Sign here, kid, and I'll make you rich.' And that's exactly what we did."

Norman Petty sold his North American publishing interests in Holly's compositions in 1976 to ex-Beatle Paul McCartney. Niki Sullivan said 50 percent of the sale money went to Petty's publishing company, Nor-Va-Jak, and 50 percent went to the individual songwriters.

Larry Holley confirms that his family never saw any of the money from the McCartney transaction. "Norman got every bit of it," he said. "He didn't even tell us he was doing it. That was a sore issue."

Still, those who are listed as Holly's cosongwriters in McCartney's purchase are doing better now than they were before 1975. Sullivan now regularly receives royalty checks from McCartney's MPL Productions for his role in writing "I'm Gonna Love You Too," and Sonny West says he's doing much better with "Rave On" and "Oh Boy." West estimates his payments from Southern Music were usually less than $1,000 per year from 1960 until McCartney bought the Holly catalog. "Ever since 1975, I've made a lot more money on it than I did before," West said.

In the years immediately before his death on August 15, 1984, Petty hinted he would set the record straight with a book he was writing about his association with Holly. Petty hoped to get Holly's mother to write about Holly's early days, with Petty writing about Holly's career from the time Petty first recorded his group. "He had tried to start on a book," Vi Petty said. "He set up a special typewriter to work on it. He was never too pleased with what he had. . . . I just don't think he ever finished what he was trying to do."

Ritchie Valens's family claims to have had problems getting royalties from Valens's manager, Bob Keane (he changed the spelling of his last name from Keene in 1970), as well. According to Ted Quillin, the KFWB disc jockey who first played "Come On Let's Go" and became close to the family, a tearful Connie Valenzuela approached him about the problem shortly after Valens's funeral. "She asked me if I could help her get some of the money that was due Ritchie from Bob Keane," Quillin said. "I went to him, [but] he didn't give her any money." Ritchie's mother told the same story to Chan Romero a few months later, after he had moved into the Valenzuela house.

Quillin said the late Ernie Freeman (who played piano on "La Bamba") once told him: "The problem with young recording stars is that they get rich before making any money." Success came so quickly for Valens that the financial reward of having a million-seller hadn't yet filtered down through the more savvy hands of the recording industry's bureaucracy.

"There weren't any musical royalties coming [right after Ritchie's death], really," Keane says. "All we had done was sell the single and they got whatever that was. I wrote them a check for $13,000 or something. That was all the royalties he was ever paid, because he never earned any more from me, except when we started with Rhino [in the 1980s]. Then Rhino paid him directly."

Keane also points out that Valens wasn't paid anything for his appearance in the film *Go Johnny Go,* and that Keane received none of Ritchie's income for appearing on the Winter Dance Party tour. Keane claims that he was always looking out for Ritchie's best interests, even to the point of advancing him the $1,000 for the down payment on the house Ritchie bought for his mother. He also says it was Keane's favorite overcoat that Valens was wearing in the fatal crash and that he ended up paying for Valens's funeral. "I paid $8,000 for the casket [and funeral]," Keane says. "Nobody had any money. The guy was in a sack back there [in Iowa]."

Donna Ludwig Fox was very disappointed in Keane's actions right after Valens's death. "I found out what a jerk he was afterwards," she says. "I think he took advantage of the family and left them almost poverty-stricken again."

Stan Ross, a close associate of Keane's over the years, says Keane's problems with Valens may have been related to his lack of experience as a manager. "I don't think he was a good manager," Ross says. "I think he was a good record producer and a record person. He was good for Ritchie on record. . . . He didn't have much of a track record as a manager."

Says Keane: "I never made a dime as a manager. The reason I was his manager was because he didn't know anything. I had to tell him what to do. All managing him amounted to was setting up personal appearances and tours to get his record going."

Keane reports he was particularly angered by a phone call he received shortly after the funeral. "He wasn't dead for two weeks before I got a call from some attorney in Beverly Hills, wanting a complete accounting," Keane said. "Some ambulance chaser said, 'Here's an opportunity,' and he got hold of the family and said, 'Let's really get this guy.'"

In fact, Keane says, the Valens family has benefited greatly from his generosity in sharing songwriting credits with Ritchie. He claims Valens never wrote a complete song all by himself. "I gave Ritchie all the [songwriting] credit," he says. "There were only two songs that I took credit for because I wrote them from scratch, "Cry Cry Cry" and "That's My Little Suzie." It really cost me a bundle. They played all his songs on that [*La Bamba* soundtrack] album and I guess they must have sold 3 or 4 million of them, and I think the family did close to $800,000 or $900,000 just on the songwriting royalties. I should have had them all."

Over the years, lawyers for the Valens estate have alleged that several contracts bearing Valens' signatures are forgeries, a contention Keane scoffs at. "This is the land of show business, my friend. The minute somebody gets a little bit famous, the stories come out like crazy. Especially when some guy is dead and can't defend himself."

For all the friction over the years, few question the role Keane played in launching Valens's career. "He got Ritchie started, he got him going in the right direction and he would have continued to be a big star," says Gil Rocha, who hired Valens to play guitar in his band, the Silhouettes.

Says Keane: "Not that I'm taking any credit, because that's just the way life was. I was there at the time that Ritchie was there, we got together and whatever happened, happened. But if it hadn't been for that meeting with me, who knows? This guy may never have happened, "La Bamba" probably wouldn't have happened. Because, when you hear the way we put it together in the studio, a lot of that stuff was my idea."

Ritchie's aunt, Ernestine Reyes, still doesn't think Keane has treated the Valens family fairly, but she says: "I have respect for the man. I have respect for him for the simple reason that he made Ritchie. He gave him what Ritchie is now and I respect him for that."

<hr />

J. P. Richardson also died before seeing any royalties from his biggest hit, "Chantilly Lace." "It sold a million. And he lived just long enough to know it," says friend Gordon Baxter. "The gold record was on the way from Mercury, but he never saw it. And J. P., Jr., was on the way with Teetsie. And he never saw him, either." The gold record was later presented to Richardson's widow; his son, Jay Perry Richardson, was born on April 28, 1959.

When Richardson's estate was appraised, it was valued at $11,111.50, including $10,000 in yet-to-be-seen royalties. Richardson left $8 in a savings account; his most valuable asset was his 1953 Dodge, which was appraised at $400. Even his guitar was worth just $100, the same as the furniture in his apartment. He owed $3,638, including $2,648 to Broussard's Mortuary for his funeral.

"Really and truly, he never had the success," Teetsie Richardson says. "He was still out on the road. There was no success as far as he was concerned. That came later."

But the financial rewards were a long time coming, according to Teetsie. "[J. P.'s manager] Bill Hall gave me money. Just enough to keep me and Debbie and Jay going. I trusted him. I didn't check the books like I should have. Being young and naive had a lot to do with it."

Record producer Huey Meaux knows what Teetsie Richardson went through. "J. P. never had a chance to enjoy much of what he did," Meaux says. "The guy that was handling him at the time also was a guy I was doing business with. He took my records and put his name on it. I was watching my songs on *The Dick Clark Show* and still cutting hair [as a barber]."

With legal assistance, Teetsie Richardson decided not to file any tort claims in the plane crash, settling for an insurance settlement of $25,000. Keeping half for herself, she deposited $6,250 in each of her children's savings accounts. For fifteen years Teetsie persisted in seeking songwriting royalties earned by her husband. On May 6, 1974, she finally won her case in Jefferson County Court. A court decree ordered half of all royalties for twenty-seven songs written by J. P. Richardson be paid directly to Teetsie, with the remaining half to be split equally between Debbie and Jay Richardson.

All three singers left musical legacies that likely will continue for many more decades. Even J. P. Richardson, whom many considered little more than a one-hit wonder in novelty song–rich 1958, has proven to have considerable staying power, particularly as a songwriter.

"Chantilly Lace" enjoyed a lengthy run itself. After its release in August 1958, it sold a million by year's end. It spent a total of twenty-five weeks on the U.S. charts, peaking at No. 6. Two of Richardson's biggest-selling hits turned out to be songs performed by others after his death: "White Lightning" by George Jones and "Running Bear" by Johnny Preston.

Preston's three biggest hits—"Running Bear," "Cradle of Love," and "Feel So Fine"—were published by Big Bopper Music, a company formed by Richardson and Bill Hall just before Richardson's death. Big Bopper Music also held the publishing on Jivin' Gene Bourgeois's 1959 regional hit "Breaking Up Is Hard to Do." Big Bopper Music was sold to polka king Lawrence Welk in 1975; Hall later ran Welk's Nashville office.

"Boogie Woogie," the ad-libbed song J. P. Richardson recorded at Jay Miller's studio in Crowley, Louisiana, in 1954, wasn't released until 1977 when Miller leased much of his material to German-based Flyright Records, which included the Bopper song on its *Louisiana Swamp Pop* album. Two other Bopper songs recorded at Miller's studio—a country ballad called "Pet Names" and a rocker called "Sippin' Cider"—have yet to be released. Another song—"Yesterday, Today and Tomorrow"—has all but disappeared. Jay P. Richardson remembers playing a 78-rpm acetate of his father's song as a youngster, but the record has never been found. He remembers the song as being very short, which may account for its never being released.

In 1986, Jay P. Richardson found his dad's guitar and briefcase in the attic of Bill Hall's mother's house in Beaumont. Hall had put the items there around the time of the funeral, and they sat there for twenty-seven years. In the briefcase, Richardson found words to several unpublished songs written by his father. Jay P. later had music written for the songs "in the Bopper style" for a possible recording.

The most covered Ritchie Valens song over the years is "La Bamba," which has been recorded by dozens of artists, including Trini Lopez, the Kingston Trio, the Tokens, and Harry Belafonte. Valens's version never rose higher than No. 22 on the *Billboard* charts, but the movie soundtrack version by Los Lobos in 1987 reached No. 1. It was the first commercial hit for the band, which had included Valens's "Come On Let's Go" on their debut mini-LP in 1983.

The infectious rhythms of "La Bamba" also formed the basis for "Twist and Shout," a song first popularized by the Isley Brothers in 1962, and which was a No. 2 hit for the Beatles in 1964. Although Valens never toured outside the United States, his influence was strong in England, where British cover artist Marty Wilde had a big 1959 hit with his version of "Donna." Wilde's success sparked an answer record by the Kittens, "A Letter to Donna."

Tommy Steele's version of "Come On Let's Go" was a British hit in 1959, the McCoys reached No. 22 with their 1966 version, and the Ramones' 1979 version was prominent in the rock cult classic film *Rock 'n' Roll High School.* Other British singers to cover Valens songs include Cliff Richard, Gary Glitter, and Shirley Bassey.

But Valens was largely out of the public's memory in the 1970s, except for a curious incident where British heavy metal group Led Zeppelin was accused of "borrowing" extensively from Valens's "Ooh, My Head" for their own composition, "Boogie With Stu." Valens's publisher settled for $130,000, plus future royalties. Ironically, Valens's song itself was "borrowed" from a Little Richard song, "Ooh, My Soul."

Due to Holly's more extensive catalog, his music has popped up with great regularity ever since his death. As the release of songs by Holly continued into the mid-1960s, many fans claimed that the new songs weren't Holly's at all. This was especially true in England.

In Ireland, a group called the Dixies covered nine Holly songs as A-sides of singles in 1964 to 1972. In 1984, they covered "I'm Gonna Love You Too" to honor the twenty-fifth anniversary of Holly's death.

One of the most successful at covering tunes popularized by Holly in the United States has been Linda Ronstadt, who placed three of his songs on the *Billboard* charts: "It's So Easy" (No. 5, 1977), "That'll Be the Day" (No. 11, 1976), and "It Doesn't Matter Anymore" (No. 47, 1975). In addition, Ronstadt's producer, Peter Asher, had a million-seller in 1965 when he was performing with Gordon Waller as Peter & Gordon, with Holly's "True Love Ways." Country singer Mickey Gilley's recording of that same song reached the top of *Billboard*'s country singles chart in July 1980.

Jerry Allison has a simple explanation for the continuing popularity of Holly's music. "The music is easy to play."

Although Buddy Holly and Ritchie Valens are well known the world over for their music, to some fans they are just as well known for "the missing tapes." In Holly's case it's a lengthy tape of an early practice session; for Valens it's the tapes he reportedly made of the Winter Dance Party.

Devoted Holly fans have long sought a four-hour tape allegedly made by Holly's friend Bobby Peeples during an early 1957 performance at either the Cotton Club or Carlsbad's Elks Club. Bill Griggs, founder of the Buddy Holly Memorial Society, keeps an empty tape box labeled as the missing tape to tantalize visitors to his Lubbock home.

With the exception of a few clips of Holly and the Crickets on national television shows, film of him is rare. In 1983, fan Bruce Christensen found some fifty seconds of 8-mm color film of Holly performing in Michigan in 1958.

Some members of the Winter Dance Party tour claim that Valens carried a small tape recorder on the tour bus, recording voice messages to send to his mother back in Pacoima. Some fans speculate that Bob Keane still has the tapes hidden away. Others claim that they were destroyed in a 1967 house fire that severely damaged the Valenzuela home.

But Keane and other Valens friends and relatives in California claim to have no knowledge of the tapes. "I don't even think Ritchie had a small tape recorder," says Gail Smith, a close family friend and employee of Keane's at Del-Fi Records. "I was with his mom almost every day and I never heard any tapes. If there were any tapes, we would have heard them. We would have played them. They were grasping at everything they could."

There were also rumors of taped performances of Winter Dance Party shows at Milwaukee and Kenosha, but no such tapes have ever turned up over the years. It's true that several disc jockeys who emceed shows of the Winter Dance Party taped interviews and promotional spots with the stars, but those, too, have disappeared.

The plane crash that killed Buddy Holly, Ritchie Valens, and J. P. Richardson was one of a series of events that saw rock 'n' roll turn away from its roots toward a more slickly packaged product. In a way, the Winter Dance Party itself offered a glimpse of the future when the replacement acts—Frankie Avalon, Fabian, and Jimmy Clanton—were brought on board to honor the remaining dates.

These singers represented the teen idols that would rule the nation's airwaves for the next five years. By the time of the crash, Dick Clark had already replaced Alan Freed as the greatest influence on what became a national hit. Shortly after the crash, Freed was swept away by payola, while

Clark gained even more prominence. By 1960, Elvis was in the army, Little Richard was a preacher, Chuck Berry was in jail, and the great package tours that once took rock 'n' rollers from coast to coast were no more. For the first time since World War II, record sales dropped.

It's hard to tell what Holly's influence would have been had he lived: Would he have continued as a solo artist, rejoined the Crickets, or formed a new group? There's evidence to support all three outcomes.

Allen Bloom says it was clear that under Irvin Feld, "Holly was going out as a single." But according to Niki Sullivan, "Buddy had called Jerry and Joe B. and I prior to leaving on that [Winter Dance Party] tour, trying to get everything put back together. He missed all three of us." Sullivan says it was two or three days before they got Holly's messages and were unable to reach him. By then, Sullivan said, Holly had a new band together. That new band included Carl Bunch on drums, who insists that Holly was taking him on a tour of Europe following the Winter Dance Party.

Perhaps Holly would have followed the same career path as Buddy Knox, whose 1950s career closely paralleled Holly's. From 1956 to 1959 Knox and his band, the Rhythm Orchids, had as many songs on the *Billboard* charts as did Holly and the Crickets. During the same period, Knox and his band were big attractions on packaged rock tours, made many appearances on TV teen dance shows, and were featured in the movie *Jamboree.* So popular was Knox in 1959 that one of his recordings, a controversial number called "I Think I'm Gonna Kill Myself," reached No. 55 on the *Billboard* charts despite being banned from airplay at many radio stations. But Knox's popularity faded fast in the teen-idol years and he was forced from the spotlight for many years until renewed interest in oldies acts gave him a new audience for his old material.

Norman Petty told acquaintances that Holly was trying to hook up with rhythm and blues singer Ray Charles not long before his death.

According to Niki Sullivan, Ella Holley later told him that Buddy was thinking of forming a publishing company with Paul Anka, and that he wanted Sullivan to write for them.

With the exception of Hawaiian singer Robin Luke, whose "Susie Darlin'" in the summer of 1958 sounded much like Holly, there were no popular emulators of the Holly sound during his brief career. After his death, however, several singers copied his style. Among them was Tommy Roe, whose 1962 No. 1 hit, "Sheila," faithfully reproduced Holly's soft vocal style. Roe's follow-up was a cover of Luke's "Susie Darlin'."

Nowhere was Holly's influence as strong as it was in England. The first tune young John Lennon learned to play on his banjo was "That'll Be the Day." It was the same song his group, the Quarrymen, recorded on their first demonstration record in 1958. A few years later, Lennon wore horn-rimmed glasses similar to Holly's in homage to the star.

Lennon's former bandmate Paul McCartney acknowledged the Beatles' and his own debt to Holly on the *Today* show of November 1, 1988:

> We were huge fans. We used to play all his music. He used three chords and that was all we knew so that was very helpful. He had a lovely country voice that we loved. We could play his stuff and we could kind of sing like him a bit, which we tried to do. John and my first songs are very Buddy-ish.
>
> He looked like the boy next door and I think that was the secret for a lot of people because until then all the rock and roll idols had looked like Elvis and unreachable. We couldn't look like that, but we could look like Buddy.

McCartney was so influenced by Holly that he bought his idol's catalog in 1976. He soon arranged for the re-release of several Holly songs and produced an LP of Holly tunes by ex-Wings bandmate Denny Laine.

Holly had a tremendous influence on other British rockers as well. Brian Poole wore Holly-type horn-rimmed glasses and did Holly imitations as front man for the Tremeloes. Hank B. Marvin, lead guitarist for Cliff Richard's backup group, the Shadows, also copied Holly's glasses and played the same model of guitar. The Shadows recorded several Holly songs in the early 1960s. A group from Hull, England, called the Hullabaloos, faithfully copied Holly's hiccuping vocal style with its only U.S. hit in 1964, a cover of "I'm Gonna Love You Too." Earlier that year, the Rolling Stones' first U.S. release was a cover of Holly's "Not Fade Away."

In later years, British rocker Elvis Costello borrowed heavily from Holly's image, with his horn-rimmed spectacles and knock-kneed posture. However, the British rock group, the Hollies, were named for the shrub widely associated with the Christmas season, not Buddy Holly.

Holly's guitar-playing also set a standard for future rockers. He was one of the first rock 'n' rollers to popularize the Fender Stratocaster guitar. Many top guitarists of later eras carried on the Stratocaster tradition, especially Jimi Hendrix.

Holly also influenced many young musicians in his hometown of Lubbock. Jimmy Dale Gilmore wasn't quite into his teens when his guitar-playing father took him to see Johnny Cash at the Lubbock show that also featured a young Elvis Presley and included Bob Montgomery and Buddy Holly as an opening act. As Holly later started to make a name for himself, Gilmore learned to play the guitar.

At about the same time, another Lubbock youngster, Butch Hancock, was learning to play the banjo. Eventually, Hancock and Gilmore teamed with a young Lubbock rocker named Joe Ely to form a group known as the

Flatlanders. Ely went on to become a well-known rock musician in the 1970s and Gilmore's 1991 album *After Awhile* was named country music album of the year by *USA Today* and the BAM Critics Poll. The same year, Gilmore was named country artist of the year by the *Rolling Stone* Critics Poll.

Another Lubbock native who went on to rock stardom was Delbert Mc-Clinton, who was playing clubs as a teenager in the 1950s, picking up tips from blues harmonica players. In 1962 McClinton got his big break, playing on Bruce Channel's "Hey Baby." Lubbock is also the hometown of pop singer Mac Davis.

Besides Tommy Dee's "The Three Stars" and Benny Barnes's "Gold Records in the Snow," there have been dozens of tribute songs to Buddy Holly, Ritchie Valens, and J. P. Richardson over the years. One of the more successful was Mike Berry's "Tribute to Buddy Holly," which hit the British charts in late 1961 when Berry was an eighteen-year-old.

But none of the tribute records matched the overwhelming success of Don McLean's "American Pie." The Holly legend was reborn in 1971 when folksinger McLean released his song, which sold 3.5 million copies in its first six months of release.

"American Pie" was an 8 minute 27 second allegory about "the day the music died." The song was too long to fit on one side of a 45, so it was split into two parts and placed on both sides. Strong airplay pushed it to the top of the *Billboard* Hot 100 on January 15, 1972, where it stayed for four weeks.

From its release, the song sparked debate as listeners tried to interpret the cryptic lyrics. McLean has steadfastly refused to reveal his interpretation. Despite its popularity, "American Pie" was ranked as the ninth-worst single ever made by authors Jimmy Guterman and Owen O'Donnell in their book *The Worst Rock 'n' Roll Records of All Time.*

<hr />

Ritchie Valens's meteoric rise to the top of the charts proved to be a strong influence to young Latino artists everywhere, but especially in his native Southern California.

Shortly after Valens's death, Chan Romero, a seventeen-year-old Valens soundalike from Billings, Montana, arrived in Pacoima. Shortly after the plane crash, a tape of Romero had been sent to Bob Keene. Keene asked Romero to fly to Los Angeles to record one of his songs, "Hippy Hippy Shake."

"Of course, because of what happened to Ritchie and Buddy and them, I was afraid to fly," Romero recalls. "So I took a train." Romero signed with Del-Fi, and soon was in the Gold Star studio, recording with some of the same musicians who previously had accompanied Valens. Romero met

Valens's family and was invited to stay in Valens's room by Ritchie's mother, Connie.

"I became part of the family," Romero says. "One morning, Connie was fixing me breakfast, and I heard her talking to a relative on the phone. She said, 'God took my son and brought me another one.'"

Keene promoted Romero as the successor to Ritchie Valens. "Hippy Hippy Shake" was released on Del-Fi in the summer of 1959 and did well in Los Angeles. Romero's follow-up, "My Little Ruby," was less successful, and his association with Keene soon ended. "I had some problems with Bob paying me my royalties," Romero said. "That's why I quit recording for him." But Keene wouldn't release Romero from his four-year contract. "That's when my career kind of came to a standstill," Romero said.

Nevertheless, Keene's reputation as a Latino starmaker was ensured. "[Keene] opened the door. That's why we all went to him," said Billy Cardenas, a successful young producer of Los Angeles–area Chicano rockers in the 1960s. "The blacks, the Chicanos out here, we all went to him. He was hard to get to, but if he heard something, he would invite you in. He had a hell of an ear." Billy Cardenas worked for Bob Keene from 1963 to 1964 before producing other area groups, such as the Premiers, Cannibal and the Headhunters, and the Blendells.

Groups like the Carlos Brothers, Ronnie and the Pomona Casuals, and the Addrissi Brothers joined Keene's roster, along with several singers who have been referred to as "Ritchie Valens clones": Eddie Quinteros, Bobby Domino, and Vic Diaz. Another young area singer who was influenced by a meeting with Valens as a teenager was Chris Montez. In 1960, at seventeen, Montez cut his first record, "She's My Rockin' Baby."

Although the Chicano sound was largely swept aside by the British invasion of the mid-1960s, Valens's influence continued into the late 1960s as his songs continued to appear on budget record labels such as Crown and Guest Star.

A group known as ? and the Mysterians, with lead singer Rudy Martinez, rode to the top of the charts in 1966 with "96 Tears." Within four years, a Chicano group from San Francisco called Santana began a lengthy career with a song called "Evil Ways."

Shortly after Valens's death, disc jockey Art Laboe held the first of several memorial dances for Valens, at the El Monte Legion Stadium. Proceeds were to go to the Valens family. Another fund-raising effort was undertaken by Valens's former girlfriend, Donna Ludwig. Under pressure from her father, Ludwig soon found herself in the Gold Star studio to record two songs for the Pop label, which was owned by popular Los Angeles disc jockey Dick "Huggy Boy" Hugg.

"I could not believe [my father] did it to me," she says. "I said, 'I cannot sing.' . . . My father said I had no choice, but I said I won't do it unless, if it makes any money, it goes to the Valenzuela family, and I signed a contract to that effect."

Hugg had local singer Jeanette Baker help develop Donna's voice. "They gave me half a pint of Jack Daniels, that was the professional guidance," Ludwig recalls. "I was shaking like a leaf and they said, 'Here, have a sip.'" The producer later added vocal backing by a local group, the Teddy Bears. The group had struck gold with its first recording, "To Know Him Is to Love Him," written by group member Phil Spector.

In May 1959, Bob Keene announced plans to raise money for a Youth Memorial Center in Pacoima through a memorial fund to be supported by sales of collectible Valens records: the so-called "Limited Valens Memorial Series." Sales of the first release were disappointing, so Keene waited until February 1960 before trying again, proclaiming it "Ritchie Valens Month." Special parties and record hops were planned, and Del-Fi released "Paddiwack Song." The song, however, failed to chart and the Youth Memorial Center was never built.

The San Fernando High School yearbook of 1960 included a photo in memory of Valens, who would have graduated that spring. There were occasional tribute shows and dances for Valens in the early 1960s, but they ended by 1962.

Later years brought belated recognition. In 1985, a mural of Valens was dedicated at Pacoima Junior High, and he was inducted into the Hispanic Hall of Fame in Chicago in 1988. After the success of the 1987 film *La Bamba,* Valens supporters pushed for a star on the Hollywood Walk of Fame. On Friday, May 11, 1990, the bronze star for Valens was dedicated in front of 6733 Hollywood Boulevard. The family raised the $3,500 for Valens's star, No. 1913 along the three-and-a-half-mile walk. More than two hundred fans showed up for the unveiling, two days before the forty-ninth anniversary of Valens's birth. Attending were actors Esai Morales and Lou Diamond Phillips.

Lubbock was extremely slow in honoring Holly. "There's not been a lot of acceptance in the hometown. Never had been," Peggy Sue Allison says.

Although Clear Lake city officials renamed a street "Buddy Holly Drive" near the Surf Ballroom in 1988, it wasn't until 1996 that Lubbock renamed part of Avenue H "Buddy Holly Avenue." Holly's birthplace was nearly destroyed in 1978 when the Lubbock Housing Department issued a demolition order for the house on February 3, ironically exactly nineteen years after his death. When an observant fan noticed what was about to happen, the house was saved and moved out of the city.

Over the years there have been occasional attempts at honoring Holly in his hometown. In 1971, Mayor James H. Granberry signed a proclamation designating July 3, 1971, as "Buddy Holly Memorial Day" in Lubbock. A concert was scheduled to raise money for a music scholarship at Texas Tech in Holly's name.

When Paul McCartney bought Holly's North American publishing rights in 1976, the former Beatle arranged for England's first "Buddy Holly Week" to celebrate what would have been Holly's fortieth birthday on September 7, 1976. McCartney flew Norman and Vi Petty to London for the event, where they were among the honored guests at a posh champagne luncheon. The original Crickets—Jerry Allison and Joe B. Mauldin—attended, as did Linda Ronstadt, Eric Clapton, Elton John, and other contemporary rock stars. At the luncheon Norman Petty presented McCartney with the cuff links Holly was wearing at the time of the fatal crash.

In 1978, after Columbia Pictures announced it would premiere *The Buddy Holly Story* in Lubbock, the city rushed to dedicate a park in Holly's name, the Buddy Holly Recreation Area, on the outskirts of town. The park is built over an old landfill, near a tin barn where Holly used to practice his guitar. The area has been a frequent target of vandals, according to Larry Holley. "They built it out in the bad part of town. It's out there where all the drunks go to have parties."

In the late 1970s, $75,000 was raised by friends and fans through tribute concerts to commission a bigger-than-life bronze statue of Buddy Holly by Utah sculptor Grant Speed. With Holly's brother Travis serving as the model, the statue was completed and placed in front of the Lubbock Civic Center. It was dedicated on September 5, 1980, as the centerpiece for what was to become a "Walk of Fame" with plaques honoring other West Texas musicians. Waylon Jennings became the first inductee into the Walk of Fame on the same day the statue was dedicated. The statue stood for three years before an identifying plaque was unveiled in September 1983.

Bill Griggs began petitioning the United States Postal Service for a Holly stamp in the late 1970s. In 1992, Texas Representative Larry Combest took up the battle. Finally, Holly and Ritchie Valens were included in the first rock 'n' roll stamps issued in 1993 as part of the Legends of American Music series.

In 1994 the city of Lubbock purchased a 156-piece collection of Holly memorabilia for $175,000 and put it on temporary public display at the Museum of Texas Tech University on September 7, 1995, which would have been Holly's fifty-ninth birthday. The city was hoping to put the items on permanent exhibit in a yet-to-be-built Lubbock Center for the Arts.

After the first rush of articles about Buddy Holly, Ritchie Valens, and J. P. Richardson in the teen press in the months following their deaths, little appeared in print about the singers over the next fifteen years.

In 1971, Collier books published a brief biography of Holly, *Buddy Holly*, by Dave Laing. The definitive biography of Holly didn't appear until the mid-1970s, however. In the early 1970s, John Goldrosen set out to document Holly's life. Goldrosen, who was eight years old when Holly died, saved his money and embarked on what would become a 20,000-mile odyssey in search of Holly's story. Goldrosen interviewed family, friends, and professional associates of Holly before writing *Buddy Holly: His Life and Music*. The book was first published by the Bowling Green University Popular Press in 1975.

Goldrosen later teamed with John Beecher, a British Holly expert, to update the book. The slick trade paperback, full of photos, was first published in Great Britain in 1986 and has been available in the United States since 1987. Holly biographies by Ellis Amburn and Philip Norman followed in the 1990s.

Bringing Holly's life to the movie screen proved even more difficult than getting his biography published. The first serious attempt was in 1973 when the American Broadcasting Company and Universal Pictures worked with Norman Petty on a made-for-television film of Holly's career. But the project bogged down when producers were unable to get the necessary character-portrayal releases.

In the mid-1970s, Twentieth Century-Fox bought a screenplay coauthored by Jerry Allison and Tom Drake. Called *Not Fade Away,* it was a fictionalized account of what happened on tours. A cast was assembled and filming began in Mississippi in late 1975. Two weeks and some $900,000 later, Fox stopped the project.

In 1975, a company called Innovisions persuaded Holly's widow they were the ones to produce a film on the singer's life and proceeded to buy movie rights based on Goldrosen's biography.

Goldrosen says Innovisions got a real bargain, purchasing the movie rights from publisher Bowling Green Press "for a few hundred bucks." Within three years, Innovisions succeeded in bringing *The Buddy Holly Story* to the screen, although it bore little resemblance to Goldrosen's biography.

Neither Norman Petty nor Clovis were anywhere to be found in the film, and Crickets Jerry Allison and Joe B. Mauldin were renamed Jesse and Ray Bob. Holly was portrayed as his own record producer (Petty said Holly was portrayed as a "tyrant"), and his parents were portrayed as being against his musical career. "It didn't even seem like Buddy at all in the movie," Larry Holley says. "They didn't ask us anything about Buddy. The only one they asked about anybody was Maria, and she just knew Buddy for five months before he got killed."

Sonny Curtis was so incensed by the movie's factual flaws that soon after seeing the film, he wrote a song called "The Real Buddy Holly Story" in an effort to set the record straight. "When I left the movie theater [premiere in Dallas] I thought, 'What a crock,'" Curtis said. "I thought Gary Busey did a great Chuck Berry, but he missed Buddy Holly all around."

John Goldrosen, who also had problems with the movie's many inaccuracies, managed to block publication of a planned book based on the screenplay. "It really would have bothered me to see that version set down in a book," Goldrosen says. "I really felt like if I let that book go forward, I was contributing to some untruths." Eventually Goldrosen was able to settle with the movie distributors because they needed Goldrosen's permission to show the movie in England.

The movie's premiere, originally scheduled to be held in Holly's hometown of Lubbock, was actually held in several Texas cities simultaneously on May 18, 1978. Most of the film's stars were at the Medallion Theater in Dallas. Not present was the film's scriptwriter, Robert Gittler, who had committed suicide a day earlier.

The film drew good reviews and excellent crowds for much of its summer run. It didn't take long to make back the $2 to $3 million it cost to film the 114-minute movie. The movie produced more than $26 million in revenues. Its star, Gary Busey, drew consistently good notices for his portrayal of Holly and was nominated for an Academy Award as best actor.

Ironically, Busey had played Jerry Allison in the ill-fated *Not Fade Away* project. "That really irritated me," Allison said. "We sort of hung out for about six months doing that movie and a bunch of stories that I told Busey came out in *The Buddy Holly Story,* except wrong."

Busey didn't win the best actor Academy Award, which went to Warren Beatty for *Heaven Can Wait,* but *The Buddy Holly Story* won the Academy Award for best adaptation of original sound.

Iowa Public Television recognized the flaws in the film and set much of the record straight with a one-hour special, *Reminiscing,* which first aired in September 1979. The program drew praise from Bill Griggs of the Buddy Holly Memorial Society: "For six years, this was the best documentary done about Buddy Holly."

In 1985, Paul McCartney, in a joint venture with the BBC and MCA, sent a camera crew to Lubbock and Clovis to produce the documentary that most Holly fans think does the best job of clearing up many of the distortions left by the commercial film.

The program first aired on the BBC on September 9, 1985, and was released as a ninety-minute videotape in the United States by Sony Video two years later as *The Real Buddy Holly Story.*

The success of the Holly movie also spawned a few plays. One short-lived play, *The Adventures of Buddy Holly,* premiered in Dallas on September 26, 1980. Another, *Buddy Holly at the Regal,* opened at the Greenwich Theatre in London on August 22, 1985, to begin a fourteen-week English run.

Most successful was another play, *Buddy,* which debuted in London in October 1989 with American Paul Hipp portraying Holly. The twenty-five-year-old Philadelphia-born Hipp was nominated for an Olivier Award for his performance, which repaid its $1.1 million investment in the first fifteen weeks. It celebrated its 1,000th performance in London on February 3, 1992, exactly thirty-three years after Holly's death. The play, written by Alan Janes, opened on Broadway in New York's Shubert Theater on November 4, 1990, and was generally panned by New York critics, largely for the cliché-ridden story line of the first half of the program, which purported to encapsulate Holly's life. The second half of the play, a reenactment of Holly's last performance in Clear Lake, fared better in most critics' eyes. The play ran for 225 performances before folding after the May 19, 1991, show. Hipp was nominated for a Tony Award as best actor in a musical, however, and the show later toured the United States, including a 1993 performance at the Surf Ballroom in Clear Lake.

The life story of Ritchie Valens took even longer to reach the screen, although Bob Keane says he was approached about a Valens film five or six times starting in the mid-1970s.

By the mid-1980s, however, California playwright Luis Valdez and his brother, Danny, persuaded the Valens family to allow them to try to film Valens's life story. Luis Valdez, an award-winning playwright with *Zoot Suit* and *Corridos,* wrote the screenplay for the movie *La Bamba,* to be directed by his brother. At auditions, actor Esai Morales originally read for Ritchie's part and Lou Diamond Phillips auditioned for the part of Ritchie's half-brother, Bob. Phillips was cast as Valens, however, with Morales taking Bob's part.

The movie was shot in forty-five days in the summer of 1986 with a budget of $6.5 million. Several Valens family members appeared in small parts. *La Bamba* became the first Hollywood feature to be released in Spanish and English versions in July 1987, and did exceedingly well at the box office, grossing more than $100 million worldwide in its first four years. Not long after *La Bamba* was released, a Valens biography was published, *Ritchie Valens: The First Latino Rocker* by Beverly A. Mendheim.

After the success of *La Bamba,* the J. P. Richardson family started receiving phone calls from film people wanting to complete the trilogy started with *The Buddy Holly Story.* "We were contacted by no less than eight different companies," says Jay P. Richardson. Michael Montgomery wrote a screenplay of the Big Bopper's life, and his son helped Montgomery research his father's colorful life.

"In the first six months after we started the project, I learned ten times more about my father than I knew before," Jay said. "I know him now. I'm doing something that should have been done a long time ago."

With a working title of *Chantilly Lace,* the project was stalled in the 1990s due to a lack of financial backing. However, Jay P. Richardson had an option agreement with another company in 1996 for a film based on a different script.

Meanwhile, Tim Knight collaborated with the Richardson family in 1989 to publish a mostly photographic review of J. P. Richardson's life through the Port Arthur (Texas) Historical Society.

Family Affairs

After Holly's death, his parents filled one room of their Lubbock home with many of his personal belongings, including his tape recorder, hi-fi, and guitar, complete with the leather cover he had hand-tooled as a youngster. They later added the gold record they were presented in 1970 for the LP *The Buddy Holly Story.* "You'd walk in that house and it was just like Buddy left there yesterday," Waylon Jennings said.

"We felt a little guilty after he was killed," Ella Holley later said. "Maybe if we hadn't encouraged him, he would have gone another way and not been killed."

Holly's father, Lawrence Odell Holley, died at the age of eighty-three in 1985 and his mother died in 1990 at the age of eighty-seven.

Larry Holley has acted as family spokesman while his brother, Travis, and sister, Pat, stay in the background. Larry has stayed in the tile business since Holly's death, while dabbling in the music business and looking after Buddy's affairs as much as possible from his home in Lubbock.

Besides working with Norman Petty in redubbing Holly's New York apartment tapes, Larry Holley recorded singer Gene Evans at Petty's in 1979. That same year, Larry and Travis Holley teamed up with Larry's children, Sherry and Randy, to record a fourteen-song album, *Holly's House: A Family Album.* In 1987, Sherry Holley's version of "Raining in My Heart" was released as a single. She recut the song in 1991 for a fourteen-song cassette, *Looking Through Buddy's Eyes,* which included twelve songs previously recorded by her uncle. Sherry Holley has appeared with the Crickets, Bobby Vee, Carl Perkins, Sonny Curtis, and Buddy Knox, and has performed in London and Scotland.

Larry Holley received his private pilot's license just two weeks before his brother was killed, and has owned five airplanes. He is still upset that his brother had to participate in the Winter Dance Party tour. "All he was seeing was chicken feed and he was having to make it on his tours. Royalty money came in through Petty, and Petty was hanging on to it. He was going to make him beg for it.

"I think if Buddy would have got hold of enough money to knock off for about two or three months, he would have slacked off and got a handle on everything and really started using his head on how he was going to run his life. But that didn't get to happen."

Maria Elena Holly, who told Buddy she was pregnant just three weeks before he left on the Winter Dance Party, had a miscarriage two days after Holly's death. Because the young couple had chosen to keep Maria's self-diagnosed pregnancy a secret until after the tour, she didn't share news of the miscarriage with her in-laws, either. She married Joe Diaz a year later. They had three children then divorced in the late 1980s.

Holley family members think Buddy would have divorced Maria, too. "I really feel like [Maria] was a bounce back marriage," Larry Holley says. "I think his true love was Echo McGuire. . . . I don't feel Buddy would have been married to [Maria Elena] for two years and neither did Mother. She said Buddy wouldn't have stayed married to her very long."

Immediately following Holly's death, Maria Elena was swamped with mail from adoring fans, much of which was answered by Holly's mother in Lubbock. Maria worked as a switchboard operator in the New York office of the Commonwealth of Puerto Rico. In the summer of 1959, Maria Elena returned to Lubbock to ensure her position as Holly's legal heir. She filed papers in the Lubbock County Courthouse to establish her claim, and sold some property Holly had bought in 1958.

Since Holly's death, Maria Elena has been an outspoken protector of his image and property. She has visited her husband's former hometown many times, but has never been to his grave. In 1987, Maria Elena testified before the Texas legislature on behalf of a bill to prohibit unauthorized use of a personality's name or image for fifty years after his or her death. The bill passed and anyone wishing to use Holly's name or likeness in Texas must receive permission from her.

Some of Holly's biggest fans are critical of Maria Elena's management of Holly's image, contending that she often "sells out" to the highest bidder. Holly biographer John Goldrosen, who first interviewed her in the fall of 1973, says that wasn't always the case, though. "We had a couple of great days together," Goldrosen says. "It wasn't until later on, when she started seeing the money that was involved in the movie and everything, that things got stickier."

Maria Elena declined to be interviewed for this book, explaining: "I'm so skeptical about interviewing for a book because they ask you about something and then they turn around, they print something else. . . . I've had very bad experiences . . . I told myself I would never do this again. . . . I have a very bad taste in my mouth with some of these things."

Maria Elena has defended her capitalizing on her late husband's name and talents in interviews, but her role in managing Holly's affairs has created a bitter split between her and Holly's family. Things went fairly smoothly between the Holley family and Maria Elena for nearly thirty years, according to Larry. "Maria Elena didn't want to keep anything that Buddy had," he says. "She didn't want any reminders. But that's all changed."

Things got tense after the Holley family leased several of Holly's personal effects to the Hard Rock Cafe in Dallas for $12,000 a year. "It rocked on for about a year," Larry Holley said. "Everybody was happy. . . . When Maria finally found out, she started realizing there was some money to be had from things like that. So she got an injunction, saying it wasn't ours to lease."

After spending some $75,000 in legal fees, the Holleys eventually joined forces with Maria Elena. "Since then we've been yoked up together," Larry says. "Not that I like it so much, but it's the only thing we could do. We can't split the stuff and she didn't want it."

After lengthy negotiations, many of Holly's personal possessions were sold on June 23, 1990, at a public auction conducted by Sotheby's in New York City. The auction netted $703,615, twice what Sotheby's expected. Half the money came from the sale of two of Holly's guitars. Gary Busey paid $242,000 for Holly's acoustic Gibson J-45, complete with the leather case Holly hand-tooled. The Fender Stratocaster Holly played on the Winter Dance Party tour sold for $110,000 to an unidentified buyer. The Hard Rock Cafe paid $45,100 for a pair of Holly's glasses, and singer Patrick Dinizio of the rock group the Smithereens paid $14,300 for the Ampex reel-to-reel tape recorder Holly used to record his "apartment tapes" shortly before his death.

Among other items sold by Sotheby's were clothing, Holly's first-grade report card, a Cub Scout belt, and handwritten homework and lyric sheets. One fan paid $5,225 for Holly's record collection and turntable. The auction catalog said it was "the personal collection of 45 r.p.m. records which Buddy Holly carried while he was on tour." Yet among the records listed were Bobby Vee's *What Do You Want?* on Liberty Records, which wasn't recorded until 1960, and Ritchie Valens's "Donna"/"La Bamba" on the Trip label, which came out decades after Holly's death.

Adrianne "Teetsie" Richardson remained in Beaumont with her daughter, Debra Joy, after J. P. was buried. On April 28, 1959, she gave birth to a son, Jay Perry. Within two years, she married Andrew Wenner of Beaumont.

As young Jay P. Richardson grew up in Beaumont, he found life in the shadow of a father he never knew difficult. "I really didn't know that much about him," Jay P. says of his father. "Mother remarried and it wasn't something that was discussed in the household. There weren't any pictures on the wall, gold records. You walked into the house, you wouldn't even know he was there.

"It was rough. I left home when I was fourteen. It was tuggin' at me, I guess. Wherever I'd go on the streets of Beaumont, I would hear, 'Oh, you're the Big Bopper's son.' I was hearing it from everybody else, but I wasn't gettin' the story from home."

When he was fifteen, Jay P. Richardson wrote a poem about his father.

SECOND-HAND MEMORIES

The only things I know about my dad
Comes from stories other folks have told.
Of course, I have all his million-sellers
On my wall coated in gold.
Thru the years past I've learned to love
A man I'll never know or ever see.
I just wish I had something more
Than these second-hand Big Bopper memories.

I often wonder what inspired him
To write a song like "Chantilly Lace."
When I ask Mom if it was her, she just smiles
And gets a faraway look on her face.
There's not a night that passes
That he doesn't walk thru my dreams and have a talk
with me;
I just wish I had something more
Than these second-hand Big Bopper memories.

I had a dream long ago
And someday I hope to follow it thru:
To travel around this world
And meet all the people my daddy knew.
Then my heart could be at rest
And my ole mind set free.
I just wish I had something more
Than these second-hand Big Bopper memories.

After seeing *The Buddy Holly Story* in 1978, Jay P. Richardson headed for Nashville. "I was going to be a star, but I didn't know my ass from a hole in the ground," he says. "As a kid, I found out that I could sound just like my father. I'd go to my grandparents' every summer at the beach about an hour from Beaumont. They had all of my dad's records and we'd sit around and I'd play them and I'd sing them for Grandma and she'd sit there with big old tears in her eyes."

His father's close friend and manager, Bill Hall, helped him in Nashville, but young Richardson quickly found out that his future didn't include musical stardom. He returned to Texas where he worked on offshore oil rigs and as a carpet installer, a trade he learned from his stepfather. Richardson quit laying carpet when he was hired as a research consultant for the proposed movie on his father. He learned a great deal about his father in the process.

"He hated [touring]," Jay P. Richardson says. "His motivation wasn't the roar of the crowd. . . . It was money. I love his music. I listen real good to his songs. He's having a good time, there's no doubt about it. That's not a show. . . . But it's not something he would have continued. . . . He wouldn't have needed that because he was going to make all the money he wanted in residuals and writing songs.

"He loved my sister like there was no tomorrow. He loved Mother. He was the ultimate family man. You just wouldn't know him by the Big Bopper. It wasn't him at all."

Jay P. Richardson made his first visit to the Surf Ballroom in June 1988 when a monument was dedicated to the four who died in the crash. There he was presented with his father's watch, found by the Albert Juhl family in their stubble field, months after the crash. When Jay P. arrived at the Surf—with his hair in a flattop, long dark jacket over light blue jeans, white shirt, and sneakers—the resemblance to his father was striking. "I couldn't believe it when I first met him," recalls Connie Alvarez, Ritchie Valens's sister. "He looked just like the pictures of his father."

Jay P. took it all in stride, meeting with fans and signing autographs while exchanging light banter and occasionally breaking into a hearty laugh. In the years since his appearance at the Surf, Jay P. has made numerous appearances around the country while managing his father's affairs through record deals. He tried to negotiate a deal with the producers of the play *Buddy* and worked out merchandising agreements with Kraft Cheese and Pizza Hut.

In February 1989, Rhino Records released a Bopper compilation, *Hellooo Baby!* The family still collects royalties from J. P. Richardson's music; his son was presented a gold record for "Chantilly Lace" from Polygram in 1990.

In the spring of 1991, Jay P. opened a nightclub called Little Bopper's in Katy, Texas, near Houston. Big Bopper memorabilia was displayed on the club's walls, and entertainment was vintage 1950s: Phil Phillips, Frankie Ford, Roy Head, Johnny Preston, Gene Thomas, Joe Barry, and Rod Bernard. Ernie Valens, Ritchie's nephew, played at the grand opening. Richardson sold the club a year later.

Plans for a Big Bopper movie stalled in the early 1990s, but Jay P. is still trying to get the project back on track. In 1996, he started performing Big Bopper tunes at conventions and recorded some of his father's songs with the Rockin' Robins for a possible CD release. Producer Mike Franklin arranged for James Burton, Ace Cannon, the Jordanaires, and the Crickets to participate in the recording sessions.

Nearly four decades after the accident that took his father, Jay P. Richardson occasionally thinks about the crash, and why it happened. "I've even thought, could it have been sabotage," he says. "It's all possible. Maybe improbable, but possible. People don't realize how they were depicted back then and what they were doing. They might have had a thousand kids there that night who loved them to death, but for every one or two kids, there were ten or fifteen adults who thought they weren't worth a damn."

When traveling, Jay P. flies only in large planes. "I made up my mind a long time ago that if the plane isn't big enough to put about one hundred people in there, then I don't get in them," he said. "Those small planes, they can have them."

Teetsie's marriage to Andrew Wenner resulted in three sons and a daughter before they divorced in the mid-1980s. J. P. Richardson's brother, Gilbert, later moved to Alaska. Another brother, Cecil Alan, tried to follow in his brother's footsteps as a songwriter as "Big Daddy" Richardson, but with little success. He died in Beaumont in 1989.

Misfortune has followed Debbie Richardson ever since her father died when she was just five years old. As a young girl, she and her father were very close, Teetsie Wenner says. "[He did the] things any ordinary father does," she recalls. "Took walks and played dolls with her."

Richardson also managed to evoke a giggle from Debbie by his teasing. "You sure are a pretty little thing," he'd say, pausing for her giggle before finishing, "just like me."

But Debbie had a nasty fall from a car as a youngster, married young, and found herself in an abusive relationship, with two young children of her own. She once had to have surgery to remove fluid from her brain. "She got mixed up with the wrong crowd, married the wrong guy," Teetsie says. As Debbie was unable to care for herself in her adult years, Cecil Richardson served as her guardian for several years before his death. She has lived in a Beaumont nursing home ever since.

At her home in Pacoima, California, Connie Valenzuela soon set up a memorial to the son she called "Ritchie Boy." She displayed his guitars in the living room and hung his black cowboy hat in his bedroom, where a closetful of his clothes remained, undisturbed. About one month after the plane crash, Connie Valenzuela opened her home to friends and relatives for nine straight nights of rosaries in Spanish.

"It was so hard after he passed away," says Ernestine Reyes, Valens's aunt. "I couldn't even listen to any of his songs." A steady stream of visitors in the weeks after Valens's death kept the family from getting on with their lives.

"Shortly after Ritchie was killed, [reporters from teen magazines] were at the house quite a bit," says Gail Smith, a close friend of the family and then-president of the Ritchie Valens Fan Club. "They were always there, taking pictures and talking to everybody. You couldn't even walk into the house without them being there."

A surprise visitor was Diane Olson, the girl from New York whom Ritchie had met while doing an Alan Freed show. "She said she was Ritchie's girlfriend," Donna Ludwig Fox says. "That's the first I had heard of her." But Ritchie had mentioned Olson to his aunt Ernestine in January, before leaving for the Winter Dance Party. When Ernestine asked Ritchie about her, he said: "She just rubbed my back."

"I think she was more like a fan in love," Ernestine says. "She madly fell in love with him. But Ritchie never told us he was madly in love with her. He just told me that she was his masseuse."

Still, Olson lived in Connie Valenzuela's house for several weeks. "She was taking advantage of the family there for a while," says Ernestine. Olson took a job in Burbank and granted the teen press several interviews during her short stay in Pacoima, talking about her aspirations for a singing career and her plans for an album based on Ritchie's life. She talked about her steady dating with Ritchie and their plans for marriage.

Although the family largely dismisses Olson's claims of a serious relationship with Valens, Gail Smith thinks Olson was closer to Ritchie than just a star-struck fan. "Diane and I got pretty close when she came out here from New York," she says. "The things she knew were very valid and I think she and Ritchie were very close."

Nevertheless, Olson disappeared just as quickly and unexpectedly as she had arrived in Pacoima. "She worked and she got enough money and took off," Ernestine says. "We have not heard from her [again]."

Connie Valenzuela used money raised from contributions and a series of benefit dances to buy a tombstone for Ritchie's grave. On May 13, 1959—which would have been Ritchie's eighteenth birthday—Connie and about a dozen members of his fan club gathered at his grave, all dressed in white, to have a photograph taken as his tombstone was set in place. "We had a big thing of flowers done up like a guitar," Donna Ludwig Fox remembers.

Connie Valenzuela returned to work to support her family until Ritchie's estate could be settled. Valens's biographer Beverly Mendheim says Connie eventually received about $40,000 in late 1960 as settlement of the estate. The family continued to make payments into the 1990s on the house Ritchie bought for his mother. Ernestine Reyes explains that "Connie borrowed money on top of it."

The family lost many of its mementos of Ritchie in a house fire in late 1967, about a week before Christmas. Nobody was seriously injured in the blaze, but the family Christmas gifts were destroyed as was just about everything of Ritchie's that the family owned, including one of his guitars. "I found his gold record back there. All burned," says Ernestine Reyes, who later had the record restored.

As the movie *La Bamba* was released in the summer of 1987, Ritchie was once again thrust into the limelight. By the end of the year, the family had reclaimed all of Valens's musical publishing rights.

The family places flowers on Ritchie's grave at least twice each year, on his birthday and on February 3.

Connie Valenzuela continued to protect her remaining children over the years and dissuaded them from flying. In fact, daughter Irma's first flight was to Seattle for the premiere of *La Bamba.* Connie indulged in an uncharacteristic bit of luxury in 1987 when she bought a late-model Cadillac, complete with personalized HI-TONE license plates. She enjoyed three months of adulation from a new generation of Ritchie Valens fans following the release of *La Bamba* before she died on October 18, 1987.

Bob Morales, Ritchie's older half-brother, settled in the Watsonville, California, area in the early 1970s. He and Rosie split in 1974. After the success of *La Bamba,* Morales moved his family from a trailer to a five-acre homestead and started an upholstery business with his second wife, Joanie. He also pursued his hobby of restoring classic cars.

Irma Norton was too young to really remember her half-brother Ritchie. "I remember Mama kept some of Ritchie's clothes in a suitcase in our garage," she said. "They were so pretty. I used to sneak into the garage and take them out of the suitcase just to look at them." Irma also settled in the Watsonville area, where she worked as a preschool teacher.

Connie Alvarez, Ritchie's half-sister, who lives in Prunedale, California, says she can't watch the end of *La Bamba*. She says she didn't look at any photos of the crash until 1991. She made her first visit to Clear Lake in January 1988 with Bob and Joanie Morales. They hiked to the crash site in bitter cold and left a bouquet of carnations, Ritchie's favorite flower, on the snow.

Alvarez has made several trips around the country on behalf of the family and found the experience to be emotionally exhausting. "It's been a highly sensitive time for us, too," she says. "You just start to feeling so used. It's not who you are, but it's who you were related to. I'll meet people who barely give you the time of day . . . but don't let somebody say, 'Oh, this is Ritchie Valens's sister,' because let me tell you, it's a different person. After three years of that, it just gets kind of old."

Rosie Morales remarried after her split from Bob. Many times since her second marriage, she has traveled from Pacoima to Ashland, Wisconsin, to visit in-laws, not realizing that Ritchie had bused through many of the same towns near the train route. She's never been in Clear Lake, although she has been tempted when her train stops in St. Paul, Minnesota, some 120 miles north of the Surf Ballroom. "Sometimes I think maybe I should stay here a few more days and try to get over there," she says.

Ernestine Reyes continued to act as a sort of family spokesman after Connie Valenzuela died in 1987. With Marcia Farley of Greenwood, Indiana, she operated a fan club for Ritchie in the late 1980s. "Keeping Ritchie's memory alive is the most important part," Ernestine says. But poor health and personal problems led to the club's demise by 1992.

Ernestine's son, Ernie, is following in Ritchie's musical footsteps. "The first time that I heard [Ernie sing], I thought he was playing Ritchie's tapes," Ernestine says. Ernie Reyes took the stage name of Ernie Valens, and started working with a band that took the name Valenz, and signed a three-album deal with Bob Keane's reactivated Del-Fi label. Ernie Valens performed at the Surf Ballroom at the February 1991 annual tribute show and returned to the Midwest later that summer to play at an Eddie Cochran festival.

While escorting Ernie to that performance, Ernestine and Lelo Reyes made their first trip to Clear Lake, stopping to visit the Surf Ballroom and crash site. While Ernie Valens hiked the half-mile from the road to the crash site, Ernestine "just watched from the motor home. . . . It was kind of sad and very depressing."

But Ernestine also carries the happy memories of Ritchie. "He's still with us, as far as I'm concerned," Ernestine says. "Even though he's down there in San Fernando Mission Cemetery, but my heart just tells me he's right here. It's very hard to forget him, that's for sure."

After Roger Peterson's funeral, Art and Pearl Peterson received letters from Ritchie Valens's family, Donna Ludwig Fox, and Buddy Holly's mother. Art gave up flying in 1963. He and Pearl retired from farming, but continued to live in the converted schoolhouse near Alta, until moving to town in the 1990s. For many years Roger was little more than a footnote to rock music's first great tragedy.

"It's just like he never existed," Pearl Peterson says. "Like he was a no-body, vanished into thin air or something." The Petersons have donated money to their church over the years in Roger's name.

Ron Peterson, the brother who helped Roger take instrument training, sneaked away from the family farm to take flying lessons after Roger's accident. He became a commercial pilot in Omaha, flying the jets Roger only dreamed of flying. About ten years after the accident, Ron applied for work at Dwyer Flying Service in Mason City. "Ron looked just like Roger," says Barb Dwyer. "I got goose bumps. . . . I wanted to hire him, but it was just too much. It brought back too many memories."

DeAnn Lenz Peterson returned to Alta where she lived for a few weeks after the crash. She turned down a job offer from a Storm Lake bank, and went to the Twin Cities where she landed a job with an airline one month after Roger was killed. She remarried in 1969 and lives in Minnesota.

Fairview School was closed around 1960 and the building was used to raise hogs. "It's a mess," Pearl Peterson says.

Larry Anderson, who was best man at Roger and DeAnn Peterson's wedding, went on to become manager of the Storm Lake airport. He was killed in a 1970 airplane accident.

Lambert Fechter, one of Peterson's instrument instructors, was killed just four months after Roger Peterson, on June 4, 1959, in an airplane accident near Hartley, Iowa, while giving instrument training to a student pilot.

Jerry Dwyer, owner of the Beechcraft Bonanza that carried Buddy Holly, Ritchie Valens, J. P. Richardson, and Roger Peterson to their deaths, was still operating a very successful flying service at the Mason City airport in the 1990s. Even after thirty-plus years, Dwyer refuses all requests for interviews.

"We get calls from everywhere—overseas," says Barb Dwyer. "And some of them are real kooks. There's kids that weren't even born when Buddy Holly died that, the way they talk, you wonder if they could do harm to you. They're not balanced mentally."

Barb says that a local urban legend that Jerry had the wreckage of the Bonanza buried under a runway at the Mason City airport during later construction is not true, but confirms that her husband has kept parts of the plane.

"We have people that say, why don't you sell pieces of the airplane, you could make a million dollars," she says. "The *National Enquirer* has approached [Jerry] several times.

"Other than this one accident, we haven't had any other incidents. And we've flown all of the presidential candidates, we get calls out of New York and everywhere. We do a lot of charter work. The FAA says we have one of the cleanest records of anybody."

Barb adds mysteriously, "If you knew all the facts about the whole thing, there's a lot that has never come out. There's a lot of things that have never come out, and they never will."

The farmhouse occupied by Albert and Elsie Juhl when the Beechcraft Bonanza crashed in the field behind it in the early morning hours of February 3, 1959. *(Courtesy Larry Lehmer collection)*

A pump stands in the front yard of the Albert and Elsie Juhl farm. The Beechcraft Bonanza narrowly missed the house before crashing behind it. *(Courtesy Larry Lehmer collection)*

Pilot Roger Peterson
(Courtesy DeAnn Lenz Peterson)

Dick Van Slyke of Ward Funeral Home talks with Surf Ballroom Manager Carroll Anderson *(foreground)* while Cerro Gordo County Coroner Ralph Smiley begins his investigation of the accident on February 3, 1959.
(Elwin Musser/Mason City Globe-Gazette)

Officials and the news media survey the aircraft wreckage on February 3, 1959. Cerro Gordo County Deputy Sheriff Lowell Sanquist kneels over a wheel while Coroner Ralph Smiley points to Deputy Bill McGill right behind him. Mason City *Globe-Gazette* reporter Jim Collison is in the dark coat with light fur collar in the center of the photo. Dick Van Slyke of Ward Funeral Home is to the right of Collison and Wendell Wilcox of the Wilcox Funeral Home is walking right in front of the wreckage. Surf Ballroom Manager Carroll Anderson is walking toward the wing of the demolished Bonanza and John G. "Andy" Anderson, editor of the Clear Lake *Mirror-Reporter,* is at the far right. *(Elwin Musser/Mason City Globe-Gazette)*

Cerro Gordo County Coroner Ralph Smiley looks at Buddy Holly's suitcase
during his investigation of the crash scene. The body of J. P. Richardson
can be seen between Smiley and the wreckage, across the barbed wire fence.
(Elwin Musser/Mason City Globe-Gazette)

This photo appeared in hundreds of papers around the country after it was distributed by the Associated Press. Cerro Gordo County Deputy Sheriff Lowell Sanquist faces the wreckage as ambulances and law enforcement vehicles approach the crash site. The bodies of Buddy Holly *(wearing light coat)* and Ritchie Valens are to the right of the wreckage.

(Elwin Musser/Mason City Globe-Gazette)

The bodies of Buddy Holly *(left)* and Ritchie Valens flank the demolished Bonanza.
(Elwin Musser/Mason City Globe-Gazette)

Federal Aviation Administration investigators Eugene Anderson and Fred Becchetti
begin combing through the wreckage of the Bonanza on Wednesday morning,
February 4, 1959, for clues to the cause of the accident.
(Elwin Musser/Mason City Globe-Gazette)

Deputy Bill McGill stands over the body of Buddy Holly *(left)* while Deputy Lowell Sanquist continues his examination *(center)*. The body of Ritchie Valens is to the right, in front of the wing and in front of the unidentified man who appears to be carrying a motion picture camera. *(Copyright © Kevin Terry)*

Several items recovered at the crash site in 1959 sat in an envelope in the Cerro Gordo County Courthouse in Mason City, Iowa, for twenty-one years before being discovered by Sheriff Jerry Allen in February 1980. Included were the frames of Buddy Holly's well-known eyeglasses, an inscribed watch presented to J. P. Richardson after his 1957 Disc-a-thon, a cigarette lighter, four dice, a watchband and the back of another watch. *(Copyright © Kevin Terry)*

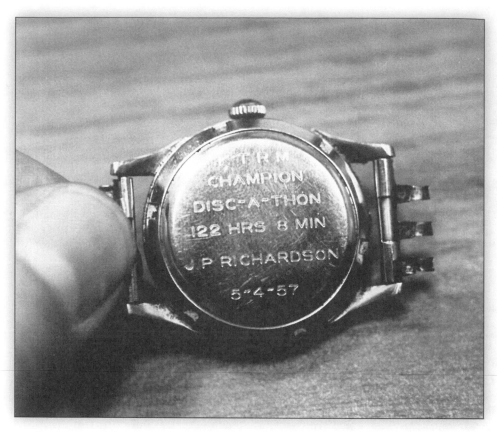

Close-up view of J. P. Richardson's watch, which sat in the Cerro Gordo County Courthouse for twenty-one years before being found in February 1980. The watch was later returned to the singer's son. *(Copyright © Kevin Terry)*

Horizontal shot of monument at crash site *(Courtesy Larry Lehmer collection)*

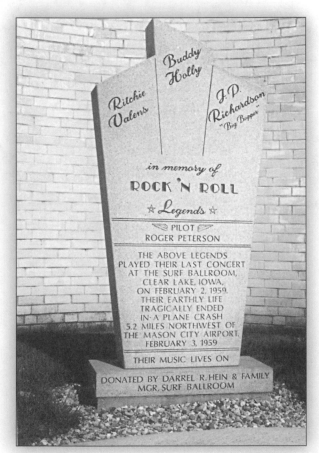

This monument at the Surf Ballroom was dedicated on June 18, 1988.
(Courtesy Larry Lehmer collection)

Buddy Holly's grave in Lubbock, with the family spelling of *Holley*
(*Courtesy Larry Lehmer collection*)

The casket containing the body of J. P. Richardson awaits burial at Broussard's Funeral Home in Beaumont. The flower arrangement with the guitar came from U.S. Army Private Elvis Presley. *(Courtesy Jay Perry Richardson)*

```
                    ITINERARY FOR J.P. RICHARDSON
                          (BIG BOPPER)
                    JAN. 23RD THRU FEB. 15TH


        JANUARY 23...GEORGE DEVINE'S BALLROOM, MILWAUKEE, WISCONSIN
        JANUARY 24...KENOSHA, WISCONSIN
        JANUARY 25...KATO BALLROOM, MANKATO, MINNESOTA
        JANUARY 26...OPEN Eu Clare, Wisconsin
        JANUARY 27...FIESTA BALLROOM, MONTEVIDEO, MINNESOTA
        JANUARY 28...PROM BALLROOM, ST. PAUL, MINNESOTA
        JANUARY 29...CAPITOL THEATRE, DAVENPORT, IOWA
        JANUARY 30...LARAMAR BALLROOM, FORT DODGE, IOWA
        JANUARY 31...ARMORY, DULUTH, MINNESOTA
        FEBRUARY 1...CINDERELLA BALLROOM, APPLETON, WISCONSIN (AFTERNOON)
                     RIVERSIDE BALLROOM, GREEN BAY, WISCONSIN (EVENING)
        FEBRUARY 2...OPEN—Clearlake, Iowa
        FEBRUARY 3...OPEN—Moorhead, Minn —
        FEBRUARY 4...OPEN—
        FEBRUARY 5...VAL AIR BALLROOM, DES MOINES, IOWA
        FEBRUARY 6...DANCELAND BALLROOM, CEDAR RAPIDS, IOWA
        FEBRUARY 7...LES BUZZ BALLROOM, SPRING VALLEY, ILLINOIS
 WCFL   FEBRUARY 8...ARAGON BALLROOM, CHICAGO, ILLINOIS = Carmen Anthony
 WIND   FEBRUARY 9...HIPPODROME BALLROOM AUDITORIUM, WATERLOO, IOWA San Doremus
        FEBRUARY 10..MELODY MILL, DUBUQUE, IOWA
 WKLO — FEBRUARY 11..MEMORIAL AUDITORIUM, LOUISVILLE, KENTUCKY—Paul Cowley
        FEBRUARY 12..MEMORIAL AUDITORIUM, CANTON, OHIO Coshocton, ohio
        FEBRUARY 13..STAMBAUGH AUDITORIUM, YOUNGSTOWN, OHIO Muskegon
        FEBRUARY 14..PEORIA, ILLINOIS
        FEBRUARY 15..SPRINGFIELD, ILLINOIS
       11 00
```

J. P. Richardson's tour itinerary with hand-written notes. Note that the
Clear Lake and Moorhead shows were penciled in at the last minute.
Radio stations and disc jockeys to contact to promote the tour were also
added by Richardson. *(Courtesy Jay Perry Richardson)*

DWYER FLYING SERVICE

MUNICIPAL AIRPORT

ESTIMATED WEIGHT AND BALANCE ON BEECHCRAFT N3794N
ON ITS LAST FLIGHT FEB. 3, 1959

	WEIGHT	ARM	MOMENT
Empty Weight	1590	77.5	123225
Gas 39 Gal	234	75	17550
Oil 21/2 Gal.	19	43	817
Pilot	165	85	14035
F. Pass	190	85	16150
R. Pass	145	117	16965
R. Pass	165	117	19305
Baggage Est.	43	140	6020
	2551 lbs.		214057

Range for this flight / 82.4 to / 84.8

Loaded C.G. / 83.09
This is an estimate to the best of my knowledge.

/s/ Hubert J. Dwyer
Hubert J. Dwyer

CIVIL AERONAUTICS BOARD
I have compared this and certify it to be a
true copy.

Signature   AIR SAFETY
             INVESTIGATOR
Title
Bureau of Safety

Detail of CAB report showing the Dwyer Flight Service's weight and balance report

A receipt for the $36 fare paid by J. P. Richardson for the ill-fated flight from Mason City was found in his wallet after the crash.
(Courtesy Jay Perry Richardson)

Headline in *Mason City Globe Gazette* announcing the crash

The Fans

London, England — Meeting Buddy Holly during his British tour in 1958 proved inspirational to young Stephen Pike.

But Holly's death in an American airplane crash last February was just too much for the fifteen-year-old to bear.

After Pike was found electrocuted in his bedroom with a stack of Holly's records on his bed and clippings about the fatal accident nearby, a coroner began an investigation.

After discovering letters written by young Stephen claiming that Holly's death had made it impossible to fulfill his future plans, the coroner ruled the death a suicide.

Fans of Buddy Holly, Ritchie Valens, and the Big Bopper have kept the singers' memories alive in the years since the accident. Most fans are content to buy their records, listen to the music, and read whatever they can about their idols. Others go further.

Norman Petty said he regularly received phone calls from someone purporting to be Buddy Holly. Bill Griggs, one of the founders of the Buddy Holly Memorial Society, receives a letter from "Holly" every February, stating he is alive and well and living in Georgia.

In September 1976, the week before the first Buddy Holly Week in Great Britain, two British fans claimed to have contacted Holly in the great beyond and reported he requested that the pair tell Norman Petty that "Buddy said hello."

Holly memorabilia has been popular ever since his death. Collectors have been known to buy anything remotely associated with the singer. When four copies of Holly's 1953 high school yearbook were discovered in a storage room at Lubbock High, a Lubbock man sold them for $150 apiece. "British fans, especially, will buy just about anything," Bill Griggs says. "They'll take anything that says Iowa and has the year 1959."

Not surprisingly, it was the British who formed the first Buddy Holly fan club, in 1958. By the time a satellite club got started in the United States in 1963, the London-based Buddy Holly Appreciation Society had some three thousand members. Although the U.S. club died within two years, a group of American fans created the Buddy Holly Memorial Society in 1976. It operated for nearly fifteen years before folding.

Bob Keene kept the Ritchie Valens Memorial Fan Club going through the mid-1960s, but efforts at creating a Ritchie Valens fan club after the success of the movie *La Bamba* sputtered in the late 1980s.

The Big Bopper, who enjoyed a bigger following overseas, never benefited from an organized fan club.

By 1996, there were no viable United States fan clubs for any of the three singers. However, the British Buddy Holly Society, which was formed in the early 1980s, was still going strong. A magazine for Crickets fans, *Crickets File,* continued to be published three times a year in England. Editor John Firminger said the magazine, which started in 1979, had around two hundred subscribers. In 1994, Jim Carr started publishing *Holly International,* a quarterly British magazine dedicated to Holly's life and music.

British record producer Joe Meek was one of Holly's biggest fans. After serving time in the British national service as a radar technician, Meek worked as a television engineer before moving on to independent record production in mid-1957. While perfecting his craft, Meek designed and built his own studio in North London. He bought used equipment using royalties from "Put a Ring On Her Finger," a 1958 song he wrote for pop singer Tommy Steele.

Meek also owned his own label in 1960 before poor distribution forced him to shut it down. An association with songwriter Geoff Goddard in 1961 led to a No. 1 British hit, "Johnny Remember Me" by John Leyton. A Leyton follow-up, "Wild Wind," reached No. 2 on the British charts.

In 1961, Meek produced one of the more enduring tribute songs to Holly, Mike Berry and the Outlaws' "Tribute to Buddy Holly." The song was a typical Meek production, heavily laden with production gimmicks he copied from his idol Norman Petty. Much of Meek's work was characterized by backward tape effects, heavy echo, and the unusual use of household sounds, such as flushing toilets and scraping combs over the edges of ashtrays. He would lock himself in his studio for days at a time and was said to be obsessed with space travel, vampires, and Buddy Holly.

Meek's biggest success came in 1962 when he wrote an instrumental called "Telstar" and formed a group, the Tornadoes, to record it. "Telstar" spent twenty-five weeks on the British charts and went to No. 1 in the United States, the first single by a British group to accomplish that feat. Follow-ups by the Tornadoes didn't come close to matching "Telstar," but Meek came back with a Top 10 hit at the height of the British invasion with the Honeycombs' "Have I the Right?" in June 1964.

It was Meek's last success, however, and a despondent Meek committed suicide by shooting himself in the head with a 12-gauge shotgun in his studio on February 3, 1967, the eighth anniversary of the death of his idol.

Memorial dances for Holly, Valens, and Richardson began at the Surf Ballroom in 1979. The first show featured Del Shannon, Jimmy Clanton, and the Drifters, with Wolfman Jack acting as master of ceremonies. Also appearing were Niki Sullivan and his seven-year-old twin sons. Ironically, a Lubbock radio station was sponsoring a disco dance in that city's Memorial Civic Center that same night, with a "soundalike" band hired to play a few Buddy Holly songs.

The Surf show drew 1,700 fans from thirty-five states, who paid $17.50 apiece for tickets. It also drew dozens of TV, radio, and print journalists from around the country. The concert lasted six and a half hours, until 2 A.M., despite temperatures of minus-22 degrees and a windchill index of minus-65.

The two-day celebration, featuring a sock hop on Friday night and a live concert on Saturday, has been a sellout every year since. Bo Diddley, Carl Perkins, Rick Nelson, Bobby Vee, and the Crickets have performed on the Surf stage at the tribute shows.

Surf manager Darrel Hein also started a Summer Dance Party in June 1988, when a granite monument to the singers and Roger Peterson was dedicated just outside the entrance to the ballroom.

The monument was opposed at first by Holly's widow because of the inclusion of Peterson's name, but Hein proceeded with his plan, paying for the monument himself. The street running east of the Surf was renamed Buddy Holly Place at the same ceremony, which marked the first occasion the families of Holly, Valens, Richardson, and Peterson were together.

The resurgent popularity of Buddy Holly, the Big Bopper, and Ritchie Valens peaked in early 1989, the thirtieth anniversary of the Winter Dance

Party and the fatal crash. Within a forty-eight-hour span, on February 3 and 4, 1989, special tributes were conducted for the singers in Fargo, in Beaumont, and in Clear Lake.

In Fargo, original Crickets Joe B. Mauldin and Jerry Allison teamed with guitarist Gordon Payne to present the music Holly was supposed to have performed across the Red River in Moorhead thirty years earlier. They were joined by Bobby Vee for the Friday night performance at the Fargo Theater.

At the same time in Beaumont, the Fabulous Thunderbirds headlined a memorial concert that drew ten thousand fans to the Montagne Center at Lamar University. Also performing were Johnny Preston and Jivin' Gene Bourgeois. Attending were Maria Elena Holly and several members of the Valens and Richardson families.

The concert also marked the unveiling of a pair of statues by Port Arthur, Texas, sculptor Doug Clark. One statue shows a grinning J. P. Richardson standing with a guitar around his waist and his arms outstretched toward his fans. The second statue shows Richardson with his arms around Holly and Valens, as if they are about to board the plane.

On Saturday, February 4, Vee teamed with the Diamonds and Freddy Cannon at the Surf. Included in the crowd was a contingent of more than a dozen Holly fans from England.

For more than three decades, fans from around the world have visited Clear Lake for a glimpse of the Surf Ballroom and the crash site. Guitar picks and flowers are routinely left at the crash site, some five miles north of Clear Lake, about half a mile west from the corner of Gull Avenue and Three-hundred-and-fifteenth Street. In winter, when snows can drift several feet deep along the old wood and wire fence, the site is often inaccessible. In February 1988, however, even temperatures well below zero couldn't deter Ken Paquette, a fan from Portersfield, Wisconsin.

Paquette fashioned a monument to the singers from stainless steel—in the shape of a guitar and three records, one for each of the singers—and deposited it on the site, despite a temperature of 16 degrees below zero. Paquette wasn't able to stabilize the statue in the frozen ground, so some Holly fans from Iowa later secured the statue by anchoring it in concrete. The monument is located on land owned by the W. H. Nicholas family of Clear Lake, which planted its own monument, four oak trees: one for each singer and one for Roger Peterson. The trees soon died, but the family planned to plant replacements.

On February 27, 1980, Cerro Gordo County Sheriff Jerry Allen found Buddy Holly's glasses and the Big Bopper's watch in the county courthouse. Also in the envelope were four dice and part of another watch. After wire services carried stories of the discovery, Holly fan Walt Guyer of Mill Creek, Delaware, tried to buy Holly's glasses and sent a check to Allen for $502.37, which he said was his life savings.

In October 1980, Maria Elena Holly Diaz filed a petition with the court saying the glasses should be turned over to her. After a hearing on March 20, 1981, District Court Judge B. C. Sullivan ordered the glasses turned over to Holly's widow. "I wish I'd have just put the damn things back and forgotten about them," Jerry Allen says.

Among those who keep the flame alive for the three singers tragically killed at Clear Lake, there are a few "superfans" who have done more to perpetuate their memories than any others.

Although Norman Petty is often credited with keeping Holly's name and music alive in the 1960s, no one has done more in the intervening years than Bill Griggs, founder of the Buddy Holly Memorial Society. Griggs, who was raised in Hartford, Connecticut, became a Holly fan for life after seeing him perform at Hartford's State Theater on March 30, 1958, during Freed's Big Beat tour.

Griggs was hit hard on hearing of Holly's death. "Rock 'n' roll stars aren't supposed to die," he remembers thinking. Griggs's interest in Holly was rekindled in 1975 when he read Dave Laing's biography, *Buddy Holly*. He also read John Goldrosen's biography of Holly and became acquainted with John Beecher, who operated the Buddy Holly Appreciation Society in England. Griggs and a few close friends formed the Buddy Holly Memorial Society in the U.S. In 1976, Griggs began publishing "Reminiscing," initially a five-sheet newsletter. By 1981, *Reminiscing* had become a full-fledged magazine, with a slick cover, typeset copy, and photographs.

In 1978, the BHMS hosted its first convention, highlighted by a reunion of ex-Crickets Jerry Allison, Joe B. Mauldin, Niki Sullivan, and Sonny Curtis.

In 1979, Griggs made his first trip to Clear Lake for the first tribute dance. While there, he drove to the crash site only to get stuck in a snow-filled ditch. Later that year, Griggs named his newborn daughter Holly Maria. Griggs moved from Wethersfield, Connecticut, to Holly's hometown of Lubbock in 1981.

Griggs is acknowledged as the biggest expert on Holly and his music and is frequently sought out as a source by reporters and writers. He has contributed to several books and articles and is coauthor with Jim Black of *Buddy Holly: A Collector's Guide*. A collector himself, Griggs has accumulated many records, photos, pieces of sheet music, and other 1950s memorabilia, much of it directly associated with Holly. His most prized posessions—one of Holly's suits, a pair of his famous horn-rimmed glasses, and a pair of Holly's black oxford shoes—are carefully displayed in a glass case.

Griggs handled the massive administration of the BHMS, which included more than five thousand members from thirty-one countries at its peak, until it disbanded in mid-1991. Even after the club folded, Griggs was receiving some twenty-five calls daily from Holly fans. "I used to fight to get the news, and now everybody calls," Griggs says, "everybody writes, and it just flows right in here and I just have to look at it. It's a nice feeling."

Griggs, who published a rock-music periodical, *The Rockin' '50s,* for several years, now makes a living through a mail-order memorabilia business. Griggs also provides visitors to Lubbock with a sight-seeing guide to the city focusing on places of interest to Holly fans.

Griggs claims to have listened to the Crickets' biggest hit, "That'll Be the Day," every day since its 1957 release. "I've never grown tired of it," he says.

A native of Eau Claire, Wisconsin, Don Larson was a regular at Fournier's Ballroom in Eau Claire, where he caught the Winter Dance Party on January 26, 1959. He was stunned to hear of Holly's death as he headed to his radio and television class the next week. "I just stood there in shock. Tears started running down my face. . . . I remember going home that night on the school bus. . . . I went into my room and shut the door. That was the first time I ever remember not coming out to have dinner with my parents."

In 1961, Larson obtained eight photos of the Eau Claire show taken by a girlfriend, Joanie Svenson. He placed them in a scrapbook where they sat for fifteen years. Since the publication of John Goldrosen's biography of Holly, Larson's photos have been printed in dozens of publications and featured on many television programs.

Larson's home in Evergreen, Colorado, is crammed with Holly memorabilia, including hundreds of albums and 45s. He proudly claims that he doesn't own an Elvis Presley album. "Buddy Holly had more talent than Elvis Presley ever dreamed of," says Larson, who works for an insurance company. "Buddy Holly was just a downright pure talent. He was an inventor of rock 'n' roll music. I've always thought that if you just take sex away from Elvis Presley, what have you got?"

Larson is an avid student of Holly, particularly the Winter Dance Party, and has assembled an informative slide presentation of the tour, which he has presented many times in Clear Lake. In 1989, Larson realized a life-long dream by retracing the Winter Dance Party route with a series of sock hops presenting music from the 1950s. Disc jockey Tom Petersack of Redondo Beach, California, accompanied Larson.

The duo covered 2,764 miles from Milwaukee to Clear Lake in a seventeen-foot rental van. Five of the eleven sock hops were held in the same buildings the original Winter Dance Party played thirty years earlier. In each city, Larson and Petersack set up a portable Holly museum, featuring much of Larson's personal collection.

Unlike the original Winter Dance Party, there was plenty of media attention for Larson's and Petersack's package. The 1989 tour never drew more than four hundred people, though, with the best turnouts at Milwaukee and Montevideo. The lowest turnout was an estimated twenty-five people at St. Paul.

Even though the 1989 tour benefited from an Interstate highway system that didn't exist in 1959, Larson and Petersack found the trip grueling. "We only had enough time to spend the night in town three times," Larson says. "And we never had time to party."

As a teenager in Marietta, Georgia, in 1958, Marcia Hopkins became an instant fan of Ritchie Valens. She bought his records, started a scrapbook, and became president of Chapter 76 of the Ritchie Valens Fan Club. "When I was fourteen and until I graduated from high school, it was because of Ritchie that I got through those years with a shred of sanity," she says. "I literally lived for the mail each day."

Marcia drew inspiration from Valens over the years as she wrote stories, poems, and song lyrics. She continued to listen to 1950s music and eventually married Jack Farley, had two kids, and worked as an executive secretary in Indiana. "But there is still Ritchie," she says. "For years there was nothing new about him. . . . Then came [the movie] *La Bamba,* and it was the 1950s all over again, with the realization that losing him was just as painful now as in 1959."

After seeing the movie, she started a new scrapbook to go with one she started in 1958. The 1980s scrapbook soon grew larger than that of 1958–61. Farley has become very close to the Valens family, and has made several phone calls to representatives of the Rock 'n' Roll Hall of Fame in an effort to have Valens considered for induction.

In 1989, she helped Ernestine Reyes form the Memorial Fan Club in Pacoima. Joanie Morales started a separate fan club from Watsonville, California, in January 1988. Both were short-lived.

Farley is also a big James Dean fan, but there's a big difference, she says. "For some reason, I have no trouble wearing a T-shirt with James Dean on the front, but I absolutely cannot wear one with a picture of Ritchie on it."

Jerry Miller was a teenager in the Mason City–Clear Lake area at the time of the crash. "I was a fan of Buddy Holly," Miller says. "[The crash] completely changed my life." Shortly after the accident, the nineteen-year-old Miller approached Jerry Dwyer in his office at the Mason City airport. According to Miller, Dwyer showed him around the airport and took him into his office where he thumbed through an aircraft book to find a photo of a Beechcraft Bonanza. Dwyer ripped the page from the book, signed it, and gave it to Miller as he discussed the incident.

"'What baffles me is that I bought that airplane for him,'" Miller recalls Dwyer saying. "'He was an excellent pilot.'

"[Dwyer] spoke in chopped sentences. He would go so far like he wanted to tell me more, and then he'd leave. When I walked out of that office I was so confused. I said there's something in this whole thing that's not right. . . . This guy was disturbed about something terribly, that he didn't want to put the whole picture together. And I said, 'I'm going to find out. These were my friends.'"

While attending college in Minneapolis, Miller researched the accident. "This thing just bothered me night and day until I began to search it out, piece by piece," he says. "I had people following me. I wrote all the information down. I went to the funeral homes. I was just a student at a theological school and they said, 'What do you want that for?' And I just said, 'They were friends of mine.' . . . Both Wilcox and Ward funeral homes cut me off completely."

Still, Miller thinks he made progress in his eighteen years of researching the accident. "I'm convinced that I know what happened," he says. "It didn't happen the way they said it did and they've covered up the lie. . . . It came down to the CIA and Civil Aeronautics Board and they just said squelch this thing. . . . It's gonna ripple across the country. Kids are gonna take their lives."

Miller is convinced that Roger Peterson flew the Bonanza into the ground because of a disturbance caused by the singers. "There seemed to be an argument on the plane before the crash," Miller says, although he admits it may be impossible to prove. "One of the singers was [trying to take control of the plane]. . . . Each one of the singers was going through their own emotional disturbance."

Miller, who is now an Assembly of God minister in Iowa, says he has addressed youth groups on the subject of Buddy Holly and has a goal of meeting with the families of the singers killed in the crash. He already has met with Roger Peterson's widow and parents. "I've listened to the heart cry of what they said," he says.

He also wants to meet Jerry Dwyer one more time before he tells the world the truth of what happened on the Bonanza that night. "It's naturally gonna be difficult and hurtful when it comes out and it's going to have some repercussions nationwide when the thing finally does hit the fan," Miller says.

As a six-year-old from Ponca City, Oklahoma, Kevin Terry was fascinated with music. By 1957, Terry was belting out rock songs at school dances, mimicking Buddy Holly's vocal mannerisms and guitar style. Terry was attending private school in Victoria, Texas, when he heard about the plane crash. Within one week, Terry had bought every record he could find by the dead artists and eagerly awaited further information on the crash. Terry returned to the Ponca City area by 1961, where he joined a local rock band.

Terry put music aside briefly in the mid-1960s to concentrate on drag racing and coin collecting, but the Holly attraction proved to be too much. In 1967, Terry started collecting Holly memorabilia. In 1978, after reading John Goldrosen's biography, Terry decided to try to contact Holly's relatives. He was soon sharing stories with Larry and the rest of the Holley family. Larry then invited Terry to attend the Lubbock premiere of the movie of Holly's life.

After meeting the family and Bill Griggs of the Buddy Holly Memorial Society, Terry realized that they knew little more about the crash that killed Holly than he did. He decided to learn more about it himself. "I've tried to retrace the events that occurred that night and find out what really happened," Terry says. "There has been a lot of speculation by various people, including Jerry Dwyer, that the crash was not caused by pilot error."

Terry estimates that he's interviewed at least eighty people connected with the crash. Terry has shared his expertise with several reporters over the years, and helped a Ponca City radio station produce a two-and-a-half-hour special on Holly. Included in his extensive Holly collection are several scrapbooks of information on Holly and the crash. Despite all his efforts, Terry still hasn't found anything to disprove the official CAB version of the accident. "We may never know what really happened," he admits.

Born in 1950, John Goldrosen's introduction to Buddy Holly came through the Beatles version of "Words of Love" on the *Beatles VI* album. "I thought it was the best song on the album," Goldrosen recalls. He started buying Holly's records to learn more about him, but found little new information.

After graduating from Harvard in 1971, Goldrosen took a year to tour the country and learn more about Holly. Goldrosen's first stop was Nashville, where he was put in touch with some musicians, including Jimmy Gilmer, Scotty Moore, and Bill Hall. "Once you met one person, they said, 'Well, here's two or three people you should meet,' and those two or three had two or three others to meet and they started to point me in the right direction," Goldrosen says.

That direction included a stop in Holly's hometown. Goldrosen ended up spending several months in Lubbock, with generous access to the Holley family's collection of memorabilia and documents. While working in Lubbock, Goldrosen heard Don McLean's "American Pie" for the first time, shortly after its release. "It kind of floored me," he says.

After meeting Norman Petty in Clovis, Goldrosen went on to Los Angeles to meet with the Crickets. On his return trip to Massachusetts, Goldrosen stopped in the Mason City–Clear Lake area. In all, he spent nearly eight months on the road.

Although he hadn't planned to write a book, that's what he ended up with. "It took the better part of two years to get the final draft together and start peddling it around," says Goldrosen, who previously had written nothing longer than papers in college. After being rejected by every major publisher, Goldrosen placed the book with Bowling Green Popular Press in Ohio. *Buddy Holly: His Life & Music* had a small press run—Goldrosen estimates it was "probably one or two thousand copies"—and is now a collector's item.

Goldrosen had a second edition of his book published by Quick Fox Press about one year after the release of the movie, *The Buddy Holly Story,* came out. Drawing on new information and dozens of new photos, Goldrosen teamed with John Beecher to release an updated version of his book in England in 1986. That book was later distributed in the United States by Penguin.

Goldrosen hasn't written another book yet, although he says he's written "some things that never got published." He is co-owner of a family-operated bookstore on Cape Cod, about an hour from his home.

George Horton, a railroad worker from Vining, Iowa, started tracking down Buddy Holly information in the early 1980s after meeting Maria Elena Holly at a tribute dance in Clear Lake. Horton has invested lots of money and time in tracking down the Holly legend in the Midwest. Many of the photos of the Winter Dance Party that have surfaced over the years are the direct result of Horton's efforts.

Horton now owns a good share of the negatives taken at the crash site on February 3, 1959, including the complete set of 4x5s taken by Lock Photographic Studios for the Insurance Company of North America.

"The music so much moved us at the time. . . . Buddy had cleaned rockabilly up, shot rock 'n' roll [into] it, and it was at last our music. We were the first group of teenagers to have our own music and we knew what we liked," Horton says.

Horton, who was thrown out of Columbus Junction High School with a bunch of buddies for having Mohawk haircuts in the 1950s, has a simple explanation for why Buddy Holly, Ritchie Valens, and J. P. Richardson have so many fans so many years after their deaths. "What we're chasing, we can't put our hands on," Horton explains. "It's one step ahead of us, and that's to catch up with the man. We're chasing through the past, but there's no way. We can't run that fast. We'll never be able to catch up with him."

Where Are They Now?

The participants in the Winter Dance Party tour have had a rich history in the music business. Many have gone on to greater fame and fortune, while some have faded from the scene.

Waylon Jennings returned to KLLL in Lubbock for a while after the accident. He then left radio briefly, working at his brother's repair shop in Littlefield. On March 21, 1961, his wife, Maxine, bore the couple's third child, a son named Buddy Dean, after Holly and film star James Dean.

By 1962, Waylon and Maxine were divorced and Jennings moved to Arizona where he returned to radio. He remarried, performed at a Phoenix nightclub, and did some recording. In 1963, Jennings recorded "The Stage," a tribute to Ritchie Valens, the Big Bopper, and Buddy Holly.

After his second marriage went sour, Jennings shared a Nashville apartment with Johnny Cash in the mid-1960s. In 1966, *Record World* magazine named him Most Promising Male Vocalist in country music. Jennings recorded several LPs in Nashville with Chet Atkins as his producer. He had his first No. 1 single with "Only Daddy That'll Walk the Line" in 1968.

On February 9, 1969, almost ten years to the day after the plane crash, tragedy struck Jennings's band. Bass player Chuck Conway was killed when the truck camper Jennings's band was riding in skidded on an icy bridge near Bloomington, Illinois.

Jennings married and divorced a third time before marrying Jessi Colter, Duane Eddy's ex-wife, on October 26, 1969. In 1970, Jennings won a Grammy Award for his recording of "MacArthur Park." In 1975, Country Music Association (CMA) members voted him Male Vocalist of the Year.

In 1976, an album featuring Jennings, Willie Nelson, Colter, and Tompall Glaser became the first country album to go platinum. *Wanted: The Outlaws* was named album of the year by the CMA; Jennings and Nelson were voted duo of the year; and Jennings and Nelson's "Good-Hearted Woman" was single of the year.

In the 1970s Jennings toured constantly, performing as many as three hundred times a year. His hard-living lifestyle was the inspiration for the 1973 movie *Payday,* a dark study of the touring life of a country music star.

In 1979, Jennings recorded the theme song for the hit CBS television series *The Dukes of Hazzard,* called "Good Ol' Boys." It became Jennings's first million-selling single. From 1974 through 1987, Jennings had sixteen No. 1 country singles.

Even though he was diagnosed a diabetic in 1981, Jennings has maintained his grueling touring pace. In 1984 he successfully kicked a twenty-one-year-old cocaine habit. A year later, Jennings teamed with old friends Cash, Nelson, and Kris Kristofferson to form the Highwaymen. An album sold more than a million copies, and a single, "The Highwaymen," rose to the top of the country charts.

Jennings had two near heart attacks and triple-bypass surgery in December 1988. After the surgery, Jennings quit smoking after forty-one years, and diversified into the food business with Waylon's West Texas Style Barbecue Sauce.

Jennings, who had dropped out of Littlefield High School at fourteen, passed the high-school equivalency exam in 1990 and became a spokesman for education as a means to combat drug use. His hometown of Littlefield declared July 4, 1990, Waylon Jennings Day and named a street and park after him. The town's water tower proclaims Littlefield as "Home of Waylon Jennings." A free concert by Jennings in 1991 drew a crowd estimated at thirty thousand to the town of seven thousand.

Although RCA Records dropped Jennings from its roster in the 1980s as crossover artists took over the country music charts, Jennings remains active with a small Texas label, Justice Records.

A lifetime of guitar picking forced Jennings to undergo surgery on both hands for carpal tunnel syndrome in June 1994. Two days later, he was on the road to one of the one hundred dates he played that year.

Jennings returned to the Surf Ballroom before a capacity audience of 2,200 on October 6, 1995. Prior to his performance, Jennings spent some time alone in the ballroom. More than three decades after the Winter Dance Party, Jennings still has memories of that tour.

"Every once in a while I'll be traveling through one of those towns and it will flash back," he says. "After [the crash] something happened to me. My mind kind of blocked it out for a long time. I didn't want to think about it. I didn't even see a picture of the plane crash for ten or fifteen years. I just happened to be looking through a book one day and there it was. That was the first time I'd seen it."

Jennings was also haunted by his final conversation with Holly in which he teased his boss about the possibility of his plane crashing. "It took me years to get over that," Jennings remembers. "You blame yourself, especially when you've said something like that. . . . Those words haunted me."

Carl Bunch played with Ronnie Smith and the Jitters for a while after returning to Odessa from the Winter Dance Party. After a short tour with Roy Orbison, he joined the army in June 1959. After his discharge, Bunch tried a number of jobs as a salesman before becoming a guard at a Georgia state prison. After a divorce, Bunch returned to Odessa to manage the family record shop and play drums in Bob Osburn's band.

Bunch later moved to Nashville, where he played drums for Hank Williams, Jr., and met his third wife, Dorothy. Bunch attended the Alabama police academy when he was forty-three. "It just about killed me," he says.

He eventually settled in southern California, where he operated Dove's Nest Ministries and worked as a substance abuse counselor before dropping from public view in the 1990s.

After returning to Odessa, Tommy Allsup worked with Ronnie Smith and Roy Orbison before taking over as artist and repertoire chief for Liberty's country music department. He produced the first Willie Nelson records in the early 1960s.

In 1964, Allsup recorded an instrumental album of Holly songs, *The Buddy Holly Songbook,* at Norman Petty's Clovis studio. He later returned to Odessa, where he started the Tommy Allsup Recording Studio.

Allsup moved to Nashville in 1968, where he did session work. Eventually, he became an independent record producer for Hank Thompson, Asleep at the Wheel, and other country acts. In 1973, he produced the final album by the legendary Western Swing bandleader and fiddler Bob Wills.

In 1979, he built a nightclub called Tommy's Heads Up Saloon in Fort Worth, Texas. The club was named after the infamous Clear Lake coin flip. In 1988, he returned to Nashville, where he returned to sessions and production work.

Ronnie Smith expected to be a star when he returned to Odessa after the Winter Dance Party. Some of the people he met on tour also thought he would.

"He was terrific," says Dion.

Waylon Jennings says: "He could have been a star. He was a real good-lookin' kid and knew how to move with the music. . . . He knew what he was doing."

"I thought Ronnie would come home and we'd be rich," says Smith's sister, Sherry. It didn't happen quite that way.

Smith's Brunswick recording, "Lookie Lookie Lookie"/"A Tiny Kiss," sold fairly well in 1959, but failed to make the national charts. Still, he made enough money to buy a white 1959 Impala with a red interior, a car that stood out on the streets of Odessa. After subsequent recordings sold poorly, Smith enrolled in the Hollywood Professional School in California, where his classmates included Mousketeers Sharon Baird and Carl "Cubby" O'Brien, actors Lauren Chapin and Tommy Nolan, the Addrisi brothers, and Mickey and Timmy Rooney. At a class dinner, Smith drew rave reviews for his singing.

But Smith had problems more serious than a sagging career in 1960. Drugs had taken control of his life, particularly glue sniffing. His family tried to get Ronnie back on track. But in 1960, there were few options for people with chemical dependency problems. "I think that was the frustrating part," Sherry Smith says. "He just couldn't help it and he needed some help."

Smith was treated at private hospitals in Odessa and Galveston before the family ran out of money. Despite the treatment, Smith was not getting better. The family committed him to the state hospital in Big Spring. However, after his commitment, Smith got worse. "He was good at getting out. He escaped," Sherry says. "Lots of times he'd jump boxcars [or] he'd ride the couplings [sixty-five miles to Odessa]."

After he was returned to Big Spring following his escapes, Smith was given electroshock treatments. "Those were horrible," recalls Sherry. "He acted like he'd just come out of surgery most of the time." The shock treatments sent Smith on an emotional rollercoaster, according to his sister. "He had some real highs and lows."

When it was apparent that Smith could not be contained at Big Spring, he was moved to another state hospital in Rusk, in southeast Texas. The family was allowed to visit Smith every two weeks. Smith's mother took food and cigarettes to her son. "Mother got to where she'd take food to other people," Sherry says. "She'd take them cigarettes and candy and Ronnie would share them with other people who didn't have visitors.

"I remember Ronnie telling me one time [as] we were just walking around, 'If you weren't crazy when you came in, you'd be crazy when you left.'"

On Thursday morning, October 25, 1962, some friends at Rusk invited Smith to play in a softball game. "He said, 'I'm just going to use the bathroom and I'll be out in a second,'" Sherry says. "And then he didn't come out." A hospital employee found Smith dead, hanging by his T-shirt. He was buried in Sunset Memorial Gardens cemetery near Odessa on October 28, 1962.

About a month before his death, Smith had handed his mother a box of his belongings for safekeeping "in case something happens." In the box were the words to a song Smith had written at Rusk, "It Was the Master Calling Me." The family had the words engraved on his tombstone:

> *Alone and afraid*
> *I watched the sunlight fade.*
> *And then I turned and slowly walked away.*
>
> *And then I heard a voice*
> *calling my name*
> *and when I turned to look,*
> *I just bowed my head in shame.*
>
> *His voice so gentle and kind*
> *He came to me and took my hand*
> *and healed my troubled mind.*
>
> *No words can ever describe*
> *The peace I felt inside*
> *Now all my fear is gone*
> *And I will never walk alone*
> *It was the master calling me.*

Dion and the Belmonts returned to New York after the Winter Dance Party, where they promptly recorded "A Teenager in Love," which became the group's first million-seller. In February 1960, they were voted the best vocal group in the fifth annual poll by *American Bandstand.* The group split later that year.

The Belmonts enjoyed some success over the next three years, but Dion far eclipsed their popularity as a solo act. He flooded the charts with a series of songs about the teenage experience: "Runaround Sue," "Lonely Teenager," "The Wanderer," "Lovers Who Wander," "Little Diane," "Love Came to Me," "Ruby Baby," "Donna the Prima Donna," and "Drip Drop." After taking several years off while recovering from a drug habit, Dion returned to the Top 10 in 1968 with his haunting ballad, "Abraham, Martin and John."

Dion concentrated on religious music for several years before appearing at Madison Square Garden in a June 2, 1972, reunion concert with the Belmonts. A live LP of the event was a bestseller in 1973, and producer Phil Spector lured him back into the studio to record rock 'n' roll in 1975. He was an early inductee into the Rock and Roll Hall of Fame, in January 1989.

In 1994, Dion formed a new band, the Little Kings, with two ex-members of the Del Lords, guitarist Scott Kempner and drummer Frank Funaro, and ex-Smithereens bassist Mike Mesaros.

After the Belmonts broke up in 1963, Carlo Mastrangelo cut a few singles on Laurie. He also recorded with a group called the Demilles in the mid-1960s and the Endless Pulse and Carlo's Crown Jewel in the late 1960s before moving to Florida. Fred Milano remained in New York and was still active in the music business in the 1990s with an updated version of the Belmonts.

After the Winter Dance Party, Debbie Stevens returned to Chicago where her husband, disc jockey Jim Lounsbury, kept her busy as a performer on his dance parties.

Stevens and Lounsbury divorced in the early 1960s and she moved to Detroit, where she became one of Motown's early recording artists under a new name, Debbie Dean. Her only national success came in February 1961 when her recording of two Smokey Robinson/Berry Gordy compositions, "Don't Let Him Shop Around"/"A New Girl," spent two weeks on the *Billboard* charts, peaking at No. 92. Subsequent releases on Motown didn't fare as well and Dean was dropped from Motown's roster of performers.

Dean stayed with the company for several more years, however, as a songwriter, and her songs have appeared on albums by Edwin Starr, the Temptations, and Martha and the Vandellas. She later moved to the Los Angeles area, where she continues to collect royalty checks from her songwriting.

Frankie Sardo had recordings on three labels in the twelve months following the Winter Dance Party, but none made the national charts. Sardo married, quit performing, and went into record production.

Sardo turned to acting in U.S. and Italian movies and off-Broadway theater in the early 1960s before moving into the nightclub business with his father, Marco, in the mid-1960s. In 1968, Sardo moved to California, where he helped produce music for the biker film *Hell's Angels '69*.

Sardo listed his occupation as movie producer when he was arrested with six other Americans and one Briton by Scotland Yard detectives in London on November 12, 1971, in connection with the theft of $30 million in securities from a Chicago company. Sardo says he was acquitted.

Sardo then took his mother's maiden name of Avianca, and has split his time between homes in Sicily, London, and New York while working as an independent film producer.

After the disastrous Winter Dance Party, Irvin Feld never booked another dance tour. "The whole tour was an experiment," says his associate Allen

Bloom. "We did this tour and it was not successful. So we just said no more of that."

In 1967, Feld finally realized his dream of owning a circus when he bought the debt-ridden Ringling Bros. and Barnum & Bailey Circus for $8 million. In 1971, Feld sold the circus to Mattel, Inc., for a reported $47 million in stock. In 1982, Feld repurchased the circus, along with the Ice Follies and Holiday On Ice shows, for $22.8 million.

Feld died in 1984 at the age of sixty-six; his son, Kenneth, took charge of the circus, and Allen Bloom served as its executive vice president.

"To this day I have very bad emotions about that whole tour because I know that had I been on that show, [Holly would] have never been on that airplane," Bloom says. "Many times I still feel a lot of guilt about it."

Sam Geller returned to Baltimore after the Winter Dance Party, where he has tried to put the tour behind him.

"I want to forget about it," he says, "It was a tragic tour. . . . I had no choice in picking out a bus or anything. The reality was we had a poor bus. It's not like I knew the people in New York and I'd call them and tell them, 'The hell with this crap.' It would never have happened. They like stiffed me. They stiffed the whole group."

Dion agrees. "[Sam] was a great guy who took the fall for the whole thing, but he wasn't at fault at all. He was blackballed because of that."

Geller took some time off before taking out some more tours for GAC, including one with Dion. His experience with the Winter Dance Party has left him bitter.

"I got the short stick of the whole thing," he says. "I'm broke."

The Crickets have continued to record in various configurations since Holly's death. Initially, Joe B. Mauldin and Jerry Allison were joined by Earl Sinks on vocals and Sonny Curtis on guitar, until Sinks left for a solo career in late 1959. Curtis took over vocal chores until being drafted in 1960.

The Crickets formed an association with the Everly Brothers, recording with them in the studio and accompanying them on tours to Australia and England in 1960. They moved to Los Angeles that year and worked extensively in sessions produced by Snuff Garrett of Liberty Records, including what would be Eddie Cochran's last recordings on January 8, 1960.

On August 16, 1960, another young singer from Lubbock, David Box, participated in the group's last recording session for Coral. Box soon left the group for a solo career and was killed in a plane crash on October 23, 1964.

The Crickets had a few minor chart successes in England. The group appeared in a couple of teen-exploitation B-movies: a British film called *Just for Fun* and a 1964 American movie, *Girls on the Beach* starring the Beach

Boys and Lesley Gore. However, the Crickets disbanded in early 1965, around the same time Jerry and Peggy Sue Allison divorced.

After getting out of the service in late 1965, Joe B. Mauldin moved to Los Angeles, where Stan Ross of Gold Star Studios hired him as a sound engineer. Sonny Curtis concentrated on his songwriting career, which included "Rock Around with Ollie Vee," "Walk Right Back," "More Than I Can Say," "A Fool Never Learns," "I Fought the Law," and "Love Is All Around," the theme for *The Mary Tyler Moore Show.*

In the late 1960s and early 1970s, Allison and Curtis used various groups of musicians as "studio Crickets," cutting an occasional record. In 1970, Curtis and Allison played on Eric Clapton's debut solo LP, and a 1973 Crickets release included British musicians Rick Grech and Albert Lee.

Mauldin, Allison, and Sonny Curtis received a big break in 1977 when Waylon Jennings, by then a major country star, asked them to join him on the road as an opening act. They worked with Jennings for several years before resuming as a self-contained act. Guitarist Gordon Payne joined the group in 1985, replacing Curtis, and the threesome have continued into the 1990s, playing the oldies circuit and cutting an album of new material in 1988, *T-Shirt.* Payne left the group in 1994.

In early 1958, Niki Sullivan recorded "It's All Over" and "Three Steps to Heaven," which resulted in a national release on Dot. The song was a local hit but failed to chart nationally despite ads in national trade publications.

"I quit. I sold my guitar," Sullivan says.

Shortly after his stint as a Cricket, Sullivan was in the navy, where he tried in vain to make the navy golf team. He worked as a store manager and salesman for several years before becoming part-owner of a hi-fi store in Lubbock. In 1978, he moved to the Kansas City, Missouri, area.

Sullivan briefly returned to the stage in 1979 when he appeared with the Whitesidewalls at the first Buddy Holly tribute dance at the Surf Ballroom in Clear Lake.

Larry Welborn, although he played on "That'll Be the Day," was never one of the Crickets. Shortly after recording Holly's first hit song, Welborn joined Joe B. Mauldin's old group, the Four Teens. In 1958, the Four Teens had a regional success on Challenge Records with "Go Little Go-Cat" and "Sparkplug." Welborn recorded some for Ben Hall in Big Spring, Texas; toured with Buck Owens; and spent a few years in Las Vegas before settling in remote southeastern Oklahoma.

Ben Hall still collects royalties on "Blue Days, Black Nights," thanks to his association with Holly. A country version of the song as sung by Hall on a home recording was included in a 1991 compact disc on the British Rollercoaster label, *Hep Cats from Big Spring.*

Hall moved to Big Spring in the early 1960s, where he was a radio and television personality. He also opened his own studio, where he recorded several young West Texas rockers, including David Box of Lubbock, who recorded two songs as a Cricket in 1960.

The biggest-selling song to come out of Hall's Big Spring studio was the million-selling "Bread and Butter" by the Newbeats in 1964. In 1968, Hall and his wife, Dena, moved to Nashville to start their own studio, which Hall was still operating into the 1990s.

Sky Corbin stayed with KLLL in Lubbock until moving to a ranch in Oklahoma. He started working part-time at KMAD in Madill, Oklahoma, in 1971, and later bought the station.

Echo McGuire married Ron Griffith on Valentine's Day, 1958, while both were attending college in York, Nebraska. They later transferred to the University of Montana, where they heard of the fatal crash.

It wasn't until reading John Goldrosen's biography of Holly in the mid-1970s that Echo realized the impact she had had on Holly. "I didn't listen to his songs," she says. "[Goldrosen] printed a lot of words to the songs and related them to my breaking up with Buddy. I didn't realize what a factor that was."

Although the Griffiths later settled just three hours from Lubbock, Echo has never visited Holly's grave. In the 1990s, the Griffiths wrote a scripture column that they distributed free to some seventy newspapers.

Waymon Mulkey, Holly's vocational teacher at Lubbock High School, had taken some 16mm film of his students at their work stations, including Holly. "When Buddy died, I took that film over and gave it to his mother," he says.

After twenty-five years of military service and eight years as a teacher, former Holly classmate Harold Womack has a different view of Holly now than he did when growing up. "Nowadays, I notice that there's not a whole hell of a lot of difference between he and I, but in those days I thought there was a vast gulf between the two of us," Womack says. "I didn't like his music. . . . Man, I was a Vic Damone guy. So I was not particularly impressed with Buddy.

"He was not a bad guy. He was not a guy that stands out in my memory as being a significant contributor to anything in our school life. I wish I'd known him better."

Nearly forty years after singing backup on Buddy Holly's first hit records, John Pickering is still disillusioned by the experience. Pickering, his brother, Bill, and Bob Lapham made up the Picks, who sang background vocals on nine of the twelve songs on *The Chirping Crickets* album.

"We were supposed to be to Buddy Holly what the Jordanaires were to Elvis," Pickering recalls. For all their work for Norman Petty, including one single for Columbia, Pickering says they received just one payment from Petty, a check for $145 for expense money, which the Picks split three ways.

The Picks received a backhanded compliment when the Crickets were named Most Promising Vocal Group of 1957 by the Juke Box Operators of America. Because Holly was the only Cricket who sang on the group's recordings to that point, the Picks were the actual vocal Crickets.

In 1984, Pickering reassembled the Picks to add backing vocals to Holly's Decca recordings, which were originally done in Nashville without any vocal accompaniments. Sadly, Bill Pickering died from an aneurysm before John Pickering released the recording from his Houston home in 1986. John Pickering estimates sales at more than four thousand in seventeen countries.

The Picks finally got some recognition in 1987, when *The Chirping Crickets* album was rereleased, this time with the Picks prominently credited on the album jacket, correcting the thirty-year-old oversight on the original recording.

John Pickering, who has worked as a geologist for most of his adult life, has also worked as a gospel singer for many of those years. Still, he wonders what might have been. "The truth of the matter is Norman [Petty] didn't do right for us," Pickering says. "He didn't follow through, he didn't take care of the Picks, he didn't keep the promise that he made. . . . I never expected any pay, that was the deal I made. But the lack of recognition for all those years, I am upset about that. I'm still upset about it."

George Atwood, a session bass player at Norman Petty's studio from 1957 through 1959, says Petty let things slide after Holly hit the big time. "After Buddy's check came in on the first go-round, the studio just fizzled. The guys that were there were starving to death.

"I saw Norman lick his chops [the day the first royalty check came in]," Atwood recalls. "In other words, 'My working days are over.'"

For Atwood, however, paychecks from Petty were rare. "Finally, one day, I just picked up my bass and went home," Atwood says.

Atwood stayed active in the music business for many years, working with Roy Orbison, Jimmy Dean, Tennessee Ernie Ford, and Ray Price. In the late 1960s he formed the High Plains Talent Agency and booked concerts. After retiring from music altogether, Atwood managed condominiums in south Texas before relocating to Idaho.

Producer Jack Hanson, who originally overdubbed the Holly "apartment tapes," died in 1977.

Although John Pickering and George Atwood may have had a difficult time squeezing money out of Pickering's childhood friend, Norman Petty did pretty well for himself after Holly's death.

By late 1959, Petty had opened a branch office in New York and maintained a part-time staff in Los Angeles. Although Petty licensed all of his previous music through BMI, Vi Petty joined ASCAP in 1959, broadening the base of operations of their publishing companies. Norman Petty also started two more publishing companies—Norman Music, Inc., and Dundee Music—which he controlled from Clovis rather than through a New York agent.

In the months immediately following Holly's death, Petty added stereo equipment to his studio and formed the nonprofit Norman Petty Foundation, which made low-interest, long-term loans to churches for the purchase of new equipment.

Petty's first musical success after Holly's death was with a young rock group called the Fireballs from Raton, New Mexico, who had minor hits with the instrumentals "Torquay" and "Bulldog" in late 1959.

In 1960, Petty bought the Mesa Theater in downtown Clovis and began converting it into a state-of-the-art eight-track recording studio. He hired an architect to design the acoustics and personally strung thousands of feet of fine metal chains of varying lengths on both sides of the theater's stage.

In 1960, Petty composed what was to be his biggest money-earner, an instrumental called "Wheels." He then recorded a hit single of the song with a group of young musicians from Plainview, Texas, the Stringalongs. In the years since, "Wheels" has been recorded more than two hundred times, reaping huge royalties for Petty and his estate. "That song kept us going for many years," Vi Petty said.

By 1962, Holly's estate had been largely settled, and the Holley family asked Petty to do something to make the tapes Holly had recorded in his New York apartment suitable for release. New York recording engineer Jack Hanson had already overdubbed the tapes, but the family was displeased with the results. Petty overdubbed Holly's acoustic guitar and vocal with instrumentation by the Fireballs, most notably the lead guitar work of George Tomsco. The result was the first "new" Holly album in almost three years, *Reminiscing,* which was released in February 1963 on Coral.

By 1963, Petty had spent some $250,000 to add a radio station studio in the Mesa Theater's lobby. From there he gave Clovis its first FM radio station, KTQM. The call letters stood for "top quality music," and pop, classical, and symphonies were aired for the better part of the twelve-hour broadcast day, noon to midnight.

Besides the release of the Holly album and the opening of his radio station, 1963 marked another milestone for Petty.

After he placed a recording called "Sugar Shack" by Jimmy Gilmer and the Fireballs with Dot records, the song became a breakout national hit that summer and went on to become top-selling record for the year. A follow-up tune, "Daisy Petal Pickin'," reached No. 15 on the *Billboard* charts in 1964, but the British Invasion that summer all but ended Petty's influence on the national rock music scene.

Petty closed his West Seventh Street studio in 1969, two years after recording his last national hit, "Bottle of Wine," by the Fireballs. Petty later added an AM radio station and built a new building to house his expanding radio empire. He also added a 24-track studio to his Mesa Theater complex.

On June 1, 1984, as Petty was waging a futile battle against leukemia, he was awarded a gold record by MCA for the album *Buddy Holly & The Crickets: 20 Golden Greats.* Petty died on August 15, 1984.

Following Petty's death, Vi Petty spent much of her time sorting through the huge amounts of material her husband had accumulated in their numerous properties in Clovis. "At one time they had five homes here in Clovis and they lived in all of them," says Robert Linville, the former member of the Roses who is an assistant manager at a Clovis Wal-Mart store. It's no wonder that the Clovis Board of Realtors recognized Petty in October 1984, naming him Citizen of the Year.

Shortly after Norman's death, Vi Petty spearheaded a restoration of the West Seventh Street Studio. In 1982, a fire had swept through the upstairs apartment next to the shuttered studio, damaging the fabled echo chamber, and cats had roamed freely through the studio itself for fifteen years. Jerry Fisher, a former associate, managed to resurrect what was left of Petty's original recording equipment. The studio was reopened for tours on what would have been Buddy Holly's fiftieth birthday, September 7, 1986.

In the years before her death due to liver failure on March 22, 1992, Vi Petty tried to protect her husband's legacy. She continued to live in the Citadel, a former Clovis church Norman Petty had bought and converted to living quarters, which also included a chapel where he could record weddings and choirs with studio clarity. One room was filled with boxes of 45s from the days when Clovis was at the center of the rock universe. Shelves bulged with press releases and photocopies of articles about her husband, his studio, and her hometown. T-shirts proclaiming Clovis as the birthplace of rock 'n' roll were available as well.

Another room was dominated by tables covered with assorted videotapes, most wrapped with white paper and a rubber band, requests from friends for copies. Against one wall stood a half dozen two-step ladders, a monument to the shopping habits of Vi Petty, who bought everything in bulk, according to Robert Linville.

Her days were full in the years just prior to her death, but in a 1988 interview Vi Petty acknowledged that carrying on her husband's memory had become a burden. "I'm not that happy without him," she said. "I'm very lonely without him. At times, staying in the business is not easy and at times I wonder if it's worth it. . . . I should be able to be retiring from a lot of all of this. Of course, I won't be completely happy if I was completely out, but to just be able to go on with what we're doing has been worth it."

Despite having written two songs that have become rock standards—"Oh Boy" and "Rave On"—Sonny West never became a major rock 'n' roll star. By the time Holly was killed in early 1959, West was playing small clubs in New Mexico. "I didn't make any money," West says. "Also, I had to play some country and western, which kind of went against my grain."

In the early 1960s, West quit playing and tried several jobs, including working on jukeboxes. He continued to write songs although, he says, "I just couldn't keep pace with what was going on or I didn't really like the music that was happening." Fans kept asking about his work at Petty's, so he obtained the master tapes from his Clovis sessions.

In 1990, West released a tape of twelve of his own songs, including eight sides cut at Petty's in the 1950s. "Oh Boy" and "Rave On" are on the West tape but, unlike Buddy Holly's versions, Norman Petty's name is left off the songwriting credits. "That's my own doings," West says. "I just thought that's really the way it is, and even though they still get the money out of it, they're not going to get their name on it. They didn't do it. And so I guess that's my little protest."

Bill Hall continued in the music business after J. P. Richardson's death, producing George Jones, Johnny Preston, Jivin' Gene, Rod Bernard, and Bennie Barnes. In 1962, he joined forces with "Cowboy" Jack Clement and operated the Gulf Coast Recording studio in Beaumont. One of the first songs they recorded was "Patches" by Dickey Lee. Brothers Johnny and Edgar Winter also did some of their early recordings in the studio.

Hall quit producing records in 1965 to concentrate on his publishing business. In 1975, Big Bopper Music was sold to Lawrence Welk. Hall died in the mid-1980s.

J. D. Miller remained active in the recording business until his death on March 23, 1996, of complications from heart bypass surgery. His tiny Louisiana studio recorded many of the great Southern blues artists, such as Slim Harpo, Lazy Lester, and Lightnin' Slim. Miller also worked on movie soundtracks and recorded more contemporary musicians, such as John Fogerty. In the two decades prior to his death, Miller reissued some fifty albums of music recorded at his studio through the British Flyright label.

His archives likely still contain some unreleased J. P. Richardson material. "Sometime back, going through some tapes, we found a tape that contained a note [from Richardson] to me," Miller said in an interview a few years before his death. "We found that in a box in a tape that he sent to me of a song he had written. Apparently he did it at home or at the radio station, just him and his guitar." The tape containing the Richardson demo was somewhere among the thousands of tapes around his studio, Miller said.

H. W. "Pappy" Daily continued to make records in Houston for his own label, Starday, as well as for major-label Mercury through 1961, when he became country music director for United Artists. In 1965 he left United Artists to form another company, Musicor, where he again joined forces with George Jones. He also enjoyed great success with a young singer named Gene Pitney. He retired in 1971 and died on December 5, 1987.

Gordon Ritter and his brother, Ken, stayed in the music publishing business for a few years, although "Purple People Eater Meets the Witch Doctor" was the only song that made money for Ken-Rick publishing. Shortly after Richardson's death, Gordon Ritter went to Atlanta where he cut another novelty tune, "The Reprieve of Tom Dooley," with Joe South playing on the session.

John Romere was a pallbearer at J. P. Richardson's funeral. Mindful that Richardson didn't care for his given name of Jiles Perry, Romere named his own son, born in 1962, James Perry so he would have the same initials as his old friend. "He didn't like his first name either, so he goes by Perry," Romere says.

Bob Keene, later Keane, would record many other musicians in the years after Valens's death, including his first big star, Sam Cooke. But Cooke left Keane's Keen label in late 1959 and signed with RCA after placing nine singles on the *Billboard* charts.

Shortly after Valens's death, Keane moved into bigger offices. In 1960, Keane started Donna Records and produced a Top 10 national hit, "Love You So," a ballad by singer Ron Holden. Keane continued to enjoy good local sales on his labels before registering a big national hit in mid-1961 with Little Caesar and the Romans' "Those Oldies But Goodies." He also continued to record lots of young Latin groups, primarily from the East Los Angeles area: Ronnie and the Pomona Casuals, Rene & Ray, the Galahads, and others.

Keane also recorded a young Frank Zappa, television star Johnny Crawford, and in the early 1960s a group of unknowns then called Kenny and the Cadets—soon to be famous as the Beach Boys. The Beach Boys made their first major public appearance at the Long Beach Auditorium on December 31, 1961, as part of a memorial dance for Ritchie Valens.

Shortly after Keane became the manager of a rock group from El Paso, the Bobby Fuller Four, Sam Cooke was fatally shot at a Los Angeles motel on December 11, 1964. It was the second tragic death of a musician whose career had taken off under Keane.

In 1965, Keane created Mustang Records and built what Keane claims was the first 8-track recording studio in Los Angeles. "Let Her Dance" by the Bobby Fuller Four was the first song recorded in the studio. The regional success of "Let Her Dance" was followed by a national Top 10 recording of "I Fought the Law," a song written by Buddy Holly's old friend and postcrash Cricket, Sonny Curtis.

Bobby Fuller followed with a cover of Holly's "Love's Made a Fool of You" in the spring of 1966 before he became the third Keane star to die tragically. On July 18, 1966, Fuller was found dead in the front seat of his new Corvette. "They called me from the office and said, 'Get over here right away. Bobby's dead,'" Keane remembers. "He was just a few blocks down the street, stretched out under the steering wheel, stiff as a board, soaked in gasoline."

The Los Angeles coroner ruled Fuller's death a suicide, despite evidence that he had swallowed gasoline and that his body bore marks of a beating. The ruling sparked controversy, and rumors of drugs and criminal activities persist to this day.

After tragically losing three major stars, Keane contemplated his future. "It's almost like, if you want to get superstitious about it, somebody saying, 'You shouldn't be in the record business,'" Keane says.

By 1968, Mustang and its sister label, Bronco, had folded and Ritchie Valens's recordings started to appear on budget labels like Crown and Guest Star. "Actually, I kind of got burned out in the music business," Keane says.

Keane went through a divorce in 1970 and, five years later, got back in the music business through his sons, Tom and John, who started recording as the Keane Brothers. The Keane Brothers recorded two albums, and eventually got a thirty-minute network television show in 1977 on CBS as a summer replacement for *Wonder Woman*.

In the years before the film *La Bamba,* Keane leased his bigger hits, such as Valens's "Donna" and "La Bamba" and Fuller's "I Fought the Law," for compilation albums.

After the success of the film in 1987, Keane reissued Valens's first three Del-Fi albums through Rhino Records. Keane also considered marketing a La Bamba Barbecue Sauce, but backed off when he uncovered trademark problems with a German manufacturer who already produced La Bamba jellies.

In the 1990s, Keane is pushing for a film on the life of Bobby Fuller and is busy releasing many of the six-hundred-plus singles he owns. Keane also found tapes from his May 1958 recording session with Ritchie Valens in the basement of his home, along with Valens's first album session at Gold Star Studio. A compact disc of the tapes, including early versions of "Come On Let's Go" and "Donna," was distributed by Ace Records of England in 1992. "Now people will be able to hear the real truth because they can see how his songs came together," Keane says.

In 1996, Keane started a public campaign to get Valens inducted into the Rock 'n' Roll Hall of Fame. Working with Westwood One and the ABC Pure Gold Network, Keane collected signatures from Valens's fans to petition the hall's selection committee.

Ritchie Valens's music will be played forever, Keane says. "Valens is immortal. Absolutely. As long as there's anybody with Latin blood, he's the guy."

Stan Ross continued churning out classic rock 'n' roll from his Gold Star Studio for many years. Among the most famous sessions to come from the studio were those of the Righteous Brothers in their early days and the lush productions of Phil Spector, who erected his famous "Wall of Sound" in Gold Star's Studio A.

"Phil was chased out of a lot of other places," Ross says. "He was kind of strange. Now they call it genius, but it's the same thing."

It was at Gold Star that Sonny Bono produced the first Sonny & Cher records, and that former Cricket Joe B. Mauldin studied to be a recording engineer under Ross.

Ross closed the studio in December 1983. In its later years, it was used for commercial work and by some heavy metal rock bands. When the business started going digital, new equipment became very expensive. "It became just another studio at that point," Ross says. "It lost some of the charm, I thought."

Ross winces at the irony of the passing of Gold Star. "We had been in business for thirty-three and a third years," Ross noted. The building was soon leveled, and a mini-mall rose in its spot.

A strike at KFWB eventually cost Ted Quillin his job. Quillin later worked as an inventor and for a Las Vegas ad agency. He says he has several patents on wind generators.

Although she ran his fan club for several years, Muriel Moore never met Ritchie Valens. "I met his family [at a fund-raising dance] after he was killed," she said in an interview. "Donna came over here after he died and sat in my den and we played the record *Donna* and she'd cry." Moore, who also handled fan mail for the *Bonanza* television show, died on November 29, 1996.

Gil Rocha rented the American Legion Hall in San Fernando in May 1959 for his new band, Gil Rocha and the New Silhouettes, to raise funds for the headstone for Valens's grave. Rocha, who still dreams of becoming a professional actor, is also the owner of Valens's first electric guitar.

"Some member of the family had given it to his next-door neighbor, who used to paint cars," Rocha said. "The guitar was all scratched up and torn up and he wanted him to repaint it. . . . Then he was moving out, he was going to throw it in the trash. So the next-door neighbor says, 'Oh no. I'll keep it.' . . . So he kept it in his garage for twelve years. He saw my picture in the paper, he walked up, and gave it to me."

Donna Ludwig Fox eventually moved to suburban Sacramento, where she is a branch manager for a mortgage company. Coworkers call her "La Bamba Mama," and she still has a thick photo album that contains a handwritten letter from Pearl Peterson, mother of pilot Roger Peterson.

Ironically, Donna lives just a few miles from Peggy Sue. The two have become good friends, but Donna would just as soon forget her days as a recording artist. "It's a terrible record," she says. "My kids haven't even heard that record. I broke every one I could find."

Chan Romero traveled with a rock band after he split from Bob Keane in a dispute over royalties. Once he was clear of Keane's contract, Romero recorded for several labels without success.

"It was about that time that I became a Christian and I just kind of put the music behind me," Romero says.

Romero returned to Billings, Montana, where he operated an auto retail business and raised his growing family of seven sons and four daughters. He and his wife did church work, and Romero wrote some three hundred gospel songs, many of which he recorded on his own label, Warrior Records.

In the mid-1980s, the Romeros moved to Palm Springs, California, to work in drug rehabilitation. Then the Georgia Satellites covered "Hippy Hippy Shake" for the soundtrack of the movie *Cocktail*. Romero said he collected more money in royalties from the soundtrack than he had collected in the previous thirty years.

Romero hooked up with Billy Cardenas in 1991 to record a new rock album with former members of the Premiers. The album included remakes of "Hippy Hippy Shake," "My Little Ruby," and the Premiers' "Farmer John."

Although it was many months after Robert Velline made his debut before he became Bobby Vee, a star was born on the day Buddy Holly, Ritchie Valens, and the Big Bopper died.

"It was almost a mystical thing," Bill Velline says. "I've thought so many times that Holly getting killed and [Bobby] going on and getting his start that night, it's almost spooky."

On that night, Vee met Burnell Bengtsson, who was managing four other young rock bands at the time, as well as running two area drive-in theaters. Bengtsson decided to give the Shadows a chance, with the promotional help of disc jockey Charlie Boone.

On Valentine's Day, 1959, Vee and the Shadows drove forty-five miles in zero-degree weather in a station wagon without a heater to their first paying gig, which netted them $60. On Vee's sixteenth birthday, Boone did a live broadcast of a Shadows' concert from one of Bengtsson's drive-ins. Soon the Shadows were in a Minneapolis studio for a recording session.

"We took them down to Minneapolis and we produced Bobby's first record—*Suzie Baby*," says Scott Beach, a radio announcer from Fargo. "When that record came out we staged a huge celebration there in Fargo with the record being flown in by the National Guard."

After "Suzie Baby" went to No. 1 in Minneapolis that summer, Liberty released the record nationally, where it went to No. 77 on the *Billboard* charts.

Vee soon signed with Liberty and was assigned to producer Snuff Garrett, who arranged for a 1960 session at Norman Petty's studio in Clovis. One of the songs from the Clovis sessions, "Devil or Angel," became a Top 10 national hit. Vee followed with another Top 10 hit, "Rubber Ball," which featured a cover version of Holly's "Everyday" on the flip side.

In 1962, Garrett paired Vee with the Crickets for an album called *Bobby Vee Meets the Crickets.* The album reached No. 42 on the U.S. charts and made the Top 10 in England, where Vee and the Crickets toured in 1962. Vee cut another LP acknowledging his Holly connection, *I Remember Buddy Holly,* which included Vee's personal tribute, "Buddy's Song." Although Vee was a huge success in England, he found himself swept aside by the British Invasion of 1964.

In 1967, Vee's "Come Back When You Grow Up" reached No. 3, however, and was to be his last million-seller.

After spending several years living in California, Vee now lives in St. Cloud, Minnesota, where he runs a high-tech recording studio. He is a regular on the oldies circuit and toured England again with the Crickets in 1988.

Otwell R. Aycock, the chief investigator of the accident for Beech Aircraft, was killed with three other people on November 21, 1962, when the plane he was piloting crashed in remote northeastern New Mexico. Aycock was forty-six. Leo Sander, who helped with the Beech investigation, was still employed by Beech in the early 1990s.

CAB chief investigator C. E. Stillwagon is dead; Eugene Anderson, A.J. Prokop, and Fred Becchetti have all retired.

Dr. Ralph Smiley, the acting coroner of Cerro Gordo County at the time of the crash, continued to practice in Mason City until 1977, when he moved to Dallas, Texas. He died in 1991. Dr. George T. Joyce, who did the autopsy on Roger Peterson, was still practicing in Mason City in the 1990s.

Glenn Kellogg, the freelance photographer who took pictures at the crash scene, joined Sheriff Jerry Allen's staff as a deputy in the early 1960s. For several years, he sold prints of his photos, until he sold his negatives.

Albert Juhl died in September 1964, and his widow, Elsie, moved to Clear Lake.

Jim Collison, the reporter who covered the crash for the *Globe-Gazette,* left the paper on July 23, 1963.

Photographer Elwin Musser remained at the *Globe-Gazette* until his retirement in 1981. Musser's photographs of the crash site earned him a nomination for a 1959 Pulitzer Prize. Nevertheless, he estimates he's printed around a hundred 8x10 sets of crash photos over the years and has been interviewed by newspaper and television reporters several times.

John "Andy" Anderson, editor of the *Clear Lake Mirror-Reporter* who took photos at the crash site, later became editor of a newspaper in Spencer, Iowa. After his death in February 1988, his widow, Louise, discovered nine negatives of the crash site among Anderson's papers. Working through an attorney, Louise Anderson offered the photos to several publications and was offered $22,500 for the set by the *National Enquirer.* A Buddy Holly collector in California offered her $45,000, but she declined.

Jerry Allen remained sheriff of Cerro Gordo County until February 1, 1981, when he resigned to take over as head of the motor vehicle enforcement office of the Iowa Department of Transportation. He later retired and remains in Iowa. Deputy Lowell Sanquist later joined the FAA and moved to Wichita, Kansas; Deputy Bill McGill took a law enforcement job in Long Beach, California; Deputy Duane Mayfield later became an aircraft insurance adjuster in Mason City. All three former deputies are dead.

Dick McKinney, who helped take fingerprints of the crash victims for the sheriff's department, left the Mason City Police Department in 1962 to join the U.S. Marshal's Service. On July 20, 1972, McKinney was beaten, robbed, and fatally shot in Cedar Rapids. He was forty-six. Ed Christensen, who oversaw the fingerprinting, is also dead.

Tommy Allsup got his billfold back in May 1972. Author John Goldrosen discovered it in Clear Lake while doing research for his book and put Sheriff Jerry Allen in touch with Allsup.

George Devine operated his Million Dollar Ballroom in the Eagles Club in Milwaukee until he was killed in an automobile accident in 1964. Devine's son, Bob, managed the ballroom into the late 1960s.

The building was still operating in the early 1990s, but not as a ballroom. The once elegant dance floor was divided into three basketball courts and the balcony area was used as a jogging track, with an extension passing directly over the stage where Buddy Holly had tried to catch up with Carl Bunch's frenetic drumming on "Peggy Sue" more than thirty years earlier.

A local legend says that Holly, the Big Bopper, and Ritchie Valens signed a NO SMOKING sign in an elevator in the Eagles Club in 1959 and that the sign disappeared shortly after their deaths. It has also been rumored for years that audiotape or color film exists of the Winter Dance Party show in Milwaukee. Bob Devine claims to have taped a number of shows at his father's ballroom, including a Dave Clark Five show in 1964, but the tapes have long since disappeared and no film has ever been seen.

Reviewer Joe Botsford is dead.

By the mid-1980s the Eagles Club in Kenosha had deteriorated. The huge ballroom overlooking Lake Michigan was idle most of the time. As repair costs mounted, older members wanted to sell the building, but younger members talked of an extensive face-lift.

Jim Lounsbury continued to do radio and television work in Chicago for another ten years following the Winter Dance Party. He later worked in New York and Fargo. In the 1990s, Lounsbury works for UPI in Washington, D.C.

Photographer Tony Szikil found himself out of the picture for nearly thirty years after taking twenty-four photos of the Winter Dance Party performance in Kenosha. Szikil's boss, Robert Sterelczyk, sold copies of Szikil's photos for many years and was usually given credit for the pictures. After Sterelczyk died in 1988, Szikil took over the business and is now receiving full credit for his work.

Shortly after seeing Buddy Holly at the Winter Dance Party, Tom Rotunda bought a Fender Stratocaster that he still owned thirty years later. Rotunda also still had the 1957 Chevy he bought right out of high school in the 1960s. Eileen Doyle thinks she still has Ritchie Valens's cigarette butt, but has misplaced it.

The Kato Ballroom was still operating in the late 1980s. Most of the booths have been replaced with tables, the wrought-iron railing at the foot of the stage is gone, and the dance floor is a bit smaller, but the building is very much the same as it was in 1959.

The Hotel Burton was destroyed in 1985 to make way for construction of a bridge.

Judy Peery attended many dances at the Kato over the years, and even though she didn't get to meet Buddy Holly, she claims to have once gotten into Tommy Sands's dressing room. She still has photos of her birthday party with Carl Bunch and the Belmonts.

Dianne Cory wishes she "would have absorbed it better," but still has the photos she took at the Kato that night, and started selling them in 1989. She has an extensive collection of photos and autographs from that era and is a frequent winner of music trivia contests on a local radio station.

Fournier's Ballroom in Eau Claire was razed in the early 1970s to make way for an apartment complex. The apartments were never built, the site sat vacant for a time, and is now a parking lot.

John F. Kennedy kicked off his 1960 Wisconsin primary campaign from headquarters in the Hotel Eau Claire and his brother Robert later stayed at the hotel, as did Richard Nixon. But by 1970, the hotel was closed, and a year later it was demolished.

Don Larson later dated Joan Svenson and the couple became engaged. Although they eventually broke up, Svenson gave Larson the photos she took at the Winter Dance Party show. For several years they were the last-known photos of Buddy Holly. "The picture has become world-famous now," Larson says. "It's been featured on *20/20* (television show), [and] on PBS specials."

The Fiesta Ballroom, the largest ballroom in Minnesota west of the Twin Cities, was destroyed by fire in the early morning hours of Sunday, September 12, 1965, after an explosion.

The Hotel Hunt underwent a major renovation and was still operating in the early 1990s as the Best Western Royale Inn.

Jane Ellefson's pictures are among the best to surface from the Winter Dance Party and have been published often over the years. Bob Bunn never did get his guitar autographed by Holly, but later had his story published by a British Holly fan club. Diane Bagus, hostess of the post-Fiesta party in Montevideo, became a professional dancer. She once danced on the field during a Bears-Packers game on national television and claims to have dated former Packer star Paul Hornung.

It took Dick Strand years to persuade Wanda Quilitz Malone to sell her autographed popcorn box. The Minneapolis pharmacist first made an offer at a class reunion. After several offers, Quilitz gave in. Strand had it professionally mounted and it now occupies a spot in his home, alongside similar autograph displays from Jayne Mansfield, Elvis Presley, and the Beatles.

The Prom Ballroom in St. Paul was torn down in 1986, and a fitness center went up on the site.

Bill Diehl continued at WDGY until 1967. He was working part-time at Minneapolis station WCCO in the 1990s and still writing movie reviews for the St. Paul newspaper.

Timothy D. Kehr did, indeed, go into the music business, working in record promotion for a number of labels: Columbia/Epic, Motown, Twentieth-Century Fox, and Polygram. In 1965, he produced the song "Liar, Liar" by the Castaways.

Sherwin Linton and his band enjoyed a lengthy run as one of the Twin Cities' top rock bands. Linton married and had a son, born in 1960. "I named my son after me, but I called him Buddy," Linton said. Linton's novelty tune, "Santa Got a DWI," was included on a Rhino Christmas compilation in the late 1980s. In 1989, Linton did an audio impression of Johnny Cash in an ad for the Iowa Lottery. So accurate was the impression that Cash's lawyers asked to have the commercials stopped.

Mike Ulahakis and Pat Ek married and moved back to Rhinelander, Wisconsin.

The Capitol Theater in Davenport, Iowa, operated as a first-run theater until 1977, when it started showing triple-X movies. A 1978 district court injunction stopped the adult films and the theater was still standing in downtown Davenport in 1990, but was rarely used. The Hotel Davenport also was still standing.

Fred Epstein went on to promote music shows for another twenty years. He sold KSTT in 1979 and retired to California.

Mark Stevens spent two years in Davenport before quitting school to join the navy. He later attended Boston University and took a radio job in Dallas. In the 1990s, Stevens is one of Houston's top-rated morning radio personalities.

After the *Tipton Conservative* failed to interview the singers when their bus broke down in Tipton, publisher H. E. Clark wrote an article for the February 12, 1959, issue of his paper explaining why: No one in the newspaper's office knew who Holly was. Clark wrote, "It is somewhat embarrassing to realize that you have become old and are also 'a square.'" Clark vowed that it wouldn't happen again. "But next time somebody calls and says they have a celebrity, there will be no questions asked—we'll go out and talk to him," Clark concluded.

Since 1959 the Laramar Ballroom has been sold several times. Thirty years later, it was managed by Denny Brown, who had attended the Winter Dance Party show.

Larry Geer, who talked Holly out of flying from Fort Dodge to Duluth, is dead.

By the 1990s, part of the Hotel Cornbelt was a correctional facility. The owners hoped to convert the rest into retail shops.

Eddie Simpson kept the photo of Ritchie Valens he pilfered from the Laramar for more than twenty-five years before misplacing it. "This is a real touchy subject around my house," he concedes.

Bill McCollough had a successful career at KWMT and booked his own mini-tours of rock acts throughout Iowa. He never soloed in an airplane and quit taking flying lessons after the February 3 crash. Over the years, he says he's carried a lot of guilt for mentioning flying to Holly.

"I really felt for years that I had been totally responsible for it [the crash]," McCollough says. He refused to talk about it for years until he mentioned it to a group of fellow disc jockeys on a trip to Florida. "This idiot from Indianapolis said, 'Hey, Bill killed Buddy Holly.' So I didn't tell it again for a while." Although McCollough no longer blames himself, he says: "It took me quite a while to come to grips with that."

In 1979, the National Guard Armory in Duluth was taken over by the city, which used it as a street maintenance toolhouse. Big trucks, graders, and heavy equipment now roll across the floor where area teens flocked to see the Winter Dance Party.

Lew Latto remained in Duluth radio and became an executive at radio stations WAKX-FM and KXTP-AM.

Bob Jensen, who attended the Duluth show just before entering the army, was inducted into the service on February 3, the same day the singers were killed. Thirty years later, he discovered that his brother had stored his record collection in an old garage. "I thought they'd be all warped, but they aren't that bad," he says.

John F. Kennedy stayed in the Hotel Duluth in September 1963, just two months before he was assassinated. The hotel was sold several times over the next two decades and many of its furnishings were sold at auction in January 1980. The building later operated as the Greysolen Plaza Hotel.

Two places where the singers stayed when the bus broke down near Hurley, Wisconsin, are no longer around. The Club Carnival in Hurley burned down and the St. James Hotel in Ironwood, Michigan, was razed and replaced by the Towne House Motor Inn.

In Appleton, Charlie Maloney replaced the Winter Dance Party with a local rock 'n' roll band to play the 1:30 to 5:30 show at the Cinderella Ballroom. Without the drawing power of Holly and the others, Maloney cut admission from $1 to 50 cents, but still drew far fewer than the two thousand fans he had hoped for. The ballroom was razed in 1988 to make way for an office building.

The Riverside Ballroom in Green Bay was still operating in the early 1990s. Lloyd and Phyllis Aude, who was pregnant at the time of the Winter Dance Party, went on to have nine children. "I was pregnant every time one of those shows came through," Phyllis Aude says.

The slides that Larry Matti took at the Winter Dance Party were shown at family gatherings for twenty years before they were "discovered" by ardent Holly fan John Stimac of Milwaukee. Since then, Matti has sold prints to the public and the photos have been used in numerous publications and on an Australian record cover.

Bill Walters, who emceed the Green Bay show, played the interviews he had taped with the singers on a tribute show on the evening of February 3, 1959. The tapes later disappeared. Walters remained active in Wisconsin radio at WCUB in Manitowoc.

Rock 'n' roll returned to the Surf Ballroom in Clear Lake on February 24, 1959, when the Mark IV Quartet performed their hits "I've Got a Wife," "Goose Bumps," and "The Shake." The Surf fell on hard times during the 1960s, however, and was closed briefly in the fall of 1967. A group of local businessmen bought the ballroom with the intention of turning it into a convention center.

Bandleader Harry "Tiny" Hill moved from Chicago to manage the Surf for a time, but the building closed again in 1973 and there was some talk of turning the seven-thousand-square-foot building into a library. Occasional dances resumed in late 1974, not long before Darrell Hein took over management.

Health problems forced Hein to give up his duties in March 1991, and longtime Holly fans Sue and Bruce Christensen moved from Florida to take over the Surf's management for the next three years. In 1994, the Surf was sold to new owners who allow the annual tribute dances to continue.

Carroll Anderson, who managed the Surf until 1967, later ran a café in downtown Clear Lake and worked as a carpenter.

Bob Hale stayed at KRIB for just a few months after the Winter Dance Party, moving on to Illinois where he eventually joined one of the hottest broadcasting staffs in the country at 50,000-watt WLS in Chicago. He later worked in Lexington, Kentucky, before returning to the Chicago area where, in the 1990s, he was playing "Hit Parade music" on a Chicago radio station and hosting a Sunday morning television show.

John Hurd, who graduated from Mason City High School in 1961, still has his autographed copy of "It Doesn't Matter Anymore." He says he's been offered $3,500 for the record, but is hanging on to it.

Keith Etzen, the junior-college student who was caught violating school rules by being at the Winter Dance Party at the Surf, was suspended from school for one week. Later that year, however, Etzen was given a good citizenship award by the local Rotary Club.

After the Winter Dance Party performance at the Surf, Dick Haukoos drove his sister and date home to Walters, Minnesota. "It was a snowy night," Haukoos recalls. "Three miles from home we ran in a ditch after dropping off my girlfriend. My sister and I had to walk home. We walked at least two miles. We couldn't get the car out."

About a week later, Haukoos took the film he shot at the Surf in for developing. "It was like a dream," Haukoos says. "I had seen them alive and there they were on the pictures. To me they were still alive."

The photos were soon forgotten, however, and tossed into a dresser drawer. In late January 1991, Haukoos discovered six of the photos, still in the dresser drawer. There were two photos apiece of Holly and Valens, one of Frankie Sardo, and one of Dion and the Belmonts, with Holly on drums.

Haukoos took the pictures to Clear Lake in 1991 when he made his first visit to a Surf tribute dance. There he showed the photos to some Holly fans. "From that moment, the word just buzzed around the whole place," Haukoos says. "I had people swarming around me, I'll bet two hundred people at a time. It was unreal."

One of those people was Bill Griggs of the Buddy Holly Memorial Society. Griggs spent part of the next morning checking with local people about details of the photos to verify their authenticity. Before leaving for his home in Lubbock, Griggs was convinced, and elated.

"After thirty-two years, this is an incredible find," he says. "We had always worried that the last photos of Buddy would be blurry and out of focus, but these are pretty good."

Haukoos is convinced there are another half-dozen photos from the same roll of film somewhere. He is still looking for the negatives. "We're pretty sure there are negatives because my mother never threw anything away," he says. His plans for the historic photos are unclear, six years after their discovery.

While deciding the pictures' fate, Haukoos continues to live near Albert Lea and work on a pet project, the Eddie Cochran Historical Organization. Cochran was born in Albert Lea. Haukoos is also busy restoring his classic cars: a 1951 Mercury, 1956 Ford, and 1951 Ford.

The Last Tour

The plane crash that killed Buddy Holly, Ritchie Valens, and the Big Bopper has been documented consistently over the years as the tragic result of a tour gone bad. A series of bus breakdowns in uncommonly frigid weather in a sparsely populated region of the United States ultimately led to the singers' decision to find a better mode of transportation. But it's possible that Buddy Holly actually made the decision to abandon the grueling conditions imposed by the bus travel in favor of quicker hops by small airplanes several days before the fatal crash.

Although it is far from conclusive, there is evidence that some members of the Winter Dance Party flew before the fateful events in the early morning hours of February 3, 1959. In Eau Claire, Wisconsin, Steve Meyer insists he drove several of the singers to the airport the morning after their January 26 performance in Eau Claire.

"I gave Buddy Holly and Ritchie Valens a ride to the airport the next morning because they were going off on their own to do a little scouting," Meyer says. "They went down to DePere, from what I recall, which is down near Green Bay where they had a show, I guess.

"I got up early in the morning and met them at their hotel and took them to the airport. . . . It was the Big Bopper, Ritchie Valens, and Buddy Holly."

If the singers flew to DePere, it was in the opposite direction from the rest of the tour, which moved 240 miles west to Montevideo, Minnesota, that day.

The subject of flying certainly was discussed on January 30, following the concert in Fort Dodge. Although Buddy Holly was talked out of flying to Duluth after the show that night, he may have flown to Duluth the next day.

Duluth is 364 miles from Fort Dodge, probably at least ten hours by bus in 1959. Disc jockey Lew Latto, who emceed the Duluth show, remembers meeting Holly in his room at the Hotel Duluth "in early afternoon." Although Latto remembers little else about that meeting, he thought "one of the Crickets was sharing the hotel room with him."

It is known that the singers spent the night before in a Fort Dodge hotel. In order to have arrived in Duluth at 3 PM, the bus would have had to leave Fort Dodge around 5 AM, an unlikely event.

Adding to the possibility of a flight to Duluth is an interview published in the *Denfeld Criterion,* a local high school newspaper, after the crash. A non-bylined story says: "When interviewed by this reporter, each of them were most cooperative. Seventeen-year-old Ritchie Valen [*sic*] offered an exciting statement of his own—'Tell everybody I'm flying!' Frankie Sardo, who recorded *Fake-out* [*sic*], explained that three of the singers on the tour, including Ritchie, were to fly to Fargo, North Dakota, and Ritchie was thrilled with the excitement of it."

Obviously, the Sardo comment is inaccurate, having been made two days before talk of such a flight developed, but it's harder to evaluate the validity of Valens's comment.

However, Fred Milano, one of the Belmonts, said Holly, Valens, and Richardson took planes before the fatal flight. "About a week they were taking planes," Milano says.

Waylon Jennings agrees with the *Denfeld Criterion* statement about Valens's flying. "Buddy had been flying with Dion and Ritchie Valens. I know Dion flew one time. They flew . . . about two or three days before the crash . . . once or maybe twice."

Dion, however, doesn't remember flying, although he considered it. "A couple of nights before [the crash], I was thinking of flying," he says. "We were mentioning a plane. To get a haircut, get some laundry done, get some sleep, and get warm. A night without any hassle."

J. P. Richardson was not fond of flying, according to Herb Kalin of the Kalin Twins. Herb and Hal Kalin performed several times with Richardson in 1958, including on the Dick Clark Saturday night show. "We had discussed a fear of flying on his part, and on our part as well," Herb Kalin recalls. "He remarked that he didn't like flying in general and he got airsick."

Gordon Baxter says that he and Richardson once talked about death and small planes when they were coworkers at KTRM. "I had even flown him in my plane and once showed him how a pilot in weather goes into a graveyard spiral."

Were it not for the death of his grandfather, Ritchie Valens could have become a victim of another major aircraft tragedy on January 31, 1957, when an F-89 Scorpion jet fighter and a DC-7 transport collided over Van Nuys, California. Wreckage from the transport rained down on the athletic field of Pacoima Junior High where some seventy-five boys were participating in a late-morning gym class. The plane, trailing smoke and spurting flames, smashed with a force felt throughout much of the San Fernando Valley.

Sheets of flame spurted from the plane after impact, burning some children. Besides the crew members of the planes, three children on the ground were killed and seventy-eight more were injured as teachers scrambled across the playground with blankets to cover the children and ambulances rushed them to valley hospitals. Valens wasn't in school that day because he was attending the funeral of his grandfather, Frank Reyes.

Although the movie *La Bamba* inferred that Valens was traumatized by the incident, his aunt, Ernestine Reyes, says, "It didn't bother him that much."

- Buddy Holly's father, L. O. Holley, later filed a workman's compensation claim against GAC, but lost.

- Last songs charted by these performers before their deaths: Hank Williams ("I'll Never Get Out of This World Alive"), Chuck Willis ("What Am I Living For?"/"Hang Up My Rock 'n' Roll Shoes"), Buddy Holly ("It Doesn't Matter Anymore"), Eddie Cochran ("Three Steps to Heaven"), Sam Cooke ("A Change Is Gonna Come").

- Included in Lot No. 634 of a Sotheby's auction on June 23, 1990, was a book, *Must the Young Die Too,* with a note to Buddy Holly from his girlfriend, Echo McGuire, on the first page. McGuire had given the book to Holly in the autumn of 1955, just before she headed to college in Abilene.

- Although the Big Bopper is generally thought of as being a very large person, he was never the biggest person on stage during the Winter Dance Party. At 5 foot 11 inches and around 210 pounds, the Bopper was overshadowed by guitar player Tommy Allsup, who stood 6 foot 3 inches and weighed about 215.

- An anagram for the song "Brown-Eyed Handsome Man," the last song the singers performed at the Surf Ballroom, is "Rhyme Man Be Dead on Snow."

- The Big Bopper played at another Surf Ballroom, in Natasket, Massachusetts, on January 2, 1959, exactly one month before playing the Surf Ballroom in Clear Lake, Iowa.

- In 1991, a Milwaukee, Wisconsin, screenwriter named Jim Eukey was working on a film script that included the Winter Dance Party. Eukey's screenplay was based on a "Wisconsin triangle" of sorts, loosely tying together the deaths of Buddy Holly, Otis Redding, and Stevie Ray Vaughan. Redding died in an airplane accident in Madison, in 1967, and Vaughan died in a helicopter accident near East Troy in 1990.

- The original headstone to Buddy Holly's grave—in the shape of an upright guitar—disappeared shortly after it was put into place. A new stone was later put on the grave.

- Other famous Texans who died before their thirtieth birthday: William Barret Travis, twenty-six, killed at the Alamo; Bonnie Parker, twenty-three, and Clyde Barrow, twenty-five, shot down by law officers in 1934; Janis Joplin, twenty-seven, drug overdose.

CORONER'S REPORTS

The official cause of death for all three singers was "gross trauma to brain," according to certificates of death filed by Dr. Ralph E. Smiley, acting coroner of Cerro Gordo County. Roger Peterson's death was attributed to "brain damage." The official time of death for all four was 1:03 AM on February 3, 1959.

At the time of his death, Ritchie Valens was wearing a black wool overcoat bearing the label HARRIS & FRANK, LOS ANGELES, and a black wool suit with the label SOBEL'S, SAN FERNANDO. He also was carrying a silver crucifix and religious medal, a brown leather pocket case with numerous receipts, several photos, $22.15 cash, two $50 checks on a Hollywood bank, and a bracelet with "Donna" attached.

J. P. Richardson was wearing a red-checked flannel shirt and light blue cotton pants. Although he didn't wear a wedding ring while performing, a gold wedding band was found on his body as well as $202.53 in cash, a pair of dice, and a guitar pick.

Buddy Holly was wearing a yellow coat and carrying $193 in cash and a pair of cuff links.

Roger Peterson was carrying $20 in cash as well as a paycheck from the Dwyer Flying Service for $130.55, dated January 31, 1959.

- Other musicians who have died in aircraft accidents: Patsy Cline, Cowboy Copas, and Hawkshaw Hawkins (March 5, 1963); Jim Reeves (July 31, 1964); Otis Redding and his band, the Bar-Kays (December 10, 1967); Jim Croce and Maury Mulheisen (September 20, 1973); Bill Chase (August 9, 1974); Ronnie Van Zandt, Cassie Gaines, and Steve Gaines of Lynyrd Skynyrd (October 20, 1977); Kyu Sakamoto (August 12, 1985); Rick Nelson (December 31, 1985); Stevie Ray Vaughan (August 27, 1990); and Walter Hyatt (May 11, 1996).

- St. Paul disc jockey Bill Diehl was so impressed by Holly's knowledge of the music business that he called him "the Glenn Miller of rock." Ironically, Miller's career also was halted at the height of his popularity by an airplane accident. A plane carrying the forty-year-old bandleader disappeared over the English Channel on December 16, 1944, as he was flying to Paris for a show in the midst of World War II. While Holly died in Iowa, Miller was born there, in Clarinda.

After filing a Freedom of Information request with the National Transportation and Safety Board in early 1988, requesting the CAB report on the accident, the author received a phone call saying the report was no longer available. Accident records are kept for just seven years, according to Mike Levins of the NTSB. Levins says they considered keeping records of prominent accidents for a longer period of time, but decided against it.

"We don't even have records of the Wiley Post accident," Levins says, referring to the plane crash that took the life of humorist Will Rogers.

However, a copy of the CAB report arrived from Cathleen Gilchrist of the NTSB two weeks later, as a result of the original request.

- The Beaumont, Texas, area produced several other rock stars after J. P. Richardson's death. Blues guitarist Johnny Winter made his musical debut on the Dart Record label in a band called Johnny and the Jammers, which included his brother Edgar. They were discovered at a Beaumont talent contest connected with the movie *Go Johnny Go,* which included Ritchie Valens. Huey Meaux produced a major national hit for Barbara Lynn in 1962, "You'll Lose a Good Thing." Rock singer Janis Joplin was born in nearby Port Arthur, Texas, on January 19, 1943. Tracy Byrd, Mark Chesnutt, and Clay Walker—all country music stars of the 1990s—are from Beaumont.

- The last song performed by Rick Nelson before his death in a plane crash on December 31, 1985, was Holly's "Rave On." Nelson used the song as the closing number of his final set on December 30 at P. J.'s Alley in Guntersville, Alabama. Nelson's twin-engined DC-3 crashed just south of DeKalb, Texas, less than twenty-four hours later.

- For several years after the accident, Ella Holley kept the gun owned by Buddy Holly and found on the Albert Juhl farm in a nightstand for protection. The gun eventually was given to Holly's widow, Maria Elena.

- A brown leather briefcase with J. P. Richardson's initials was found in the wreckage of the Bonanza. It contained a pint of whiskey, a sixty-tablet bottle of Bufferin, a Stanley nylon bristle hairbrush, a three-inch diameter imported mirror from West Germany, three adjustable Bopper ties, a Big Bopper guitar strap, and musical arrangements for Big Bopper songs.

- The same Beechcraft Bonanza was used in the movies *The Buddy Holly Story* and *La Bamba.*

- Autograph expert William Lineham of Concord, New Hampshire, said in 1991 that a Buddy Holly signature was worth around $1,000, more if it was on a photograph, album, or handwritten letter. Other autograph experts place a signed Holly album in the $3,500 range. Ritchie Valens and J. P. Richardson signatures are worth about $500, Lineham says, although he once sold an autographed Valens demo record for $2,500.

- Del Shannon's last performance was at a February 3, 1990, memorial show for Holly, Valens, and Richardson at the Fargo Civic Auditorium. Five days after appearing with Bobby Vee and the Crickets, Shannon committed suicide.

On September 23, 1958, Buddy Holly recorded an eerily prophetic interview with Alan Freed for his October 2 television show on WNEW-TV in New York. During the interview, Freed and Holly reminisced about the Big Beat tour of that spring.

FREED: Buddy, we had a lot of fun. We did a lot of flying.

HOLLY: Yeah, we sure did. You know I was just in a town the other day, in Cincinnati. You remember when we landed there and the helicopter had crashed that day that we got in there?

FREED: That's right, Buddy, we played, I think we rode every kind of airplane imaginable.

HOLLY: We sure did.

FREED: Those DC-3s were really something.

HOLLY: Uh-huh. With the [making noises] *ummhp ummhp.*

FREED: Oh boy, oh boy. Without the seat belts, we'd have been right through the top, that's for sure.

HOLLY: Sure would.

- Despite his popularity, Holly never had a No. 1 single as a solo artist in America. The song highest on the charts was "Peggy Sue," which reached No. 3 on the *Billboard* charts.

- The Airport Commission of Mason City erected a nine-foot-tall plaque just east of the terminal building at the Mason City Municipal Airport in 1996 to celebrate the fiftieth anniversary of the airport in Iowa's sesquicentennial year. The plaque, titled NORTH IOWA AVIATION HISTORY, mentions visits to the area by Charles Lindbergh and Amelia Earhart in the early days of aviation, but makes no mention of Roger Peterson, Buddy Holly, J. P. Richardson, or Ritchie Valens.

- Holly's early records with the Crickets called the band an orchestra. The instrumentation consisted of two guitars, a bass, and drums.

- Bobby Keyes of Slaton, Texas, hung around Holly's rehearsals as a youngster, fetching soda and sandwiches for the musicians. Keyes later had a musical career of his own, playing with the Rhythm Orchids, Bobby Vee, Leon Russell, and the Rolling Stones as a saxophone player.

- Bob Dylan has said in several interviews that he was in attendance at the Winter Dance Party stop in Duluth, Minnesota, on January 31, 1959. Dylan's hometown of Hibbing, Minnesota, was just seventy-five miles northwest of Duluth.

- Despite the fact that they didn't sing, the Crickets were named the most promising vocal group of 1957 by the Juke Box Operators of America in an annual poll conducted by *Cash Box* magazine. The Decca recording of "That'll Be the Day" is the only one on which the Crickets sing.

- The biggest hit ever produced by Tommy Allsup's Odessa, Texas, studio was the 1969 smash hit, "In the Year 2525," by Denny Zager and Rick Evans. Recorded for just $500, the single went on to sell more than 4 million copies.

- In his early days as a rock performer, Sonny West went by the name Sonnee West thanks to a simple typographical error on his first record. He added the incorrect spelling on his guitar "and then we just decided to go with that," he says.

- One of Bob Keane's early employees was Herb Alpert, who was an apprentice artists and repertoire man at Keen Records after getting out of the service in 1958. With Sam Cooke and Lou Adler, he helped write four straight Cooke hits: "Love You Most of All," "Everybody Likes to Cha Cha Cha," "Only Sixteen," and "Wonderful World."

- Jimmy Self, a close friend of Norman Petty and one of the first artists to record in Petty's Clovis studio, wrote "Blue Christmas," a big hit for Elvis Presley.

- Bill McAlister, the mayor of Lubbock who proclaimed the first Buddy Holly Week, is the son of Mac McAlister, who owned Clovis, New Mexico, radio station KICA in the 1940s when Norman Petty had a radio show as a teenager.

- Niki Sullivan and Buddy Holly were distant cousins through marriage. The relationship was unknown to both singers until October 3, 1957, when the Biggest Show of Stars tour stopped at Waco, Texas. Several relatives of the singers happened to be seated near each other at that show and discovered the connection through casual conversation.

- Bob Keane went through two name changes in his professional career. In 1951, he performed on the radio as Bob Kuhn and his orchestra. "On the first show, the announcer said Bob Coon and the producer says, 'You'll have to change your name or they'll think you're black,'" Keane says. He changed Kuhn to Keene, after a popular Woody Herman tune, "Peachy Keen." In 1970, when he was producing a Hawaiian musician who was managed by a numerologist, the manager said: "You've got too many *e*'s in your name. It's bad luck." So, Keene became Keane.

- Bill Kimbrough, the session drummer on "Chantilly Lace," also designed J. P. Richardson's stage outfits, all of which had a name. His three-quarter-length, simulated leopardskin coat was named "Melvin," the zebra-patterned outer coat was "Igor," and his knee-length, tiger plush jacket was "Zelda." Kimbrough included several pairs of shoulder pads with each outfit, contributing to their outrageous appearance. Kimbrough and a group called the Townsmen had a minor regional success on Pappy Daily's D label in late 1958 with "Chantilly Lace Cha Cha Cha."

- The wallet owned by Tommy Allsup and carried by Buddy Holly in the fatal crash is now on display at the Hard Rock Cafe in Dallas.

- Ritchie Valens and J. P. Richardson each cut their biggest hits at separate Gold Star studios. Valens recorded at Stan Ross's fabled Gold Star Studio in Los Angeles, while Richardson recorded at Bill Quinn's Gold Star Studio in Houston. Quinn's studio was the first major studio in the South and was where another major Beaumont star, Harry Choates, recorded his Cajun classic, "Jole Blon." Huey

Meaux eventually bought the studio through bankruptcy proceedings and renamed it Sugar Hill Studios.

- The first mention of Buddy Holly in the Lubbock *Avalanche* newspaper was the day after his birth. Unfortunately, it recorded his arrival as a baby girl.

The only known motion picture footage of the crash site is owned by Fox-Movietone in New York. The 16mm black-and-white footage lasts just 1 minute 20 seconds and includes a sweep of the site, a man holding a piece of the wreckage, the bodies being removed to the ambulances, and the ambulances driving away. The footage is available commercially at varying rates, beginning at $1,500 per minute.

APPENDIX A

The Plane

The Beechcraft Bonanza was designed by Beech engineers in the mid-1940s with several performance goals: the ability to carry four people and their baggage on flights of a practical length at speeds comparable to commercial airliners, and the capability of instrument flying. The result, according to Beech, was an innovative plane with an all-metal airframe, low-wing design, retractable tricycle landing gear, and a unique "V-tail" design. Wind tunnel testing helped Beech engineers create a sleek machine with a cabin that "was designed as a strong, crash-resistant compartment, with 80 percent of the airplane's weight below or ahead of the passenger compartment," according to Beech.

A 165-horsepower Continental six-cylinder engine powered the plane, which used a controllable propeller that allowed for a low sound level in the forty-two-inch-wide cabin. Two prototype aircraft were subjected to strenuous lab testing, estimated by Beech officials to be equivalent to 20,000 hours of flying and 100,000 landings. The first flight of a prototype on December 22, 1945, resulted in a cruise speed 10 mph faster than wind tunnel calculations. According to Beech, the test pilot said it was "the best airplane we have ever built."

Even before technical details of the plane were released in 1946, Beech had received five hundred orders for the Bonanza. That number grew to 1,500 before the first plane was delivered, after the Civil Aeronautics Agency issued its Approved Type Certificate for the Bonanza on March 25, 1947.

The first 1,500 Bonanzas produced from 1947 to 1948 are known as the Straight 35. The Bonanza that carried Roger Peterson, Buddy Holly, J. P. Richardson, and Ritchie Valens to their deaths was one of these early models, manufactured on October 17, 1947, in Wichita, Kansas.

The first modifications came in 1949 with the A35 model. Successive models had different letter prefixes and, in some cases, suffixes. More than 10,000 V-tail Bonanzas have been manufactured. The Bonanza was an instant success and held many records.

1949 Capt. Bill Odom set a world record for nonstop distance flying by a light airplane by flying 4,957 surface miles from Honolulu, Hawaii, to Teterboro, New Jersey, in 36 hours 2 minutes. This plane went on permanent display in the National Air and Space Museum in the Smithsonian Institution in Washington, D.C., in 1975.

1951–1952   Congressman Peter F. Mack, Jr., flew a Bonanza around the world, visiting thirty countries.

1952   Paul Burniat of Brussels, Belgium, set a world speed record for light aircraft of 225.776 km per hour in a Bonanza.

1953   Bonanzas won the first four places in the annual Jaycee Transcontinental Air cruise from Philadelphia, Pennsylvania, to Palm Desert, California. In 1954, Bonanzas took the first three places.

1954   Ann Waddell turned in fastest speed in annual Skylady Derby from Raton, New Mexico, to Kansas City, Missouri.

1955   Waddell won the Skylady Derby again.

1956–1958   Bonanzas took first place for three successive years in the Powder Puff Air Derby.

1958   Capt. Pat Boling set a world record for nonstop distance flying by a light airplane with 6,856 surface miles from Manila, Phillipines to Pendleton, Oregon, in 45 hours 43 minutes.

1959   Beech officials say the Bonanza was selected as one of the hundred best-designed, mass-produced products of modern times. The ten-thousandth Bonanza rolled off the assembly line in Wichita on February 18, 1977. A cutaway airframe of a Bonanza went on display at the Smithsonian Institution in Washington, D.C., in 1980.

Factory Specifications of the 1947 Bonanza 35

GROSS WEIGHT: 2,550 pounds

ENGINE: Continental E-185-1 (6-cylinder)

HORSEPOWER: 185

CRUISE SPEED AT 10,000 FEET: 152 knots (175 mph)

SERVICE CEILING: 18,000 feet

STANDARD FUEL: 39 gallons

FUEL EFFICIENCY: 14.5–18.8 miles/gallon

RATE-OF-CLIMB AT SEA LEVEL: 950 feet per minute

EMPTY WEIGHT: 1,558 pounds

USEFUL LOAD: 992 pounds

MAXIMUM SPEED: 160 knots (184 mph)

MAXIMUM STRUCTURAL CRUISING SPEED: 139 knots (160 mph)

NEVER EXCEED SPEED: 176 knots (203 mph)

MANEUVERING SPEED: 113 knots (130 mph)

MAXIMUM GEAR EXTENSION SPEED: 87 knots (100 mph)

MAXIMUM FLAP EXTENSION SPEED: 87 knots (100 mph)

STALL SPEED FULL FLAPS (IAS): 48 knots (55 mph)

FUSELAGE LENGTH: 25 feet 2 inches

WING SPAN: 32 feet 10 inches

According to *The Aviation Consumer Used Aircraft Guide* of 1981, "the Bonanza was the first high-performance post-war design . . . and is still considered by many to be the best single-engine airplane flying." The Bonanza's roomy cabin and well-designed windows made for excellent visibility and comfortable flying for front-seat passengers. Passengers in the rear seats were a bit cramped, however, and some pilots claimed the V-tail caused excessive fishtailing in turbulence.

The Bonanza was known for its sensitive handling qualities. From *The Aviation Consumer Used Aircraft Guide*:

> The V-tail airplane has very light ailerons and low lateral stability, what the test pilots call high spiral divergence. Once a wing drops a little, it tends to keep going. In instrument weather and turbulence, this low rolling stability can put the pilot into the "graveyard spiral" quickly.

Many Bonanzas (including Jerry Dwyer's) carried thirty pounds of lead in the nose to keep the plane within its narrow center of gravity envelope. However, according to *The Aviation Consumer Used Aircraft Guide*:

> With any passengers in the back seat, a Bonanza can be very close to its aft c.g. limit, and it's not uncommon for V-tails to be flown illegally beyond their aft limit. An aft c.g. further reduces the V-tail's already low longitudinal stability, making the airplane even more sensitive in pitch and making wheel forces even lighter.

Bonanzas also present handling problems if loaded improperly. The thirty-pound weights in the nose are sometimes not enough to compensate for the weight of two adults and baggage in the rear of the Bonanza.

———•———

The serial number of Jerry Dwyer's Beechcraft Bonanza was D-1019; its registration number was N3794N. Here are some key events in the history of D-1019.

OCTOBER 20, 1947: Beech applies for airworthiness certificate.

OCTOBER 23, 1947: Plane sold to Butler Co. of Chicago, who sold same day to Rohn Flying Service, Peoria, Illinois.

JANUARY 2, 1948: Sold to Lyle Hosler Advertising Agency, Peoria, Illinois.

FEBRUARY 7, 1949: Sold to Earl Houk, Scottsbluff, Nebraska.

JANUARY 30, 1952: Sold to American Aviation Co., Des Moines, Iowa.

MARCH 13, 1952: Sold to Des Moines Flying Service, Des Moines, Iowa.

APRIL 11, 1952: After 636 hours 45 minutes flying time, original engine is replaced with reconditioned Continental model E-185-8.

FEBRUARY 27, 1954: Sold to Community Builders, Des Moines, Iowa.

OCTOBER 20, 1954: "Complete major overhaul" on engine after 789 hours on engine; 1,425:45 on airplane.

JULY 5, 1955: New prop blades installed; hub assembly torn down, cleaned and inspected; prop balanced; nose gear removed and rebuilt; both brake master cylinders rebuilt.

FEBRUARY 6, 1956: Sold to Billy Phillips, Des Moines, Iowa.

AUGUST 2, 1956: Cabin door outer skin reinforced at lower hinge.

NOVEMBER 12, 1956: Sold to Century Mutual Insurance Co., Des Moines, Iowa.

MARCH 20, 1957: Sold to Richard Mumey, Des Moines, Iowa.

MARCH 22, 1957: Directional gyro and Sperry artificial horizon installed.

SEPTEMBER 27, 1957: Lear arcon and Lear radio installed.

JULY 8, 1958: Sold to Hubert J. Dwyer of Dwyer Flying Service, Mason City, Iowa. Engine had 667 hours since overhaul; airplane had 2,092:45 flying time. Plane passed inspection by Charles E. McGlothlen.

SEPTEMBER 13, 1958: After 94.8 hours flying by Dwyer Flying Service, plane passes 100-hour inspection by McGlothlen.

OCTOBER 3, 1958: Registration issued to Dwyer.

NOVEMBER 22, 1958: "Engine torn down for major overhaul." 818.6 hours since last overhaul; 1607.6 hours on engine; 2,244:05 on airplane.

JANUARY 3, 1959: Overhaul completed; flap indicator bulb replaced; new main tires installed; aircraft passes 100-hour inspection by McGlothlen.

JANUARY 10, 1959: Plane hasn't flown since engine overhaul. Passes periodic inspection and is deemed airworthy by Hubert J. Dwyer.

JANUARY 14, 1959: Oil changed.

JANUARY 26, 1959: Oil changed by Roger Peterson. Plane had flown 22.3 hours since overhaul.

FEBRUARY 3, 1959: "Aircraft completely demolished in accident." Plane had flown 40 hours since overhaul; 17.7 hours in previous week; 1,647.6 hours on engine; 2,284:05 on airplane.

APPENDIX B

Roger Peterson's Flying Career

From United States Department of Transportation, Federal Aviation Administration, and Civil Aeronautics Board Records

SEPTEMBER 18, 1954: Passed third-class physical by R. P. Noble, M.D.

OCTOBER 3, 1954: Peterson applies for student license; his father also signs.

OCTOBER 11, 1954: Issued student pilot certificate by John W. Hunt. From back of certificate: Passed written test on December 1, 1954 (Lawrence A. Westphal); soloed in Aeronca 7 AC on December 5, 1954 (Westphal); soloed in J3 Cub C65 on July 30, 1955 (Carl Keller); private pilot written examination was posted on September 21, 1955 (Fred Becchetti).

SEPTEMBER 21, 1955: Peterson is issued an airman identification card by Fred Becchetti.

OCTOBER 16, 1955: Issued temporary Private Pilot license for Airplane Single-Engine Land by Hal C. Blacksten. Action endorsed by agent John W. Hunt on October 19. Test taken in Piper J-3-C-65. At time Peterson had 31:30 in this aircraft, 24 as pic. Total flying time: 15 dual, 29:30 pic, 5:10 dual cc, 10:10 pic cc.

OCTOBER 19, 1956: Passed CAA physical by R. P. Noble, with note: "Audiometer shows loss of hearing in lower ranges below 512 in left ear." Had 90 hours total flying time, 20 hours in last six months.

DECEMBER 4, 1957: Scored 88 on written test for Commercial Pilot Airline. Gave address as Rose School of Aviation, Box 7071, Tulsa, Oklahoma.

FEBRUARY–MARCH 1958: Enrolled in Instrument Course at Graham Flying Service at Graham–Rickenbacker Field in North Sioux City, South Dakota.

Roger Peterson enrolled in the Instrument Course at our school and flew with us during February and March of 1958, and worked as lineman in his spare time. Roger received most of his training in light aircraft at a country airport and had had no radio training before coming here. When he began his training he seemed to be slightly overconfident of his own ability. We gave him his instrument training in a Piper Tri-Pacer. He handled the airplane well on instruments but when things would go badly with a flying lesson he would become disoriented in his radio procedure. All of this harked back to his lack of radio experience.

We gave him 42 hours of training while he was here and during that time we did not notice that there was any tendency to fall off to the right in his flying.

Charles F. Meyer

Early 1958

According to my records, I gave Roger Arthur Peterson 8 hours of instrument dual flight instruction in preparation for his Commercial Pilot Certificate.

Mr. Peterson was below average at the end of this time in that he had tendencies up into the 6th hour of developing severe vertigo, and allowing the aircraft to go into diving spirals to the right.

Lambert L. Fechter, Hartley, Iowa

MARCH 21, 1958: Failed phase III of the Instrument Rating Flight Test given by Melvin O. Wood at Sioux Falls, South Dakota. Test was witnessed by his flight instructor, Leonard G. Ross (probably of Graham Flying Service). Aircraft used was a Piper PA-22.

Applicant had difficulty copying and interpreting ATC Clearances. Failed to orientate himself and comply with Air Traffic Control instructions given by Sioux Falls Approach Control.

Failure to properly tune and use his omni radio, became confused and was unable to establish on course.

Failed to establish holding procedures and identify station passage.

Lost control of the aircraft, on two occasions, while reading approach charts and descended below his assigned altitude in a spiral attitude. At this point the flight test was discontinued, and no approach procedure, missed approach procedure or emergency procedure was accomplished.

This applicant was very susceptible to distractions and became upset and confused during phase III of the flight test.

The applicant's deficiencies were thoroughly discussed with him and his flight instructor.

Melvin O. Wood

MARCH 29, 1958: Passed second-class physical by R. P. Noble, M.D., but a hearing deficiency was noted for the right ear. Showed total flying time as 270 hours, 100 in last six months.

APRIL 2, 1958: Issued temporary Commercial Pilot license, by examiner Hal C. Blacksten. Action endorsed on April 4 by Clarke S. Hall, certificate mailed on May 16. Test taken in Cessna 120. Flight hours at time: 60:35 dual, 215 pic, 5:10 dual cc, 91:25 pic cc, 43:55 instrument (actual), 0:45 dual night.

APRIL 29, 1958: Regional Medical Officer Chas. W. McMillin, M.D., gave Peterson 90 days to take a flight test to see if he can receive a waiver for his defective hearing. Did not take flight test until November 4.

MAY 7, 1958: Scored 82 on first part, 70 on second part of written test for FIA 3967.

JULY 23, 1958: Peterson's application for a Limited Flight Instructor rating was disapproved because he failed the oral portion of the exam. His logbook indicated: 316:30 of solo flying, 45:25 instrument and 67:30 dual time. Upon re-application, he was to be re-examined on Phase 1 Oral and Phase 2 Flight. Notice was signed by Clarke S. Hall. Peterson was living at 307 N. 4th Street, Clear Lake, Iowa, at the time.

NOVEMBER 4, 1958: Issued Commercial Pilot license, with the note "Airplane Single Engine Land, holder does not meet night flight requirements of ICAO, issued on the basis of medical flight test." Examiner was A. J. Prokop. Airplane used was a Cessna 175 (N7110M). Peterson had 40 hours in this aircraft (all pilot in command), other hours: 72 dual, 502 pic, 5 dual cross-country, 360 pic cc, 45 instrument (hooded), 2 dual night, 25 pic night.

His first test was to contact the Tower, using the VHF receiver. The volume was turned down and he received his instructions and complied with them satisfactorily. After takeoff he was told to turn to the Newton VOR station; at the particular time a broadcast was being given and he was told to repeat what was being said.

This was done satisfactorily with the volume turned up just a little above normal. Conversation was conducted and it was found that above the noisy aircraft I had to speak a little more loudly. He immediately recognized any throttle change that I made.

In view of the above, he was issued a certificate with the notation "Issued on the Basis of Medical Flight Test," since his hearing was not impaired sufficiently to place further restrictions on the certificate.

—A. J. Prokop

NOVEMBER 19, 1958: Chas. W. McMillin, M.D., regional medical officer of the CAA, issued a medical waiver to Peterson.

JANUARY 6, 1959: Took 3:15 of instrument dual instruction from Lawrence A. DenHartog of Eagle Grove at Mason City in DenHartog's Tri-Pacer, N3763P.

After takeoff, I had the colored goggles in my lap, and shortly thereafter, Mr. Peterson reached over and put them on. He had trouble orientating himself and flying the aircraft for at least 15 minutes after putting on the goggles. I would say that he had a false courage or was a little over-confident.

Mr. Peterson had previously come to the Eagle Grove airport to make arrangements for the above-mentioned instruction. I was not present at the time, but he informed my wife that he wouldn't need much time, and that he had received high grades on his written and had also received previous instrument time, and stated that all he would need was a little brushing up. My wife related to me what he had said, and I thought he would be pretty good, so the first thing I was going to have him do was some holdings.

However, after taking off, I felt it was necessary to practice considerable straight and level flying for some time before practicing turns and holdings. Then after the 3:15 hours of instruction, given by me, I think Mr. Peterson was disappointed in himself and may have thought I was a little rough as a flight instructor on instruments.

On the afternoon, previous to the aircraft accident, I called Mr. Peterson at the Dwyer Flying Service, Mason City, Iowa, on the telephone and he told me that he had been busy getting his flight instructor rating but planned to take additional instrument instruction from me the next week.

(I definitely feel that Mr. Peterson got "vertigo" at the time of the accident, and that the aircraft got away from him.)

—Lawrence A. DenHartog

JANUARY 27, 1959: Issued temporary airman certificate as Limited Flight Instructor. Passed test in Cessna 172 on January 25 with Hubert J. Dwyer instructing. Endorsed by John W. Hunt on January 27. At time: 81:30 dual, 610 pic, 5:10 dual cc, 313 pic cc, 51 instrument (hooded), 1 dual night, 35:35 pic night.

FEBRUARY 4, 1959: In the aircraft accident report signed by Air Safety Investigator C. E. Stillwagon, Roger Peterson was credited with 710 hours 45 minutes of flying time, 208:50 in the 90 days before his death. Of those most-recent hours, 48:10 were in the Bonanza, 14:40 were at night and 7:00 were on instruments.

The Dwyer Flying Service, which started in 1953, had an air carrier operating certificate with an air taxi rating issued by the Federal Aviation Agency. The certificate permitted the carrying of passengers for hire within the continental United States in accordance with visual flight rules, both day and night.

Notes and References

Chapter 2: Big Beat from Texas

Based on interviews with Jerry "J. I." Allison, Tommy Allsup, George Atwood, Allen Bloom, Sonny Curtis, Echo McGuire Griffith, Bill Griggs, Ben Hall, Larry Holley, Buddy Knox, Robert Linville, Wayne Maines, Joe B. Mauldin, Bobby Mayfield, Waymon Mulkey, Vi Petty, John Pickering, James Pritchard, Peggy Sue Rackham, Roy Rucker, Niki Sullivan, Larry Welborn, and Harold Womack.

page 9: "If the public ... a strong chance." *Billboard,* 1956.

page 11: "Whatever we may think ... plays for you." *Downbeat,* September 19, 1956.

page 17: "After I saw ... have to go." Chris May, *Rock 'n' Roll,* p. 108.

page 21: "Rock solid are ... is here." *Melody Maker,* 1958.

page 21: "Without doubt ... of the time." Keith Goodwin, *New Musical Express,* 1958.

page 22: "15 persons ... out of control." *Variety,* May 7, 1958.

Chapter 3: The Big Bopper

Based on interviews with Gordon Baxter, Jack Baxter, Jerry Boynton, James Broussard, Sonny Burns, Bonnie Cornwell, Bud Daily, J. C. Dorrell, Molly Dorrell, Bill Hall, Hal Harris, Don Jacobs, Herb Kalin, Tim Knight, Harry Luke, Huey Meaux, J. D. Miller, John Neil, Nick Noble, Cecil Richardson, Jay Perry Richardson, Gordon Ritter, Ken Ritter, John Romere, Charlie Schmucker, Roy Dixon Shotts, and Adrianne "Teetsie" Wenner.

Chapter 4: Getting Ready

Based on interviews with Nick Acerenza, Jerry "J. I." Allison, Tommy Allsup, Carmine Anthony, George Atwood, Howard Bedno, Allen Bloom, Carl Bunch, Sonny Curtis, Dion DiMucci, Woodrow Due, Paul Gallis, Sam Geller, Bill Griggs, Bill Hall, Larry Holley, Waylon Jennings, Buddy Knox, Robert Linville, Joe B. Mauldin, Vi Petty, Peggy Sue Rackham, Cecil Richardson, Jay Perry Richardson, John Romere, Frankie Sardo, Mrs. T. B. Skarning, and Adrianne "Teetsie" Wenner.

page 37: "Tim Gale ... Gale added." *Cash Box,* 1958.

page 39: "Norman told Buddy ... a lot of men." John Goldrosen, *Remembering Buddy,* p. 118.

page 45: "Waylon Jennings ... in Littlefield." *Lamb County Leader,* January 22, 1959.

Chapter 5: La Bamba

Based on interviews with Fred Aguilera, Connie Alvarez, Sal Barragan, Howard Bedno, Eusebio "Sailor" Canche, Donna Ludwig Fox, Earl Glicken, Pete Gonzalez, Sal Gutierez, Carol Kaye, Bob Keane, Art Laboe, Muriel Moore, Rosie Morales, Irma Norton, Armando "Lefty" Ortiz, Earl Palmer, Ted Quillin, Ernestine Reyes, Gil Rocha, Stan Ross, and Gail Smith.

page 55:"Ritchie Valens ... only in Spanish." *Cash Box,* November 15, 1958.

page 56: "As soon as ... that moment." *Movie Life,* June, 1959.

page 56: "It's happening ... too confusing." Beverly Mendheim, *Ritchie Valens: The First Latino Rocker,* p. 135.

page 57: "Ritchie and I ... my T-Bird." Mendheim, p. 104.

page 57: "I want you ... my mother." Mendheim, p. 105.

Chapter 6: The Tour Begins

General tour information from interviews with Carl Bunch, Dion DiMucci, Sam Geller, Waylon Jennings, Fred Milano, and Frankie Sardo.

Milwaukee information based on interviews with Orv Bathke (Larry Ladd), Bob Devine, Mark Shurilla, and John Stimac.

Kenosha information based on interviews with Mike Bjorn, Tammy Davidson, Eileen Doyle, Mark Ellefson, Kathy Jennings, Jim Lounsbury, Dan Lydon, Joan Mesner, Carol Pawlaczyk, Hank Rice, A. J. "Tony" Ritacca, Tom Rotunda, Edie Sadowski, Joe Santiloni, Debbie Stevens (Dean), and Tony Szikil.

Mankato information based on interviews with Dianne Cory, Bill Diehl, Paul Lyons, Jerry Martinka, Judy Peery, Curt Schueneman, Diane Seitz, and Cathy Chatleain Sembauer.

Eau Clair information based on interviews with Greg "Mouse" Bement, Joan Svenson Calkins, Pat Harvey, Don Larson, Kathy McLaughlin, Steve Meyer, Glenn St. Arnault, Tom Tronsdal, and Curt Tweith.

Montevideo information based on interviews with Newton Anderson, Roger Anderson, Diane Bagus, John Beltz, Bill Botten, Gordon Bright, Bob Bunn, Gladys Burns, Jane Ellefson, Jerry "Doogie" Erickson, Wanda Flickenger, Lorraine Folkestad, Edie Sickles Foos, Donnie Gayken, Glenn Gayken, Ronnie Hadrath, Gordy Hildahl, Ione Hunt, Irene Keilen, Gail Strouts Kessel, Loran Kratz, Lee Kvanli, Ruth Benson Leppke, Wanda Quilitz Malone, Arloa Hunt Molstad, Della Pillatzki, Larry Pray, Sandra Ryer, Donald Skogrand, Dick Strand, and Art Wersal.

pages 62–64: "It was crazy ... a fine blast!" Joe Botsford, reprinted with the permission of the *Milwaukee Sentinel,* January 24, 1959.

page 66: "A horde of ... Frankie Sardo. Wow!" Bill Diehl, *St. Paul Pioneer Press,* January 25, 1959.

Chapter 7: The Tour Goes Bad

General tour information from interviews with Tommy Allsup, Carl Bunch, Dion DiMucci, Sam Geller, Waylon Jennings, Fred Milano, and Frankie Sardo.

St. Paul information based on interviews with Ray Cook, Bill Diehl, Harry Given, Timothy D. Kehr, Sherwin Linton, and Milke Ulahakis.

Davenport information based on interviews with Dave Cooper, Fred Epstein, Judy Epstein, Susan Epstein Laforce, Mark Stevens, and Bill Wiederkehr.

Tipton information based on interviews with Betty Murray Aegerter, Betty McGregor, Bob McGregor, Gene Sissel, George Tevis, and Esther Wenck.

Fort Dodge information based on interviews with Denny Brown, Katie Cain, Tom Cairney, Dick Derrig, Jerry Estes, Bob Geer, Bill McCollough, Gary Onnen, John Shafar, Eddie Simpson, Sherwyn Thorson, and Arnie Ulstad.

Duluth information based on interviews with Bob Howden, Bob Jensen, Roger Krob, Lew Latto, Donna Lindholm Olson, and Ron Sapik.

page 82: "The group ... everyone else." *Tipton Conservative,* February 5, 1959.

page 84: "Buddy would call ... needed the money." Paul Galloway, *Chicago Tribune,* June 24, 1988.

Chapter 8: The Tour from Hell

General tour information from interviews with Jerry "J. I." Allison, Tommy Allsup, Carl Bunch, Dion DiMucci, Sam Geller, Larry Holley, Waylon Jennings, Joe B. Mauldin, Frankie Sardo, and Adrianne "Teetsie" Wenner.

Hurley/Ironwood information based on interviews with Gene Calvetti, Mrs. Clarence Grigg, and Dave O'Donahue.

Green Bay information based on interviews with Lloyd Aude, Phyllis Aude, Roger Bader, Butch Denissen, Dianne Heyroth, Karl Johannson, Wilbur LaHaie, Larry Matti, Butch Mellen, Judy Bender Oestreich, Terry Oestreich, Darold Rogers, Tom Rotter, Mary Geniusse Saunders, Bill Walters, Mrs. Bernard Wavrunek, and Helen Wiederkehr.

Clear Lake information based on interviews from Carroll Anderson, Keith Etzen, Bill Gasperi, Marge Vavric Gutzner, Bob Hale, Dick Haukoos, John Hurd, Nels Larsen, Karen Martinson Lien, Mrs. Harvey Luth, Sharon O'Neill, Bob Speakar, Dave Spilman, and Vic Stanbrough.

page 96: "He didn't tell me he was going to fly." Goldrosen, p. 144.

Chapter 9: The Flight

Based on interviews with Jerry Allen, Bruce Anderson, Carroll Anderson, Gordon Baxter, Bob Booe, Glenn Buchanan, Donald Buck, Thomas "T. K." Cameron, Jim Collison, Sky Corbin, Barb Dwyer, Reeve Eldridge, Art Fischbeck, Mrs. Harley Francis, Jim Frederickson, Maxine Funk, Ruth Pickering Gerber, Lorene Gilbert, Bob Hale, Larry Holley, Mrs. Robert Hoy, Waylon Jennings, Delbert Juhl, Elsie Juhl, Bob Keane, Glenn Kellogg, Dean Kemmerer, Ed Lamson, Duane Mayfield, Charles McGlothlen, Elwin Musser, John Neil, Art Peterson, DeAnn Peterson, Janet Peterson, Pearl Peterson, Ron Peterson, Joel Punke, Connie Ramirez, Roy Dixon Shotts, Dr. Ralph Smiley, Niki Sullivan, Warren Tilton, Glen Truax, Keith Van Hove, Adrianne "Teetsie" Wenner, and Lucille Wilcox.

pages 102–3: "The first thing ... was fully capable." Civil Aeronautics Board interview, February 4, 1959.

page 103: "We then ... Roger in first." Ibid.

pages 103–4: "They started ... straight North heading." Ibid.

page 104: "I stepped back ... optical illusion." Ibid.

pages 105–6: "The first place ... guide them in." Ibid.

page 110: "I yelled ... in her lap." Radio interview on Magic 104, Chicago, February 3, 1989.

Chapter 10: A Star Is Born

Based on interviews with Tommy Allsup, Eugene Anderson, Bobby Dale Bastiensen, Gordon Baxter, Scott Beach, Burnell "Bing" Bengtsson, Pat Berg, Allen Bloom, Bob Booe, Charlie Boone, James Broussard, Carl Bunch, Jim Collison, Dion DiMucci, Donna Ludwig Fox, Sam Geller, Larry Holley, Marvin A. "Ike" Iverson, Waylon Jennings, Elsie Juhl, Bob Keane, Rod Lucier, Charles McGlothlen, Fred Milano, Bruce Nokleby, Art Peterson, Pearl Peterson, A. J. Prokop, Peggy Sue Rackham, Ernestine Reyes, Cecil Richardson, Jay Perry Richardson, Leo Sander, Frankie Sardo, Mrs. T. B. Skarning, Gail Smith, Sherry Smith, Debbie Stevens (Dean), David Taylor, Bobby Vee, Bill Velline, and Lucille Wilcox.

pages 119–21: "Four persons ... roll favorites." Mason City Globe-Gazette, February 3, 1959.

page 124: "All [the dead ... an eerie feeling." Bill Griggs, Reminiscing, September 1979.

pages 125–26: "I originally ... and I did." Gregg Barrios, Los Angeles Times, July 19, 1987.

page 127: "a cleffer of some distinction." Billboard, February 9, 1959.

page 127: "We always ... terrible thing." Ibid.

Chapter 11: New Directions

Based on interviews with Jerry "J. I." Allison, Tommy Allsup, Gordon Baxter, Allen Bloom, Sonny Curtis, Barb Dwyer, Larry Holley, Waylon Jennings, Delbert Juhl, Elsie Juhl, Bob Keane, Robert Linville, Joe B. Mauldin, Muriel Moore, Ernestine Reyes, Cecil Richardson, Jay Perry Richardson, Sherry Smith, and Adrianne "Teetsie" Wenner.

page 128: "Rock 'n' roll ... is nothing, nothing." Time, February 16, 1959.

page 131: "There'll be ... bills he owed." Dorothy Killgallen, syndicated columnist, March 14, 1959.

Chapter 13: The Controversy

Based on interviews with Fred Aguilera, Jerry Allen, Jerry "J. I." Allison, Tommy Allsup, Bruce Anderson, Eugene Anderson, Bob Booe, Carl Bunch, Dion DiMucci, Barb Dwyer, Reeve Eldridge, Sam Geller, Ruth Pickering Gerber, Bob Hale, Mahlon A. "Curly" Hintzman, Larry Holley, Waylon Jennings, Dr. George T. Joyce, Delbert Juhl, Joe B. Mauldin, Charles McGlothlen, Fred Milano, DeAnn Peterson, Pearl Peterson, Ron Peterson, A. J. Prokop, Leonard Ross, and Debbie Stevens (Dean).

page 143: "fired all four bullets into the air" and "all discharged perfectly." Clear Lake Mirror-Reporter, April 9, 1959.

page 143: "These investigations ... on the accident." Ibid.

pages 143–44: "The pistol ... plane wreck." Mason City *Globe-Gazette*, April 10, 1959.

page 144: "I was ... that gun." Mason City *Globe-Gazette*, February 1, 1989.

page 147: "This *really* ... him again." Mendheim, p. 29.

page 149: "decreased pitch ... by surprise." *The Aviation Consumer Used Aircraft Guide*, p. 96.

page 150: "the North ... several minutes." Civil Aeronautics Board interview, February 4, 1959.

page 151: "When he ... radio procedure." Letter to Civil Aeronautics Board, February 19, 1959.

page 151: "Mr. Peterson ... to the right." Letter to Civil Aeronautics Board, February 10, 1959.

page 151: "We gave ... his flying." Letter to Civil Aeronatics Board, February 19, 1959.

page 152: "Applicant had ... flight test." Federal Aviation Agency memorandum to Civil Aeronautics Board, February 12, 1959.

page 153: "After takeoff ... next week." Letter to Civil Aeronautics Board, March 2, 1959.

Chapter 14: Legacies

Based on interviews with Jerry "J. I." Allison, Tommy Allsup, George Atwood, Gordon Baxter, Allen Bloom, Billy Cardenas, Sonny Curtis, Donna Ludwig Fox, John Goldrosen, Bill Griggs, Sal Gutierez, Larry Holley, Bob Keane, Tim Knight, Buddy Knox, Art Laboe, Joe B. Mauldin, Huey Meaux, J. D. Miller, Vi Petty, Charlie Phillips, John Pickering, Ted Quillin, Peggy Sue Rackham, Ernestine Reyes, Jay Perry Richardson, Gil Rocha, Chan Romero, Stan Ross, Gail Smith, Niki Sullivan, Adrianne "Teetsie" Wenner, and Sonny West.

page 169: "We were ... look like Buddy." *Today* television show, November 1, 1988.

Chapter 15: Family Affairs

Based on interviews with Connie Alvarez, Barb Dwyer, Donna Ludwig Fox, John Goldrosen, Larry Holley, Sherry Holley, Maria Elena Holly, Waylon Jennings, Rosie Morales, Irma Norton, Art Peterson, DeAnn Peterson, Pearl Peterson, Ron Peterson, Ernestine Reyes, Cecil Richardson, Jay Perry Richardson, Gil Rocha, Gail Smith, and Adrianne "Teetsie" Wenner.

page 178: "We felt ... not been killed." Nene Foxhall, *University Daily* (Texas Tech student newspaper), November 3, 1972.

Chapter 16: The Fans

Based on interviews with Jerry Allen, Marcia Farley, John Firminger, John Goldrosen, Bill Griggs, Darrel Hein, George Horton, Bob Keane, Don Larson, Jerry Miller, Muriel Moore, Jay Perry Richardson, and Kevin Terry.

Chapter 17: Where Are They Now?

Based on interviews with Jerry Allen, Jerry "J. I." Allison, Tommy Allsup, Carroll Anderson, Eugene Anderson, Louise Anderson, George Atwood, Lloyd Aude, Phyllis Aude, Diane Bagus, Burnell "Bing" Bengtsson, Allen Bloom, Denny Brown, Carl Bunch, Bob Bunn, Joan Svenson Calkin, Billy Cardenas, Bruce Christensen, Jim Collison, Sky Corbin, Dianne Cory, Sonny Curtis, Bud Daily, Bob Devine, Bill Diehl, Dion DiMucci, Eileen Doyle, Jane Ellefson, Fred Epstein, Keith Etzen, Donna Ludwig Fox, Bob Geer, Sam Geller, Harry Given, Echo McGuire Griffith, Bob Hale, Ben Hall, Bill Hall, Dick Haukoos, Darrel Hein, Ione Hunt, John Hurd, Waylon Jennings, Bob Jensen, Dr. George T. Joyce, Elsie Juhl, Bob Keane, Timothy D. Kehr, Glenn Kellogg, Don Larson, Lew Latto, Sherwin Linton, Robert Linville, Jim Lounsbury, Wanda Quilitz Malone, Jerry Martinka, Larry Matti, Joe B. Mauldin, Duane Mayfield, Bill McCollough, Fred Milano, J. D. Miller, Muriel Moore, Waymon Mulkey, Elwin Musser, Gordon Payne, Judy Peery, Vi Petty, John Pickering, A. J. Prokop, Ted Quillin, Peggy Sue Rackham, Gordon Ritter, Ken Ritter, Gil Rocha, John Romere, Chan Romero, Stan Ross, Tom Rotunda, Leo Sander, Frankie Sardo, Mark Shurilla, Eddie Simpson, Dr. Ralph Smiley, Sherry Smith, Debbie Stevens (Dean), Mark Stevens, John Stimac, Dick Strand, Niki Sullivan, Tony Szikil, Mike Ulahakis, Pat Ek Ulahakis, Bobby Vee, Bill Velline, Bill Walters, Larry Welborn, Sonny West, and Harold Womack.

page 220: "It is somewhat ... 'a square.'" *Tipton Conservative,* February 12, 1959.

page 220: "But next time ... talk to him." Ibid.

Chapter 18: The Last Tour

page 225: "When interviewed ... excitement of it." *Denfeld Criterion,* February 1959.

page 229: "Buddy, we ... Sure would." Alan Freed television show, WNEW-TV, New York, September 23, 1958.

Appendix A: The Plane

page 235: "The Bonanza ... airplane flying."*Aviation Consumer Used Aircraft Guide,* p. 93.

page 235: "The V-tail ... spiral' quickly." Ibid., p. 95.

page 235: "With any ... even lighter." Ibid., p. 95.

Bibliography

Books

Airguide Manual. Long Beach, CA: Airguide Publications, Inc., 1971.

Allen, Bob. *George Jones: The Saga of an American Singer.* Garden City, NY: Doubleday & Company, Inc., 1984.

Amburn, Ellis. *Dark Star: The Roy Orbison Story.* New York: Carol Publishing Group, 1990.

American Panorama: East of the Mississippi. Garden City, NY: Doubleday & Company, Inc., 1960.

Barron, Lee. *Odyssey of the Mid-Nite Flyer.* Omaha, NE: kr & associates, 1987.

Beecher, John, and Malcolm Jones. *The Buddy Holly Story.* Distributed with MCA Records *Buddy Holly* boxed set.

Berry, Chuck. *Chuck Berry: The Autobiography.* New York: Harmony Books, 1987.

Berry, Jason, Jonathan Foose, and Tad Jones. *Up from the Cradle of Jazz.* Athens, GA: The University of Georgia Press, 1986.

Boeckman, Charles. *and the beat goes on.* Washington: Robert B. Luce, Inc., 1972.

Bronson, Fred. *The Billboard Book of Number One Hits.* New York: Billboard Publications, Inc., 1985.

Carlisle, Dolly. *Ragged But Right: The Life and Times of George Jones.* Chicago: Contemporary Books, 1984.

Carr, Patrick. *Illustrated History of Country Music.* Garden City, NY: Country Music Magazine Press, 1979.

Chapple, Steve, and Reebee Garofolo. *Rock 'n' Roll Is Here to Pay.* Chicago: Nelson-Hall, 1977.

Chronicle of the 20th Century. Mount Kisco, NY: Chronicle Publications, Inc., 1987.

Clark, Alan. *Ritchie Valens: 30th Anniversary Memorial Series.* West Covina, CA: The National Rock 'n' Roll Archives, 1989.

Coleman, Ray. *Lennon.* New York: McGraw-Hill, 1985.

Current Biography. New York: H. W. Wilson Co.

Denisoff, R. Serge. *Tarnished Gold: The Record Industry Revisited.* New Brunswick, NJ: Transaction Books, 1986.

―――. *Waylon: A Biography.* Knoxville, TN: The University of Tennessee Press, 1983.

DiMucci, Dion, with Davin Seay. *The Wanderer: Dion's Story.* New York: Beech Tree Books, 1988.

Duncan, Robert. *Only the Good Die Young.* New York: Harmony Books, 1986.

Eisen, Jonathan. *The Age of Rock 2.* New York: Random House, 1970.

Fowler, Gene, and Bill Crawford. *Border Radio.* New York: Proscenium Publishers Inc., 1990.

Fox-Sheinwold, Patricia. *Too Young to Die.* New York: Weathervane Books, 1979.

George, Nelson. *Where Did Our Love Go?* New York: St. Martin's Press, 1985.

Goldrosen, John, and John Beecher. *Remembering Buddy: The Definitive Biography of Buddy Holly.* New York: Penguin Books, 1986.

Govenar, Alan. *Meeting the Blues.* Dallas, TX: Taylor Publishing Co., 1988.

Guralnick, Peter. *Feel Like Going Home.* New York: Outerbridge & Dienstfrey, 1971.

————. *Lost Highway.* Boston: David R. Godine, 1979.

————. *Sweet Soul Music.* New York: Harper & Row, 1986.

Hemphill, Paul. *The Nashville Sound.* New York: Simon & Schuster, 1970.

Hendler, Herb. *Year by Year in the Rock Era.* Westport, CT: Greenwood Press, 1983.

Hirshey, Gerri. *Nowhere to Run.* New York: Penguin Books, 1984.

Holley, Larry. *The Buddy I Knew!* Self-published, 1979.

Hopkins, Jerry. *Elvis: A Biography.* New York: Warner Books, 1971.

————. *The Rock Story.* New York: Signet, 1970.

The Illustrated History of Rock Music. New York: Simon & Schuster, 1984.

Iowa: A Guide to the Hawkeye State. New York: Hastings House, 1959.

Jackson, John A. *Big Beat Heat.* New York: Schirmer Books, 1991.

Jancik, Wayne. *One-Hit Wonders.* New York: Billboard Books/An Imprint of Watson-Guptill Publications, 1990.

Jones, Mablen. *Getting It On: The Clothing of Rock 'n' Roll.* New York: Abbeville Press, 1987.

Knight, Tim. *Chantilly Lace: The Life and Times of J. P. Richardson.* Port Arthur, TX: Port Arthur Historical Society, 1989.

Lazell, Barry. *Rock Movers and Shakers.* New York: Billboard Publications, Inc., 1989.

Lewis, Myra, with Murray Silver. *Great Balls of Fire: The Uncensored Story of Jerry Lee Lewis.* New York: William Morrow and Company, Inc., 1982.

Lewis, Peter. *The Fifties.* New York: J. B. Lippincott Company, 1978.

Logan, Nick, and Bob Woffinden. *The Illustrated Encyclopedia of Rock.* New York: Harmony Books, 1977.

Lydon, Michael. *Boogie Lightning.* New York: The Dial Press, 1974.

Makower, Joel. *Boom! Talkin' About Our Generation.* Chicago: Contemporary Books Inc., 1985.

Mann, Alan. *The A–Z of Buddy Holly.* London: Aurum Press Ltd., 1996.

Marsh, Dave, et al. *The First Rock & Roll Confidential Report.* New York: Pantheon Books, 1985.

————. *The Heart of Rock & Soul.* New York: New American Library, 1989.

The Marshall Cavendish Illustrated History of Popular Music. Freeport, NY: Marshall Cavendish Corp., 1989.

Martin, Linda, and Kerry Segrave. *Anti-Rock: The Opposition to Rock 'n' Roll.* Hamden, CT: Archon Books/The Shoe String Press, Inc., 1988.

May, Chris. *Rock 'n' Roll.* London: Socion Books.

Mendheim, Beverly. *Ritchie Valens: The First Latino Rocker.* Tempe, AZ: Bilingual Press, 1987.

Merritt, Jeffrey. *Day By Day: The Fifties.* New York: Facts On File, 1979.

Millar, Bill. *The Drifters.* New York: Collier Books, 1972.

Miller, Douglas T., and Marion Nowak. *The Fifties: The Way We Really Were.* Garden City, NY: Doubleday & Company, Inc., 1977.

Minnesota: A State Guide. New York: Hastings House, 1947.

Murrells, Joseph. *Million Selling Records.* New York: Arco Publishing, Inc., 1985.

Nash, Bruce M. *Whatever Happened to Blue Suede Shoes?* New York: Grosset & Dunlap, 1978.

National Cyclopedia of American Biography. New York: James T. White & Co.

Nite, Norm N. *Rock On.* New York, Thomas Y. Crowell Company, 1974.

———. *Rock On: Volume II.* New York: Thomas Y. Crowell Company, 1978.

Norman, Phillip. *Rave On: The Biography of Buddy Holly.* New York: Simon & Schuster, 1996.

Nugent, Stephen, and Charlie Gillett. *Rock Almanac.* Garden City, NY: Anchor Books, 1978.

Oakley, J. Ronald. *God's Country: America in the Fifties.* New York: Dembner Books, 1986.

Palmer, Tony. *All You Need Is Love.* New York: Grossman Publishers, 1976.

The Penguin Encyclopedia of Popular Music. Edited by Donald Clarke. New York: Penguin Books USA, 1990.

Pollock, Bruce. *When Rock Was Young.* New York: Holt, Rinehart and Winston, 1981.

Preiss, Byron. *The Beach Boys.* New York: Ballantine Books, 1979.

Redd, Lawrence N. *Rock Is Rhythm and Blues (The Impact of Mass Media).* East Lansing, MI: Michigan State University Press, 1974.

Rohde, H. Kandy. *The Gold of Rock & Roll: 1955–67.* New York: Arbor House, 1970.

Rolling Stone Rock Almanac. New York: Collier Books, 1983.

Shaw, Arnold. *The Rockin' '50s.* New York: Hawthorn Books, Inc., 1974.

———. *Black Popular Music in America.* New York: Schirmer Books, 1986.

Shore, Michael. *The History of American Bandstand.* New York: Ballantine Books.

Sklar, Rick. *Rocking America.* New York: St. Martin's Press, 1984.

Smith, Steve. *Rock: Day By Day.* London: Guinness Books, 1987.

Stambler, Irwin, and Grelun Landon. *Encyclopedia of Folk, Country and Western Music.* New York: St. Martin's Press, 1969.

———. *Encyclopedia of Pop, Rock & Soul.* New York: St. Martin's Press, 1977.

Swenson, John. *The John Lennon Story.* New York: Leisure Books, 1981.

Szatmary, David. *Rockin' in Time.* Englewood Cliffs, NJ: Prentice-Hall, Inc., 1987.

Texas: A Guide to the Lone Star State. New York: Hastings House, 1945.

Texas Travel Handbook. Texas Highway Department.

Theroux, Gary, and Bob Gilbert. *The Top Ten: 1956–Present.* New York: Simon & Schuster, 1982.

Tobler, John. *The Buddy Holly Story.* London: Plexus Publishing Limited, 1979.

———. *Who's Who in Rock & Roll.* New York: Crescent Books, 1991.

Tosches, Nick. *Hellfire: The Jerry Lee Lewis Story.* New York: Delacorte Press, 1982.

———. *Unsung Heroes of Rock 'n' Roll.* New York: Charles Scribner's Sons, 1984.

Ward, Ed, Geoffrey Stokes, and Ken Tucker. *Rock of Ages.* New York: Rolling Stone Books/Summit Press, 1986.

Waters, Thomas F. *The Streams and Rivers of Minnesota.* Minneapolis, MN: University of Minnesota Press, 1977.

Whitcomb, Ian. *After the Ball.* New York: Simon & Schuster, 1972.

White, Charles. *The Life and Times of Little Richard.* New York: Harmony Books, 1984.

Who's Who in America. Chicago: Marquis-Who's Who.

Wisconsin: A Guide to the Badger State. New York: Hastings House, 1954.

The World Almanac Book of the Strange. New York: Signet, 1977.

Worth, Fred L. *Rock Facts.* New York: Facts On File Publications, 1985.

The Year in Music: 1978. New York: Columbia House, 1978.

Zalkind, Ronald. *Contemporary Music Almanac 1980–81.* New York: Schirmer Books, 1980.

Articles

Hoffman, Jim. "We Belong Together,"*Photoplay,* May 1959.

Holly, Maria Elena. "A Farewell to Buddy Holly," unknown magazine, probably 1959.

Larkin, Lou. "Why Did They Have to Die?," *Motion Picture,* May 1959.

Meltsir, Aljean. "Portrait of a Family in Grief," *Motion Picture,* May 1959.

Myers, David. "The Life and Death of Ritchie Valens," *Modern Screen,* May 1959.

Nash, Bonnie. "The Night I Sang With Richie Valens," *Dig,* April 1959.

Sherlock, George. "We'll Remember Ritchie," *Teen,* date unknown.

Spencer, Dee. "When Ritchie Valens Died, We Died Too," *Movie Life,* June 1959.

Magazines

Billboard

Buddy Magazine (Dallas, TX)

Cash Box

Downbeat

Goldmine (Krause Publications, Iola, WI)

Melody Maker

Movie Life

New Musical Express

Reminiscing (magazine of the Buddy Holly Memorial Society)

Rockin' '50s (Bill Griggs, Lubbock, TX)

Time

Variety

Newspapers

The Capital Times, Madison, WI

The Chicago Tribune, Chicago, IL

The Coshocton Tribune, Coshocton, OH

The Courier, Waterloo, IA

The Courier-Journal, Louisville, KY

The Daily Globe, Ironwood, MI

The Daily Telegram, Eau Claire, WI

The Denfeld Criterion, Denfeld High School, Duluth, MN

The Des Moines Register, Des Moines, IA

The Des Moines Tribune, Des Moines, IA

The Dubuque Telegraph-Herald, Dubuque, IA

Duluth Herald, Duluth, MN

Duluth News-Tribune, Duluth, MN

The Fargo Forum, Fargo, ND

Globe-Gazette, Mason City, IA

The Green Bay Press-Gazette, Green Bay, WI

The Iron County Miner, Hurley, WI

Kenosha Evening News, Kenosha, WI

The Lamb County Leader, Littlefield, TX

The Los Angeles Times, Los Angeles, CA
Mankato Free Press, Mankato, MN
The Messenger, Fort Dodge, IA
The Mid-Week Bulletin, Kenosha, WI
The Milwaukee Journal, Milwaukee, WI
The Milwaukee Sentinel, Milwaukee, WI
The Mirror-Reporter, Clear Lake, IA
The Montevideo American-News, Montevideo, MN
The Morning Democrat, Davenport, IA
The Muskegon Chronicle, Muskegon, MI
The Peoria Journal Star, Peoria, IL
The Pioneer Press, St. Paul, MN
The Pioneer Press & Dispatch, St. Paul, MN
The Post-Crescent, Appleton, WI
Record-Herald, Wausau, WI
Rhinelander Daily News, Rhinelander, WI
The Sioux City Journal, Sioux City, IA
The State Journal-Register, Springfield, IL
The Tipton Advertiser, Tipton, IA
The Tipton Conservative, Tipton, IA
The University Daily, Texas Tech University, Lubbock, TX
Wisconsin State Journal, Madison, WI

Index

ABC (American Broadcasting Company), news of plane crash, 108
"Abraham, Martin and John" (Dion), 203
Academy Award, for *The Buddy Holly Story*, 175
Adler, Lou, 230
Adventures of Buddy Holly, The, (play), 176
After Awhile (Gilmore album), 170
Aguilera, Fred, 147
air traffic controller, 103–4
Allen, Jerry, xi, 106, 144, 217
    objects found by, 192–93
Allens, Arvee (Ritchie Valens), 56. *See also* Valens, Ritchie
Allison, Jerry, 7, 8, 10–12, 14, 15, 18, 22, 23, 40, 78, 96, 128–29, 133, 144–46, 166, 173, 193, 205–6
    and *The Buddy Holly Story*, 175
    Fargo memorial, 192
    marriage, 24–25
    Not Fade Away, 174
    and Petty, 38, 158, 161
    and "That'll Be the Day," 156, 159–60
    and tours, 19, 20, 22, 24
Allison, Peggy Sue Gerron, 24–25, 39, 40, 126, 172, 206, 215
"All Shook Up" (Presley), 30
Allsup, Thomas Douglas "Tommy," xi, 24, 40, 43, 45, 62, 71, 119, 123, 133, 201, 226, 230
    and financial arrangements, 128–29, 159
    and flight from Mason City, 96, 97
    and Holly, 46, 84, 150
    gun given to, 144
    and Milano's gun, 84–85
    and Petty, 155
    and tour bus, 85, 115–16
    wallet of, 97, 110, 217, 231
Alpert, Herb, 230
Alvarez, Connie (half-sister of Valens), xiii, 182, 185–86
Amarillo, Texas, Presley concert, 7
Amburn, Ellis, 174
American Bandstand, 18, 39, 54
American Federation of Musicians
    and Winter Dance Party, 65
"American Pie," McLean, 179, 197
Anderson, Bruce, 100, 143
Anderson, Carroll, xi, 94, 95, 97, 104, 108, 110, 222
    and flight arrangements, 101, 103
Anderson, Eugene, 121–22, 126, 144, 148, 216

Anderson, John "Andy," 217
Anderson, Larry, 187
Anderson, Louise, 217
Andrews, Lee, 16
Angola, Indiana, 24
Anka, Paul, 18, 21, 168
    "Diana," 19
Apollo Theater, New York, 17
Appleton, Wisconsin, 86, 90
Aragon Ballroom, Chicago, 126–27
Arthur Murray Show, The, 21
Asher, Peter, 166
Associated Press, report of crash, 119–21
Atco Records, and Darin, 23
Atkins, Chet, 199
Atwood, George, 43, 158, 208
auction of Holly possessions, 180
Aude, Lloyd and Phyllis, 91, 222
Australia
    Crickets tour, 21
    sales of Holly's records, 129
    tour plans, 129
autographs, value of, 229
Auxner, Ed, 65
Avalon, Frankie, 117, 123, 127, 167
Avianca, Frankie, 204. *See also* Sardo, Frankie
The Aviation Consumer Used Aircraft Guide, 149
Aycock, Otwell R., 125, 126, 216

background music, Holly and, 158
Bagdasarian, Ross (David Seville), "Witch Doctor," 32–33
Bagus, Diane, 73–74, 219
Baker, Jeanette, 172
Baker, LaVern, 18
Bandstand Matinee (television program), 64
bank account controlled by Petty, 40, 155–56, 159
Barnes, Benny, 32, 130
Barrow, Clyde, 227
Barry, Joe, 183
Bassey, Shirley, 166
Baxter, Gordon, 27, 28, 30, 31, 32, 35, 125, 164, 225
    "Gold Records in the Snow," 130
Baxter, Jack, 28
Beach, Scott, 216
Beach Boys, 205–6, 212
Beatles, 168–69
    "Twist and Shout," 166
Beaumont, Texas, xi, xv, 228
    memorial concert, 192
    news of plane crash, 108
Be–Bop–a–Lula (Vincent), 10

Becchetti, Fred, 121–22, 126, 216
Bedno, Howard, 47
Beech (plane manufacturer), investigation of accident, 125, 126
Beechcraft Bonanza, 233–37
    flown by Peterson, 101
Beecher, John, xi, 174, 193, 198
"Beggar to a King" (Barnes), 32
"Beggar to a King" (Richardson), 32
Belmonts (vocal group), 69, 147, 203. See also Dion and The Belmonts
    on tour, 83.
Bengtsson, Burnell, 118, 119, 216
Bennett, Bill, 146
Berg, Pat, 118, 119
Bernard, Rod, 183
Berry, Chuck, 18, 22, 167
Berry, Mike, "Tribute to Buddy Holly," 170
Big Beat tour, 22, 193
Big Bopper, 28. See also Richardson, J. P.
    fan club, 44
Big Bopper Music, 44, 165, 211
Big Bopper Show (radio program), 28
"Big Bopper's Wedding" (Richardson), 36
Biggest Show of Stars tour, 18–20, 38, 123
"Big Mamou" (Davis), 34
Billboard, 9, 36, 127
    and Valens records, 53, 55
Bill Halcy and His Comets, 8
biographies
    of Holly, 174–76
    of Valens, 176
birthplace of Holly, saved from demolition, 172
Black, Jim, Buddy Holly: A Collector's Guide, 193
Blecher, Joseph, 91
Blecher, Marie, 91
Bloom, Allen, 17, 18, 42, 117, 128, 129, 168, 204–5
"Blue Christmas" (Presley), 230
"Blue Days, Black Nights," Hall, 206
"Blue Days, Black Nights" (Holly), 8
blues music, Holly and, 7
"Blue Suede Shoes" (Presley), 9
Bobby Fuller Four, "Let Her Dance," 213
Bobby Vee Meets the Crickets (album), 216
"Bo Diddley," 17
Boling, Pat, 234
Booe, Bob, 105, 108, 110, 146, 151
"Boogie With Stu" (Led Zeppelin), 166
"Boogie Woogie" (Richardson), 29, 165
book given to Holly, 226
Boone, Charlie, 117, 118, 216
Boston, Big Beat tour, 22
Botsford, Joe, 62–64, 218
"Bottle of Wine" (Fireballs), 210
Bourgeois, Jivin' Gene, 165, 192
Bowen, Jimmy, 12–13
Box, David, 205, 207
Boynton, Jerry, 27, 28, 29, 33–35

Braddock, Jim, 64
Bradley, Owen, 8, 156
Brady, Violet Ann, 13–14. See also Petty, Violet Brady "Vi"
"Bread and Butter" (Newbeats), 207
"Breaking Up Is Hard to Do," 165
briefcase found in wreckage, 228
British tour, Crickets, 21–22
broadcasting marathons, 78, 80
    Richardson's Jape–a–thon, 29–31
Broussard, James, 29
Brown, Denny, 220
"Brown-Eyed Handsome Man," 96
Bruno (fashion photographer), 41
Brunswick Records, 15, 16, 17, 23, 30, 132
Buchanan, Glenn, 111
Buck, Louie, 30
Buddy (play), 176
"Buddy and Bob," 6
    as openers for Presley, 7, 8
Buddy Holly (Laing), 174, 193
Buddy Holly: A Collector's Guide (Griggs and Black), 193
Buddy Holly: His Life & Music (Goldrosen), 174, 198
Buddy Holly & The Crickets: Golden Greats (album), 210
Buddy Holly Appreciation Society, xi, 190
Buddy Holly at the Regal (play), 176
Buddy Holly Memorial Society, xi, xiv, 190, 193–94
Buddy Holly Recreation Area (Lubbock), 173
"Buddy Holly's Crickets," 119, 124
Buddy Holly Society (British), 190
Buddy Holly Songbook, The (instrumental album), 201
Buddy Holly Story, The (album), 127
Buddy Holly Story, The (film), xi, 133, 173, (film), xi, 133, 173, 174–75
"Buddy's song" (Vee), 216
"Bulldog" (Fireballs), 209
Bunch, Carl, 43, 46, 47, 67, 69, 84, 117, 123, 128–29, 132, 144, 146, 147, 168, 201
    and Winter Dance Party tour, 45–46, 62, 71, 72, 124
    frozen feet, 90
    tour bus, 69–70, 81, 85, 86, 88
    tour members, 71, 74, 75
Bunch, Dorothy, 201
Bunn, Bob, 73, 74, 219
Burlison, Paul, 10
Burnette, Johnny, 10
Burns, Clarence, 72–73
Burns, Sonny, 34
Burton, James, 183
bus, Winter Dance Party tour. See tour bus
Busey, Gary, 175, 180
"Bye Bye Love" (Everly Brothers), 18
Byrd, Tracy, 228
CAB. See Civil Aeronautics Board

Cain, Katie, 83
California, Valens appearances, 54
Cameron, Thomas, 99
Campbell, Jo Ann, 123
candy bars, at crash site, 146
Cannon, Ace, 183
Cannon, Freddy, 192
Capitol Records, 10
Capitol Theater, Davenport, Iowa, 79, 220
Cardenas, Billy, 171, 215
Carol Kay and the Teen-Aires, 123
Carr, Jim, 190
cars purchased by Holly, 20, 24, 38
Cash, Johnny, 169, 199, 200
Cash Box, 14, 36, 37, 53, 55, 230
"Cattle Call" (Dinah Shore), 31
Cedar Rapids, Iowa, Winter Dance Party,
    125
Challenge label, 52
Champagne Music Makers, 91
Champs (rock group), 51–52
"Change Is Gonna Come, A" (Cooke), 226
"Chantilly Lace" (Richardson), 25, 34, 35, 36,
    44, 164, 165
        gold record, 127, 182
        Milwaukee performance, 63
Chantilly Lace (LP), 130
"Chantilly Lace Cha Cha Cha" (Kimbrough),
    231
Charles, Ray, 168
Chatleain, Cathy, 67, 69
Chernier, Clifton, 29
Chesnutt, Mark, 228
Chicago, Winter Dance Party, 126–27
Chirpin' Crickets (album), 71, 207, 208
        cover shot, 18
Choates, Harry, "Jole Blun," 231
Christensen, Sue, 222
Christensen, Bruce, 167, 222
Christensen, Ed, 112, 217
cigarette butt discarded by Valens, 66
Cinderella Ballroom, 221–22
Citadel (Petty home), xiv, 210
Civil Aeronautics Board (CAB)
        investigation, 110, 121–22, 124
        report, *134,* 135–41, 228
            media and, 142–43
Clanton, Jimmy, 117, 123, 167, 191
        and tour bus, 124
Clapton, Eric, 173, 206
Clark, Dick, 39, 64, 167
        American Bandstand, 18, 39, 54
Clark, Doug, 192
Clark, H. E., 220
Clark, Sanford, 35
"Class Room" (Sardo), 42
Clear Lake, Iowa, xi, 92, 191–93
        Winter Dance Party, 93–97
Clear Lake *Mirror-Reporter,* 143
Clem Brau (polka band), 67
Clement, "Cowboy" Jack, 211

clothes
        of Crickets, 18
        of Holly, 8
        See also costumes for stage perfor-
            mance
Clovis, New Mexico, recording studio, xiii,
    13–14, 38, 132
Club Carnival, Hurley, Wisconsin, 89–90, 221
Cochran, Eddie, 18, 40, 205, 223, 226
Cocktail (film), 215
coincidences, strange, 226–27
Collins, Larry and Lorrie, 14
Collins, Tommy, 9
Collison, Jim, 111–12, 124, 217
        story of crash, 119–21
Colter, Jessi, 199
Columbia Records, 16
        Petty and, 158
Combest, Larry, 173
Come and Get It, Ferber, 89
"Come Back Baby" (Crickets), 38
"Come Back When You Grow Up" (Vee), 216
"Come On Let's Go," recordings by various
        artists, 166
"Come On Let's Go" (Steele), 55
"Come On Let's Go" (Valens), 42, 51, 52–53
continuous broadcasting record, 29–31
Conway, Chuck, 199
Cooke, Sam, 51, 212, 213, 226, 230
Coral Records, 10, 15, 17, 19
        The Buddy Holly Story, 127, 129
        posthumous Holly releases, 129
Corbin, Sky, 109, 207
Corbin, Slim, 43, 109
Cornwell, Bonnie, 27, 28
coroner's reports, 227
Cory, Dianne, 68–69, 219
co-songwriters with Holly, income of, 162
Costello, Elvis, 169
costumes for stage performance, 17, 45
        Holly, 6
        Valens, 55
Cotton Club (Lubbock), 7, 11
"Cotton Picker" (Watts), 32
Council Bluffs Daily Nonpareil, xi
country music
        Dion and, 71
        Holly and, 7
        Richardson and, 31–32
country music tours, 8, 9, 11
"Cradle of Love" (Preston), 165
Crandall, Eddie, 8, 9
crash site, 192
        motion picture footage, 232
        photographs, xii, 198, 217
crash theories, 145–48, 196, 197
Crawdaddy magazine, x, xi
Crawford, Johnny, 212
"Crazy Blues" (Richardson), 32
Crickets (Holly's band), xv, 5, 15, 16, 21–22,
    23, 159, 205–6, 230

Crickets (*continued*)
    "Biggest Show of Stars" tour, 18–19
    competition for name, 129
    Petty and, 156–5, 161
    recordings, 15, 38
        "Come Back Baby," 38
        "Reminiscing," 38
        "That'll Be the Day," 15, 16,
            17, 19, 21, 194
    split with Holly, 40
    television appearances, 39
    Winter Dance Party group, 46, 63
    after plane crash, 123
    report of deaths, 109, 116
    reunion, 193
    tribute shows, 191
    See also, Holly, Buddy; Holly and the
        Crickets
Crickets File (fan magazine), 190
Crowley, Louisiana, recording studio, 28
"Cry Cry Cry," Keane and, 163
"Crying, Waiting, Hoping" (Holly), 129
Curtis, King, 38
Curtis, Sonny, 7, 8, 10, 11, 40, 128–29, 133,
    161, 193, 205–6
    and *The Buddy Holly Story,* 175
    and first Holly record, 9–10
    "I Fought the Law," 213

"D" label records, 32, 34, 103
Daily, Bud, 31
Daily, H. W. "Pappy," 31, 32, 34, 211
"Daisy Petal Pickin'," 210
Dale, Dave, 122
Dale, Dick, 51
Dallas, Texas, xiv
dance party tour, 41–42. *See also* Winter Dance
    Party tour
Danny and the Juniors, 22
Darin, Bobby, 23, 123
Davenport, Iowa, 78, 79–81
Davis, Link, 34
Davis, Mac, 170
Dean, Debbie, 204. *See also* Stevens, Debbie
Dean, James, 195
Deane, Buddy, 54
Decca Records, 8–10, 12, 16, 23
"De De Dinah" (Avalon), 123
Dee, Tommy, "The Three Stars," 123
DeLeon, Texas, Presley concert, 7
Del-Fi label, 51, 55
    Ernie Valens and, 186
    posthumous Valens releases, 129, 130
Denato, Pat, xii
Denfeld Criterion, 225
DenHartog, Lawrence A., 152–53, 242–43
Denny, Jim, 8
Derrig, Dick, 82, 83
Des Moines, Iowa, 124
Des Moines Register, xii
"Devil or Angel" (Vee), 216

Devine, Bob, 217–18
Devine, George, 217
    Million Dollar Ballroom, 62–64
Diamonds (group), 22, 192
"Diana" (Anka), 19
Diaz, Joe, 179
Diaz, Maria Elena Holly, 193. *See also* Holly,
    Maria Elena Santiago
Dick Clark Saturday Night Beech-Nut Show, The,
    35
Diddley, Bo, 91
Diehl, Bill, 66, 68, 76, 220
Dillinger, John, 89
Ding Dongs (Darin and Kirshner), 23
Dinizio, Patrick, 180
Dion, 66, 73, 74, 83, 92, 95, 147, 203–5, 225
    and Smith, 124, 201
    and tour bus, 67, 70, 71, 88
Dion and the Belmonts, 42, 63, 71, 75, 77,
    96, 116, 203
    Valens as drummer, 91
disc jockeys, 130
    Richardson as, 27–31
Dixies (Irish group), 166
Dixon, Jack (Buddy Knox), 161
Domino, Fats, 18
"Donna" (Richard), 127
"Donna" (Valens), 42, 53–55, 56, 74
    gold record, 96, 130
    Milwaukee performance, 63
"Donna" (Wilde), 166
Donna Records, 212
"Don't Cha Know" (Giordano), 41
"Don't Let Him Shop Around," (Debbie
    Dean), 204
"Don't Pity Me" (Dion and the Belmonts), 42
Dorrell, J. C., 36
Dove's Nest Ministries, 201
Downbeat, and rock music, 11
Doyle, Eileen, 66, 218
Drake, Tom, *Not Fade Away,* 174
dream of airplane crash, 46
Drifters (group), 191
Driscoll, Danny, 47
drug rumors, 146–48
drugs, Smith and, 202
Due, Woodrow, 44–45
Dukes of Hazzard, The, theme song, 200
Duluth, Minnesota, 85, 86–87
    flight to, 224–25
Duncan, Hi-Pockets, 109
Dundee Music, 209
Dwyer, Barbara Jean, 111, 127, 131–32, 143,
    150, 187–88
Dwyer, Hubert J. "Jerry," 95, 100, 111,
    119–20, 127, 143, 149, 187, 195–96
    crash theories, 145
    and fatal flight, 102–6, 108
    suit against, 131–32
Dwyer Flying Service, 100, 243
Dylan, Bob, 230

Eagles Ballroom, Kenosha, Wisconsin, 64, 65–66
Eagles clubs
    Kenosha, 218
    Milwaukee, 217–18
"Early in the Morning" (Ding Dongs), 23
"Early in the Morning" (Holly), 23, 25
Eau Claire, Wisconsin, 70–71, 194
echo chamber for Petty's studio, 15–16
Echols, Oris "Pop," 157
Edison Hotel, New York, 16
Ed Sullivan Show, The, 20, 21
    Presley and, 11
    education, Jennings and, 200
Ehlert, Bob, 47, 64, 91, 94, 115
Ek, Pat, 77, 220
Eldridge, Reeve, 104–5, 154
Ellefson, Jane, 73, 219
El Monte Legion Stadium, 54, 171
Ely, Joe, 169–70
"Empty Cup, An" (Holly and Crickets), 19
England, 21–22
    Holly's influence, 168–69
    popularity of Holly, 133, 189–90
    sales of Holly's records, 129
    Valens' influence, 166
Epstein, Fred, 79, 220
    errors in crash reports, 142–43
Estes, Jerry, 83
Etzen, Keith, 223
Eukey, Jim, 226
European tour plans, 128, 129
Evans, Gene, 178
Evans, Rick, 230
Everly Brothers, 18, 40
    Crickets and, 133, 205
    songs by, 41
"Everybody Likes to Cha Cha Cha" (Cooke), 230
"Everyday" (Vee), 216
"Evil Ways" (Santana), 171

Fabian, 127, 167
Fabulous Thunderbirds, 192
"Fake Out" (Sardo), 42
fans, 44, 189–98
fan clubs
    for Holly, 190
    for Valens, 55, 130, 186, 195
Fargo, North Dakota, memorial concert, 192
Farley, Jack, 195
Farley, Marcia, 186
"Fast Freight" (Allens), 56
Fechter, Lambert L., 151, 187, 240
Federal Aviation Administration (FAA) investigation, 121–22
"Feel So Fine" (Preston), 165
Feld, Irvin, 5, 38, 41, 128, 204–5
    "Biggest Show of Stars, The" 18–20
    and Crickets, 16, 129
    and Winter Dance Party, 116, 117

Feld, Kenneth, 205
Fender Stratocaster guitars, 169
    owned by Holly, 8, 180
Ferber, Edna, Come and Get It, 89
Fiesta Ballroom, Montevideo, Minnesota, 72–73, 219
films
    of Holly, 167
    about Holly's career, 174
    about Richardson, 177
    about Valens, 176
fire at Valenzuela home, 185
Fireballs (rock group), 132, 209–10
Firminger, John, 190
"First Kiss, The" (Norman Petty Trio), 16
Fisher, Jerry, 210
Flatlanders (group), 170
flight
    from Mason City, 102–6
    path of crash, map of, 98
    plans for fatal flight, 103, 104
    wreckage, distribution of, 107
Florida, Crickets tour, 21
flying
    Buddy Holly and, 149–50
    Larry Holley and, 178
    Peterson and, 100–101
    Valens and, 57
Flyright Records, 165
Fontana, D. J., 7
football, Richardson and, 26
Ford, Frankie, 183
Fort Bliss, Richardson at, 29
Fort Dodge, Iowa, 82–85
foul-play rumors, 143–44
Fournier's Ballroom, Eau Claire, Wisconsin, 70–71, 194, 219
Four Teens (Texas group), 206
Fox, Carl, 93
Fox, Donna Ludwig, 126, 184–85, 215. See also Ludwig, Donna
    and Keane, 163
"Framed" (Valens), 52
Franklin, Mike, 183
Frederickson, Jim, 100
Freed, Alan, 18, 54, 167, 229
    Christmas holiday show, 20, 21, 56
    tours, 21, 22
Freeman, Ernie, 162
Freeman, Orville, 76
Fryou, Adrianne "Teetsie," 27. See also Richardson, Adrienne "Teetsie" Fryou
Fuller, Bobby, 213
Funaro, Frank, 204
fundraisers for Valens family, 171–72
funerals, 125, 126

GAC. See General Artists Corporation
Gale, Tim, 37, 127
Garlow, Clarence, 29
Garrett, Snuff, 205, 216

Gaul Motor Co., Tipton, Iowa, 81
Gayken, Glenn, 72
Geer, Bob, 82–83
Geer, Larry, 82–83, 84, 221
Geller, Sam, 42, 47, 72, 93, 97, 205
    and drug use on tour, 147
    news of plane crash, 116
    and tour bus, 74, 86, 94
    breakdown, 88–89, 90
General Artists Corporation (GAC), 24, 41, 55
    GAC-Super Productions, 41
Gerron, Peggy Sue, 24–25. *See also* Allison,
    Peggy Sue Gerron
Gibson, Don, 35
Gilbert, Lorene, 109
Gilchrist, Cathleen, 228
Gilley, Mickey, "True Love Ways," 166
Gilmer, Jimmy, 197
    "Sugar Shack," 210
Gilmore, Jimmy Dale, 169–70
Giordano, Lou, 5, 41
    "Stay Close to Me," 30
Girl Can't Help It, The (film), 11
Girls on the Beach (film), 205–6
Gittler, Robert, 175
Given, Harry, 76
Glad Music, 32
Glaser, Tompall, 199
glasses worn by Holly, 192–93
Glitter, Gary, 166
Goddard, Geoff, 190
Godfrey, Arthur, *Talent Scouts,* 16
Go Johnny Go (film), 56, 123, 162
"Gold Records in the Snow" (Barnes), 130
Goldrosen, John, x, xi, 96, 197–98
    and Allsup's wallet, 217
    Buddy Holly: His Life and Music, 174
    and *The Buddy Holly Story* (film), 175
    and Maria Elena, 39, 179
Gold Star Studios, 51–52, 53, 55, 214,
    231–32
"Go Little Go-Cat" (Four Teens), 206
Gonzalez, Pete, 49
"Good-Hearted Woman" (Jennings and Nel-
    son), 199
"Good Ol' Boys" (Jennings), 200
Goodwin, Keith, 21–22
Gore, Lesley, 206
"Gotta Travel On," 62, 96
Graham Flying School, 100
Grammer, Billy, 62
Granberry, James H., 173
Grant, Milt, 54
Grech, Rick, 206
Green Bay, Wisconsin, 90–92
Greysolen Plaza Hotel, 221
Griffith, Ron, 20, 207
Griggs, Bill, xiv, 124, 144, 167, 173, 175,
    193–94, 197, 223
    and fans of Holly, 189, 190
Griggs, Holly Maria, 193

Guess, Don, 8, 11, 12
guitars
    owned by Holly, 169, 180
    Valens and, 49, 50, 215
Gulf Coast Recording studio, 211
gun
    discovered at crash site, 143–44
    owned by Holly, 228
Gunshot Ridge (film), 18
Guterman, Jimmy, *The Worst Rock 'n' Roll
    Records of All Time,* 170
Guyer, Walt, 193

Hale, Bob, 94–97, 108, 145–46, 222
Hale, Kathy, 97
Haley, Bill, 9
Hall, Ben, 7, 206–7
Hall, Bill, xi, 32, 34, 36, 44, 164, 165, 197,
    211
    and Jay P. Richardson, 182
Hall, W. Earl, 111
Hammond, Leland, xi
Hampton, Lionel, 64
Hancock, Butch, 169–70
"Hang Up My Rock 'n' Roll Shoes" (Willis),
    226
Hanson, Charlie, 62
Hanson, Jack, 129, 208, 209
Hardin, Charles, 135
Hard Rock Cafe, Dallas, Texas, 180
Harris, Hal, 45
Haukoos, Dick, 223
"Have I the Right?" (Meek), 191
Hawkins, Dale, 35
Head, Roy, 173
"Heartbreak Hotel" (Presley), 9
Hearts, The, 16
Hein, Darrell, 191, 222
Hellooo Baby! (album), 182
Hendrix, Jimi, 169
Hep Cats from Big Spring (British CD), 206
High Plains Talent Agency, 208
high school, Holly and, 6–7
"Highwaymen The," 200
Hill, Harry "Tiny," 222
Hillbilly Allstars, 27
Hinson, Buck, 34
Hintzman, Mahlon A. "Curly," 146
Hipp, Paul, 176
"Hippy Hippy Shake" (Georgia Satellites), 215
"Hippy Hippy Shake" (Romero), 170–71
Holden, Ron, "Love You So," 212
Holiday on Ice, 205
Holley, Ella (mother), 5, 109, 168, 178, 228
Holley, Lawrence Odell (father), 5, 15, 109,
    178, 226
Holley, Larry (brother), 8, 23, 41, 43, 97, 122,
    149, 178, 197
    and *The Buddy Holly Story,* 174–75
    and Buddy's finances, 178–79
    and Buddy's songwriting, 157

and Lubbock park, 173
and Maria Elena, 179–80
news of Buddy's death, 109–10
and Petty, 158, 159, 161, 162
Randy (Larry's son), 178
Sherry (Larry's daughter), 178
Holley, Pat (sister), 178
Holley, Randy, 178
Holley, Sherry, 178
Holley, Travis (brother), 15, 173, 178
Holley family, 178
and Maria Elena, 179–80
Hollies (British rock group), 169
Holly, Buddy, 5–25, 39, 43, 46, 74, 84, 91,
  145, 147, 155, 168–70, 229, 231
  biographies, 174–76
  birth announcement, 232
  birthplace, 172
  book from Echo McGuire, 226
  and Bunch, 72, 75
  and Darin songs, 23–24
  death of, ix–x, 1–2, 106, 122, 227
  funeral, 126
  news of, 109, 119–21
  Diehl and, 68, 76, 77–78
  as drummer for Belmonts, 96
  estate of, 131, 132
  fans of, 189
  and fatal flight, 95, 103, 149–50
  financial arrangements, 159
  flights before fatal crash, 224–25
  glasses of, 192–93
  grave headstone, 227
  gun belonging to, discovered at crash
    site, 143–44
  Jennings and, 80, 97, 200–201
  last photographs, 219
  last song charted, 226
  marriage, 24–25, 37–38, 46, 84
  and Mastrangelo, 92
  memorials for, 172–73
  missing tapes, 167
  Petty and, 38, 40, 93, 155–58, 159
  postage stamp, 173
  as producer, 38
  recordings:
      "Blue Days, Black Nights," 8
      "Crying, Wanting, Hoping,"
        129
      "Early in the Morning," 23, 25
      "I'm Changing All Those
        Changes," 10
      "It Doesn't Matter Anymore,"
        39, 129, 226
      "It's So Easy," 39
      "Looking for Someone to
        Love," 159
      "Love Me," 8
      "Modern Don Juan," 12
      "Moondreams," 39
      "Now We're One," 23

"Oh Boy!," British release, 21
"Peggy Sue," 19, 21, 230
"Peggy Sue Got Married," 129
posthumous releases, 129, 166,
  209
"Raining in My Heart," 39
"That'll Be the Day," 5,
  159–60
"True Love Ways," 39
unreleased material, 155
"You Are My One Desire," 12
"You're the One," 43
See also Crickets; Holly and the
  Crickets
social life, 40–41
songs written by, 10, 30, 131
split with Crickets, 40
teeth capped, 77
telephone call from Clear Lake, 96
touring band, 43
Vee and, 119
and Winter Dance tour, 5, 43,
  62–63, 69, 71, 73, 81, 83, 89,
  94–95, 96
Holly, Maria Elena Santiago, xiii, xiv, 24–25,
  37–38, 46, 84, 96, 126, 132, 179–80, 192,
  193
  and Buddy's gun, 228
  money from tour, 128
  and Pettys, 39
Holly and the Crickets, recordings of
  "An Empty Cup," 19
  "Maybe Baby," 19
  "Oh Boy!" 21, 162
  "Rave On," 23
  "Rock Me My Baby," 19
Holly International, 190
Holly's House: A Family Album, 178
Hollywood Professional School, 202
Hollywood Walk of Fame, star for Valens, 172
Honeycombs (British group), 191
Hooker, Robert, 108–9
Hope, Bob, 21
Hopkins, Marcia, 195
Horton, George, xii, 198
Hotel Burton, Mankato, Minnesota, 67, 69, 218
Hotel Cornbelt, Fort Dodge, Iowa, 83, 221
Hotel Davenport, 80, 220
Hotel Duluth, 86, 221
Hotel Eau Claire, 70, 219
Howard Theater, Washington, D.C., 16–17
"How Deep Is the Ocean," 20
"Huggy Boy" (Hugg), 171–72
Hullabaloos (British group), 169
Hunter, Dave, 78, 80
Hurd, John, 95, 223
Hurley, Wisconsin, 88–89
Hynes, John B., 22, 23

Ice Follies, 205
"I Fought the Law," Curtis, 213

"If You Can't Rock Me" (Stevens), 64
"I'll Never Get Out of This World Alive" (Williams), 226
"I'll Wait for You" (Avalon), 123
"I'm Changing All Those Changes" (Holly), 10
"I'm Gonna Love You Too," royalty income, 162
"I'm Gonna Love You Too" (Dixies), 166
"I'm Gonna Love You Too" (Hullabaloos), 169
"I'm into My Teens" (Collins brothers), 14
"I'm Stickin' with You" (Bowen), 12–13
Innovisions, *The Buddy Holly Story*, 174
insurance
    for Mason City, 111–12
    settlements, from plane crash, 132
    interim jobs, 15
I Remember Buddy Holly (Vee album), 216
Ironwood, Michigan, 89
Isley Brothers, "Twist and Shout," 166
"It Doesn't Matter Anymore" (Holly), 39, 95, 129, 223, 226
"It Doesn't Matter Anymore" (Ronstadt), 166
"I Think I'm Gonna Kill Myself" (Knox), 168
"It's All Over" (Sullivan), 206
"It's So Easy" (Holly), 39
"It's So Easy" (Ronstadt), 166
"It's the Truth Ruth" (Richardson), 130
"It Was the Master Calling Me" (Smith), 203
Iverson, Marvin A. "Ike," 125
"I Wonder Why" (Dion and the Belmonts), 42, 63

Jackson, Clarence, 70
Jackson, Wanda, 9
Jack's Tires, 28
Jacobs, Dick, 39
Jacobs, Don, 35–36
Jagger, Mick, 133
James, Sonny, 9
Janes, Alan, Buddy, 176
Jape-a-thon, 29–31, 149
Jennings, Buddy Dean, 199
Jennings, Jessi Colter, 199
Jennings, Julie Rae, 45
Jennings, Maxine, 199
Jennings, Terry Vance, 45
Jennings, Tommy, 109
Jennings, Waylon, 38, 43, 62, 89, 123, 128–29, 130, 146, 173, 199–201, 206, 225
    and flight from Mason City, 96–97
    and Holley home, 178
    and Holly, 150, 93
    Moorhead performance, 119
    and news of plane crash, 116
    and Petty, 39
    report of death, 109
    and Smith, 201
    and Winter Dance Party tour, 45–46, 67, 71, 74, 80, 85, 96
Jensen, Bob, 221
Jensen, Thor, 111

Jitters (band), 132
John, Elton, 173
"Johnny Remember Me" (Leyton), 190
Johnson, Ben, 126
Johnson, Rick (Gordon Ritter), 33, 34
Johnston, Bruce, 54
"Jole Blon" (Choates), 231
"Jole Blon" (Jennings), 38, 46, 130–31
Jones, Bill, 50
Jones, George, 32, 34, 36, 130, 211
    at KTRM, 27
    "White Lightning," 165
Joplin, Janis, 227, 228
Jordonaires (singing group), 183
Joyce, George T., 112, 122, 145, 147, 151, 217
Juhl, Albert, 104, 121, 132, 143, 144, 217
Juhl, Delbert, 104, 106, 121, 132, 144
Juhl, Elsie, x, 105, 106, 121, 132, 217
Jules Herman Orchestra, 76
"Just a Dream" (Clanton), 123
Just for Fun (British film), 205
Justice Records, 200

Kalin, Hal and Herb, 225
Kato Ballroom, Mankato, Minnesota, xv, 67–68, 218–19
Kaye, Carol, 52
KCRG (Cedar Rapids radio), 108
KDAV (Lubbock radio), 6
Keane, Bob, 176, 190, 212–14, 231. *See also* Keene, Bob
    and Valens finances, 162–64
Keane, John and Tom, 213
Keene, Bob, 51, 89, 110, 127, 130, 162, 171, 172. *See also* Keane, Bob
    name changes, 231
    and Romero, 170–71
    and Valens, 51–56, 125
    Keene label, 51
Kehr, Timothy D., 77, 220
Kellogg, Glenn, 217
Kempner, Scott, 204
Kennedy, John F., 219, 221
Kennedy, Robert, 219
Kenny and the Cadets (Beach Boys), 212
Kenosha, Wisconsin, 64–66
Kenosha News, 65
Keyes, Bobby, 230
KFDA (Amarillo television), 16
KFDM–TV (Beaumont, Texas), 33
KFWB (Southern California radio), 52, 53, 214
KFXM (Bakersfield radio), 123
KICA (Clovis radio), 13
Killgallen, Dorothy, 131
Kilgore, Texas, Presley concert, 7
Kimbrough, Bill, 34, 231
KLLL (Lubbock radio), 38, 43, 109
    Jennings and, 130, 199

KMAD (Madill, Oklahoma radio), 207
Knight, Tim, xv, 177
Knox, Buddy, 12–13, 14, 18, 40, 168
    and music business, 161
    and Petty, 156, 161
    and tours, 18–19
Korum, Bob, 118
Kratz, Loran, 74
KRIB (Clear Lake radio), 94, 108
Kristofferson, Kris, 200
KSTT (Davenport radio), 79
KTQM (Clovis radio), 209
KTRM (Beaumont radio), 26–29, 108–9, 125
    Jape–a–thon, 29–31
KVOW (Littlefield radio), 109
KVOX (Moorhead radio), 115
KWMT (Fort Dodge radio), 83
KXYZ (Houston radio), 35

"La Bamba," recordings of, 166
La Bamba (film), 172, 176, 185, 195, 226
"La Bamba" (Valens), 53, 55, 56, 74
    Duluth performance, 86–87
Laboe, Art, 171
Laine, Denny, 169
Laing, Dave, *Buddy Holly,* 174, 193
Lamar College, Richardson at, 26
Lapham, Bob, 207
Laramar Ballroom, Fort Dodge, Iowa, 82–84, 220
Larry Ladd's Entertaining Band, 62
Larsen, Nels, 95
Larson, Don, 71, 194–95, 219
Latino artists, influenced by Valens, 170
Latto, Lew, 221, 224–25
leathercraft, Holly and, 6, 8
    wallet, 8
Led Zeppelin, and Valens song, 166
Lee, Albert, 206
Lee, Dickey, "Patches," 211
Lee, Terry, and the Poor Boys, 119
Legends of American Music (postage stamps), 173
Lennon, John, 133, 168
Lenz, DeAnn, 99–100. *See also* Peterson, DeAnn Lenz
Leppke, Ruth Benson, 72
"Let Her Dance" (Bobby Fuller Four), 213
"Letter to Donna, A" (Kittens), 166
Levins, Mike, 228
Lewis, Charles R. "Doc," 34
Lewis, Jerry Lee, 22
Leyton, John, 190
Liberty Records, 201, 216
Lineham, William, 229
Linton, Sherwin, 78, 220
Linville, Robert, xiv, 38, 132–33, 210
    and Holly's split with Petty, 39
lip-synching, 35, 39
Little Bohemia resort, 89
Little Bopper's (nightclub), 183

Little Caesar and the Romans, 212
Littlefield, Texas, 109, 200
"Little Girl" (Valens), 129, 130
Little Kings (Dion's band), 203
"Little Red Riding Hood" (Richardson), 36
Little Richard, 167
Lone Rock, Wisconsin, 71, 92
"Lonesome" (Watts), 32
Lookie Lookie Lookie (Jitters), 132–33
"Lookie Lookie Lookie" (Smith), 201
"Looking for Someone to Love" (Holly), 159
Looking Through Buddy's Eyes (cassette), 178
Los Lobos (band), and Valens songs, 166
Louis, Joe, 64
Louisiana Hayride (radio show), 12
Louisiana Swamp Pop (album), 165
Lounsbury, Jim, 64–66, 204, 218
"Love Me" (Holly), 8
Love Me Tender (film), 11
"Love Me Tender" (Presley), 11
"Lovesick Blues" (Williams), 6
"Love's Made a Fool of You" (Fuller), 213
"Love You So," 212
Lowery, Bill, 34
Lubbock, Texas, xiii, xiv, 6–8, 12, 43, 169, 194, 197
    and Holly, 172–73, 191
Lubbock Avalanche, 11
    Holly's birth announcement, 232
Lubbock Evening Journal, 11
Lucier, Rod, 115, 117, 118
Ludwig, Donna, 50, 53–54, 55, 57, 171–72, 214. *See also* Fox, Donna Ludwig
Luke, Robin, "Susie Darlin'," 168
Luth, Harvey, 94–95
Lyceum Theater, Clovis, Texas, 15
Lymon, Frankie, 22
Lynn, Barbara, 228

McAlister, Bill, 231
McAlister, Mac, 231
"MacArthur Park" (Jennings), 199
McCartney, Paul, 131, 133, 169, 173
    purchase of Holly's compositions, 162
    The Real Buddy Holly Story, 175–76
McClinton, Delbert, 170
McCollough, Bill, 82, 83, 84, 221
McCoys, "Come On Let's Go," 166
McGill, Bill, 106, 217
McGlothlen, Charles, 101, 102, 110–11, 122, 124, 144, 146, 150, 151
McGlothlen, Judye, 101–2, 111
McGregor, Bob and Betty, 81
McGuire Sisters, "Sugartime," 157
McGuire, Echo, 6, 7, 8, 12, 19, 20, 179, 207
    book given to Holly, 226
McKinney, Dick, 112, 217
McLean, Don, "American Pie," 179
McLendon, Gordon, 34
McPhatter, Clyde, 16, 18, 43

Maines, Wayne, 6
Malone, Wanda Quilitz, 219
Maloney, Charlie, 221–22
Manhattan, Holly apartment in, 37–38
Mankato, Minnesota, 66–69
Mark IV Quartet, 222
Martinez, Rudy, 171
Martinka, Herb, 67
Martinka, Jerry, 67–68
Marvin, Hank B., 169
Mason City, Iowa, xi
    Dwyer's Flying Service, 100
    Municipal Airport, 230
    night conditions, 151
Mason City *Globe–Gazette,* x, 122, 124,
  143–44
    and plane crash, 111–12, *114,*
      119–21
Mastrangelo, Carlo, 69, 91–92, 124, 204
    Moorhead performance, 119
Mathis, Johnny, 15
Matti, Larry, 91, 92, 222
Mauldin, Joe B., 15, 23, 24, 40, 78, 96, 128–29,
  133, 144, 158, 173, 192, 193, 205–6, 214
    income from "That'll Be the Day,"
      159–60
"Maybe Baby" (Holly and Crickets), 19
    British recording, 22
Mayfield, Duane, 106, 110, 217
Meaux, Huey, 164, 228, 231–32
    media, and plane crash, 108–12,
      119–21
    CAB report, 142–43
Meek, Joe, 190
Melody Maker, 21
memorabilia of Holly, 173, 190
    Larson's collection, 194
    Terry's collection, 197
memorials
    dances, 191, 212
    for Holly, 172–73
    for Valens, 171–72
Mendheim, Beverly A., 56, 57, 185
    Ritchie Valens: The First Latino Rocker,
      176
Mercury Records, 32, 34, 130
Mesaros, Mike, 204
Mesa Theater, Clovis, New Mexico, xiii–xiv,
  209–10
Mesner, Joan, 66
Mettler, Dick, 122
Meyer, Charles, 151
Meyer, Steve, 70–71, 224
Midwest, tour of, 42
Milano, Fred, 69, 70, 116, 147, 204
    and flights by singers, 225
    gun carried by, 84–85
Miller, Glenn, 228
Miller, J. D., 28–29, 165, 211–12
Miller, Jerry, 195–96
Miller, Mitch, 14–15, 16, 158

Miller, Tom, *Crawdaddy* story, x, xi
Million Dollar Ballroom, Milwaukee, 62–64,
  217–18
Milton Berle Show, Presley's performance on, 9
Milwaukee, Wisconsin, 61–64
missing tapes, 167
mistakes in crash accounts, 142–43
"Modern Don Juan" (Holly), 12
Moffett, Oscar, 106
"Monkey Song, The" (Richardson), 32
Montegut, Louisiana, 45
Montei, Herb, 53
Montevideo, Minnesota, 71, 72–74
Montez, Chris, 171
Montgomery, Bob, 6, 133, 169
Montgomery, Michael, screenplay about
  Richardson, 177
monuments, Clear Lake, Iowa, 191, 192
"Mood Indigo" (Norman Petty Trio), 13–14
"Moondreams" (Holly), 39
Moore, Muriel, 55, 130, 214
Moore, Scotty, 197
Moorhead, Minnesota, 93, 115
    Winter Dance Party, after crash,
      118–19
Morales, Bob (half-brother of Valens), 48, 49,
  54, 56, 57, 96, 185
Morales, Esai, 172, 176
Morales, Joanie, 185, 195
Morales, Rosie, 49, 50–51, 54, 185, 186
Mulkey, Waymon, 6, 207
Murillo, Mary, 49
Murray, Betty, 81
music, on tour bus, 71
music industry, 12
    record sales, 20
    young musicians and, 10, 159–63
musicians killed in aircraft accidents, 227
Musser, Elwin, 111–12, 217
Mustang Records, 213
Must the Young Die Too, 226
"My Little Ruby" (Romero), 171

Nashville, Tennessee, xi, 8, 10, 12
National Guard Armory, Duluth, 86–87, 221
Neal, Jack, 6
Neiderhauser, Ben, 124
Neil, Jack, 28
    and Jape-a-thon, 29–30
Neil, John (son of Jack), 27, 33, 35, 108
    and "Chantilly Lace," 35
Nelson, Rick, 191, 228
Nelson, Sander "Sandy," 54
Nelson, Willie, 199, 200, 201
"New Girl, A" (Debbie Dean), 204
New Musical Express, 21–22
New York City, 5, 16, 54
New York Crickets, 133. *See also* Crickets
Nichols, Red, 91
Nichols, W. H., family, 192
Nokleby, Bruce, 118–19

"No One Knows" (Dion and the Belmonts), 42

Norman, Philip, 174

Norman Music, Inc., 209

Norman Petty Foundataion, 209

Norman Petty Trio, 13, 16, 19

Norton, Irma (half-sister of Valens), xiii, 185

Nor-Va-Jak
    Petty's publishing company, 162
    record label, 14

Not Fade Away, Allison and Drake, 174

"Not Fade Away" (Rolling Stones), 169

novelty tunes, 32–33

"Now We're One" (Ding Dongs), 23

"Now We're One" (Holly), 23

Odom, Bill, 233

O'Donnell, Owen, *The Worst Rock 'n' Roll Records of All Time,* 170

Off the Record (BBC program), 22

"Oh Boy" (West), 211

"Oh Boy!" (Holly and Crickets), 21, 162

Oliver, Chester, 157

Olson, Diane, 56, 184

Olson, Simon, 74, 76

O'Neill, Sharon, x

"Only Daddy That'll Walk the Line" (Jennings), 199

"Only Sixteen" (Cooke), 230

Onnen, Gary, 84

"Ooby Dooby" (Orbison), 10, 13

"Ooh, My Head" Valens, 166

"Ooh, My Soul" (Little Richard), 166

Orbison, Roy, 13, 14, 156, 201
    "Ooby Dooby," 10, 13

Orenstein, Harold, 40

Osburn, Bob, 201

overseas sales, Holly's records, 129

Owens, Buck, 206

"Paddiwack Song," 54, 172

Palmer, Earl, 52

Paquette, Ken, 192

Parker, Bonnie, 227

Parker, "Colonel" Tom, 9, 20, 125

Parsons, Bill, 127

"Party Doll" (Knox), 12

"Patches" (Lee), 211

Patton, W. L., Insurance Agency, 111–12

Payday (movie), 200

Payne, Gordon, 192, 206

Peeples, Bobby, 167

Peery, Judy, 68–69, 218–19

"Peggy Sue" (Holly), 19, 21, 230
    Milwaukee performance, 62, 63

"Peggy Sue Got Married" (Holly), 129

Peoria, Illinois, 127

Perkins, Carl, 9, 191

Perry, Norman, 37

Peter & Gordon, "True Love Ways," 166

Petersack, Tom, 194–95

Peterson, Art (father), xii, xiii, 99, 100, 101, 111, 186–87
    Peterson, DeAnn Lenz (wife), xii–xiii, 100–102, 105, 111, 147, 154, 187. *See also* Lenz, DeAnn

Peterson, Janet (sister), 99, 101

Peterson, Pearl (mother), xii, xiii, 99, 152, 154, 186–87

Peterson, Roger Arthur (pilot), xii–xiii, 95, 99–102, 143, 147, 150, 227, 239–43
    CAB report, 138–39
    death of, 1–2, 106, 112, 122, 145
    funeral, 125
    news report, 119–21
    flight preparations, 102–3
    hearing difficulties, 152
    instrument training, 151–53
    monument to, 191
    night-flying experience, 153

Peterson, Ron (brother), 100, 154, 187

"Pet Names" (Richardson), 165

Petty, Norman, 5, 13–15, 132, 133, 156–57, 158, 173, 189
    business dealings, 23–24, 38, 40, 131, 155–58, 159–62, 208–10
    and Crickets, 16, 17, 19, 23, 96, 128, 158
    and Holly, 14, 15, 41, 93, 162, 168
    posthumous releases, 133
    Larry Holley and, 178–79
    and Maria Elena Holly, 39
    Pickering and, 207–8
    recording studio, 15–16, 132

Petty, Violet Brady "Vi," xiii–xiv, 13, 39, 157–58, 160, 209–11

Phillips, Charlie, "Sugartime," 157

Phillips, Lou Diamond, 172, 176

Phillips, Phil, 183

Phillips, Sam, 10

photographs
    of crash site, 217
    of Holly, last known, 219
    of Winter Dance Party, 194, 198, 218, 219, 222, 223

Pickering, Bill, 207–8

Pickering, John, xv, 156, 207–8
    and Petty, 158, 160–61

Pickering, Ruth, 104, 106, 153–54

Pickering, Vicky, xv

Picks (vocal group), xv, 207–8

Pierce, Webb, 10

Pike, Stephen, 189

Pitney, Gene, 211

plane crash investigations, 125, 126
    CAB report, 134, 135–41
    media and, 142–43

poker, on tour bus, 70

Pollock, Jim, xii

Poole, Brian, 169

postage stamps, 173

poverty of Valens' family, 49
Prairie du Chien, Wisconsin, 92–93
Pray, Larry, 73
Presley, Elvis, 7, 8, 9, 11, 12, 14, 20, 76, 125, 167, 169, 194
    wallet for, made by Holly, 8
Preston, Johnny, 130, 165, 183, 192
Prism Records, 41
Pritchard, James, 7
Prokop, A. J., 110, 121–22, 126, 144, 152, 216
Prom Ballroom, St. Paul, Minnesota, 75, 76, 219
publicity photos, 17–18, 41
    for Chirping Crickets album, 18
publishing company formed by Holly, 41
Punke, Gus, 106
"Purple People Eater, The" (Wooley), 33
"Purple People Eater Meets the Witch Doctor," 211
"Purple People Eater Meets the Witch Doctor" (Johnson), 33
"Purple People Eater Meets the Witch Doctor" (Richardson), 33–35
"Purple People Eater Meets the Witch Doctor" (South), 34
"Put a Ring On Her Finger," Meek, 190
Pythian Temple studio, New York, 39

Quarrymen, The (Lennon's group), 168
Quilitz, Wanda, 74
Quillin, Ted, 52, 54, 162, 214
Quinn, Bill, 34

racism, on tour, 19
radio personality, Richardson as, 26–31
"Raining in My Heart" (Holly), 39
"Raining in My Heart" (Sherry Holley), 178
Ramirez, Concepcion Reyes Valenzuela (mother of Ritchie Valens), 48. See also Valenzuela, Concepcion Reyes
Ramirez, Connie (half-sister of Ritchie Valens), 48, 54, 110
Ramirez, Irma, 54
Ramirez, Mario, 54
Ramirez, Ramon, 48, 49
Ramones, "Come On Let's Go," 166
Raring, Louis "Skip," 147
"Rave On" (West), 157, 160, 211, 228
    royalty income, 162
"Rave On" (Holly and Crickets), 23
Ray Charles Singers, 129
RCA, "X" label, 14
RCA Records, and Jennings, 200
"Real Buddy Holly Story, The" (Curtis song), 175
Real Buddy Holly Story, The (television documentary), 176
"Real Cool Cat, A" (Burns), 34
record company formed by Holly, 41

recording studios
    Allsup's, 201
    Clovis, New Mexico, xiii, 132, 209–10
    Holly's plans for, 43
    Richardson and, 44
    recording techniques, and Crickets' sound, 158
Redding, Otis, 226–27
rehearsals for Winter Dance Party, 45–46
"Reminiscing" (Crickets), 38
Reminiscing (fan magazine), 193
Reminiscing (Holly album), 209
Reminiscing (television documentary), 175
"Reprieve of Tom Dooley, The," 212
reviews of the Crickets, 21–22
Reyes, Ernestine (aunt of Valens), 49, 50, 53, 54, 56, 57, 164, 184, 185, 186, 195, 226
Reyes, Ernie, 186. See also Valens, Ernie
Reyes, Frank, funeral of, 226
Reyes, Lelo, 49, 50, 57, 186
Rhino Records, Hellooo Baby! 182
rhythm 'n' blues, 28
Rhythm Orchids (Knox's band), 168
Rhythm Teens (Kenosha group), 65
Richard, Cliff, 127, 166
Richardson, Adrianne "Teetsie" Fryou, 27, 29, 32, 45, 109, 164–65, 180–81, 183
    and Jape-a-thon, 30
    and tours, 36, 90
Richardson, Cecil Alan "Big Daddy" (brother), xi, 26, 27, 28, 30–31, 34, 44, 183
Richardson, Debbie (daughter), 36, 180, 183
Richardson, Gilbert (brother), 183
Richardson, J. P. (Big Bopper), 25–29, 31, 33–35, 42, 44, 74, 75, 76, 89, 90, 94, 95, 129, 147–49, 226
    death of, 1–2, 106, 122, 227
    news of, 108–9, 119–21
    funeral, 125
    film about, 177
    and flying, 96, 224–25
    finances, posthumous, 164–65
    musical legacy, 155, 165
    recordings, 165
    sleeping bag, 93
    tours, 36, 90
        "Beggar to a King," 32
        "Big Bopper's Wedding," 36
        "Boogie Woogie," 29, 165
        "Chantilly Lace," 25, 34, 35, 36, 44, 127, 165, 182
        "Crazy Blues," 32
        "It's the Truth Ruth," 130
        "Little Red Riding Hood," 36
        "The Monkey Song," 32
        posthumous releases, 130
        "The Purple People Eater Meets the Witch Doctor," 33–35

"Someone Walking Through My Dreams" 130
"Someone Watching Over You," 130
"Teenage Moon," 32
"That's What I'm Talking About," 130
unreleased material, 212
sleeping bag bought by, 93, 115–16
as songwriter, 36, 130
stage costumes, 231
statue of, 192
Stevens, and, 79–80
television appearances, 65
watch belonging to, 192
and Winter Dance Party, 5, 47, 63, 71, 73, 77, 80, 83, 92
Clear Lake performance, 95, 96
tour bus, 93
Richardson, Jay Perry (son), xiii, xiv–xv, 164, 180, 183
and father, 165, 181–82
Richardson, Jiles Perry, Sr. (father), 26
Righteous Brothers, 214
Ringling Bros. and Barnum & Bailey Circus, 205
riot at Boston concert, 22
Ritchie Valens: The First Latino Rocker (Mendheim), 176
Ritchie Valens (album), 129
Ritchie Valens Memorial Fan Club, 190
Ritter, Gordon, 30, 33, 34, 211
Ritter, Ken, 33, 212
and "Chantilly Lace," 34, 35
Riverside Ballroom, Green Bay, Wisconsin, 90–92, 222
Robbins, Marty, 8
Rocha, Gil, 49–50, 54, 164, 214–15
Rock and Roll Hall of Fame, 203
Rock 'n' Roll High School (film), 166
Rock 'n' Roll Trio, 10
Rock Around the Clock (film), 76
Rockin' 50s magazine, xiv, 194
Rockin' Rebels (Montevideo band), 73
"Rock Me My Baby" (Holly and Crickets), 19
rock music, 10–11, 21, 31, 94, 167–68
banned in Boston, 22–23
Holly and, 7, 198
Milwaukee, Wisconsin, 62, 63–64
Richardson and, 32, 44
"Rockola Ruby" (West), 15
Roe, Tommy, "Sheila," 168
Rolling Stones, "Not Fade Away," 169
Romere, Dixie, 44
Romere, John, 34, 44, 212
Romero, Chan, 162, 170–71, 215
Ronnie Smith and the Jitters, 201
Ronnie Smith and the Poor Boys, 43, 124
Ronstadt, Linda, 166, 173
Rose, Henri, 51
Roses (singing group), xiv, 38, 133

Ross, Leonard G., 143, 152, 240
Ross, Stan, 51, 52, 163, 206, 214
Ross Aviation School, 100
Rotunda, Tom, 65, 218
royalties, 131, 162
from Holly's records, 159–60
from Richardson's music, 164–165, 182
from Valens' songs, 163
"Rubber Ball" (Vee), 216
Rucker, Roy, 7
"Running Bear" (Preston), 130, 165
Rush, Ray, 41
Ryer, Sandra, 72

St. Paul, Minnesota, 75, 76–78
St. Paul Pioneer Press, 66, 68
"Salty Dog Rag," 96
Sander, Leo, 125, 126, 216
Sanquist, Lowell, 106, 110, 144, 146, 217
"Santa Got a DWI" (Linton), 220
Santana, 171
Santiago, Maria Elena, 24–25. See also Holly, Maria Elena Santiago
Santiloni, Joe, 66
Sapik, Ron, 86–87
Sardo, Frankie, xiv, 42, 62, 74, 84, 116, 204
Winter Dance Party tour, 69, 71, 92, 95
Moorhead performance, 118
and tour bus, 69, 88
Sardo, Marco, 204
Schueneman, Curt, 69
Searchers, The (movie), 10
seating arrangements on fatal flight, 103, 148
"Second-Hand Memories" (Jay P. Richardson poem), 181
Self, Jimmie, 14
"Blue Christmas," 230
Seville, David (Ross Bagdasarian), "Witch Doctor," 32–33
Shadows, (British group). 169
Shadows, The (Bobby Vee's band), 118–19, 216
Shadows, The (Cliff Richard's band), 127
Shannon, Del, 191, 229
"Sheila" (Roe), 168
"She's My Rockin' Baby" (Montez), 171
Shotts, Roy Dixon, 29, 108
Silhouettes, The, 49–50, 147
Simpson, Eddie, 83–84, 221
Simus, John, 51
Sinks, Earl, 40, 128–29, 133, 205
Sioux City, Iowa, 124
"Sippin' Cider" (Richardson), 165
Skarning, T.B., 115
sleeping bag bought by Richardson, 93, 115–116
Smiley, Ralph E., 111, 112, 120, 217, 227
Smith, Gail, 54, 57, 130, 167, 184
Smith, Ronnie, xiv, 123, 124, 128–29, 132, 146, 201–3

Smith, Sherry, xiv, 201, 202
"Someone Walking Through My Dreams" (Richardson), 130
"Someone Watching Over You" (Richardson), 130
songwriter
  Curtis as, 206
  Debbie Dean as, 204
  Holly as, 8, 40, 41
  Richardson as, 32, 36, 165
  Sonny West as, 211
songwriting credits
  Petty and, 156–57
  of Valens' songs, 163
Sonny & Cher, 214
South, Joe, 34, 212
"Sparkplug" (Four Teens), 206
Spector, Phil, 172, 203, 214
Speed, Grant, statue of Holly, 173
Spencer, Dee, 56
"Splish Splash" (Darin), 23
Springfield, Illinois, 127
"Stage, The" (Jennings), 199
stage costumes
  of Holly, 6, 17
  of Richardson, 231
Starday Records, 32, 34
statues, 173, 192
"Stay Close to Me" (Giordano), 30, 41
Steele, Ted, Thanksgiving concerts, 123
Steele, Tommy, 55–56
  "Come On Let's Go," 166
Sterelczyk, Robert, 218
stereo recordings, Holly's first, 39
Stevens, Debbie, 64, 117, 123, 146, 204
Stevens, Mark, 79–80, 220
Stillman, Jim, 117–18
Stillwagon, C. E., 121, 126, 143, 148, 216
Stimac, John, 222
Stirling, Leon "Peaches", 29
Stone, "Pappy" Dave, 7
Strand, Dick, 73, 219
Strasberg, Lee, Actor's Studio, 41
Stringalongs (Texas group), 209
Stull, Billy, xiii
"Sugar Shack" (Gilmer and the Fireballs) 210
"Sugartime" (McGuire Sisters), 157
"Sugartime" (Phillips), 157
suicide, 201
  of Holly fans, 189, 191
Sullivan, B. C., 193
Sullivan, Niki, 7, 12, 14–18, 109, 168, 191, 193, 206
  and "Biggest Show of Stars," 18, 19–20
  and Petty, 157, 160, 162
  relationship to Holly, 231
  royalty income, 159–60, 162
Summer Dance Party, 36, 191
"Summertime" (Cooke), 51
Sunday Night at the Palladium (British television), 21

Sunday Party, The (radio program), 6
Surf Ballroom, Clear Lake, Iowa, x–xi, 93–97, 182, 186, 200, 222
  memorials, xiii, 192
  tribute dances, xi–xii, 191, 206, 222, 223
  visits by fans, 192
"Susie Darlin'" (Luke), 168
"Susie Darlin'" (Roe), 168
"Suzie Baby" (Vee), 216
Svenson, Joan, 194, 219
Swanson, Phil, 84
"Sweet Rockin' Baby" (West), 15
Szikil, Tony, 66, 218

Talmadge, Art, 34
Taupe publishing company, 41
Teddy Bears (singing group), 172
"Teenage Moon" (Richardson), 32
"Teenager in Love, A" (Dion and the Belmonts), 203
teenagers
  at concert, 68–69
  dances for, 41, 67–68, 72–73, 82
Teen-Agers (New York group), 9
  television appearances, 21
  "Buddy and Jack," 6
  Crickets, 18, 20, 39
  Holly interview, 229
  Presley, 9, 11
  Richardson, 33, 35, 36
  Valens, 54
  Winter Dance Party members, 65
television films, 174
  Reminiscing, 175
"Telstar" (Meek), 190
"Tequila" (Champs), 52
Terry, Kevin, xiii, 196–97
Tevis, George, 81
Texas Crickets, 133. See also Crickets; Holly and the Crickets recordings
Tex-Mex sound, 13
"That'll Be the Day" (Holly and Allison), 10, 159–60, 168
  songwriting credits, 156–57
"That'll Be the Day" (Crickets), 5, 14–15, 16, 21, 194
  sales, 17, 19
"That'll Be the Day" (Richard), 127
"That'll Be the Day" (Ronstadt), 166
"That's My Little Suzie" (Valens), 129
  Keane and, 163
"That's What I'm Talking About" (Richardson), 130
Thiele, Bob, 15
Thomas, Gene, 183
Thompson, Hank, 8, 11
"Those Oldies But Goodies" (Little Caesar and the Romans), 212
"Three Stars, The" (Dee), 123
"Three Steps to Heaven" (Cochran), 226
"Three Steps to Heaven" (Sullivan), 206

"Til I Kissed You" (Everly Brothers), 133
Tiny Kiss, A (Jitters), 132
"Tiny Kiss, A" (Smith), 201
Tipton, Iowa, 71
Tipton Conservative, The, 81–82, 220
"To Know Him Is to Love Him" (Teddy
  Bears), 172
Today (television program), 22
tombstone for Valens' grave, 184–85
Tommy's Heads Up Saloon, 201
Tomsco, George, 209
Torchy Swingsters (Petty's group), 13
Tornadoes (British group), 191
"Torquay" (Fireballs), 209
tour bus, Winter Dance Party, 47, 61, 67,
  69–72, 79, 82, 94, 115–16, 124
    breakdown of, xiv, 88–89
    frozen heaters, 81–82
    gun on, 84
tours, 21–23, 24, 42, 92–93
    "Biggest Show of Stars," 18–20, 38,
      123
    country music, 8, 9, 11
    map of, 60
    Richardson and, 36, 44
    See also Winter Dance Party tour
Travis, William Barret, 227
"Treasure of Love" (Jones), 36
Tremeloes (British group), 169
tribute dances, Surf Ballroom, 206, 222,
  223
tribute songs, 130, 170, 190
"Tribute to Buddy Holly" (Meek), 190
Tripp, Peter, 78
"True Love Ways" (Gilley), 166
"True Love Ways" (Holly), 39
"True Love Ways" (Peter & Gordon), 166
T-Shirt (Crickets album), 206
Tweith, Curt, 71
Twin Cities, Minnesota, 76–78
"Twist and Shout," 166

Ulahakis, Mike, 77, 220

Valdez, Danny, 176
Valdez, Luis, 176
Valens, Ernie (Ernie Reyes), 183, 186
Valens, Ritchie, xi, 42, 48–53, 55–56, 74, 76,
  77, 89, 95–96, 118, 147, 164, 176
    death of, 1–2, 106, 122, 125, 126,
      227
    news of, 110, 119–21
    estate of, 131, 132
    and family, 54, 56
    fan clubs, 130, 186
    finances, posthumous, 162–64
    and flying, 96, 97, 224–26
    influence of, 170–72
    memorials for, 171–72, 212
    musical legacy, 155, 166
    photograph of, 84
    postage stamp, 173

recordings:
    "Come On Let's Go," 42, 51,
      52–53
    "Donna," 42, 53–55, 56, 130
    "Fast Freight" (Allens), 56
    "Framed," 52
    "La Bamba," 53, 55, 56
    "Little Girl," 129, 130
    missing tapes, 167
    posthumous releases, 129
    reissued material, 213–14
    "That's My Little Suzie," 129
    "We Belong Together," 130
  sisters of, xiii
  television appearances, 65
  winter coat, 90
  Winter Dance Party, 5, 47, 57, 61,
    63, 66, 69, 70–71, 74, 80, 81,
    86–87, 92, 95
Valenz (band), 186
Valenzuela, Concepcion Reyes (mother of
  Ritchie Valens), 48–51, 54, 130, 131,
    162–63, 184–85
    and death of son, 110, 125–26
    and Romero, 171
    and Winter Dance Party, 57, 61
Valenzuela, Joseph Steve (father of Ritchie
  Valens), 48
Valenzuela, Richard Steven (Ritchie Valens),
  48–49. *See also* Valens, Ritchie
Variety, 22, 36, 74
Vaughan, Stevie Ray, 226–27
Vaughn, Jack, 13, 14
Vee, Bobby (Velline, Robert), xi, 117–19,
  191, 192, 215–16
Vee, Sue, 69
Velline, Bill, 117–18
Velline, Robert (Bobby Vee), 117–18, 215. *See
  also* Vee, Bobby
"Venus" (Avalon), 123, 127
Vidorian, The (Vidor, Texas), 149
Vincent, Gene, 10, 35

Waddell, Ann, 234
Walker, Clay, 228
Walk of Fame, Lubbock, Texas, 173
Wallace, Hal, 9
Waller, Gordon, 166
wallet belonging to Allsup, 97, 110, 217, 231
Walters, Bill, 91, 92, 222
Wanted: The Outlaws (album), 199
Warrior Records, 215
Washington, D.C., Crickets tour, 16–17
Waterloo, Iowa, 24
Watts, Wortham "Slim," 27, 31, 32
Waylon's West Texas Style Barbecue Sauce,
  200
WDGY (Minneapolis radio), 68, 76
weather for Winter Dance Party tour, 47, 71,
  85, 92
    Clear Lake, Iowa, 94, 97
    Davenport, Iowa, 79, 80–81

weather for Winter Dance Party tour (*continued*)
    Minnesota, 67, 69, 72, 75, 78, 86
    at time of plane crash, 1–2, 102, 136, 139–4
    Wisconsin, 61, 64, 65, 70, 90
Webb, Don, 132
"We Belong Together" (Valens), 130
Webster, Harold, ix
weight and balance of plane, 148–49
Weir, J. E., 122
Welborn, Larry, 6, 12, 14, 15, 206
Welk, Lawrence, 91, 165, 211
Wenck, Esther, 81
Wenner, Andrew, 180, 183
West, Sonny, 15, 157, 162, 211, 230
    and Petty, 160
WGN-TV (Chicago television), 64
WGRC (Louisville radio), 34 35
"What Am I Living For" (Willis), 226
"Wheels" (Petty), 209
"When Sin Stops Love Begins" (Jennings), 38
"White Lightning" (Jones), 130, 165
Whitman, Slim, 12
Whoopee John (polka band), 67
Wilde, Marty, "Donna," 166
"Wild Wind" (Leyton), 190
Williams, Hank, 6, 226
Williams, Hank, Jr., 201
Williams, Larry, 22
Willis, Chuck, 226
Wills, Bob, 201
Winter, Edgar, 211
Winter, Johnny, 211, 228
Winter Dance Party tour, x, xii, 42, 47, 57, 129, 146, 155
    Clear Lake, Iowa, 93–97
    Davenport, Iowa, 79–80
    Des Moines, Iowa, 124
    Duluth, Minnesota, 86–87, 230
    Eau Claire, Wisconsin, 70–71, 194
    final stops, 126–27
    financial arrangements, 43, 130
    Fort Dodge, Iowa, 82–84
    Green Bay, Wisconsin, 90–92
    Kenosha, Wisconsin, 64–66
    Mankato, Minnesota, 68–69
    map of tour, 60

Milwaukee, 61–64
mistakes in ads, 142
Montevideo, Minnesota, 73
Moorhead, Minnesota, 115, 118–19
photographs of, 198, 218, 219, 222, 223
rehearsals for, 45–46
replacements, 117, 127
route retraced, 194–95
St. Paul, Minnesota, 76–78
Sioux City, Iowa, 124
tapes of, 167
thirtieth anniversary, 191–92
tour bus, 47, 61, 67, 69–72, 79, 82, 94, 115–16, 124
    breakdown of, xiv, 88–89
    frozen heaters, 81–82
    gun on, 84
Valens' income from, 162
WISN (Milwaukee radio), 62
"Witch Doctor" (Seville), 32–33
WLIP (Kenosha radio), 65
WOC (Davenport radio), 79
Wolfman Jack, 191
Womack, Harold, 6, 207
Wood, Melvin O., 240, 151–52
Wooley, Sheb, "The Purple People Eater," 33
"Words of Love" (Beatles), 197
Worst Rock 'n' Roll Records of All Time, The (Guterman and O'Donnell), 170
wreckage of plane, 106, *107*, 137
WSPT (Minneapolis radio), 76
WTIX (New Orleans) Fun Night, 35–40

Yankovic, Frankie, 64
"Yesterday, Today and Tomorrow" (Richardson), 165
"You Are My One Desire" (Holly), 12
Young, Faron, 9
Young, Martin, 81–82
young musicians, and music business, 10, 159–63
"You're the One" (Holly), 43
"You Send Me" (Cooke), 51
"You've Got Love" (Holly and Crickets), 19

Zabukovec, Frank, 65
Zack, Ed, 79
Zager, Denny, 230